Leicester–Nottingham Studies in
Volume 8

WHEN MEN WERE MEN

The history of classical antiquity is a history of men. We have been taught
to see it as *the* history of Western civilization, not simply as *a* history: just
one of the many strands of a broader past which makes us what we are
today. This volume questions the deep-set assumption that men's history
speaks and has always spoken for all of us, by exploring the story of classical antiquity as an explicitly masculine story.

When Men Were Men covers a wide range of periods and places, from
Archaic Greece through Classical Athens to Imperial Rome and Roman
Egypt. It employs a variety of critical approaches and methodologies and
focuses on a broad range of source material to examine masculinity in the
classical world. Among the topics explored are gender differentiation in
Archaic Greece, the '*machismo*' of the Athenian Empire, the masculinity of
the Hellenistic king and the Roman emperor, the male body in Roman
Egypt, masculinity and male social roles in Roman Boiotia, and soldiers,
masculinity and power in Republican and Imperial Rome.

When Men Were Men presents a beautifully illustrated and innovative
study of masculine dominance in the classical world.

Lin Foxhall is Reader in the School of Archaeological Studies at the
University of Leicester. She is the co-editor, with A. S. E. Lewis, of
Justifications not Justice: The Political Context of Law in Ancient Greece
(1996).

John Salmon is Senior Lecturer in Ancient History at the University of
Nottingham. He is the author of *Wealthy Corinth* (1984), and co-editor,
with Graham Shipley, of *Human Landscapes in Classical Antiquity* (1996).

WHEN MEN WERE MEN

*Masculinity, power and identity in
classical antiquity*

Edited by
LIN FOXHALL and JOHN SALMON

LONDON AND NEW YORK

First published 1998
by Routledge
2 Park Square, Milton Park, Abingdon, Oxon, OX14 4RN

Simultaneously published in the USA and Canada
by Routledge
270 Madison Ave, New York NY 10016

Transferred to Digital Printing 2010

Routledge Ltd is a Taylor & Francis Group company

British Library Cataloguing in Publication Data
A catalogue record for this book is available from the British Library

Library of Congress Cataloging in Publication Data
When Men were Men: masculinity, power and identity in classical
antiquity, edited by Lin Foxhall and John Salmon.
p. cm. – (Leicester–Nottingham Studies in Ancient Society: v. 8)
Includes bibliographical references and index.
1. Masculinity – History. 2. Men – Greece. 3. Men – Rome. 4.
Civilization, Classical.
I. Foxhall, Lin. II. Salmon, J. B. iii. Series: Leicester–Nottingham Studies
in Ancient Society: v. 8.
HQ1090.7G8W49 1998
305.31'09 – dc21

ISBN10: 0–415–14634–8 (hbk)
ISBN10: 0–415–61936–X (pbk)

ISBN13: 978–0–415–14634–0 (hbk)
ISBN13: 978–0–415–61936–3 (pbk)

98–14169
CIP

Publisher's Note
The publisher has gone to great lengths to ensure the quality of this reprint
but points out that some imperfections in the original may be apparent.

Contents

CONTENTS

Figures

Contributors

Richard Alston teaches Roman history at Royal Holloway College. He has published *Soldier and Society in Roman Egypt* (1995), *Aspects of Roman History AD 14–117* (1998) and various articles on the Roman army and urbanism in Roman Egypt.

Paul Cartledge is Reader in Greek History in the University of Cambridge and a Fellow of Clare College. He is the author, co-author, editor and co-editor of a dozen books, including *Xenophon: Hiero the Tyrant and Other Treatises* (Penguin Classics), *Hellenistic Constructs: Essays in Culture, History and Historiography* (University of California Press) and *The Cambridge Illustrated History of Ancient Greece* (CUP) (all 1997). His most recently published (both 1998) titles are *Democritus and Atomistic Politics* (Orion) and *KOSMOS: Essays in Order, Conflict and Community in Classical Athens* (CUP).

Susan Fischler is Lecturer in Ancient History in the Department of Ancient History and Archaeology at the University of Birmingham. She is the co-editor, with L. Archer and M. Wyke, of *Women in Ancient Societies: An Illusion of the Night* (1994).

Nick Fisher is Senior Lecturer in the School of History and Archaeology, University of Cardiff. His principal publications are *Hybris* (1992), *Slavery in Classical Athens* (1993) and *Social Values in Classical Athens* (1976), as well as several articles on Greek political and social history. He is currently preparing a translation and commentary on Aischines' speech *Against Timarchos*.

Lin Foxhall is Reader in Ancient History in the School of Archaeological Studies at the University of Leicester. She is the co-editor, with A. S. E. Lewis, of *Justifications not Justice: The Political Context of Law in Ancient Greece* (1996).

Jane F. Gardner is Professor of Ancient History at the University of Reading, and has written three books on the relation between personal status and legal capacity: *Women in Roman Law and Society* (1986), *Being a Roman Citizen* (1993) and *Family and* Familia *in Roman Law and Life* (1998).

Jill Harries is Professor of Ancient History at the University of St Andrews. She was Visiting Fellow at All Souls College, Oxford and Leverhulme Research Fellow in 1996–7. She is the author of *Sidonius Apollinaris and the Fall of Rome* (1994), *Law and Empire in Late Antiquity* (1998), and edited (with Ian Wood) *The Theodosian Code: Studies in the Imperial Law of Late Antiquity* (1993).

Keith Hopwood is Lecturer in Classics at University of Wales, Lampeter. His research centres on Roman, Byzantine and early Turkish Asia Minor with particular reference to town–country and sedentarist–pastoralist relationships. His work has appeared in Classical, Byzantine and Oriental publications. He is the editor of *Ancient Greece and Rome: A Bibliographical Guide* (Manchester University Press, 1995) which was nominated for the Besterman Medal.

Eireann Marshall studied at Barnard College and the University of Birmingham, and is completing her doctorate on Cyrenaica at the University of Exeter, where she currently lectures. She has published several articles on Cyrenaica and is currently editing a volume on classical art.

Dominic Montserrat is Lecturer in Ancient History at Warwick University. He is the author of *Sex and Society in Graeco-Roman Egypt* (1996) and edited *Changing Bodies, Changing Meanings* for Routledge. He is currently working on a book about Western cultural fantasies of ancient Egypt.

Jim Roy is Senior Lecturer in the Department of Classics at the University of Nottingham, and has recently contributed chapters to G. Shipley and J.B. Salmon, *Human Landscapes in Classical Antiquity* (1996), and M. H. Hansen, *The Polis as an Urban Centre and as a Political Community* (1997).

John Salmon is Senior Lecturer in Ancient History at the University of Nottingham. He is the author of *Wealthy Corinth* (1984), and co-editor, with Graham Shipley, of *Human Landscapes in Classical Antiquity* (1996).

Hans van Wees is Lecturer in Ancient History at University College London. He is the author of *Status Warriors: War, Violence, and Society in Homer and History* (1992) and editor, with Nick Fisher, of *Archaic Greece: New Approaches and New Evidence* (1998).

Preface

The god, from the very beginning, designed the nature of woman for the indoor work and concerns and the nature of man for the outdoor work. For he prepared man's body and mind to be more capable of enduring cold and heat and travelling and military campaigns, and so he assigned the outdoor work to him. Because the woman was physically less capable of endurance, I think the god has evidently assigned the indoor work to her. And because the god was aware that he had both implanted in the woman and assigned to her the nurture of newborn children, he had measured out to her a greater share of affection for newborn babies than he gave to the man. And because the god had also assigned to the woman the duty of guarding what had been brought into the house, realising that a tendency to be afraid is not at all disadvantageous for guarding things, he measured out a greater portion of fear to the woman than to the man. And knowing that the person responsible for the outdoor work would have to serve as defender against any wrong doer, he measured out to him a greater share of courage. [...] And the law declares honourable those duties for which the god has made each of them more naturally capable.[1]

Thus in the fourth century BC Xenophon described the ideal roles of an upper class Athenian man and woman. Though these roles are ordained by divine and human law, Xenophon's didactic treatise makes it clear that they must also be learned and repeatedly re-instilled. As Xenophon goes on to describe the functioning of the household and its members it becomes clear that although gender roles are innate they vary according to social class, and are less strict among slaves whose instincts and work assignments are not so neatly categorized but depend upon their owners' needs and their assessments of a slave's behaviour.

Did gender roles also change over time? Would a synchronic approach (that is, 'la longue durée') to this question prove more fruitful than the diachronic approach implied by the chronological arrangement of the twelve articles in the present volume? Jill Harries' contribution opens with a quotation from Plutarch, who lived in Greece some 600 years after Xenophon. Yet his observation that the woman is sedentary, domestic and difficult to move is consistent with Xenophon's views. Three of the articles indicate that the violence of an Athenian hoplite was not dissimilar from that of a Roman legionary. It comes as no surprise that Hellenistic and Roman monarchs grappled with the same problems and often found the same solutions to gender definitions and representations in imperial cult. Thus it would be instructive to read the discussions of ruler cult by Jim Roy and Susan Fischler in tandem. The ancient world was conservative, and periods of violent transition were often marked by nostalgia for an (often fictitious) more stable past. The literary classics dominated the thinking of later intellectuals and constituted the curriculum of well-educated monarchs. Alexander the Great consciously shaped himself as a reincarnation of his putative ancestor Achilles, for both conquered Asia by the spear. Although Hans van Wees demonstrates that weeping had become unfashionable for men during the archaic period, some 900 years after the fall of Troy Alexander wept copiously while lying on the corpse of his friend Hephaistion (Arrian, *Anabasis* 7. 14. 3). This display of emotion by the most powerful man in the Mediterranean world may well have established a new paradigm for male grief. Thus Alexander's troops have tears in their eyes after he harangues them (Arrian, *Anabasis* 7. 11. 5, Quintus Curtius 10. 5. 1).

Men's studies is still in its infancy. This rich collection of articles allows the reader to experiment with various historical paradigms and interpretative models. But the subjects of our concern had few choices. In antiquity, gender roles were prescribed and deviations from them severely punished. One conclusion may be drawn from all the contributions: as a social system, patriarchy exercises implacable authority over men as well as women.

NOTE

1 Xenophon, *Oeconomicus*, 7. 23—5, 30 (excerpted); trans. Sarah B. Pomeroy, *Xenophon Oeconomicus: A Social and Historical Commentary*, Oxford: Oxford University Press 1994, 143, 145.

Sarah B. Pomeroy

Introduction

Lin Foxhall

> Man seems to have wanted, directly or indirectly, to give the universe his own gender as he has wanted to give his own name to his children, his wife, his possessions.
>
> (Irigaray 1993, 31)

The history of classical antiquity is a history of men, though it is never studied that way. We have been taught to see it as *the* history of Western civilization, not simply as *a* history, one of many strands of a broader classical past, which makes us what we are today. The aim of this book is to question the deep-set assumption that men's history speaks and has always spoken for all of us, by exploring the story of classical antiquity as an explicitly masculine story.

We have abundant sources, however ideologically charged they may be, for the views of men in the Greek and Roman world. Almost every piece of evidence we possess, whether literary, epigraphical, iconographic or material, is the product of men's thoughts and actions. Even the surviving remains of Greece and Rome are the mostly the remnants of men, since women by and large were responsible for ephemeral things which are not so often preserved in the archaeological record (Foxhall and Stears 1998; Foxhall 1995b). This has long been recognized by those studying women in antiquity: the logical corollary must be that to understand the lives of women, slaves or any of the many kinds of 'others' excluded from the structures of power perpetrated by dominant masculine ideologies it is essential to study the perpetrators not only as rulers, soldiers and masters, but also as men (see Cartledge, Marshall, this volume).

Ironically, the initial stimulus for the study of men and masculinity has been the 'second wave' feminism of the later 1960s and 1970s, perhaps the most powerful theoretical and political trajectory of our era. Women, previously invisible and mute for the most part, were revealed by a range of social and historical disciplines to be significant actors, producers and reproducers in past and present worlds (see Pomeroy 1975, for example, on classical antiquity, recently reprinted as a modern 'classic'). In the first instance,

1

scholarly interest was weighted towards women's domestic activities and their roles within the family. Following the discovery of the 'other sex' came the 'revelation' of other sexualities, and the idea that our modern notion of (hetero/homo)sexuality was not necessarily applicable to the classical past. Though women were still at the forefront of most studies, spotlights now shone on sex and sexuality, in part thanks to the publication of Foucault's *History of Sexuality*, the first volume of which appeared in French in 1976 (translated into English in 1978). Concomitantly, a range of changing views about how power and authority were exerted in societies (again, partly stimulated by Foucault's work) merged with these new perspectives on gender, sex and sexuality (for instance, Winkler 1990a; Halperin 1990). The study of sexuality has most recently developed to include 'queer theory' and the 'gay gene', that is, the notion of a 'natural' homosexuality inherent in certain individuals.[1]

The difficulty of investigating women in isolation became ever more apparent, and by the mid 1980s gender studies had become the purported focus (for an account of gender as a category of historical analysis, see Scott 1986). Works which specifically targeted men and masculinity as objects of study appeared rather late in the day, and in the Anglo-American scholarly tradition first emerged en masse in the 1980s.[2] Men's studies have taken several different lines of approach. All have been politically inspired, founded to some extent on reactions to feminist thought. The spectrum has ranged from the backlash of the 'weekend warriors', with emphasis on the acceptability of 'traditional', aggressive and oppressive male behaviour, to 'new men' approaches portraying men as trapped by the constraints of masculine roles and expectations, which inhibit their development as humans.[3]

It is probably still fair to say that studies of men and masculinity are most important and abundant in the social sciences which focus on contemporary society, largely, though not exclusively, in the West.[4] Psychoanalysis and psychoanalytic approaches have been particularly influential, constituting a main theme of men's (and gender) studies in many social sciences. Some aspects of this body of theory have had a major impact on other areas of gender studies beyond the social sciences, for example object relations theory, as propounded by Nancy Chodorow (1978). However, disciplines concerned with past societies have to date rarely focused on men as men. Nor do contemporary studies generally engage with the past at any historical distance greater than the nineteenth century, or at best the early modern period. Frequently 'historical causation' in relation to modern male roles and ideologies is linked to the development of Western capitalism and the processes of industrialization, often in a highly schematized way.[5]

Nonetheless, classical antiquity often holds a special place for contemporary researchers in terms of the history of ideas and ideologies. Ancient myth and classical philosophy in particular have been subjected to a kind of ancestor worship, providing templates for gender hierarchies in general and especially men's superior places in them. The impact of psychoanalytic theory is mainly responsible for this, since part of its claim to universality has from the outset been based on the appropriation of classical models. However, recognition of the Greek and Roman inspiration behind the historical moment of the Enlightenment – significant as the birth of modernity for thinkers such as Foucault (1985, 1986), Habermas and others who have profoundly influenced the literature on women, men and gender over the past quarter century – also sets classical antiquity on a pedestal of its own. Unfortunately, that pedestal is all too frequently of spurious modern manufacture, and the original settings of the ancient viewpoints on men and women have been lost or forgotten. A major goal of this volume and its companion, *Thinking Men: Masculinity and its Self-Representation in the Classical Tradition*, is to recontextualize classical perspectives on gender hierarchies within our fuller understandings of ancient societies. The historical and ideological pathways between our world and that of the ancient Greeks and Romans become more perceptible in the light of that larger context, the direct evidence for which largely consists of the viewpoints of men. Hence the need arises to examine these viewpoints as emanating from male people, especially the élite ones who dominate, not just as emerging from Greek and Roman 'history'.

In recent years, scholarship on gender, men and women has questioned and begun to deconstruct the notion that we can talk about unified or uniform categories of 'men' and 'women'. The title of Connell's recent synthetic study, *Masculinities* (1995) (not 'masculinity'), is typical, reflecting the tendency to fragment the monolithic polar categories of 'man' and 'woman' in favour of a more complex spectrum of categories (for example, Herdt 1994b). It is plain for any broadly historical discipline that historical moment, life stage, age, class, status, wealth, race/ethnicity and so on profoundly shape what can be understood as the masculinity or femininity of any individual.

Similarly, it is now clear to most of us that gender roles are socially and politically constructed, not 'natural'. The questions of whether or not gender is socially constructed, or whether or not biological and physiological phenomena are subject to cultural mediation, are no longer worth asking, since the answer to both must be 'yes'.[6] What and how 'biological sex' might or might not contribute to gender roles, however, is at the heart of much potentially fruitful debate.

Despite these recent trends, I still find it deeply disturbing that dominant ideologies (along with ideologies of dominance) have everywhere always been masculine, never feminine. Though it may be possible to show that only certain men are able to act out what have been dubbed 'hegemonic masculinities',[7] thereby gaining and maintaining the advantage of power over other men as well as women, and that women sometimes attain positions of power

LIN FOXHALL

(Roy, Fischler, this volume) I still wonder to what extent so-called multiple masculinities are really only variations on a single theme. Where has there ever been a human society or institution run by principles or structured in hierarchies which could be characterized (by the society itself or by others) as positively 'feminine'?[8] And could this be one reason why the paradigms of masculinity based on what has come down to us from classical antiquity have wielded such power to shape the thoughts and ideals of modernity?

Certainly for the classical world, though dominant, 'hegemonic', masculine ideologies may have been élite in origin, it would be too simple to say that they remain located amongst the élite, or that other males are starkly emasculated by their exclusion from the most concentrated arenas of power. Indeed, the most élite males may operate in a realm beyond the normal constraints of masculinity, with distinctive relationships with the women related to them (see below and Roy, Fischler, this volume). Cartledge (this volume) demonstrates the complexities and ambiguities of what exactly constitutes the 'hegemonic masculinity' of classical, imperial Athens. Specifically because notions of power are so often integrated with particular kinds of gender roles, they can be replicated in other social locations beyond those in which they were founded and remain most potent. What non-élite men always have in common with dominant élites is their manhood, and this is demonstrably true for the classical world (see Alston, Gardner, this volume).

This is not to say that masculinity is somehow 'natural' or undifferentiated, or that the perceptions of how power is gendered are the same for those at the top (or the inside) of any system as for those at the bottom (or outside). Rather the logic of power and its reproduction, entangled as it is with some fundamental, generally agreed concept of maleness (itself culturally specific and not necessarily agreed in all times and places), suggests that within any specific context relative hierarchies will be constructed on the principle of male superiority. So, for example, in antiquity violence played an ambivalent and disputed part in the behaviour and expectations of men across the social spectrum, demonstrated by Fisher's study (this volume) of élite Athenian men, and by Alston's paper (this volume) on Roman soldiers, who fall outside the category of 'full-status' men by the standards of the Roman upper classes. For both groups, violence is integrated into the definition of manhood, however problematically, in part because it is never a characteristic of the feminine. The weeping heroes of Homer maintain their masculinity, despite potentially 'feminine' emotional displays, through their prowess in battle (van Wees, this volume). If you are male there is always someone who can be defined as lower than yourself if they do not count in some degree as a man (see Hopwood, Montserrat, this volume).

Indeed, part of the very definition of masculinity and male power (hegemonic or otherwise) frequently includes the control of specific women whose associated submission manifests, symbolizes and highlights male

4

superiority. The ways in which Hellenistic queens complement kings (Roy, this volume), or the ways in which relationships of wives, daughters and mothers to emperors are expressed in Roman Imperial cult (Fischler, this volume) provide good examples. It is significant that in neither case was masculine hegemony entirely unchallenged, but though women, especially the élite, might sometimes buck the authority of patriarchal power for a while, they have never been able to break it once and for all: though Ismenodora was unconventional in 'abducting' a younger husband, she was not revolutionary (see Harries, this volume).

'Subaltern' males virtually always collude with the ideals of hegemonic masculinity at least in the suppression of women: I cannot think of an historical example which contravenes this principle. Male slaves (Montserrat, this volume) or bandits (Hopwood, this volume) were still men, not women. One need not seek refuge in cultural essentialism to argue that however disempowered the lowly, their one claim to sharing in the privileges of their masters and superiors rested in their maleness, though no doubt the latter might not have considered such manhood to bear much resemblance to their own. So, for example, though Roman soldiers were at one level merely tools of the state, with their right to exert the political and social aspects of the manhood appropriate to Roman citizens circumscribed, many nonetheless constructed the equivalent of civilian patriarchal relationships with their women and households, despite the legal and political problems this caused (see Alston, this volume). Even men set apart from others by physical damage or disability (Gardner, this volume) or sexual tastes (Walters in Foxhall and Salmon 1998) remained men, not women, in terms of political hierarchies and social relations of power (see below).

The notion that essential categorical difference between 'man' and 'woman' exists, grounded in the two shapes in which most human bodies are created, is universal, embedded in all human languages and cultures. What is plainly culturally specific is the infinitely complex elaboration of essential categorical difference, including the precise terms of the categories themselves, the creation of sub-categories, crossing categories, the full spectrum in which gender roles, personas and behaviours which may be overlapping, blurred, transcended or even obliterated. This principle is embodied by those males who choose a sexual identity, and in some cases its associated gender traits and behaviours, which is deemed alternative or unacceptable in the terms of hegemonic masculine ideals. One example of such a role is that of the *kinaidos*, perceptively studied by Winkler (1990a). However, in classical antiquity, it is clear that the possession of an identifiably male body to a large extent negated the effects of chosen social role in the overall gender hierarchies, placing him still superior to all women. Roman men were identified as men by being born with male bodies, carrying male genitals, and despite any subsequent social and physical events, his maleness (and with it his hierarchal position) usually remained intact (Gardner, this volume). And the body of a sexually receptive Roman slave is still a male body, deriving its meanings from the fact that it is not female, though it may be in some respects feminized. In that way the slave, Epaphroditus, had a kind of 'self' denied to women, though it may not be easy for us to see from the documents (Montserrat, this volume).

There are areas which all or virtually all masculinities share in common with each other and, more to the point, do not share with any aspect of femininity. Three which I shall highlight here (by no means the only ones) are the construction of the individual self, the appropriation of reproduction, and the invention (or imagination?) of rationality.

The construction of the individual self

Whether or not one agrees with those branches of psychoanalytic theory which claim that men perceive and construct the boundaries of their personal being differently, more sharply, than women,[9] social and political 'selves' are certainly structured differently along gendered lines. In classical antiquity, fully political 'selves' were always male (Gardner, this volume). The success of masculine values rests in their ability to arrange and rearrange the goalposts so that self-interest is always paramount and 'selves', more broadly speaking, cannot be other than male, even if 'other' males are problematic.[10] Plutarch celebrates the women of his world for a combination of feminine modesty and 'masculine' self-control (Harries, this volume): the positive feminine trait is a contradiction in terms.

Though it has been argued[11] that 'selfless self-sacrifice' often characterizes manhood, in fact such 'selfless' acts valorize the male individual 'self' entirely in masculine terms, via pathways not open to women unless they have been at least partially transformed into men. So, for example, though one could argue that soldiers are cannon-fodder exploited by élites and states for their own ends and that the age-old glorification of death in battle is merely a deceptive myth, the fact remains that war memorials, from classical Athens to modern America, monumentalize individual men or, more rarely, women with man-like courage. Though the self-sacrifice of some men, notably lower status ones, is certainly ignored on public monuments (see Cartledge, this volume), the vast numbers of women whose lives were ruined by their personal sacrifices are never memorialized: the women who lost husbands, fathers and brothers, or who were victims of capture, rape and slaughter in war have no 'self' worthy of preservation for posterity. Even the unknown soldier has a self, but the unknown wife or rape victim does not. The political and ideological collectivity of these selves, as expressed by the 'national' ideals of heroic warfare, are thus also entirely male. Moreover, the use of violence is to some extent always legitimate for men and underpins all masculine hegemonies, as it is simultaneously denied to women. It is significant that many of the papers in this volume focus on the way in which men (or certain men) use, abuse or uphold an exclusive claim to wielding violence (Cartledge, Fischler, Fisher, Hopwood, Montserrat, Roy, van Wees).

The appropriation of reproduction

This ability of masculine hegemonies to reproduce themselves adaptively results in the appropriation of reproduction in all senses to exclude women, and in political and social senses to exclude males who are not 'men' who matter. In the ancient world civic and/or territorial entities themselves (usually personified as feminine) are portrayed as generated by masculine powers, divine, heroic and human, as represented by the myths of the foundation of Kyrene (Marshall, this volume). One fundamental problem with this reproductive strategy is that ultimately women are crucial to physical reproduction and therefore cannot be entirely ignored in social and political reproductive strategies (though they can, as in the case of Kyrene just cited, be relegated to passive roles): the ideological circumvention of this problem is at the heart of many masculine behaviours and discourses of power in all societies. Repeatedly rituals, representations and rhetoric promote the fantasy of male reproduction without women, from the initiation of Sambia boys into manhood (Herdt 1987) to the imaginings of the character of Aristophanes in Plato's *Symposium*. Where women's reproductive roles cannot be dismissed, they are regularly suppressed, for example within lineages drawn up along male lines, or relegated to confined sacred spaces and occasions, which are in effect socially constructed windows with bars, though this is not to imply there is no resistance.[12] Nowhere in the classical (or the modern) world does birth into social/political manhood, any kind of manhood, from any social sector, erupt from womankind. Boys may have mothers, but (political) men have mentors, sponsors, colleagues and 'friends'.

The invention (or imagination?) of rationality

The notion of rationality is perhaps the most important part of the classical heritage to be incorporated into modern thought. One could argue (though a surprising number of classical scholars do not) that ancient rationality was masculine in gender in all senses (Lloyd 1984, 1–9, 18–33). Rationality in the sense of a pure, disembodied, decontextualized logic, capable of leading to the (male) human control of pure reason and truth, the *logos*, was a notion limited to a small, eccentric group of élite men, with relatively little impact on the rest of society. The idea that such value-free knowledge in an absolute sense exists has been bombarded by feminist critiques in recent years. Notable among these is the feminist dismantling of 'value-free' scientific reasoning,[13] which demonstrates clearly that culturally specific notions of gender hierarchies permeate the metaphors we use to represent the underlying workings of the universe. Such views have also been challenged by recent writing on masculinity in the West (for instance, Seidler 1989, 14–21, 183–6).

Similarly, the notion of 'reason' as a quality inherent in, or more fully developed in men (a concept which certainly has classical roots) has been a leitmotif of Western culture (Jordanova 1980). Certainly the ancients and their successors envisaged the *logos* as a masculine characteristic, reproduced via masculine genealogies. Women rarely enter these intellectual genealogies, and when they do it is only by 'becoming' men, donning the male dress of pure reason, like the female philosophers whom Plutarch admired (see Harries, this volume). However, the standards by which gendered rationality is evaluated are again movable goal posts, for male behaviour, even when apparently 'irrational', such as extreme grief, is saved from being regarded as dangerously out of control (as similar behaviour by women would be perceived) by the fact that these particular men are warriors – a role denied to women (see van Wees, this volume).

The feminist thinker Luce Irigaray (1985, 1991, 1993) takes the view that women have been conditioned to operate as multiplicities rather than (like men) as unities, arguing that such 'classic' rationality as demands singularity of identity, non-contradiction and the constructions of oppositions is a characteristically male invention. Women can participate in it fully only if they give up their womanhood (see Harlow, Clark, in Foxhall and Salmon 1998). One could go even further, to postulate that the kind of categorization of the world implied by either ancient philosophical or modern scientific rationality is a mode of thought which seeks, indeed pretends, to dominate the universe (Lloyd 1984, 7–17). The *telos*, the logical implication of these modes of reasoning, is that it is ultimately possible to know everything and thereby control it (since to know is to control), stepping outside the particulars of human time and space in which we find ourselves located (French 1994, 18–22).[14] The imaginings of such power are surely fantasies, and the new gods which result, whether they are the modern ones of science or the fire, earth, air and water of the pre-Socratics, are equally specious.

The papers in this book represent a range of approaches to studying the masculine ideologies which both form the basis of our sources and constituted the framework of most ancient institutions. They focus on a wide variety of source materials, periods and places. The ancient frameworks explored here have been encompassed in (and used to justify) many practices and institutions of the more recent past and the present. The structures of masculine dominance on the classical world are still with us in many forms: our aim is to see them for what they are so that we can begin to understand where they have taken us.

Notes

1 *TLS* 1 November 1996, 14; Edwards 1994, and cf. Walters in Foxhall and Salmon 1998.
2 For example, Hearn 1987; Herzfeld 1985; Herdt 1981; Brittan 1989; Seidler 1989.
3 For the latter, cf. Connell 1995, 204–24, and van Wees, this volume
4 See Connell 1995: 27–39; for cross-cultural perspectives, see e.g. Gilmore 1990; Herzfeld 1985; Herdt 1984; Cornwall and Lindisfarne 1994.
5 For example, Connell 1995, 186–99; Seidler 1989.
6 Such questions do, of course, continue to be asked by certain lines of scholarship. Examples include cruder forms of sociobiological 'history' (e.g. Knight 1991) and some of the more extreme views on the 'gay gene' (see *TLS* 1 November 1996, 14).
7 Cornwall and Lindisfarne 1994, 3; Cartledge, Montserrat, this volume.
8 Cf. Marshall, Fisher, Cartledge, van Wees, this volume.
9 Lacan 1977, and cf. Brittan 1989, 71–3; Irigaray 1985.
10 Cf. Cartledge, Fisher, this volume; Foxhall in Foxhall and Salmon 1998.
11 Gilmore 1990; cf. van Wees, this volume.
12 Foxhall 1995a, 1995b; Irigaray 1993, 16.
13 For example, Lennon and Whitford 1994; Haraway 1986, 1989, 1991; Blier 1986; Fee 1986.
14 French 1994, 22: 'In living things, said Aristotle, the form is the soul for the soul is the source of life. To be a living thing is to have soul. To live, feed, grow and generate one's kind is to have a vegetative soul, to live as a plant. To perceive and move in addition is the soul of a an animal. To have a rational soul is to be a man [*sic*]'.

1

A brief history of tears: gender differentiation in archaic Greece

Hans van Wees

Men are reinventing themselves as victims. Champions of male liberation insist that in the war of the sexes all recent casualties have been on their side, and indeed that many of the deaths have been self-inflicted. 'As boys experience the pressures of the male role, their suicide rate increases 25,000 percent', says one.[1] A man's lot is not a happy one, we are told, because he is made to sacrifice his health and happiness for the sake of others. As if it were not enough having to provide for his family and put up with all the occupational hazards and mental stress involved, he is expected to be an 'unpaid bodyguard': 'You know that is your job as a man – every time you are with a woman . . . any woman, not just your wife'.[2] The so-called mythopoetic wing of the men's movement traces male altruism right back to Greek legend, with the aid of a garbled version of the story of how Kleobis and Biton died helping their mother, and a bit of dubious Indoeuropean etymology claiming that the Greek word hero meant 'basically a slave whose purpose was to serve and protect'.[3]

All this, of course, is merely the latest spin given to an old and widespread ideal of masculinity. Ethnographic evidence from across the world shows that 'manhood ideologies always include a criterion of selfless generosity, even to the point of sacrifice. Again and again we find that "real" men are those who give more than they take; they serve others' (Gilmore 1990, 229). A recent anthropological survey charitably concludes that the ideal is not far removed from reality, and that men are trained to live up to its exacting standards because their sacrifice is needed for the common good. 'Men nurture their society by shedding their blood, their sweat, and their semen.' '*Cui bono*? Who benefits? Everyone.' (Gilmore 1990, 230, 168). It is tempting to be cynical, but arguing about how useful or useless men really are would be beside the point. The real question in the study of masculinity is why gender ideologies encourage men to display certain socially desirable qualities, while they fail to encourage, or positively discourage, a display of the same qualities by women.[4]

With that question in mind, we shall investigate an intriguing aspect of ancient Greek gender differentiation: the norms according to which men and women were supposed to express and suppress grief. A comparison between the extrovert grieving by men as well as women in Homer and the much more restrained expression of sorrow by men in classical Athens reveals a significant change in the ideology of masculinity. The process can be reconstructed not only from literary evidence but also from the series of scenes of mourning found in Athenian art from the eighth to the fifth century BC. Increasing differentiation in the expression of emotion, it will be suggested, was part of a general widening of the gender gap, which provided new justification for the superior status of men, which in turn was part of a still more general redefinition of social hierarchies.

Homer's weeping warriors

Big boys are not supposed to cry or go running to their mothers for help when they are being bullied. So we are a little embarrassed when Akhilleus, a grown man and the greatest warrior of his generation, sits on the beach 'crying tears' and 'groaning heavily' while his mother strokes him consolingly and promises to make that bully Agamemnon pay for what he has done to her son.[5] Ever since antiquity, people have felt the urge to make excuses for our hero. Alexander Pope summed up the gist of most ancient comment when in a note on his translation of *The Iliad* (1715) he explained that:

> It is no Weakness in Heroes to weep, but the very Effect of Humanity and Proof of a generous temper. . . . But this general Observation is not all we can offer in excuse for the Tears of Achilles: His are Tears of Anger and Disdain . . . of which a great and fiery temper is more susceptible than any other; and even in this case, *Homer* has taken care to preserve the high Character, by making him retire to vent his Tears out of sight.
>
> (Pope 1715, note *ad* 1. 458)[6]

There is, however, no getting away from the fact that all Homer's heroes display sadness and despair far more extrovertly and frequently than classical and modern audiences have regarded as normal and appropriate for men.[7]

The world of heroes is a fantasy, of course, and how much of it is based on the poet's own world remains a matter of debate. Yet whatever else may be fictional in the epics, the manner in which emotions are expressed is a part of culture so deeply ingrained that it is commonly perceived as human nature, and it is highly unlikely that Homer and his audiences could have imagined heroes whose emotional behaviour was fundamentally unlike their own. We may suspect that the poet at times intensifies emotions for literary effect,[8] but if so, this merely confirms that his original audiences, unlike his subsequent readers, found extrovert displays of grief by men perfectly acceptable.

Physical expressions of grief in Homer range from slapping one's thighs, through shedding tears, to tearing out one's hair and writhing on the ground. An impressive range of vocal expressions is suggested by a string of verbs, including *klaiein, oduresthai, olophuresthai, muresthai, oimōzein, goan, stenakh(iz)ein*, and, for women only, *kōkuein*. The precise nature and pitch of the emotions conveyed by these verbs is not always easy to determine. *Olophuresthai*, for instance, has been rendered as 'lament', 'sigh', or merely 'speaking in a doleful voice', according to the translator's sense of what is called for in the circumstances. Yet it may be misleading to impose our notion of propriety on Homer, and it seems likely that *olophuresthai* is a stronger expression of emotion than some of these translations suggest. It is, among other things, how Ares and Patroklos, slapping their thighs, respond to news of serious disasters (15. 114, 397–8). Similarly, *stenakh(iz)ein*, which is conventionally translated 'groan' when it refers to the sound made by wounded men, is also used of lamenting women. Do women 'groan' in mourning, or do men 'wail' in pain? Again, we may have to imagine wounded heroes as making rather more noise than we would consider dignified.[9]

Sometimes the display of emotion by men in Homer remains within limits acceptable even to us. We can empathize easily enough with Diomedes' tears of anger when he loses his whip and sees his chances of winning the chariot race slip away (*Il.* 23. 385–7), or the tears of helplessness shed by Odysseus and his companions at the sight of their friends being torn apart by the Cyclops (*Odyssey* 9. 294–5), or the tears of joy at many a happy reunion.[10]

Much more startling is the sight of military leaders in tears when the going gets tough – not only in battle (*Il.* 8. 245; 17. 648), but even in assembly, where Agamemnon addresses his men 'shedding tears like a well of dark water' and 'groaning heavily' (*Il.* 9. 14–16). Fear, too, makes men cry. A crowd of outstanding young warriors observed the Trojan onslaught and 'tears sprang to their eyes, for they did not think there was any escape from harm' (*Il.* 13. 88–9). Agamemnon, watching the enemy campfires at night, 'emitted frequent groans from the bottom of his heart, and his mind trembled . . . . He pulled out much hair from his head by the roots' (*Il.* 10. 9–15). As Odysseus tells the story, he and his crew wept whenever they saw danger approaching. 'We sailed into the straits lamenting' at the sight of the maelstrom Kharybdis (*Od.* 12. 234). 'They wept loudly and shed abundant tears' on finding that they had landed on an inhabited island, where half of them eventually set off to face the unknown, 'crying; and they left us behind lamenting' (*Od.* 10. 201–9). Later, despairing at the thought of having to travel to the Underworld, the men 'sat down on the spot, lamenting, and tore out their hair' (*Od.* 10. 567). Odysseus himself was no less upset ('I sat down on the bed and wept, and I no longer wanted to live'), but pulled himself together when he had had 'enough of weeping and writhing' (*Od.* 10. 497–9).

The most powerful expressions of male emotion are found in spontaneous reactions to personal loss (as opposed to more formal expressions of grief in funerary ritual, to which we shall return). Word of the death of Patroklos leaves Antilokhos unable to speak and unable to stop crying (*Il.* 17. 695–700; 18. 17, 32). The loss of his best friend makes Akhilleus wail and groan, as he throws himself on the ground, covers his face and clothes with dust, and pulls out his hair. Bystanders worry that he might kill himself (*Il.* 18. 23–35). Menelaos and Odysseus, too, are reduced to crawling around in the sand and to a suicidal state of mind, one at the thought of losing his brother, the other despairing of ever coming home.[11] Priam not only wails, beats his head, and pulls out his hair at the sight of Hektor in mortal danger (*Il.* 22. 33–4, 77–8), but responds to the death of his favourite son by spending day after day in the part of his courtyard where livestock are fed, wallowing in the dung left by the animals and smearing it on his head and neck.[12]

Despite what might seem an extreme lack of inhibition, some degree of self-control is practised and admired. The Trojans are instructed not to 'weep' (*klaiein*) when they collect their dead from the battlefield, presumably in order not to give the enemy the satisfaction of witnessing their distress; so they shed tears in silence (*Il.* 7. 426–8). One notes the implication that crying tears is normally accompanied by sounds of wailing. An exceptional hero may be able to restrain even his tears in the most difficult situations. A story told to illustrate the unique bravery of Akhilleus' son tells how he alone remained steady and dry-eyed when all the other Greeks hidden inside the Trojan Horse were wiping their tears and shaking with fear (*Od.* 11. 526–30). Similarly, it is an illustration of the self-control for which Odysseus is famous that he manages not to cry when to do so would have betrayed his identity. Although he is deeply moved by the sight of his wife breaking down in tears, 'his eyes stayed as firm as horn or iron' (*Od.* 19. 209–11).[13]

In another episode, Odysseus is twice unable to contain his emotions when at a feast among the Phaiakians he hears a singer tell tales of the Trojan War. Each time he tries to hide his tears by burying his face in his cloak, 'for he felt inhibited before the Phaiakians' (*Od.* 8. 83–92, 521–31).[14] This is at first sight surprising, given that tears flow so freely otherwise, but it emerges elsewhere that feasts are indeed occasions when tears are not acceptable. When over food and wine hosts and guests begin to cry as they remember their dead, one of them soon tells the others that, although there is nothing wrong with mourning loved ones, 'I do not enjoy wailing *in the middle of a meal* [*metadorpios*]' (*Od.* 4. 193–8). At a feast, the paramount concern is evidently to preserve a cheerful atmosphere. A host might take offence should anyone spoil it, as Odysseus himself remarks: 'I should not sit in another man's house wailing and lamenting . . . or else one of the maids, or you yourself, might take offence, and think that I am swimming in tears because my head is heavy with wine' (*Od.* 19. 118–22). One hostess resorts to slipping drugs into people's drinks to stop them crying, which not only confirms that tears are taboo on festive occasions, but also shows that there is no sense that a man ought to restrain his emotions by force of will (*Od.* 4. 219–32).

Crying may thus be thought unpleasant, and in some situations impolite. It may be said that it 'will not achieve anything' (*Od.* 4. 544), or that it has 'no practical use' (*Od.* 10. 202, 568; *Il.* 24. 524). People quite often stop, or are made to stop, crying and indulging in grief because there is some business to take care of; otherwise, they might have wept till dark, or dawn.[15] The one reason for not crying which is *never* given is that it is *unmanly*.

In two passages, there is a hint that women and children cry more easily than men. Odysseus reproaches Greeks for 'crying to one another about going home, like little children or widowed women' (*Il.* 2. 289–90), and Patroklos, 'shedding hot tears like a spring of dark water' at the sight of the Greek losses, bumps into Akhilleus, who says mockingly that he looks 'like a little girl running along after her mother, asking to be carried, pulling at her dress' (*Il.* 16. 2–11). But these represent the mildest of rebukes. Odysseus immediately adds that no one could blame the troops for feeling this way (*Il.* 2. 291–7), while Akhilleus 'pitied' Patroklos in his distress (*Il.* 16. 5). Tellingly, in the *Odyssey* the hero's own tears can be compared at length to those of a woman whose husband has fallen in battle (*Od.* 8. 523–30), without the least suggestion of effeminacy.

The narrative, in fact, does not suggest that women cry more easily than men. Penelope may spend all her days weeping for her lost husband, but during his seven-year stay with Kalypso, Odysseus behaves much like his wife. He spends all day sitting on the beach, 'his eyes never dry of tears . . . crying and groaning' (*Od.* 5. 151–8). Again, Hektor's mother may lament and tear out her hair when she sees him fall in single combat, but his father laments, tears out his hair, beats his breast, and throws himself down in the dung (*Il.* 22. 77–81, 405–14). If anything, the male reaction seems the more emotional. If Homer does perceive men as less tearful than women, the difference is very slight.[16]

It is only in the more formal lamenting over the dead that a clear distinction emerges. It has been observed that, by comparison with the violence of the first reaction to the loss of family or friends, the actual funerary ritual is conducted 'more calmly'.[17] In fact, it is only men who remain relatively composed as they deal with the bodies of their dead. Women, by contrast, display grief most intensely during the so-called *prothesis*, the period during which the body lies in state. Some women even resort to self-mutilation.

The contrast is clearest during the funeral rites for Hektor. After many days of abject self-abasement, Priam is perfectly in control of himself as soon as his son's body arrives at Troy. Presumably he cries along with everyone else, but otherwise his only role is to make arrangements and give orders (*Il.* 24. 715–17, 777–81). By contrast, Hektor's mother and wife stand at his bier, once more tearing out their hair (710–12). After singers have sung a dirge (*thrēnos*), the two women are joined by Hektor's sister-in-law and each utter a lament (*goös*) over his body (720–76). A large crowd of both men and women is present (707–8), but it is predominantly the women who 'groan' in response to dirge and laments (722, 746, 760). After the final lament, however, the entire crowd joins in (777).

Like Priam, Akhilleus abstains from any expressions of grief more violent than crying and 'groaning', while he is in charge of the arrangements for mourning Patroklos. The same is true of the other Greeks. There is no more self-abasement, or wild tearing out of hair. Instead, we meet two much more restrained tributes to the dead. Akhilleus makes his companions drive their chariots three times around Patroklos' bier: 'let us draw near with our chariots and horses, and weep for Patroklos, for that is the privilege of the dead' (*Il.* 23. 8–9). Later, they each cut off a lock of hair which they place on his bier when the body is carried out to be cremated; this is cited several times as a common custom.[18]

Again it is clear that the main burden of mourning normally lies with women, for Akhilleus announces that the body of Patroklos will be wailed and wept over day and night by Trojan and Dardanian captives of war (*Il.* 18. 338–42), and at one point they are indeed shown lamenting him (*Il.* 19. 282–302). Yet, presumably due to the absence from the Greek camp of any women other than slaves, it is men, led by Akhilleus himself, who are the most prominent mourners. During Akhilleus' own *prothesis*, glimpsed in preview and flashback, the parts played elsewhere by women are taken by goddesses who put in an appearance. The Muses sing a dirge; Thetis and her sisters lament.[19]

As in Troy, women grieve more intensely than men. Unlike any of the men, both goddesses and slaves beat their chests (*Il.* 18. 31, 51), and one captive resorts to an extreme gesture: 'with her hands she lacerated her chest and soft neck and fair face' (*Il.* 19. 284–5). This violent form of grieving is mentioned again when a warrior boasts that any man facing him will die: 'his wife's cheeks are lacerated, . . . and he . . . lies rotting, surrounded by more vultures than women' (*Il.* 11. 393–5).

In Homer, lamentations may be kept up by a whole army or community for a long time – nine days for Hektor (*Il.* 24. 664, 784), seventeen days and nights for Akhilleus (*Od.* 24. 63–4). Such prolonged, widespread, and inten-sive mourning can hardly be entirely spontaneous, and a degree of artificiality is acknowledged by the poet when he remarks that those less closely involved ostensibly weep for the dead man, but really for their own suffering and losses (*Il.* 19. 301–2, 338–9). In this ritual form of grieving, then, a clear gender distinction is created, which expects women to mourn more conspicuously and more intensely than men. Outside the ritual setting, however, such a contrast is as yet barely noticeable.

The discovery of male self-control

A famous deathbed scene in Plato's *Phaedo* has a group of men struggling to retain their composure in a manner that strikes a chord with every modern reader, and could not be further removed from the abandoned grieving of Homer's heroes. When Sokrates calmly takes poison in the presence of his friends, they react as follows:

> For some time, most of us had managed to keep ourselves from crying, but when we saw him drinking and finishing the poison, we no longer could. A flood of tears escaped me despite myself, so that I covered my face and wept aloud . . . . Even before me, Krito had got up and left because he had been unable to control his tears. Apollodoros had never stopped crying even earlier on, and at that moment he let rip. With his heart-rending cry, he broke down all present, except Sokrates himself, who said: 'What are you doing? You amaze me. It precisely for this reason that I sent away the women, so that they would not misbehave like this . . . . Be quiet and be strong.' When we heard this, we were ashamed and stopped crying.
>
> (117 C 5–E 4)

No other classical Greek author is quite so adamant about the importance of keeping a stiff upper lip. In his *Republic*, Plato goes so far as to propose the deletion from Homer of the verses describing Akhilleus' tears, Priam's rolling in the dung, and the like, since they set a bad example and might induce young men 'to chant lots of dirges and laments about petty mishaps, without inhibition or control' (388 A 4–D 7). An emphatic distinction is again made between the sexes in this respect: 'As you are aware, when any of us suffer personal misfortune . . . we pride ourselves on being able to stay calm and strong, since we regard that as the mark of a man, and the opposite as typical of a woman' (605 D 7–E 1).

Plato sets higher standards of self-control than most of his contemporaries. Xenophon is not averse to highlighting the tears shed by his heroes. In his historical novel, the great king Kyros is given to tears of pity, while in his history Agesilaos weeps at the death of his friend and fellow king, Agesipolis. Xenophon even offers a parallel to Agamemnon's tearful speech to the assembly: the mercenary leader Klearkhos once appeared before his followers and 'wept for a long time' before addressing them.[20] Fourth-

century BC law court and political speeches, too, often refer to men
appealing for sympathy by crying, both in private and in public. Such
emotional display may be denounced as insincere, as a rhetorical trick, but it
is only Plato who insists that those who descend to such behaviour are
'nothing but women'.[21]

Outside the realms of philosophy, then, the demands of emotional
control seem relaxed by the standards of modern Western culture, but they
are nonetheless more stringent, and certainly more gender-bound, than they
are in the Homeric world. A small but telling detail is that in classical
Athens etiquette requires one to hide one's tears by covering one's face in
most social situations – not just on festive occasions, as in the *Odyssey*. The
gesture tends to draw attention to one's distress as much as conceal it, but its
wide application does suggest the growth of at least a token taboo on crying
in company.[22]

Since Plato criticizes not only Homer but also 'other tragedians' for
playing on their audiences' emotions and milking the sorrow of their heroes
with long speeches, songs and dramatic gestures (*Republic* 605 C 9–D 6), it is
remarkable that even the tragic poets do not give tears free play. Both
Sophokles and Euripides do indeed bring Herakles on stage weeping and
crying out loud in agony ('*Ē, ē!*' *'Iō, iō!*' '*Aiai!*'), but they make him insist
that he had never before in his life shed a tear. Sophokles' Herakles expresses
particular embarrassment at 'wailing like a girl' and finding himself 'nothing
but a woman'. A passing reference in Homer, by contrast, takes it for
granted that even a hero like Herakles would cry regularly: 'he used to weep
[*klaieske*] to the heavens', says Athena, whenever he was in trouble in any of
his Twelve Labours.[23]

If tears are still common in the late fifth century BC, they are evidently no
longer unproblematic. In Euripides' tragedies, Agamemnon and Menelaos,
too, cry on stage, but they differ from their Homeric counterparts in
agonizing over the propriety of such behaviour. Menelaos tries not to weep
or excite pity by 'turning into a female through tears', but hesitates for a
moment: 'They do say that it becomes a well-born man to shed tears in
misfortune. Yet this fine thing – if it is a fine thing – I shall not prefer to
strength of spirit'. Agamemnon is still less certain: 'I am ashamed to shed
tears, but I am equally ashamed not to cry, poor me, faced with the greatest
misfortunes'.[24] The ideal, it would seem, is not to suppress one's emotions
altogether, as Plato would have it, but to strike a balance between a show of
sensitivity and a show of self-control.

While men in tragedy are more restrained than men in epic, the reverse is
true of women. Besides passing frequent comment on women's inclination
to cry, the tragedians lose no opportunity to conjure up images of women
lacerating themselves. 'My crimson cheek is marked with the gashes of nails,
a newly cut furrow.' 'I shall sink bloodied nails into the skin of my cheek.'
'Hellas . . . placed her hands upon her head, and with bloody strokes of the

nail soaked the soft skin of the cheek.' What was a rare occurrence in Homer has become commonplace in tragedy, a phenomenon all the more remarkable in view of the evidence that, in reality, lacerating oneself was not an acceptable way of expressing grief in fifth-century BC Athens.[25] The contrast between conspicuous displays of grief by women and men's qualms about crying at all creates a no doubt exaggerated image of the difference between the sexes. The important point, however, is that there must be a perceived gender gap for the poets to exploit in this way. It follows that Athenian men, however much they may still cry in private and in public, are now constrained by the knowledge that the expression of emotion beyond certain ill-defined boundaries will be branded as effeminate.

The gap, it should be noted, is one of class as well as gender. When wondering whether to cry or not to cry, Agamemnon comments that this is a question easily answered by the lower classes. 'Low birth has one advantage. For such people it is easy to cry, and to talk about all their problems. To a man of noble birth, all that is wretched. Our lives are governed by dignity, and we are slaves to the mob' (Eur. *IA* 446–50). In other words, men of high status feel obliged, and are expected by their inferiors, to show more self-control than most. The same point is made by Plato, when he insists that laments and dirges in poetry should not be uttered by 'men of repute' or 'famous men': 'we may assign them to women, though not to admirable women, and to those of the men who are of low standing [*kakoi*]'. The intended result is that upper class men 'will find that sort of behaviour intolerable'.[26] Although most commonly described as a gender characteristic, the capacity for emotional control is thus class-bound, too, and may cut across gender boundaries. Eminent women should try to restrain themselves; lower class men can more easily let themselves go.

A comparison of the representation of heroes in epic and tragedy thus reveals in Athenian drama an ideal of male self-control and a notion of the effeminacy of tears which are foreign to the *Iliad* and *Odyssey*. When did this new concept of masculinity emerge? The literary evidence bridging the gap between Homer and the fifth century BC is thin, but a few surviving fragments show that the classical ideology of gender goes right back to the earliest lyric poets, around the middle of the seventh century BC. 'Neither a single townsman nor the community at large, Perikles, will enjoy good cheer and find fault with the groans of mourning', is Arkhilokhos' response to a shipwreck which has claimed the lives of many men, 'for our lungs are swollen with pain. Yet the gods have created a remedy for incurable ills: stout endurance . . . . So you must bear up, while we, as quickly as possible, dispel *effeminate* grief' (*gynaikeion penthos*, F 13 West). Characters in Homer would have argued that prolonged grieving is no use, but here, instead, we are told for the first time that grieving is something for women, not men.[27]

Tears and effeminacy are not otherwise linked explicitly in archaic poetry, but there is much emphasis on emotional restraint. Less than a generation after Arkhilokhos, Semonides counsels: 'If people would listen to me, we should not be so in love with misery, and torment ourselves by dwelling upon what is bad and painful' (F 1 West). Quite extreme is another bit of advice: 'If we had any sense, we would not think of him, now that he is dead, for more than a single day' (F 2 West). The Theognid corpus, some of which may go back to the late seventh century BC, has more in the same vein. 'Endure misfortune, Kyrnos . . . . Do not let it show too much. Letting it show, Kyrnos, is a bad thing' (355–9). 'No one is totally happy in every way, but the good man endures his misfortunes and does not make a spectacle of himself' (441–2 = 1162ab). 'Drink whenever the others drink; if you are sick at heart, let no one know of the weight on your mind' (989–90).

Both the self-control expected of men and the lack of emotional control expected of women thus already feature in the earliest poetry after Homer and Hesiod. The literary sources, then, supported by iconographic evidence to which we shall now turn, indicate a radical change in the representation of gender in the seventh century BC.

Images of grief: emotional restraint and violence in funerary ritual

Even in the Homeric world, where women were not otherwise markedly more given to tears than men were, a clear gender gap opened up in mourning: it was women who played the leading role in laying out and lamenting the dead, and it was women who expressed their grief most extrovertly. This type of gender differentiation has been a feature of Greek culture from Mycenaean to modern times. Figurines and moulded vase ornaments in the shape of mourning women appear in Mycenaean art, and again in Greek art from as early as 1000 BC onwards. Painted scenes of mourning feature on coffins from Mycenaean Tanagra, as they do on many Geometric, archaic, and classical Athenian pots and plaques used as grave goods, offerings to the dead, or tomb decorations: in all of these, women predominate. Indeed, the first preserved human figure drawn in post-Mycenaean Greek art is a mourning woman.[28] The general pattern, then, is clear, and the continuities are obvious.

Less obvious and little studied, yet historically even more interesting, is the fact that certain changes take place within this basic division of emotional labour. A survey of images of mourning, and more particularly of depictions of the *prothesis* – the lying-in-state of the dead body, on a bier surrounded by mourners – will reveal two important trends. First, the gender gap widens as the display of emotion by women in funerary ritual grows in intensity between the late eighth and the mid-seventh century BC. The gap remains wide even when emotional display is eventually toned down. Second, between the late eighth and the early sixth century BC, male and female mourners are ever more segregated, until the *prothesis* becomes a purely private and female affair, while the funeral remains a public event and is increasingly dominated by men. These developments can be traced in any detail only in Athenian art, but there is evidence to suggest that they are not confined to Athens, nor to art alone.

Some mourners in Geometric art are shown touching the corpse or bier; others are waving a branch or whisk to keep flies away from the dead body; others again are engaged in ritual processions or dances. The vast majority, however, stand, sit, or kneel around the bier making one of the two standard gestures of lamentation: they raise either one hand or both hands to the head. The stylization of the pictures makes it impossible to tell precisely what these actions represent: beating one's head and pulling at one's hair are possibilities, but it may equally well be that the hands are indeed simply placed on the head (as they are in many later, more naturalistic pictures), or that the image is an abstraction intended to convey all these gestures at once. In any case, the images are clearly meant to convey emotional distress, and it seems fair to say that the two-handed gesture conveys distress more strongly. Two hands are surely sadder than one, when thrown up in despair.

In the last phase of Attic Geometric, Late Geometric II (LGII, 735–700 BC), these gestures of lamentation are clearly gender-bound. Figures easily identifiable as women by their long dresses, and sometimes also by two small brushstrokes indicating breasts, always use the two-handed gesture (Figure 1.1c, d). The remaining figures – some identified as men by their swords, and the others no doubt men, too – always raise only one hand to the head (Figure 1.2b, c).

Whether the same distinction is already made in earlier vase-paintings, from Late Geometric I (LGI, 760–735 BC), is not entirely clear. At this stage, few figures can be positively identified as female, since dresses are not yet part of the repertoire and breasts are the only indication of femininity. Male figures again can only be positively identified by their swords, since in scenes of mourning we never find the tiny brushstroke used elsewhere to indicate the penis. In LGI, as in LGII, definitely female figures raise both hands, while definitely male figures raise one hand in lamentation (Figures 1.1b, 1.2a). Our problem is to account for the great number of figures whose sex cannot be identified by physical characteristics or dress (Figure 1.1a). The absence of breasts does not necessarily mean that they are men, since most female figures in LGII have no breasts either (Figure 1.1d). Their visible legs do not, as one might imagine at first glance, imply that they are naked, and thus presumably men, since in LGI even unmistakably female figures sport seemingly naked legs (Figure 1.1b).[29] These highly stylized 'neuter' figures, therefore, could be either men or women. Given that, in both LGI and LGII, the sexes make distinct gestures of lamentation whenever we can distinguish them by dress or physical characteristics, it seems reasonable to identify men and women by these gestures even when we cannot otherwise tell the sexes apart. In other words, it is likely that the gender distinction which is universal in LGII does apply to all figures in LGI as well: among the 'neuter' figures, those who raise one hand are male, and the large numbers who raise two hands are female.[30]

If this is correct, the representation of men in Athenian funerary scenes between 760 and 640 BC changes little by comparison with the transformation undergone by women.[31] Throughout, the gesture of male mourners standing round the bier remains the raising of one hand, usually the right, to the top of the head, or to the forehead; the other hand may be held out towards the corpse, but more commonly simply hangs down (Figure 1.2). The same pose is struck by men moving in line, probably performing a funeral dance, as depicted on LGII and Early Protoattic vases (EPA, 700–675 BC).[32]

There are also men who, generally without making gestures of lamentation, form a procession of chariots, horsemen, and warriors, either fully armed or equipped only with a sword. In LGI, it is quite clear that these are processions circling round the bier, since they are often part of the *prothesis* scene itself (Figure 1.3), though also found by themselves in separate frames.[33]

In LGII, a procession is only once more pictured as part of the main scene, but independent lines of chariots and men proceeding round the vase remain common; they are still common in Early and Middle Protoattic work

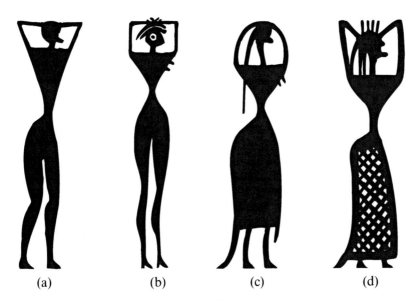

(a)   (b)   (c)   (d)

Figure 1.1 Female mourning gestures: Late Geometric
(a) style of the Dipylon Master (LGI)
(b) style of the Hirschfeld Workshop (LGI)
(c) after Florence 86.415/85/86 and Uppsala 137 (LGII)
(d) style of the Workshop of Athens 894 (LGII)

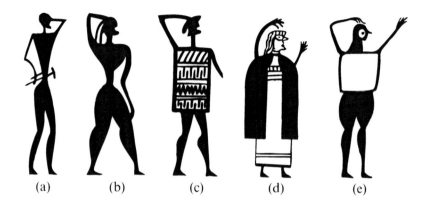

Figure 1.2 Male mourning gestures: Late Geometric and Early Protoattic
(a) style of the Dipylon Master (LGI)
(b) style of the Workshop of Athens 894 (LGII)
(c) after Philadelphia Painter (Myrrhinous amphora) (LGII)
(d) after Phaleron fragment (EPA)
(e) after Kerameikos 1153 (EPA)

(MPA, 675–640 BC), but not thereafter.[34] These independent processions, too, are part of the funerary ritual, as is shown by the gestures of lamentation made by some of the participants (Figures 1.4, 1.5).[35] It would seem that what the Attic painters had in mind was something very much like the chariot procession around the bier mentioned in Homer as a regular 'privilege of the dead'.[36]

From the start, women are represented in a markedly different manner. The one constant factor is that in ritual lamentation they appear to display greater emotion than men. The two-handed mourning gesture which characterizes women in Late Geometric art must express, as suggested, more intense or at least more extrovert grieving than the male gesture does,[37] and subsequent changes only reinforce the distinction.

In LGI, most women stand round the bier, but many of them sit on stools. Two touching scenes almost certainly show the deceased's wife, with their child in her lap, seated by his body – in one picture on a simple stool, in the other on an impressive 'throne' (Figure 1.6). A very few women kneel or squat on the ground.[38] In striking contrast, no one ever sits down to lament in a LGII *prothesis* scene. The figures on either side of the bier always remain standing, and of the figures shown 'below' (that is, in front of) the bier, most of whom had previously been standing or sitting, the vast majority now kneel on the ground (Figure 1.7).[39]

This is by no means a trivial change. The *Odyssey* treats sitting on the ground rather than on a chair as a pointed demonstration of sorrow: on hearing that her son has left on a dangerous journey, Penelope 'was swallowed up by soul-destroying grief, and she could no longer bear to sit on a

Figure 1.3 Prothesis, LGI krater, Louvre A517
Source: Photo: La Licorne. Courtesy of Musée du Louvre

stool, although there were many in the house, but she sat on the threshold of her room, lamenting pitifully' (4. 716–19). Like Penelope, female mourners of the LGII period are apparently too agitated to contemplate sitting down during the long *prothesis*, and many are so distressed that they sink to the ground. The painters of this phase, it would seem, portray women who mourn more intensely than they used to.

This trend is temporarily reversed in EPA painting, which as often as not features women striking the one-handed pose that was used to characterize men (Figure 1.8).[40] In the only scene from the period to juxtapose male and female mourners, the women make a curious intermediate gesture, with one hand raised to the head and the other to shoulder-level (Figure 1.9). A gender distinction thus remains in force, but it is rather muted, and women seem to express their grief a little less extrovertly.

The next development is all the more dramatic. Only three *protheseis* survive from the Middle Protoattic phase, but in all three we find an entirely new pose: one hand is raised and stretched out, while the other is raised to the level of the cheek. The painters have taken particular care to show the fingers making a clawing gesture. These women are unmistakably lacerating their faces with their fingernails (Figures 1.10, 1.11).[41]

Two of the *protheseis*, and a third scene depicting mourners in exactly the

Figure 1.4 Procession with mourning charioteer, EPA bowl, Kerameikos 1158
Source: Photo: DAI

Figure 1.5 Procession with mourning hoplite, MPA 'Hoplites' bowl, Aigina Museum
Source: Photo: DAI

Figure 1.6 Mourners with children, seated at the bier (LGI)
(a) after New York 14.130.14
(b) after Athens NM 802

Figure 1.7 Kneeling mourners (LGII)
(a) after Berlin, Staatliche Museen 1963.13
(b) after Karlsruhe B 2674
(c) after Baltimore 48.2231

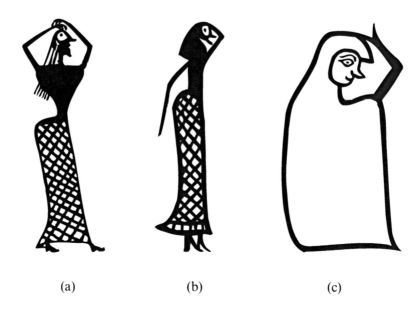

(a) (b) (c)

Figure 1.8 Female mourning gestures: Early Protoattic
(a) after NY.210.8
(b) after Würzburg 80
(c) after Mainz University 156 (krater D)

same pose, are painted on mugs found in an offering trench in the Kerameikos cemetery, dated to *c.*660 BC. The third, which actually shows blood on the women's cheeks, appears on a jug recovered from a trench of *c.*650 BC. In this second trench was also found a remarkable offering stand (*thymiatērion*) in the shape of a woman holding up a bowl. Unlike other such figures, this one supports the bowl with only one hand: she holds the other against her temple, from which blood flows down to her chin in two red streaks (Figure 1.12).[42]

The sudden concentration of images portraying self-mutilation, an extreme display of grief, calls for more comment than it has provoked so far. Scholars have tended to assume that cutting one's face, neck, and chest had always been a customary form of mourning, which for artistic reasons had never been represented until 'the Protoattic artist gradually freed himself from the stylized postures and gestures and created the first images of intense human grief'.[43] Yet we have seen that the development was not gradual. Figures were already much less stylized in the EPA period, but the trend was to show women in *less* emotional poses, and when they raised a hand it was never to the cheek. The sudden vogue for pictures of women lacerating their faces, therefore, is a surprising new departure. At the very

Figure 1.9 Funeral dancers and mourners, EPA amphora, Kerameikos 1370
Source: Photo: DAI

Figure 1.10 Prothesis, two fragments of MPA mug, Kerameikos 1280
Source: Photo: DAI

28

Figure 1.11 Prothesis, MPA mug, Kerameikos 80
Source: Photo: DAI

least it indicates that a new importance is attached to the custom. It might even mean that the practice had only recently been adopted in Athens.

It so happens that two non-Athenian terracotta figurines survive, dating to the same period (*c*.670–650 BC), and also representing women lacerating themselves. One, from Rhodes, displays 'scratches, filled with red, on breast and cheeks' (Figure 1.13); the other, from Thera, represents a woman who 'has just finished making five bloody scratches on her right cheek, and now pauses, her right hand ready at the top of her left cheek, to start gouging again' (Figure 1.14).[44] The simultaneous appearance of these figurines suggests that at this time laceration may have been newly popular in quite a few parts of Greece.

Around the middle of the seventh century BC the gender gap thus seems wider than ever. Men feature only in an occasional funerary procession, while women monopolize the ritual of lamentation and display their grief more violently than at any time before.

The female monopoly on scenes of lamentation continues in the next two phases, the Late Protoattic and Early Black-Figure periods (640–580 BC); men do not appear in a single scene with funerary connections.[45] On the other hand, the lacerating gesture does not remain the standard female pose

Figure 1.12 Female mourner, MPA *thymiatērion* stand, Kerameikos 145
Source: Photo DAI

in Attic art. In paintings, both on vases and on plaques, the mourners seem rather restrained, as they place both hands on their heads with 'formally correct, trained gestures'.[46] Yet graphic images of self-mutilation do continue to appear. A vase attachment in the shape of a mourning woman's head, from the late seventh century BC, has three dark red streaks running from her temples to the corners of her mouth, her chin, and her neck, while similar streaks run from her forehead down her nose (Figure 1.15). The rims of a jug and a bowl, of 600–590 BC, are decorated with figurines which, despite striking a stylized pose with two hands raised to the head, have their foreheads and cheeks painted with red scratches (Figure 1.16). A table for a board game, dated to 590–580 BC, has a mourning woman on each corner, her cheeks painted red.[47]

Things change again from 580 BC onwards. Women are shown in a much greater variety of poses, and often seem more emotional than in the preceding phase, but despite this there is no longer any evidence for the custom of laceration.[48]

One of the few scholars to have commented on the change attributes it to artistic taste: 'the black-figure painter shrinks from the colourful gore' (Kurtz 1984, 327). An alternative explanation, which to my surprise I have not seen suggested elsewhere, might be that the change reflects a well-known legal ban on female self-mutilation at funerals. It is said that, in 594 BC, Solon 'forbade those who beat themselves [in lamentation] to inflict skin-

Figure 1.13 Figurine of female mourner from Rhodes, 670–660 BC, London BM 14
Source: Photo: British Museum

wounds'. An old Roman law dictating that 'women shall not scratch their cheeks' supposedly copied Solon's very words. This particular prohibition was not repeated in subsequent Athenian funerary laws, which rather suggests that it had been effective.[49] Tradition has it that even earlier attempts had been made to modify mourning ritual. Epimenides of Phaistos, a religious expert invited over from Crete in the late seventh century BC, had reportedly tried to make the Athenians 'gentler in their

31

Figure 1.14 Figurine of female mourner from Thera, 650 BC, Thera 392
Source: Photo: DAI

grieving', by introducing certain sacrifices and 'prohibiting the severe and barbaric behaviour which had previously afflicted most women' (Plut. *Solon* 12. 8). According to the literary evidence, then, self-mutilation was a controversial custom for some time until it was successfully outlawed. The artistic evidence for 660–580 BC could very well reflect this state of affairs, ranging as it does from female mourners with blood running down their faces to

Figure 1.15 Head of female mourner as vase attachment, late seventh century BC, Cahn collection HC1038
Source: Photo: Courtesy of of Dr Herbert A. Cahn

mourners who appear to lament quietly and decorously, until the more violent images of grief disappear shortly after the date of Solon's reforms.[50]

A second significant development from 580 BC onwards is the reappearance on the scene of men.[51] They are transformed. Gone are not only the chariot processions, but also the traditional gestures of mourning. With very few exceptions, men are shown as a group, walking towards the bier, but showing no signs of grief. Instead, they keep one hand covered by their cloaks and raise the other towards the dead man as if in salutation. Their composure stands in stark contrast to the women's display of emotions ranging from quiet despair to wild grief (Figure 1.17).[52]

In the previous period, the absence of men, and the violence of women's emotions in mourning, had suggested strongly developed gender differentiation. The banning of self-mutilation softens the contrast, but the transformation of the men more than compensates. Their return certainly does nothing to bridge the gender gap. On the contrary, the female monopoly on grieving remains intact, and the contrast between the sexes gains an extra dimension: women continue to be shown as the emotional

Figure 1.16 Head of female mourner as vase attachment, 590 BC, Jug,
Kerameikos 40
Source: Photo: DAI

sex, but in addition, men – their calm movements proof of emotional equilibrium – are now explicitly portrayed as the sex capable of restraint and
self-control.

The other major trend to be discerned in funerary art is the development
of gender segregation. In the first phase of the Late Geometric style,
roughly two-thirds of surviving *prothesis* scenes do in fact feature both
women and men, whether in processions or gathered round the bier.[53] The
arrangement of the men around the bier varies. In one scene, all the men
stand to the right, apparently bearing offerings, while the women stand to
the left, but elsewhere the sexes are not kept apart. Men may appear immediately behind the women, or directly beside the bier itself, either among the
women or in front of them. Conversely, another scene features two female
mourners moving along with the men's chariot procession.[54] In these early
vase paintings, then, gender segregation in mourning is not rigid.

In the second phase of Late Geometric, boundaries begin to be drawn.
Warrior and chariot processions are now separated from the *prothesis* itself
and assigned to other zones of the vases. Funeral dances, also pictured in
separate zones, are added to the repertoire. The effect is to create two
distinct all-male spheres of activity,[55] and to shift the balance a little
towards a women-only *prothesis*: only about half of these still feature
mourners of both sexes.[56] In these remaining 'mixed' *protheseis*, almost as

Figure 1.17 Black-Figure prothesis. 500 BC, funerary plaque, Louvre L 4 (MNB 905)
Source: Photo: La Licorne. Courtesy of Musée du Louvre

many men as women stand mourning by the bier,[57] but they are kept strictly apart. All women stand to the right of the bier, apart from a few placed 'under' it, and all men to the left (Figure 1.18). The sexes thus no longer mingle in mourning as they had done.[58] While one cannot assume that in reality, too, men and women would necessarily stand on opposite sides of the bier, the mere fact that artists introduce a form of gender segregation into their pictorial schemes implies that the sexes are now thought of as playing separate roles in the mourning ritual.

Their separation becomes ever more pronounced in the Protoattic period. In EPA, we find but a single funerary scene featuring both men and women: a line of male funeral dancers, superimposed on a line of female mourners, each in its own frame (Figure 1.9). Otherwise, the admittedly fragmentary evidence shows us either groups of women lamenting, or groups of men in funeral dances or parades. A unique Theban *hydria* from 680–670 BC, however, shows a *prothesis* scene in which men and women are only roughly separated (Figure 1.19).[59] This could be taken to mean that early in the century, at any rate, segregation was not yet clear-cut, but equally one could argue that Athenians, or at least Athenian artists, may have been keener to keep the sexes apart than their Boeotian neighbours were.

In Middle Protoattic, funeral dances disappear, reducing the role of men to parading, and, as we have already seen, during the next sixty years men seem to play no role at all. Again, the eventual reintroduction of men into *prothesis* scenes sharpens rather than blurs the impression of segregation. In Black-Figure painting, women alone stand mourning at the bier. Men, with the occasional exception of an aged man waiting to receive them, are always shown in a procession just arriving at the place where the body is lying in state. The majority are on foot, but youths on horseback may accompany them. They are presumably to form the funeral cortège (Figure 1.17).[60] The effect is once more to highlight the distance between the sexes: these images show us men who emphatically do not join the women at the *prothesis*, but instead play their own role in the funerary ritual.

Moreover, the crowds of men in these paintings are at times seen moving past a column, indicating the entrance to either a courtyard or a room (Boardman 1955, 55–6). That is to say, they are arriving from outside, while the women have been mourning inside the dead man's house. There is a contrast with earlier vase paintings, and Homer, where the *prothesis* takes place outdoors – or else there would have been no room for chariots to circle the bier – and accordingly women lament their dead in public. When the change took place is hard to tell. It may be that the disappearance of chariot processions after 640 BC reflects a move towards making the *prothesis* a private ritual, but if so, the transition was not completed until 594 BC, when another law attributed to Solon stipulated that *prothesis* was to take place 'inside' (*endon*). The law proceeded to bar from the dead man's house, from the procession to the grave, and from the funeral, any woman under the age

Figure 1.18 Prothesis, three views of LGII oinochoe, Louvre CA 3283
Source: Photo: La Licorne. Courtesy of Musée du Louvre

Figure 1.19 Prothesis, Boeotian Subgeometric hydria, 680–670 BC, Louvre A 575
Source: Photo: La Licorne. Courtesy of Musée du Louvre

of sixty who was not a cousin's daughter or a closer relative. Women who did join the cortège were instructed to walk behind the men.[61]

The result of this trend, and this legislation, was that in mourning women were no longer merely segregated from men, but segregated for the first time into a specifically private and domestic role, leaving men to dominate the public part of the funerary rites.[62] The juxtaposition in sixth-century BC art of groups of women gathered inside and groups of men approaching from outside, neatly mirrors this final twist in the construction of gender in archaic Athenian mourning ritual.

Vase paintings are not snapshots of real life, and scholars have rightly warned that one should not simply assume that images in funerary art faithfully reflect current funerary practice. Geometric and Protoattic art, in particular, have been thought to portray some 'heroic' version of a funeral, rather than the real thing. On the other hand, we have seen that in the early sixth century BC developments in artistic representation do closely match developments in contemporary behaviour as prescribed by law. Nor does anything suggest heroization or epic influence of any kind when one considers the representation of female mourners in earlier art. The custom of laceration is not a fiction, as Solon's law shows, nor is its predominance in the art of the mid-seventh century BC likely to have been inspired by an oral tradition about heroic funerals, since the custom is only briefly mentioned in Homer. Again, there is nothing in Homeric scenes of lamentation that could have inspired the sudden change from seated to kneeling mourners in Geometric vase painting. As for the men, funeral dances certainly do not feature in the epic tradition, which leaves only the chariot parade round the bier as a possible heroic fiction. Yet there is nothing intrinsically fantastic about even this practice, given a habit of staging the *prothesis* outdoors as implied by Solon's law, and given the occurrence of chariot processions in religious contexts in early Greece.[63]

Since images of funerary ritual in Athenian art do not quite correspond to their Homeric counterparts, and keep changing in ways not easily explained in terms of mere artistic convention, we must surely conclude that they are not generic pictures of fictional heroic funerals. In all probability, these images – selective, stylized, idealized as they no doubt are – reflect ritual mourning according to local norms and customs. If so, we are able to detect in the iconography how, over a span of a century and a half, gender relations in Athens evolved from the limited differentiation and segregation of the mid-eighth century BC to the sharp conceptual and social boundaries familiar from classical Greek culture but first developed between the mid-seventh and early sixth centuries BC.

Conclusion: reasons to be tearful

The history of mourning can only be fully understood as part of the history of tears, which in turn must be seen as part of the history of gender in archaic Greece.

Up to a point, however, changes in mourning customs can be, and usually have been, explained as a by-product of escalating rivalries between aristocratic families using funerary ritual to demonstrate their status and power. At funerals, not only the size of the burial mound and the lavishness of funeral feast, offerings, and games indicated the status of the dead man and his family, but also the duration of the *prothesis*, the number of mourners, and the intensity of the lamentations. Tears, being the 'privilege' (*geras*) of the dead, were a sign of 'respect' (*timē*). Self-mutilation was a sign of the highest respect. The tears of women thus played a part in the power struggles of men: for a family burying its dead, a public *prothesis* and funeral attended by crowds of women lacerating themselves would be an effective act of self-assertion against its rivals.

Solon's legislation may therefore be understood as aiming to limit the scope for disruptive competition between men by curtailing the role of women 'as a medium of display' (Humphreys 1993, 86). Lowering the emotional pitch of mourning may in addition have been designed to reduce the chances of funerals turning violent, spilling over into fights and inciting feuds.[64] Moreover, by the standards of a developing egalitarian ideology, the highest funerary honours came to be thought of as excessive for even the most prominent citizen, and fit only for heroes, tyrants or 'the barbarians in Asia'[65] – and such a more egalitarian ideology may well have begun to emerge in the early sixth century BC, if not earlier.

The intensification of mourning over the previous century and a half may be seen in part as the result of aristocratic competition as well; the surges in popularity of self-mutilation in art around the middle of the seventh century BC, and again around the time of Solon, may have corresponded to peaks of rivalry in contemporary funerary display.

Yet this cannot be the whole story. It is surely no coincidence that we come across a sudden proliferation of images of women lamenting desperately, scratching their faces till they bleed, at a time when we first meet the rejection of tears as 'effeminate' in literature, too. What is more, it is in all probability also during the seventh century BC that the emotional nature of women came to be enshrined in the cult of Adonis, the most conspicuous feature of which was the loud wailing of women standing on the roofs of their houses, lamenting the death of the young hero in a manner first attested *c*.600 BC in the poems of Sappho:

> He is dying, Kythera, the beautiful Adonis. What shall we do?
> Beat your breasts, girls, and rend your garments.
> Woe, Adonis![66]

The intensification of funerary display of grief is evidently part of a development affecting female behaviour more generally: as the masculinity of self-control is being discovered, women are beginning to act out a new role as the 'emotional' sex.

The removal of the *prothesis* from the public sphere, too, is part of a general trend affecting gender relations. Like the banning of laceration, it may be in part an attempt to close down an arena of aristocratic display, but it cannot be fully explained without taking into account other contemporary developments tending to the seclusion of women.

There has been much debate about the extent to which women in classical Athens really lived secluded lives, but it seems clear that such a life was held up as the ideal, however rarely it may have been attained in practice. In Homer, by contrast, some of the most highly idealized women walk about town without the company of men, though they do veil themselves in public and are escorted by a couple of servants. Nausikaa, an unmarried girl, actually leaves town with her maids to take a cartful of laundry to the river, bringing a box full of 'all sorts of food and dainties' as well as a goatskin full of wine and a *lēkythos* of olive oil (*Od.* 6. 72–80). The first sign of restrictions on women's outdoor activities comes, once again, in a law attributed to Solon. Forbidding a woman, as it does, to leave her house with more than three outer garments, more than an obol's worth of food and drink, or any basket taller than a foot-and-a-half, the law might almost have been designed to prevent just such expeditions as Nausikaa's.[67]

A degree of seclusion developed even within the house, to the extent that the room for dining and drinking came to be defined as the 'men's room', the *andrōn*, from which women were excluded, at least in the presence of guests. In Homer, the host's wife is entitled, indeed expected, to be present at feasts when visitors are being entertained. The same expectation still underlies Semonides' seventh-century BC diatribe against women.[68] The exclusion of women probably came about not long before 600 BC, by which time, vase-paintings suggest, banquets and drinking parties had become all-male occasions.[69]

Gender distinctions exist everywhere, but cultures differ greatly in their perceptions of what constitutes the gap between men and women and of how wide that gap is. Clearly, gender differentiation as such was not an invention of the seventh century BC, but iconographic and literary evidence indicate that its nature, as perceived by the Greeks, changed dramatically in the course of the seventh and early sixth centuries BC. Developments in funerary ritual, the emergence in literature of the notion that tears are effeminate and self-control masculine, the introduction of the Adonis cult, the growing seclusion of women, and their exclusion from commensality – all these point to a major historical process which saw an increasingly sharp segregation of male and female spheres, and a redefinition of men and women as psychologically virtually different species.

One must ask why the idea that fundamental and innate differences separate the sexes should have taken root so strongly in seventh-century BC
Greece. Helpfully, the significance attributed to gender distinctions in classical Greece is set out clearly by our sources, which frequently contrast men's
natural ability to make rational decisions, dependent on their capacity for
keeping emotions and appetites rigorously in check, with women's natural
inability to do either. This contrast serves not only to assign to men a higher
status, but it explicitly serves also to justify the exercise of power by men
over women. The argument is that it is essential to one's wellbeing that one's
life be governed by rational decisions, and therefore that it is in the best
interests of women that their lives be governed by men, who are able to
make for them the rational choices of which they themselves are incapable.
In its most articulate form this doctrine of natural superiority is found in
Aristotle's *Politics*, but the general principle was commonly recognized and
not confined to philosophical thought.[70]

In this light, it is quite obvious why, in classical Greece, men should have
been encouraged to maintain their composure at all times, while women
were expected to weep at the slightest provocation. Men may have spoken
with disapproval of the over-emotional behaviour of their wives and daughters, and women may have enjoyed their freedom to vent their feelings, but
ultimately the women's tears, lamentations, and ritual wailing for Adonis
had the effect of reinforcing the men's claims to natural superiority, and
justifying their power.

In classical thought, the notion of innately superior rationality further
served to justify a whole range of power relations: the power of parents over
children, of masters over slaves, and, for the undemocratically-minded, the
power of élites over masses. As Plato put it:

> One will certainly find a great many of all sorts of appetites, plea-
> sures, and pains in children, women, and slaves in particular, and,
> among so-called free men, in the worthless masses . . . . But simple
> and moderate appetites, guided by rational thought (*logismos*)
> according to good sense and sound opinion – these occur only in
> the minority who are the best by nature and who have been best
> educated.
>
> (*Resp.* 431 B 8–C 7)

The same principle, moreover, asserted the innate superiority of Greeks over
foreigners, and helped legitimate attempts to subject barbarians to Greek
rule. To a degree, then, women were assimilated to all these other subordinate groups, in opposition to free, adult, upper class, Greek men. Yet it was
felt that not all inferiors were of a kind, and in particular that Greek women
ranked more highly than slaves or barbarians.[71]

We have no archaic sources which spell out current perceptions of gender and other hierarchical relations, but what happened in the seventh and sixth centuries BC is best explained on the assumption that something very much like the classical ideology was then being formulated. I would suggest that men began to assert greater control over their wives, sisters, and daughters; that they increasingly sought to confine women to the private sphere; and that they justified the new balance of power by redefining the 'natural' traits of each sex.

In this process, female and barbarian characteristics may have been associated right from the start. The Adonis cult was an Eastern import, a Greek version of the cults of Baal and Tammuz found among the Phoenicians, Assyrians, and Babylonians. The ritual of self-laceration, too, may be of non-Greek origin. If it did indeed gain popularity in the mid-seventh century BC, as I have argued, contemporary Near Eastern customs are a probable source of inspiration. The late seventh-century BC prophet Jeremiah speaks of 'gashing oneself' in grief as a common habit among Israel's neighbours, and even in Israel itself where it was officially forbidden.[72] Bearing in mind that the general impact of the Near East on Greek material culture at the time was such that the seventh century BC has come to be known as the 'Orientalizing' age, it seems highly likely that Eastern, perhaps more specifically Phoenician, models encouraged the adoption of laceration as the ultimate expression of respect for the dead.[73] Significantly, the Greeks did not simply copy the practice: in the Near East, men as well as women resorted to self-mutilation in mourning. It was the Greeks who added a gender dimension. By having only women honour the dead with displays of extreme emotion, they bracketed women with barbarians as inferior by nature, and born to be ruled by their betters.

An outright identification of women and foreigners, however, rejected by classical thinkers, may have posed certain problems already in the archaic age. This could account for the controversy which evidently surrounded the custom of laceration and in the end led to its being banned. As well as offending against a growing ideal of less competitive and more egalitarian relations among men, it may have gone too far in associating aristocratic Greek women with barbarians and common people. A retreat from the extremes of emotional display better met the conflicting demands of gender, class and ethnic hierarchies.

With so many pressures pulling in different directions, it is not surprising that, from their turning point in the mid-seventh century BC, gender relations remained in a flux, if not an actual state of crisis, for two generations or more. In Athens, Solon's legislation appears eventually to have been quite successful in creating a new *modus vivendi*, soon afterwards graphically illustrated in art. When, by 580 BC, the dust settles, controlled and rational behaviour has established itself as a vital ingredient of true masculinity. For centuries to come, the Greek version of the idea that 'real men serve others' held that real men would put their superior minds at the disposal of the emotionally unstable and intellectually feeble – and in return ask only to rule over these inferior beings.

There could be no more precise illustration of the new concept of manliness than the disdain of Zoilos of Amphipolis, a contemporary of Aristotle's, for Akhilleus' despair in the *Iliad*. 'He should have known in advance that everyone runs the same risks in war', he says, sternly rationalizing away any cause for sadness. 'This sort of excessive grieving is effeminate.' Then, casting around for a single image to express the unmanly, slavish, and foreign nature of tears, he spits out, in final condemnation, 'Not even a barbarian nurse would behave like that'.[74]

Acknowledgements

This chapter has benefited from the generous advice and criticism of Paul Cartledge, Helene Foley, Alan Johnston, John Salmon, James Whitley, and an anonymous referee, as well as from the many helpful comments offered by participants in seminars in Leicester, London, and Swansea, at which various incarnations of this paper were delivered. Responsibility for the views expressed here remains exclusively my own.

Notes

1 Farrell 1994, 15. An accompanying footnote explains that the statistic 'is derived by comparing the 0.1 suicides per 100,000 boys under the age of nine to the 25.8 suicides per 100,000 boys between ages 20–24' (268, n. 8).
2 From F. Hayward, 'The Male's Unpaid Role: Bodyguard And Protector', as cited in Farrell 1994, 21.
3 The story was 'related by Robert Bly [of *Iron John* fame] during a breakfast discussion' and is cited by Farrell (1994, 43), who contributes the etymology (ibid., 44).
4 Gilmore (1990, 231) ends up dismissing the problem: 'here we have to stop, for this is a question for the philosopher, not the social scientist'.
5 Akhilleus' tears: *Iliad* 1. 349, 357, 360, 362, 364. His mother stroking him: 1. 361.
6 His translation skips the passage where Thetis strokes her son. Cf. scholia *ad Il.* 1. 349, 360, and e.g. *ad Il.* 19. 5: 'Fine men are always quick to tears'. Hostile comment: below, 46.
7 The evidence set out briefly below has been studied at length in several recent studies: Monsacré 1984a, 1984b; Waern 1985; Arnould 1990; see also Neuberger-Donath 1996.
8 Holst-Warhaft (1992, 105) notes the repeated fainting of heroic knights at the sight of dead comrades in e.g. the *Chanson de Roland* or *Le morte d'Arthur*: probable instances of the literary intensification of emotions.
9 'Groaning' of the injured: *Il.* 8. 334; 13. 538; 14. 432. Even Ares 'groans' (*Il.* 21. 417) and *olophuretai* (*Il.* 5. 871) when injured. However uncertain its precise meaning, Willcock (1986, 203) is probably right to argue that Monsacré's rendering of *stenakhein* as 'to sob' (*sangloter*; 1984a, *passim*) is not appropriate. Arnould (1990, 20–2) claims that men do not actually shed tears *in pain*, with the exception of Thersites (*Il.* 2. 266–9), who is the 'worst' man in the army. There

are also, however, the tears of Eumelos, an eminent figure, when his chariot crashes; the context does suggest that he is in pain (*Il.* 23. 396–7). Note that the heroes are quick to withdraw when wounded, and not above fainting: Van Wees 1996, 7.

10 Tears of joy: e.g. *Od.* 10. 408–20, 453–4; 16. 213–20; 21. 222–6; 23. 205–8, 231–41.

11 Menelaos sat down on the beach, wept, and wanted to die, until he 'had his fill of weeping and writhing' (*Od.* 4. 538–41). Odysseus, believing he had been dumped on some foreign island rather than taken home, 'grieved for his fatherland, crawling on the beach and wailing greatly' (*Od.* 13. 219–21); earlier, he had considered drowning himself when, in sight of home, his ship was blown off course again (*Od.* 10. 49–52). Cf. also Laertes' covering his head with dust when reminded of the loss of his son (*Od.* 24. 315–17).

12 *Il.* 24. 163–5 (smeared), 635–40 (many days; 'among the mangers', *en khortoisi*). He had earlier wallowed in the dung at the city gate (*Il.* 22. 414).

13 Telemakhos later matches his father in self-control, and contains his tears: *Od.* 17. 489–91.

14 'Inhibited': *aideto*. *Aidōs* ranges in meaning from 'shame' to 'respect', a sense of inhibition being the common element (Cairns 1993, especially 13; Riedinger 1980); to adopt the common translation 'felt ashamed' here might suggest that Odysseus regards crying as intrinsically embarrassing, which it clearly was not. Telemakhos foreshadows his father's behaviour when he, too, buries his face in his cloak to hide his tears in the presence of his host (*Od.* 4. 113–16, 153–4).

15 For example, *Od.* 16. 220; 21. 226; 23. 241; and the long scene in which Odysseus persuades Akhilleus that grief should not interfere with a sensible diet (*Il.* 19. 154–233). See Waern 1985, 226–7.

16 Monsacré (1984a, 159–184) and Neuberger-Donath (1996) identify subtle differences between male and female tears in Homer, but as Holst-Warhaft (1992, 107–8) notes, this is stretching the evidence.

17 Andronikos 1968, 11. He tries to explain away some quite violent displays of emotion by women. Most studies of mourning (see n. 28, below) do not make the necessary distinction between funerary and other expressions of grief.

18 *Il.* 23. 135–6; *Od.* 4. 197–8; 24. 45–6. Akhilleus, too, plans to cut his hair (*Il.* 23. 45–6); what is unusual is his decision to cut off a lock which was supposed to be dedicated to the river Sperkheios (*Il.* 23. 140–53).

19 This combines features of *Il.* 18. 50–72 (foreshadowing Akhilleus' death) and *Od.* 24. 43–64.

20 Kyros: *Kyroupaideia* 5. 5. 10; 7. 3. 6, 8, 11, 16; cf. 1. 4. 2, 26, 28. Although he is a Persian, Kyros is surely set up as a model for Greeks as well; it is possible, however, that tears of pity were more acceptable than tears of grief. Agesilaos: *Hellenika* 5. 3. 20; 7. 1. 32; Klearkhos: *Anabasis* 1. 3. 2. Arnould (1990, 106–8) notes that Klearkhos' soldiers' response is to be 'amazed', and suggests that Agamemnon-style public weeping is no longer regarded as appropriate; however, Klearkhos' appeal is successful, and the soldiers are initially amazed because they do not know what the matter is, rather than because their commander's behaviour is strange in itself.

21 *Apology* 35 B 3; Appeal for sympathy: e.g. Lysias 32. 10; Isocrates, 19. 27, 14. 47. False appeals: e.g. Isoc. 17. 18; Demosthenes 38. 27; Aeschines, 2. 156.

22 Briefly discussed by Arnould 1990, 58.

23 Euripides, *Heracles Furens* 1354–7; Sophocles, *Trachiniae* 1071–5; Hom. *Il.* 8. 364.

24 *Hel.* 991–2, 947–53; *IA* 451–3. Arnould 1990, 103–5; Dover 1974, 167–8, 195.

25 See nn. 48–49, below. Quotations from Aischylos, *Choephoroi* 24–5; Eur., *Hel.* 1089 and 370–4. References to laceration: Garland 1985, 141–2; Foley 1993, especially 110–11. References to female tearfulness: Dover 1974, 100–1.

26 Pl. *Resp.* 387 D 1–2, 387 E 9–388 A 2; Foley 1993, 102–3 n. 4. Note also the gradual transformation of the concept of *sōphrosyne* from 'good sense' in Homer to 'self-control' in Plato: North 1966.

27 Noted by Arnould 1990, 102; Foley 1993, 102–3 n. 4. The poet is clearly speaking of a general atmosphere of mourning rather than of ritual lamentation during the lying in state of the dead, already associated with women in Homer.

28 Coldstream 1968, 21. Figurines of *c.*1000 BC: Schmidt 1967, 168–73, pl. 58. 2. Analyses of mourning and *prothesis* in Mycenaean and early Greek funerary art: Cavanagh and Mee 1995, 45–51; Vermeule 1991, 104–18; cf. Iakovidis 1966, 45–50; Geometric: Rombos 1988, 77–91, tables at 35, 337–47; Ahlberg 1971; archaic and classical: Shapiro 1991; Kurtz 1984; Zschietzschmann 1928; archaic plaques: Boardman 1955. Mourning: in ancient and modern Greece: Holst-Warhaft 1992, 98–126; Alexiou 1974, 4–21; ancient: Seaford 1994, especially 74–92; Humphreys 1993, 83–8; Garland 1989 and 1985, 23–34; Kurtz and Boardman 1971, 142–9; Andronikos 1968, 1–20; Reiner 1938, 8–70.

29 It may be noted that large jutting chins are also characteristic of LGI and II figures of both sexes, and should not therefore be mistaken for beards.

30 This is the conclusion of Ahlberg's scrupulous examination (1971, 261–7). She admits only one exception: a scene on krater frg. Athens NM 812 (Ahlberg 1971, no./pl. 18), where all figures strike the 'female' pose, but only some of them have the two tiny brushstrokes that indicate breasts. Perhaps one should consider the possibility that the painter was simply careless; see also below, nn. 31, 37, 58.

31 I owe to James Whitley two important observations. One: it remains conceivable that the 'neuter' figures represent males, and if so, the change in the representation of gender in mourning ritual from LGI to LGII is even more radical than I suggest below. It would follow (a) that mourners in LGI were male, whereas in LGII most were female, and (b) that gender-specific mourning gestures are first created in LGII; in other words, that both the predominance of women in mourning ritual and their greater display of emotion are reflected in art only from 735 BC. Two: developing gender differentiation is *not* mirrored in grave goods and grave markers, which are more clearly 'gendered' *before* LGII (see Whitley 1991, 179–83).

32 Male mourners at the bier: LGI: Ahlberg 1971, nos./pls. 2, 7–8, 19–20, 22); LGII: Ahlberg 1971, nos./pls. 32–5, 38, 41, 43, 47–8. Lines of lamenting dancers: LGII: Ahlberg 1971, nos./pls. 35, 38–9, 41–3, 58; EPA: Kübler 1970, no. 9, pl. 7 (Kerameikos 1153); King 1976, pl. 14, fig. 16; cf. Rombos 1988, 35, 347 (Kerameikos 1370); Cook 1935, pl. 49b = Ahlberg 1971, pl. 64d (frg. from Phaleron). For their interpretation as dancers, see Ahlberg (1971, 179): it is 'self-evident and has never been doubted'. One might note, however, that the mourners do not hold hands or carry branches, as is usual in other dances.

33 See Ahlberg 1971, nos./pls. 4–8, 13–16, 19. That processions circle the bier, rather than parade past it, is evident where processions 'departing' to the right proceed all the way round the vase to 'arrive' at the *prothesis* again from the left, thus neatly creating a circling effect without the aid of perspective. The clearest instance is the single LGII vase exhibiting this scheme (Oxford 1916.55; Ahlberg 1971, no./pl. 33); see n. 35. Similarly on two earlier vases, except that here the procession is cut up into frames (Sydney 46.41; Louvre A552 = Ahlberg 1971, nos./pls. 14; 16). Ahlberg (1971, 168–70, 296) surprisingly insists that processions parade past, but do not circle, the bier; presumably she wishes to create space for

her argument that those standing beside the bier are in fact moving round it (1971, 299–300).

34 Kübler (1970, 202–4) gives the middle of the seventh century BC as the cut-off point; although Morris (1984) does not comment on it, her 'Hoplites bowl' of c.640 BC (pl. 11, no. 585 [here Figure 1.5]) would appear to be the latest featuring a procession with a funerary connection (see n. 35).

35 The single LGII vase featuring a procession as part of a *prothesis* scene is Oxford 1916.55, cited in n. 33; Coldstream (1968, 56 n. 5) notes that this vase is something of a throwback in several respects. LGII processions in separate frames: Ahlberg 1971, nos./pls. 35–43, 46, 58cd, 59, 60a, de. Sheedy (1992, 27) points out that from LGII onwards vases were smaller and that, as a result, 'the big set pieces, the *prothesis* and the chariot procession, had then to be abbreviated'. The raised hands of the mounted warriors on amphora Essen K 969 (Ahlberg 1971, no./pl. 40) may represent a form of mourning gesture. EPA processions with funerary connections: New York 10.210.8 (Cook 1935, pl. 47; below scene of mourning women); Athens, frgs. from Phaleron (Cook 1935, pls. 48ab, 49a; raised hands); Kerameikos 1152 (Kübler 1970, no. 5, pl. 6; probable frg. of male mourner preceding chariot and horseman); Kerameikos 1158 (Kübler 1970, no. 3, pl. 4; lamenting gesture [here Figure 1.4]). MPA procession with hindmost warrior making a gesture of lamentation: Morris 1984, pl. 11, no. 585; dated towards 640 [here Figure 1.5]. Other EPA/MPA scenes which I would regard as funerary processions despite the lack of positive indications other than the fact that most come from offering trenches for the dead: Kübler 1970, 202–4.

36 *Il.* 23. 8–9, see above. The suggestion of a circling movement, as well as the absence of a corpse, count against the alternative theory that these processions represent the *ekphora*, the carrying out of the dead for burial (*contra* Kübler 1970, 36). Except on Athens 806 (Ahlberg 1971, no./pl. 20), the postures of horses and men do not suggest that they are racing as part of the funeral games (*contra* Kübler 1970, 202), though the occasional appearance of warriors jumping onto the chariots is remarkable (e.g. LGII amphora Stathatou collection 222 = Ahlberg 1971, no./pl. 40; MPA vases Kerameikos 75, 76, 79 = Kübler 1970, nos. 28, 27, 31, pls. 16–19, 27–8).

37 Rombos (1988, 341) points to at most three possible instances of women, whose hands are otherwise free, making one-handed gestures.

38 Wife and child: Athens NM 802; New York 14.130.14 [Figure 1.6] (Ahlberg 1971, nos./pls. 7, 25). Other seated women: Ahlberg 1971, nos./pls. 2, 3, 4, 7 (a second figure), 8, 13 (in large numbers), 14, 15, 22. Women kneeling: 2, 8 (incl. wife and child?), 18; squatting: 23.

39 On 13 LGI vases, the figures below the bier stand or sit; on only 3 do they (also) kneel or squat. On 13 LGII vases their counterparts kneel; on only 5 do they stand. The development was noted, but not interpreted, by Ahlberg (1971, 123–5). Ahlberg notes that figures below the bier are often differentiated from other female figures (1971, 128–32), and argues that they are often, but not always, professional mourners. It seems to me that the rather different style of painting (less elaborate hair, no cross-hatching on clothing) is likely to be due to the compression required in the confined space under the bier. Even if one takes the distinction seriously, it seems more probable that the figures nearest to the bier are close relatives rather than professional mourners. The issue does not, however, affect my arguments.

40 A trend noted by Kübler (1970, 40). As well as in Figs 1.8b, c and 1.9, the one-handed gesture appears in a *prothesis* (Victoria D23/1982; Rombos 1988, pl. 14) alongside the established two-handed gesture. The latter appears also in Figure

8a; in a second *prothesis* (King 1976, pl. 15e = Ahlberg 1971 no./pl. 44); and almost certainly on a frg. from the Kerameikos (Kübler 1970, no. 218, pl. 107).

41 As is generally agreed. Neumann (1965, 89), Kübler (1970, 199), and Kurtz (1984, 327), note the novelty of the gesture in art.

42 Mugs from the earlier trench (β/IX): Kerameikos 80, 1279, 1280 (Kübler 1970, nos. 21–4, pls. 12–15); jug and *thymiatērion* from later trench (γ/XI): Kerameikos 145, 149 (Kübler 1970, nos. 46, 49, pls. 36–42; and cf. pp. 454–5, 457–8, for the interpretation). A woman on the so-called 'Oresteia' or 'Aigisthos' krater of *c.*650 (formerly Berlin A32; *CVA* Berlin, Antiquarium 1, pls. 18–21; Morris 1984, pl. 13) makes precisely the same gesture as the mourners on the Kerameikos mugs: see Morris (1984, 60) for the date and interpretation. I can find nothing in Kübler's photographs or descriptions to support Kurtz's claim (1984, 317), that 'the clay women on the handles' of some of the above vases also sport 'pale cheeks . . . dabbed in red paint' (as some later figures do, see below).

43 Kurtz 1984, 327. Boardman (1955, 55) also sees the new pose as reflecting a difference in style only; he asserts that these vases do not otherwise 'contribute to our knowledge of funeral practice'. So too Neumann 1965, 89. Ahlberg (1971, 264–5) not only assumes that laceration was a long established practice but even wrongly claims that some Geometric figurines have blood painted on their cheeks and foreheads. Only Vermeule (1991, 104–18) has actually tried to demonstrate that self-mutilation was continuously practised from Mycenaean to archaic Greek times (cf. Cavanagh and Mee 1995, 47, 58). To my mind it is not clear in Mycenaean art that certain marks *are* lacerations, or that some of the 'lacerated' figures are *women*. In any case, without further evidence until *c.*660 BC, continuity cannot simply be assumed.

44 Quotations from Higgins 1967, 29 (see pl. 11d; BM, cat. no. 14), and Vermeule 1991, 104 (see Figs. 11–12). The Thera figurine (Thera 392) is also discussed by Higgins, who dates it to the mid-seventh century BC (1967, 40; see pl. 15h); John Salmon suggests to me that the unique and highly dramatic pose of the figurine might indicate an artist conscious of portraying a new phenomenon. A third seventh-century BC figurine, from Crete, described by Vermeule (1991, 116, Fig. 41) as possibly a blood-spattered mourner, is more probably some 'spotted demon' (Boardman 1961, 103–4).

45 The late seventh- and early sixth-century BC *loutrophoroi* listed by Karydi (1963) feature mourning women only: thus, for example, the vase from Vari, published in *Archaiologikon Deltion* 18 (1963), pls. 49–51; Munich 7629 (in *CVA*, Munich 3 = Zschietzschmann 1928, no. 78, pl. 9); and Boston 24.151 (dated in *CVA*, Boston 2, to 600–580 BC). The same goes for the earliest plaque series in Boardman's survey (1955, nos. 1, 3–5), though he mentions a fragment of a male head (no. 2, unpublished) which might be an exception. The lists of Protoattic themes compiled by Houby-Nielsen (1992, Table 7) and Whitley (1994, Table 3.6) mention no male mourners. A figure on a recently published fragment of a plaque in the Cahn collection in Basle (HC1028; in *Frühe Zeichner* 1992, no. 6, dated to 650–625 BC) is in every respect indistinguishable from the standard female mourner, except for the fact that the skin is painted red. If this a man, as the catalogue entry has it, he is the only male ever to be shown in this pose (at least after LGI; see above, 20–1 with n. 31).

I owe to Alan Johnston a reference to an exception from outside Attica: a cup from Kommos (Crete), dated to 650–625 BC, which shows a *prothesis* flanked by a hoplite and a man in a tunic, whose left hand is raised towards his face; the vase is damaged at this point, but it seems to me that he may be grasping a lock of his own long hair (rather than 'a bouquet of flowers'; Shaw 1983, 445–7; fig. 1 and pl. 61, 3).

46 So Vermeule (1991, 103; cf. fig. 8) *à propos* of Boston 24.151, which shows a pose typical of the period.

47 Attachment: Cahn collection (HC1038; *Frühe Zeichner* 1992, no. 10). Jug and bowl: Kerameikos 40 and 41 (Kübler 1970, nos. 106–7, pls. 93–4). Gaming table (presumably made specifically as a funerary gift): Kerameikos 45 (Kübler 1970, no. 129, pl. 102). The dates are those suggested by Kübler in his earlier discussions of the finds (1959, 66, 122: 'beginning of the 590s' for the jug and bowl; 79, 123: 'beginning of the 580s' for the gaming table); he subsequently suggested lower dates ('late 590s' and '570s' respectively: 1970, 381, 383), but these have not found much favour (cf. Morris 1984, 15–16).

48 Zschietzschmann's survey mentions only the gestures of '*beating* the head and forehead with the flat of the hand, the cheeks and neck with *clenched fist*' (1928, 23). Reiner (1938, 45 n. 1) is wrong to claim that Zschietzschmann's nos. 72 and 99 (pls. 12, 17) do depict women 'scratching' their faces; Karydi's claim that Kerameikos 1682 shows scratched faces (1963, 94) is not supported by its description in Lullies 1946/7, 73; Neumann (1965, 89) mistakes the wrinkles of an aged mourner on Athens NM 1170 for scratches.

49 Plutarch, *Solon* 21. 6; Cicero, *De Legibus* 2. 23. 59 and 2. 25. 64. Contrast Solon's injunction to carry out the dead before daybreak ([Dem.], 43. 62), which had to be reiterated by Demetrius of Phaleron (Cic. *Leg.* 2. 26. 66). Note also that Plato feels no need to prohibit self-mutilation in his set of ideal funerary laws, although he specifically does forbid the singing of dirges, and lamenting outdoors (*Leges* 960 A 1–2): presumably the practice of laceration is simply no longer current. In the light of this evidence, as well as that of the vase paintings, we should conclude that references to lacerated cheeks in Athenian tragedy do not reflect contemporary practice, but constitute an archaism: Foley 1993, 107–43.

50 On the traditional chronology adopted here, there is a gap of more than a decade between Solon's law and the last mutilated mourners in art, which seems plausible enough. A low chronology putting Solon in the 570s would suggest a very rapid impact – unless one were to adopt a low chronology for the vases, too.

51 Their earliest appearance would seem to be on a fragment of a plaque attributed to Sophilos (Boardman 1955, no. 6; Bakir 1981, no. A.23–25), and they are a common feature throughout the rest of the century.

52 See the surveys in Kurtz 1984, 324–8; Boardman 1955, 55–8; Zschietzschmann 1928, 24–5. Again, there are exceptions, as Alan Johnston points out to me: a few male mourners clasp their foreheads with one hand (e.g. Zschietzschmann 1928, pl.15, nos. 89 and 92; *Frühe Zeichner* 1992, no. 130 [HC955]).

53 The total number of LGI vases in Ahlberg's collection of *prothesis* scenes is 26 (1971, nos./pls. 2–26, and the Kriezi Street amphora noted at 311, 314). Most of these are fragmentary; six vases are too fragmentary to be used for our purposes (nos. 9–12, 17, 26). Of the remaining twenty, six or seven (depending on how one interprets the vase discussed in nn. 30, 58) feature women only; thirteen or fourteen feature both sexes.

54 Ahlberg 1971, nos./pls. 2, 7 (behind women), 8, 19 (among women), 20 (ten men preceding four women, to the right of the bier), 22 (men right, women left), and 14 (women 'under' chariot horses).

55 Ahlberg (1971, 177–9) strains to find one LGII and one EPA example of *female* funeral dancers, apparently because she finds it 'very strange' (179) that there should be no female counterpart to the many male dancers. Neither instance is in fact convincing: whereas the men are always clearly moving, the women – whose feet are usually shown – are to all appearances standing still, and are surely mere mourners.

51

56 Ahlberg's collection includes 21 LGII vases (nos./pls. 27–43, 45–8; no. 44 is now regarded as Early Protoattic), the majority of which survive largely intact: ten of these feature both sexes (see next note). The absolute numbers are, of course, small, and the relative proportions therefore need not mean much.

57 Counting only the figures immediately beside the biers, and only largely complete scenes: thirteen men: twenty women (Ahlberg no./pl. 32); six: seven (48); three: three (33); two: two (41, 43); one: one (34, 38); women outnumbered: three: two (35); eleven: nine (47). The balance is tipped in favour of women by the additional female figures under the bier.

58 Only two LGII vases representing both sexes adopt a different scheme. Thorikos TC 65.666 (Ahlberg no./pl. 30) keeps the sexes separate in a different way. Hamburg 1966.89 (Ahlberg no./pl. 43) has one woman and one man on each side of the bier. LGI, New York 14.130.15 (Ahlberg no./pl. 22) is the only vase to separate men and women in this way (though the sides are reversed), unless one counts Athens NM 812 (Ahlberg no./pl. 18). On the view that the left-hand figures on the latter vase are men, it would be a unique LGI instance of a common LGII scheme – a fact which counts in favour of regarding them as women instead (see above, n. 30).

59 Louvre A 575 (Ahlberg no./pl. 52); dated by Coldstream 1968, 211. Alexiou (1974, 6) misunderstands Zschietzschmann (1928, 20) when she asserts that this vase 'shows the hair actually coming out'.

60 See surveys cited in n. 52 above.

61 [Dem.] 43. 62; Plut. *Sol.* 21. 6. Cf. Pl. *Leg.* 960 A: (lament in private only); Cic. *Leg.* 2. 26. 66 (Pittakos' law, *c.*600 BC, against attending the funerals of non-relatives).

62 This is not to say that women were *excluded* from the public part of the funerary ritual, for literary sources make it clear that they did attend, as do the very few surviving images of *ekphora* and burial: Ahlberg 1971, nos./pls. 53–5; Zschietzschmann 1928, nos. 91–2, pl. 15 (Paris, Bibliothèque Nationale 353, 355, from the late sixth century BC; the full pictures in *CVA*, Bibl. Nat. 2, pls. 71–3, show that the burials in question are accompanied by a funeral dance performed by hoplites).

63 Strabo (10. 448) cites an archaic Greek inscription, recording a religious procession comprised of 60 chariots, 600 horsemen, and 3,000 footsoldiers. On the likelihood that Homeric descriptions of chariots, even of their use in war, reflect contemporary practice, see Van Wees 1994, 9–13, 140–1.

64 Seaford 1994, 86–92; Alexiou 1974, 21–2. It should be said that these risks are purely hypothetical: no funerals which turned violent are attested, though the custom of bringing out a spear at the funeral of a murder victim is suggestive (Dem. 47. 69; Seaford 1994, 90).

65 So Herodotus 6. 58, on the exceptional rituals enacted for dead Spartan kings, which Xenophon regarded as suitable for heroes rather than mortals (*Lakedaimoniōn Politeia* 14 [15]); see Cartledge 1987, 332–42. See Athenaios 259 E for tyrants demanding exceptional funerary honours for their friends.

66 Sappho, FF 140, 168; cf. F 211 L–P. At approximately the same time, the cult myth of the love of Adonis and Aphrodite was mentioned in a lost work by Epimenides, the reformer of Athenian mourning ritual, according to a fragment from Philodemos' *On Piety* (Henrichs 1972, 92). The fragment also provides evidence for the date of the introduction of the cult, since it implies that this cult myth did not feature in either Homer or Hesiod. According to Apollodoros (3. 14. 3–4), Hesiod did mention Adonis, but called him a son of Phoinix and Alphesiboia, quite unlike any of the later versions which made him the son of Myrrha or Smyrna and variously named kings of Assyria or Cyprus. Most prob-

ably, then, the 'canonical' version of the myth was not yet current in the early seventh century BC because the cult had not yet established itself.

67 Plut. *Sol.* 21. 5. The law further allows women to travel at night only in a cart illuminated by a lamp. All this does seem designed to hamper women's freedom of movement, rather than to reduce their role as a 'medium of display': no limitations on, for instance, the wearing of jewelry or expensive clothing are mentioned. It is, of course, possible that further restrictions were imposed by other laws, though it would be surprising for Plutarch and his sources not to have noted these. Classical ideal of seclusion and actual freedom of action: Cohen 1989; Foxhall 1989; Just 1989, 105–25; Hunter 1994, 9–42.

68 Semonides, F 7, 19 (Bitch Woman keeps yapping, even among guests [*xeinoi*]), 29 (a guest seeing Sea Woman 'within the house' may – wrongly – praise her), 106–7 ('Wherever there is a wife, men cannot readily receive a guest who comes to the house'). Wives at Homeric feasts: Van Wees 1995, 154–63, 178–9.

69 Dentzer 1982, 123–5; Fehr 1971. Murray (1994) shows that some elements characteristic of sympotic behaviour go back well into the eighth century BC; the exclusion of women is not necessarily among them.

70 Classical gender ideology is well set out by Just 1989, 153–93; cf. Dover 1974, 98–102.

71 Aristotle (*Pol.* 1. 1252 a 35–b 9), insists that women, slaves and barbarians, though all naturally inferior to free Greek men, constitute quite distinct categories. For the ideology in general, see Just, as cited in n. 70.

72 'Gashing' (*jitgōdēd*): Jeremiah 16. 6–7 (Israel), 41. 5 (Shekhem, Shiloh, Samaria), 47. 5 (Philistines), 48. 37 (Moab), 49. 3 (Ammon). Forbidden by law: Leviticus 19. 28, 21. 5; Deuteronomy 14. 1. Self-mutilation – with weapons – was also a feature of the cult of Baal: 1 Kings 18. 28; Hosea 7. 14 (and attested much earlier in the Ugaritic myth of Baal and Anat).

73 The custom may have been known and sometimes practised earlier, as its brief mention in Homer suggests. In my view, the *Iliad* is to be dated to the first half of the seventh century BC (for the most recent arguments in favour of this date, see Van Wees 1997; 1994, 138–48; Osborne 1996, 147–60; West 1995; Dickie 1995; Crielaard 1995, especially 273–4; Sale 1994, 13 n. 10; 91 n. 103, 97–8), and I would suggest that Homer is referring to a custom recently introduced but not yet well-established, since it does not feature in the main scene of mourning, during the *prothesis* of Hektor. On a more conventional eighth-century BC (or earlier) date for Homer, one would have to conclude that the custom has played a role in Greece for longer, but its marginality in the epics would still contrast sharply with its predominance in mid-seventh century BC Athens, and Eastern influence might still help account for its spread. In any case, Classical Greeks continued to associate laceration with barbarian habits: e.g. Aesch. *Cho.* 423–4; Eur. *IT* 180; cf. Holst-Warhaft 1992, 130–3, 149–51; Reiner 1938, 59–61.

74 Zoilos, *FGrH* 71 F 11 (*ap.* Schol. A *ad Il.* 18. 22).

2

The *machismo* of the Athenian empire – or the reign of the *phaulus*?

Paul Cartledge

Colonialism and imperialism

It was only a matter of time, perhaps, before specialists in ancient Greek history caught up with the palpable trend towards the study of masculinity and manhood within the burgeoning overall field of gender and sexuality studies.[1] Yet, in another sense, manhood or masculinity has always been there, right at the centre of Greek history and historiography, inasmuch as war was an inescapable and indeed desired focus of Greek civic life. For war, according to the universal Greek normative preconception, was by definition exclusively the business of men. So close was the ideological fit between the two, indeed, that war was seen as a field for the display precisely of *andreia*, that is, virility or manliness in general, and specifically the peculiarly masculine cardinal virtue of martial courage and pugnacity.[2] However, as the editors of a recent collection of historical studies of 'masculinities in Britain since 1800' have well expressed it, although ' "Manful assertions" – whether of verbal command, political power or physical violence – have often been the traditional stuff of history, . . . this truth is more often accepted than analysed' (Roper and Tosh 1991, 1).

One area in which such analysis is actually being widely applied is that of colonialism and imperialism, sometimes labelled subaltern studies. Few topics engender such vigorous debate within current literary and cultural-historical studies, and there is now nothing startlingly unusual in the mere fact of applying here a gender/sexuality approach.[3] It is taking much longer for students of the ancient world to go and do likewise, although a most promising start has been made, precisely in the area of war and gender that concerns me, by Carol Dougherty's investigation of what she calls the 'colonial discourse', conducted with special reference to the tropes of rape and possession both of foreign women and of foreign land by Greek founders and settlers during the archaic period (1993; cf. Cartledge 1995b). Contrast, however, Dougherty's pioneering work with the standard historiography of war and imperialism in the Greek world during the classical period and later. That it should be written from a gender/sexuality standpoint or even with a gender/sexuality dimension is still not exactly an *idée reçue*.[4] The standard histories of the fifth-century BC Athenian empire, for example, seem mostly to forget or ignore the fact that imperialism is a culture and an ideology as well as a political, economic and military practice – that is, not only does imperialism affect culture but there is a culture of imperialism.[5] Or, if they are aware at least of that, as was Moses Finley, for example, they nevertheless do not – unlike the ancient Athenians – place gender at the centre of their representations and reconstructions.

There are, however, exceptions – there are always exceptions. One is Nicole Loraux's brilliant account of Athenian attitudes to citizenship and the division of the sexes, in which she studies the representations of the imperially marked Acropolis in both the performing and the visual arts (1984/1993; cf. Cartledge 1996a). Another, yet closer to my present theme, is the work of Edith Hall, which directly applies a cultural studies-inspired concern with tropes of self-defining literary discourse to the negative representation of the oriental barbarian Other as effeminate or 'unmanned' in polar opposition to the Greeks' definition of themselves as manly and warlike in fifth-century BC Attic tragedy (Hall 1989, 1993a). Closest of all, though, is the avowedly popular work of Eva Keuls, whose *Reign of the Phallus* (originally 1985) would seem to be the only vaguely systematic treatment available. Yet for various reasons – not all of them to do with invincible masculine prejudice against, and/or reluctance to accept, some of her more exotic feminist theories – this remarkable study appears to have had little or no impact on general historiography.[6] Still in 1989 Keuls could protest, not without justice, against the failure to acknowledge duly that 'classical Athens was a militarily aggressive, expansionist state, which treated its slaves more harshly than many other societies, enslaved its women and tyrannized its "allies" '.[7]

Too little has changed since then. Hence, in part, this present attempt to apply a gender/sexuality approach to Athenian imperialism of the fifth century BC, with respect to two questions in particular that as far as I am aware have never before been seriously raised, let alone adequately investigated. These are, first, the implications of imperialist *machismo* – insofar as Keuls was correct to claim that Athens' imperialism was distinctively phallocratic, what would or might that have implied for relations between, not Greeks and barbarians (Edith Hall's problematic), but Greeks and Greeks, that is, the Athenians and their allies (or 'allies', as Keuls prefers)? Second, if it is uncontroversial that among the Athenian citizenry it was the 'naval mob' (*nautikos okhlos*: Thucydides 8. 72. 2; Aristotle, *Politics* 4. 1291 b 4, 5. 1304 a 22) who were chiefly responsible for acquiring, extending and maintaining the Athenians' naval empire, how does that military prepotence square with the Athenians' moral-political ideal, or dominant military ideology, of civic masculinity – namely, that of hoplite (heavy-armed infantry) *andreia*?

Freedom and control

The metaphor of Greek colonialism as sexual domination in the form of penetration and rape has recently been thoroughly explored by Carol Dougherty, as noted above, with special reference to the commissioned odes composed by the lyric poet Pindar to celebrate victors in the four major Panhellenic – and all-male – athletics festivals. To her chosen body of textual evidence one might want to add those divine rapes of Greek myth that can be read as allegories of human conquest of foreign peoples and territories.[8] At a more mundane level, the trope of 'spear-won' (*doriktētos*) land carried an obvious gendered overdetermination, as erect male spear penetrated yielding female earth: Alexander the Great was therefore doing nothing out of the way in making that symbolism literally explicit as he began his supposedly Panhellenic invasion of effeminate Asia in 334 with a penetrative spearcast.[9] But may these images and insights legitimately be applied to the fifth-century BC Athenian empire? If 'to behave as a free man' necessarily involved being 'dominant and active', so that 'there was nothing shameful about conquering' (Svenbro 1988/1993, 189), was it the freedom or the masculinity that counted for more in the Athenians' and Greeks' scale of honour and shame, or did both count equally?

An earlier investigation of Greek self-identification through historiography led me to the firm conclusion that freedom was the archetypal and architectonic Greek value, the one in terms of which all others were judged and from which they were ultimately derived (Cartledge 1997, cf. 1993a). But gender or normative gendering ran freedom a close second. The combination of the two was therefore especially potent, and nowhere was it more virulently expressed than in the martial imagery of conquest by Greeks of oriental barbarian males. Since the latter were deemed to be effeminate by nature, as well as custom, it was only right and proper that they should be treated symbolically if not physically like women (of whom as a 'race' the Greek male stereotype was less than wholly flattering).[10] Perhaps the *locus classicus* of the visual representation of this trope is an Athenian red-figure *oenochoe* (wine-jug) of the mid-fifth century BC, all the more telling for not being an especially glamorous or out-of-the-way object.[11] On one side (Fig. 2.1 (left)), a nearly naked man, a young adult Greek soldier, rushes forward holding his penis erect (or semi-erect – observers disagree) in his right – that is, the positively gendered and militarily active – hand. On the other side (Fig. 2.1 (right)), a soldier in unmistakably Persian clothes and gear submissively offers his buttocks to the approaching aggressor while raising his hands in a feminine gesture of distress and, looking face-on to the viewer, says or rather wails (as if in a cartoon bubble) 'I am Eurymedon, I stand bent over'.[12]

The scene is unparalleled; that is, there are no other visual representations precisely like this known to be extant. Its exact significance, too, is open, as visual representations generically are, to more than one interpretation.[13] However, the underlying ideological schema seems clear enough: the polar opposition of masculine Greek and effeminate Persian, variations on which are known to have been played in all the central and public arenas where discursive representations of Athenian identity were negotiated. And the date of the scene, besides, is utterly appropriate.

For round about the time that our *oenochoe* was painted, the Athenians made some sort of peace with Persia on behalf of their alliance, and direct hostilities between the two sides ceased for a generation. That peace or cessation of hostilities the Athenians energetically represented both visually and verbally as a tremendous victory, and the buildings on the Acropolis of Athens that we today may tend to take for granted as generically Athenian are in fact the very local and specific outcome of a sustained programme of imperial building determined upon by the Athenian Assembly under the inspiration chiefly of Pericles. They were, moreover, financed very directly from the imperial 'peace dividend' – that is, from the surplus of monies paid over in tribute since the 470s BC by Athens' allies into a central war-chest housed, since its transfer from the island of Delos in 454 BC, on the Acropolis.[14] Good contemporary written evidence is lacking, as usual, but there is enough to suggest, what we might in any case have guessed, that the building programme was controversial, not so much among the voting members of the Athenian Assembly as among the allies. Hence came, in response, the construction (in more than one sense) of the Parthenon as a sort of Imperial War *Mouseion*, or shrine of the Muses: a cultural artefact, that is, designed both to illustrate and to propagate the Athenians' inclusive view of the peace as a Panhellenic victory of Greek civilization over oriental despotism. This explains, for instance, the prominent representation of defeated Amazons, a mythic foe who were not just oriental barbarians, but mannish female oriental barbarians, and, therefore, an even more formidable foe than standard-issue effeminate Persian males.[15]

The problem – our problem – is that the Athenians did not lord it only over the Persians and other barbarians. Suppose we now turn from Greek, or Athenian, relations with barbarians to relations between the Athenians and the other Greek members of their anti-Persian military alliance. From about 450 BC the Athenians began to speak of 'the cities which the Athenians control', meaning the Greek cities of their supposedly free allies, and to do so officially and publicly, where the allies could overhear them (Hornblower and Greenstock 1984, nos. 147–9). It must be added at once that *kratein*, the Greek verb used in this phrase for 'control', did not

Figure 2.1 Two views of the Eurymedon Oinochoe, Museum für Kunst und Gewerbe, Hamburg, inv. no. 1981.173
Source: Photo: Museum (Maria Thrun)

automatically carry despotic or tyrannical connotations – the cognate noun *kratos* was indeed the term for the power whereby the Athenians ruled or rather administered themselves democratically.[16] But whereas civic, democratic self-rule at home definitionally involved both ruling *and* being ruled turn and turn about, the Athenians' control over the subject-cities was a one-way, non-reciprocative and certainly less than wholly democratic process. It was all too easy therefore for dissident allies to represent the Athenians' non-responsible rule over them as equivalent to despotism, using language that conjured up the bogey of slavery, in outright contradiction of the very ideological foundation stone of Greek identity and self-consciousness. One rather telling indication of the extent and impact of this dissident allied response is the care with which Herodotus prefaced his considered judgment that the Athenians had been the real 'saviours' of the Greeks during the Persian Wars with the admission that he knew it would be 'invidious' or 'hateful to many' (7. 139. 1, 5); another pointer in the same direction is Thucydides' admittedly rather sweeping assertion that popular opinion inclined to support Sparta against Athens at the outbreak of war in 431 BC, on the grounds that the Spartans had declared themselves to be fighting for the liberation of Greeks from the Athenians' tyrannous suzerainty (2. 8).[17]

It was possible, in other words, for Athenian allies to represent their political status in foreign affairs as equivalent to that of the servile subjects of an oriental despotism, and that, as we have seen, would have raised issues of symbolic gendering – passivity, penetrability – aggravated in those cases where revolted allies had been punished by the confiscation or some other perceived violation of their territory (Hornblower and Greenstock 1984, p. 145 d). Indeed, as we learn indirectly from the document that served as a 'charter' for the renewed Athenian naval alliance of the fourth century BC, it was Athenian occupation of or distraint upon allied land that had been one of the allies' main complaints against the Athenians' fifth-century BC imperialism (Hornblower and Greenstock 1984, no. 60, lines 35–48). The Athenians' response was to attempt to put clear blue water between their allies and all other Greeks with whom they dealt and *a fortiori* all non-Greeks, by upgrading the allies to the honorific status of colonists, with all the implications of genetic kinship and religious communion that this relationship traditionally bore. Henceforth, representatives of the allied cities would parade alongside Athenian citizens and other residents of Athens in the two major civic religious festivals, the annual Great Dionysia and the quadrennial Great Panathenaia. At the former, moreover, the allies' symbolic masculinity would be explicitly affirmed and reinforced through the ceremonial *phallophoria*, the carrying of model phalluses, signifying their incorporation as associate members of the Athenian phallocratic hegemony.[18]

However, the structural strains and tensions of an inherently unequal relationship could not be entirely eased even by this most vigorous ideological massaging. In the first place, allied egos are unlikely to have been flattered by the fact that such participation was compulsory. Besides, allied representatives at the Dionysia had to carry, in addition to the phalluses, tokens of the money they paid over to the alliance as tribute, which had come to be viewed at least by the payers as a hated badge of their servitude. For the Great Panathenaia, moreover, there were further required contributions payable only by the allies, and not by the Athenians: a suit of hoplite armour to symbolize their military role and a heifer to sacrifice to the virgin Athena, Athenian patron goddess of the alliance in succession to Apollo of Delos.

The asymmetry between rulers and ruled was further reinforced at the Games that followed the sacrifice, and here again a gender element was centrally involved. Most of the Panathenaic events were open to all-comers – indeed, the Athenians had a stake in making the Games as comparable in their universality and prestige to the Olympic and the other three major Panhellenic games as they possibly could. But there were also in the programme Athenians-only events, organized on a tribal basis, and among these was the *euandria*, a contest of manly beauty or strength.[19] Was the risk of Athenian defeat by an allied team in such an ideologically sensitive contest simply too uncomfortable to contemplate, one wonders? Or was it rather that here was another arena reserved exclusively for Athenian manhood to demonstrate its superior masculine prowess, corroborating symbolically the real *kratos* the city of Athens wielded even over its supposed 'colonists'?

Violence and power

According to an 'anthropological view' proposed by the late Ernest Gellner, violence, including martial violence, was 'the central organizing principle of society' in ancient Greece, since it was politicized violence (1991, 62). Political power, that is to say, rested on the organization of violence. Sociologically speaking, moreover, classical Athens had in the terminology of Stanislav Andreski a high MPR or 'Military Participation Ratio': in wartime, that is, practically every available free adult male, citizen or non-citizen, bore arms – or at any rate fought in some capacity (Andreski 1968, especially 43–8). Politically, therefore, it mattered very much where the specific gravity of Athens' principal military fighting force was centred. The contemporary commentator nicknamed 'the Old Oligarch' (he was, certainly, an ideological oligarch) was characteristically frank about it: 'it is the common people (*dēmos*) who man the ships and confer power on the city – helmsmen, signalmen, captains, look-out men, and shipwrights – these are the ones who confer power on the city much more than the hoplites, the well-born (*gennaioi*) and the better class (*khrēstoi*)'.[20] He therefore conceded, far more controversially, that the Athenian *dēmos* deserved its political *kratos* (power, sovereignty). This *de facto* congruence between military function and political clout was reaffirmed more soberly and sociologically, for the Greek city in general, by Aristotle.[21] Nevertheless, despite the rise of the 'naval mob' to military prepotence, Athens' dominant military ideology remained a hoplite ideology. This was most obviously so among the *gennaioi* and the *khrēstoi*, the self-styled 'beautiful and good' (*kaloikagathoi*), who were to justify their anti-democratic counter-revolution of 411 BC in part on the grounds that it was they, and not the masses, who served the city best 'with both their personal resources and their bodies'.[22] But it was by no means a uniquely élite ideology. Indeed, it seems that not only the hoplites themselves but some, perhaps many of the sub-hoplite thetes may have internalized it for much or most of the time.[23] At any rate, the dominance of hoplite ideology in democratic Athens is fully confirmed by examples drawn not only from anti-democratic rhetoric and political theory but also from the two main publicly approved democratic discourses of drama and oratory, as well as by visual representations both official and unofficial. In the verbal examples at least, the essential gender component of the ideology is transparently clear.

If Athenian drama was importantly the city of Athens talking to itself, then it talked to itself as an 'imagined community' not of sailors but of hoplites (Anderson 1991). Two dramatic passages will have to suffice. In tragedy, the gender dimension of the dominant male hoplite ideology is captured perfectly in the ironic transgression of it by Euripides' Medea, an oriental barbarian woman, who ventured to compare male claims to a monopoly of hoplite *andreia* with a woman's monopoly of the pangs of childbirth and scandalously found the former wanting: 'I'd rather take my stand behind a shield three times than bear one child'.[24] In comedy, the chorus of Aristophanes' *Wasps* (1060–3) invokes the well-worn Marathon theme and in characteristic comic mode makes crudely explicit the implicit gendering of the hoplite ideology: 'The prowess we showed in battle, and the superb manly prowess we showed just in precisely this [indicating their artificial comic phalluses] respect. That was of the past [the Marathon hoplite battle]'. A few lines later (1076–7) the chorus-leader picks up the refrain: 'We . . . are the only genuine aboriginal native Athenians, a most manly breed'.[25]

In oratory, Nicole Loraux's study of the Athenian *Epitaphios* or Funeral Speech in both the fifth and the fourth centuries BC has demonstrated among much else how Athenians could consider someone to be less of an Athenian if he specialized in non-hoplite warfare (1981/1986, 34). A speech of Aischines, in self-defence against a charge of treason, nicely exemplifies the deployment of the *topos* of the *kinaidos* as the cultural anti-type of the normative hoplite: whereas the hoplite is the properly manly male, subduing his emotions and appetites for the sake of the group, the *kinaidos* is the womanly male, lacking above all sexual self-control.[26] In painted pottery for use in symposia or as grave-goods, the hoplite is everywhere, not of course depicted in the interests of accurate military history-painting but rather in order to make a sociological point about Athenian military hierarchy: painters 'emphasize the individual role of the [hoplite] warrior in relation to other classes in the city rather than his collective activity on the field of battle' (Lissarrague 1989, 44).

So far as political theory is concerned, Plato offers particularly revealing testimony. On the one hand, being Plato, he does not shrink from questioning in the *Laches* and in the first three books of the *Laws* the standard, hoplite definition of courage, but more representative of Athenian thought generally is the passage of *Laws* (4. 706–7) in which Plato's surrogate, the Athenian Stranger, disparages the naval battles of Salamis and Artemision to the greater glory of the hoplite battles of Marathon and Plataea; this is but an unusually colourful variation on the standard upper-class denigration on moral grounds of the undeniable practical role of lower-class sailors.

Nor was the downgrading of nautical thetes confined to verbal or visual art. For example, although the navy became the city's principal fighting arm from the Persian Wars onwards, it is not certain that thetes were included in official casualty-lists.[27] When war-orphans brought up at state expense were paraded at the Great Dionysia on their coming of age, the military equipment with which they were endowed was that of the hoplite (just as it was a hoplite panoply that allies were required to contribute to the Great Panathenaia, above).[28] When in the fourth century BC Athens had forfeited naval hegemony and was forced to employ more varied and flexible military tactics and strategy, a regular 'national service' was introduced for eighteen- and nineteen-year-olds in the form of the predominantly hoplite, land-based *ephēbeia*, but it seems probable that thetes, at least half of the Athenian citizens, never became ephebes, even though 'the whole city was an agent of war'.[29] And so on and so forth. In short, being a man in classical Athens is being a hoplite man, the hoplite is the masculine norm (cf. in contrast, the Roman 'masculinization' of soldiers, Alston, this volume). Being a member of the class of sub-hoplite thetes whose military function was naval was to be little if at all less of an 'other' warrior in terms of the Athenian civic 'imaginary' than was being an archer or peltast.[30]

But how does this hoplite ideology square with Athenian military–political practice? Or rather how did the nautical thetes respond to the mismatch between their *de facto* military–political prepotence and the hoplites' ideological hegemony? The many tactical innovations of the fifth and fourth centuries after Marathon and the multiple social, political and ideological tensions flowing therefrom are well brought out in Pierre Vidal-Naquet's nuanced diachronic analysis of the Athenian hoplite 'tradition'.[31] To that analysis I would only add two glosses and one other item of evidence. The first gloss concerns the composition of an Athenian trireme crew. One trireme alone was always crewed exclusively by Athenian citizens, namely the sacred state trireme detailed for official, and sometimes secret, business.[32] The crews of the remainder always contained a strong or dominant citizen component, but rarely if ever would the citizen rowers not be accompanied by hired foreigners and, even more controversially, slaves. In one sense, the trireme was a sort of microcosm of democratic solidarity, a 'cradle of liberty'; but from another point of view it was vulnerable to the literal taint of guilt by servile association.[33]

My second gloss concerns the Athenians' opening Peloponnesian War strategy. Vidal-Naquet rightly emphasized the destabilizing effects of the growth of Athenian naval power: 'the fleet was simultaneously a model and an agent of imbalance, destroying the old [hoplite] organization'; if it raised the military status of thetes, and moreover turned some of them into state-equipped hoplite marines and others into hoplite-status colonists, at the same time it 'also paradoxically mobilized the upper class' as captains and financial sponsors of trireme warships (Vidal-Naquet 1981/1986, 93). What has not always been fully appreciated, however, is the challenge posed to the dominant masculine hoplite ideal by the strategy and tactics laid down by Pericles for the conduct of the Peloponnesian War. Thucydides, who supported but probably somewhat misrepresented them, noted and regretted the Athenians' decision to sue for peace as early as 430 BC in order to prevent further devastating Spartan invasions of Attica.[34] But he failed to bring out the ideological stigma of womanish cowardice that the Periclean strategy of sitting tight behind the city walls as the enemy plundered their fields under their very noses must necessarily have inflicted on hoplites schooled in the masculine battlefield heroics of Homer's *Iliad*.

On the other hand, Thucydides does give a hint, in a doubtless fictitious pre-battle speech that he placed in the mouth of the brilliant Athenian admiral Phormion in 429 BC, of the sort of thetic riposte that might have been made in order to counteract dominant hoplite ideology: 'Stick to your posts in your ships (*eutaktoi . . . menontes*), keep good order (*kosmon*), be on the alert for any word of command . . . put your trust in discipline (*sigē*, literally 'silence')'.[35] Phormion, in short, is here made to appropriate traditional hoplite language counterculturally to an untraditional naval and thetic context.

It is with another such presumed thetic riposte that I conclude. On a *stamnos* (wine-jar) of about 440 BC (shown in Fig 2.2) one Archenautes ('Master Mariner') is depicted in the act of sacrificing.[36]

His name is extremely rare, even in Athens. His father, possibly one of the Salamis sailors celebrated almost uniquely in Aischylos' *Persians* of 472 BC, was apparently proud to proclaim thereby his own nautical station – unlike Aischylos in his own person, who fought at Salamis but whose epitaph, perhaps written by himself, tellingly mentioned only the quintessentially hoplitic Marathon.[37] Archenautes' father was not, one hopes, alone in being so self-consciously proud of his class's *de facto* naval reign. But the contrary

Figure 2.2 The Archenautes Stamnos
Source: Photo: British Museum

evidence of Anthemion gives one pause, and there is no gainsaying the, to us paradoxical, fact that *nautai* were – in the Athenians' conventional, moral–political parlance – *phauloi*, 'worthless', the reverse of the Old Oligarch's *gennaioi* and *khrēstoi*.[38]

Acknowledgements

It was an honour for me to kick off the 1994–5 Nottingham–Leicester Ancient History Seminar in a double act with Nick Fisher, and a pleasure to find that we are still together in print. '*Phaulus*' in my title is a derogatory Greek adjective meaning 'low-class'; it was chosen partly to pick up and respond to the title of Keuls 1993 – *The Reign of the Phallus*. For their kind invitation, and subsequent editorial labours, best thanks are owed to my friends Lin Foxhall and John Salmon. This chapter is dedicated to the memory of Ernest Gellner.

Notes

1 Instances of the trend are Roper and Tosh 1991; Nye 1993; Williams 1993.
2 Cartledge 1997, index s.v. 'bravery'; Loraux 1989/1995: passim.
3 Examples include Hulme 1985; Kabbani 1986; Hyam 1990; Dawson 1991; Greenblatt 1991. On gender and war specifically, see Cooke and Woollacott 1993; Bourke 1995; Damousi and Lake 1995; Trexler 1995.
4 More or less standard modern accounts and discussions of war and (Athenian) empire in English include Meiggs 1979; Rhodes 1985; McGregor 1987; Rhodes 1992; Davies 1993, especially 64–86; Mattingly 1996. (The picture would not be altered if non-English-language scholarship were included in the reckoning.) On the relevant ancient historiography: see Finley 1985b, 67–87 (chapter entitled 'War and Empire'); Wickersham 1994.
5 Said 1993; cf. Said 1978/1995. An exception is Finley 1985c, 76–109 (chapter entitled 'Democracy, consensus and the national interest').
6 Shapiro 1986; Knox 1989, 110–15.
7 Keuls 1989, 226; one of her specific targets was McGregor 1987.
8 Dougherty 1993a, especially 61–80 (chapter entitled 'The Lay of the Land'), index s.v. 'rape'; Zeitlin 1986. See also Marshall, this volume.
9 Diodoros Sikulos 17. 17. 1; Justin, *Philippic Histories* 11. 5. 10. On earth as gendered symbol, see further duBois 1988.
10 Hall 1989, 1993a; cf. Georges 1994, index s.v. 'Barbarian stereotype'. On the Greek stereotype of woman, see Cartledge 1997, 63–89; and on the 'race' of women, Loraux 1984/1993, 72–110.
11 Schauenburg 1975; Dover 1978, 105; Francis 1990, 39 and fig. 12; Hall 1993a, 111; Keuls 1993, 293 and fig. 261; Kilmer 1993, 264, R1155; Svenbro 1988/1993, 194.
12 Translation by Dover 1978, 105. Symbolism of the right hand: Cartledge 1997: 14, 67.
13 For a sample illustration of this general interpretative problem, see the essays collected in Goldhill and Osborne 1994; and for visual images of gendering in particular, cf. those in Kampen 1996.
14 Bibliography on the Acropolis building-programme and its imagery is immense; for a range of recent perspectives, see Castriota 1992, especially 184–202 ('The [Parthenon] Frieze and the Ethics of Imperialism'); Harris 1996; Spivey 1996, 123–71.
15 Recent discussion of the Amazons' cultural significance is cited and deconstructed in Henderson 1994, especially 135.
16 Moreover, the first attested appearances of the formula are in honorific, not punitive, documents. For a nuanced discussion of democratic *kratos*, see Meier 1990, index s.v. 'Power'.
17 On the implications of the language of tyranny in Greek inter-state discourse, see Cartledge 1997, 150.
18 Dionysia: Hornblower and Greenstock 1984, no. 135, line 12; Keuls 1993, 78 and fig. 71. Great Panathenaia: Hornblower and Greenstock 1984, nos. 76, lines 56–7; 85, lines 41–3; ?106, heading (lost); 135, lines 11–12.
19 Panathenaic Games generally: Kyle 1992; Neils 1994. *Euandria*: Crowther 1985.
20 Ps.-Xenophon, *Constitution of the Athenians* 1.2, trans. Gagarin and Woodruff 1995, 134; cf. 1.6.
21 *Pol.* 4. 1289 b 36–9, 4. 1297 b 12–28, 6. 1321 a 5–25.
22 Thuc. 8. 65. 3. *Kaloikagathoi*: 8. 48. 6.
23 The pride with which Anthemion son of Diphilos publicly celebrated and commemorated his rise from the thetic class to that of the Hippeis (Cavalrymen)

with a statue and an epigram seems to indicate a strong negative attitude to thetic status: ?Aristotle, *Constitution of the Athenians* 7. 4, with Rhodes 1981.

24 Euripides, *Medea* 250–1, trans. Gagarin and Woodruff 1995, 61. On 'bed' versus 'war' in the Greek imaginary see Loraux 1989/1995: 23–43.

25 Aristophanes' comedy is stuffed to the gunwales with nautical imagery, but as Henderson 1991, 165, has noted, references to the battle of Salamis 'often come in the context of . . . the woman on top' – the world turned upside down, that is, in normative Greek gender terms.

26 Aischines 2. 150–1; cf. Winkler 1990a, 50.

27 Raubitschek 1943, 48 n. 102; cf., on the symbolic significance of casualty-lists, Goldhill 1990, 110–12.

28 Goldhill 1990, 106–14.

29 Vidal-Naquet 1981/1986, 99. The fullest study of the *ephēbeia* known to me is an unpublished 1994 Oxford doctoral thesis by H. de Marcellus, who has persuaded me that no general and integrated system of military–moral education was introduced until the mid-330s BC but has failed to persuade me that all Athenians, including thetes, were obligatorily included therein; see rather Sallares 1990, 121. On the practice and sociopolitical significance of hoplite warfare in Greece generally, from the archaic to the late classical period, see Hanson 1989; Hanson 1995, 221–89, 327–56.

30 Lissarrague 1988. Civic 'imaginary': Loraux 1984/1993, 3–22. On the topic of civic inequalities at Athens, both ideological and institutional, see further Raaflaub 1996 and Cartledge 1996b.

31 Vidal-Naquet 1981/1986, 85–105; cf. Ridley 1979.

32 Thuc. 8. 73. 5, with Gabrielsen 1994, 109.

33 Trireme as 'cradle of liberty': see Strauss 1996. For a contrary emphasis on the servile element, see Graham 1992; Hunt 1998; cf. the generally negative picture drawn by Bourriot 1972, especially 22–30.

34 2. 59. 2, which he immediately counters with Pericles' 'last', self-justificatory speech (2. 60–4), the message of which the historian himself endorsed (2. 65. 7–9).

35 2. 89. 9; cf. de Romilly 1995, 172–3, who comments in regard to 2. 89. 3 on how extraordinary it was for Phormion to discourse on the merits of education for sailors.

36 Osborne and Byrne 1994, 68, s.v. 'Arkhenautes (1)' (contrast the popularity of Arkhestratos). The *stamnos* (London, British Museum E455) was assigned by J.D. Beazley to his 'Polygnotus Group'; if Arkhenautes was indeed, as is possible, a *kalos* name (cf. Dover 1978, 111–24), that would probably indicate a considerable rise in the social scale for the son by comparison with his father's assumed thetic status.

37 Aischylos, *Persai*, especially 302–432, with Hall 1996.

38 Anthemion: above, n. 23. The general issue of ideological hegemony within the Athenian democracy, especially in the fourth century BC, is the subject of Ober 1989, an outstandingly original and deservedly influential book. The thrust of this paper may, however, go somewhat to qualify some aspects of Ober's more optimistic construction.

3

Violence, masculinity and the law in classical Athens

Nick Fisher

Masculinity in Athenian culture

Ideals, images and issues of masculinity, gender difference and '*machismo*' are the subject of much current debate, ambiguity and confusion.[1] The mainstream culture of classical Athens no doubt, like many traditional societies, gives the firm impression of the dominance of less ambiguously and less apologetic masculinities than does modern Britain. Yet contradictions and debates on the appropriate exercise of one's masculinity existed there too. Many expressions of manhood took the forms of aggressive or violent behaviour; on the other hand, prevailing political values of the democracy upheld ideals of respect for law, tolerance and community spirit between citizens, and in principle offered protection for its poorer or weaker members from outrage or attacks on their property. Hence it is worth asking what procedures and mechanisms to restrain and deal with '*macho*' violence existed, how effective they may have been, and whether they were conceived as supporting and building on accepted ideals of assertive masculinity, associated with the honour of the male householder and citizen, or whether they sought rather to undermine or replace them.

The most striking image of masculine aggression to be found in the law court speeches comes in the account of a drunken fight between rich Athenians, some at least of whom were violently drunk, and who had clashed violently before. Ariston, the speaker of Demosthenes' speech against Konon, gives a graphic description of the beating inflicted on him by his enemies, who, allegedly, left him with a cut lip, and internal rib and lung injuries; the culmination of the assault was the triumphant gloating, 'the clearest sign of their *hybris*', which was most graphically displayed when the middle-aged Konon imitated a victorious, crowing, fighting-cock (Dem. 54.1–10, especially 8). The role in Athenian culture of cockfighting, both public (at the City Dionysia) and private, in affording the excitements of sport and gambling, and providing powerful, if ambivalent, images of masculine, aggressive and phallocentric assertiveness, has been much illuminated recently in accounts stimulated in part by discussion of the Getty Birds kalyx-krater, in part by Clifford Geertz's influential essay on Balinese cockfights.[2] How were such expressions of aggression regarded, and what responses to them were appropriate for male Athenians who sought both to defend their honour and to display a democratic devotion to the rule of law?

A masculine culture?

A starting point is a brief résumé of what have been taken to be prominent elements of a dominantly masculine culture, which I have taken largely from works by the social anthropologist David Gilmore, who undertook field-work in Andalusia, edited a symposion discussing and problematizing the concepts of honour and shame and the supposed unity of the Mediterranean, and wrote a cross-cultural survey on *Manhood in the Making*.[3] Thus it is suggested that in such cultures men would, on growing up, come to accept most or all of the following:

1   *A clear view of the great difference between male and female natures, the superiority of the male, and the consequent sharp ideological segregation of roles, and often attempts at physical segregation of women of the household in most areas and periods of life.* There is little need to argue either for the prevalence and importance of such ideas in Athens, or for the view that practice may have often differed from ideology.[4]

2   *The need to perform adequately as a husband, and to father children (especially sons).* For Athens one need only cite the example of the change of the husband's attitude at the birth of his son in Lysias' first speech (1. 6).

3   *The need to be seen to play male, dominating, penetrating roles in sexual behaviour and comparably in the expression in public of sexual attitudes, and hence to avoid being seen as feminine, effeminate or effete.* The importance of such attitudes in Athens has been the subject of many recent studies, which explore, above all, many complexities and contradictions, especially those introduced by culturally acceptable, if circumscribed and ambivalent, forms of homosexual behaviour.[5]

4   *The need to engage in competitions of manliness, and in many cases to prepare for this by elaborate rites of passage, which frequently involve feats of endurance and/or other initiation ceremonies, with or without sexual acts between boys and elder youths.* For Greece the survival in various forms in different cities of original initiation rituals is a contested issue, which for Athens focuses on the evidence for initiation into the phratries at the Apatouria, and its allegedly associated myths of

69

the 'black hunter', and on the stages of development of the *ephēbeia*;[6] still more contested is the debate on whether the origin of the cultural predominance of the 'pederastic' mode among homosexual relationships in Greece is to be traced to such initiation rituals.[7]

I am tempted to favour a positive response to all these questions, but cannot argue them here. In the classical period, free boys were trained for full admission to the prime cultural settings such as *gymnasia* and *symposia*, in many cases by their responses to pederastic pursuit from older members of these associations, while in many of the public festivals boys and ephebes were expected to display in varied competitions their development towards full manhood – most eloquently and dramatically in the Panathenaic competition in manly beauty and strength, the *euandria*.[8]

5 *The obligation to maintain an independence of occupation and ability to sustain the position of the close family.* For Athens, again there is no need to argue or illustrate the centrality of such ideas, with the additional pressure weighing on citizen householders to strive if possible to be slaveowners, and at all costs to avoid seeming to work in a 'slavish' way for another.[9]

6 *The pressure on an adult man to display throughout his life repeated feats of courage, by which above all one proved oneself a man, or 'played at' being a man, often linked to the need to defend or increase the wealth and status of the community in organized fighting.* In Athens, the standard phrase in the praise of the war-dead, above all the hoplite infantry – 'they (showed they) were good men' (*andres agathoi egenonto*) – the need to avoid the formal dishonour (*atimia*), or the informal comic mockery, associated with displays of cowardice such as leaving the ranks or dropping one's shield, are all eloquent testimonies to the strength of this ideological pressure.[10]

7 *Finally, the ability to respond adequately to insults, directed against oneself and one's masculine image, or against one's dependants, especially one's female relatives; concomitantly, the potency to display sexual virility in the male public arenas, at least in word and gesture, if not always in act.* It is with the (often contradictory) representations of these areas of masculine and honour-driven imperatives that this paper is concerned. Provisionally, then, it seems that Athenian males were likely to feel that a good deal of their 'honour', social identity and worth depended on their scoring highly according to these widely accepted standards of masculinity, that is on their proving themselves, repeatedly, to be at least adequate, and preferably more than adequate, on these criteria.

Further preliminary remarks on the applicability and use of modern ethnographic studies to Athenian culture may be made. First, discussion of values, feelings and actions in all the areas adumbrated above is very commonly conducted through manipulation of the Greek concepts which are usually 'translated' in English into the categories of 'honour' and 'shame': for ancient Greeks this involves above all concepts associated with *timē* – honour (including the negative *atimia* – dishonour, and *philotimia* – love of honour, ambition, public recognition) and *aidōs* or *aischynē* – shame (and many other words indicating insult or humiliation). Allegedly comparable concepts are found in similar and significant contexts in many so-called 'Mediterranean' societies. These are admittedly complex and culturally varied concepts, and 'honour' and 'shame' are far from identical across languages and cultures, and certainly not restricted to the Mediterranean region; but it remains a plausible view that these concepts share sufficient similarities across many such societies, as well as significant local variations and major cultural differences, for comparative work, if conducted with sufficient care, to lead to positive results.[11]

Second, care in this area is needed precisely because societies do not necessarily display a high level of interpersonal violence in civic life even if they undeniably have strong institutionalized and internalized beliefs (at least among men) both in firm 'natural' differences between the genders, and also in the need, in order to preserve the family's status, for all members to display the appropriate qualities and virtues in public. Many such societies may indeed have in the recent past been characterized by extensive or interminable feuds between communities, or vendettas between agnatic groups or networks of friends (for example, Albania, the Bedouin in Cyrenaica, or the Lebanon). In such societies, the formal legal systems were often perceived to be inadequate; rather than have recourse to a court hearing or an arbitration procedure (or faced with a defeat in such a setting), members of a family or social group felt a binding obligation, and a deep desire, to exact direct revenge, by the infliction of theft, wounding or death on members of the enemy family/group.[12]

Other studies suggest that demonstrations of masculinity and modes of preserving status can be radically renegotiated in response to changing political conditions. The Ghiyarti of Eastern Morocco, for example, have given up traditional ways of displaying manhood such as the feud, to maintain honour or gain scant resources, and have turned to more cooperative and legal means of showing their independent manhood, such as competitive wealth-seeking, displaying hospitality, and supporting friends and clients (Marcus 1987). A fine example of communities which combine high levels of sensitivity to masculine honour and aggressiveness with very low levels of actual physical violence are the Andalusian small agro-town communities described by Gilmore (as they were before the end of the Franco régime). Social life on the surface is polite, and fights are rare; but the community is suffused by verbal hostility and harmful 'magic'. The reasons for the relative absence of violence have apparently little to do with a respect for legal processes; rather they prefer to express antagonism and satisfy their sense of *machismo* through gossip, ritualized violence and insults at festivals, in order to maintain the general civility and cohesiveness of their small, close-knit community against the outside world. This conformity is apparently sustained by the memories of the horrors of the Spanish Civil War, and also by fear of the central police and authorities (Gilmore 1987a).

In modern Greek communities there are considerable variations in the balance achieved between the pressure to assert manliness in defence of honour, regardless of the law, and the pressure to keep to the law, internalize its values, and exercise self-restraint (cf. Herzfeld 1987, 159). Nowhere is there anarchy or unstructured violence, but the degree of involvement in legal procedures varies considerably. On the one hand, Campbell's Sarakatzani, living as transhumant shepherds on the fringes of Greek village communities, placed a high value on readiness to react to insults with violence; but limits were accepted, and the unmarried males establishing their manhood were expected to be much quicker to engage in a fight or a feud than the married householders. But since they regarded the courts as alien and largely corrupt, they would not choose to satisfy honour by going to law, if they could avoid it, and preferred to settle things themselves.[13] The 'Glendiots' of Crete studied by Herzfeld, shepherds in the upland interior of Crete, disdained going to law to resolve disputes, and praised successful trickery of the distant state authorities; they expected to prove themselves at times as men in the traditional form of rustling, but the practice was regulated by formalized conventions, and was often met not with escalation, but with limited counter-raiding or negotiation and the formation of alliances (Herzfeld 1985). On the other hand, many less marginalized communities, such the villagers of Euboia studied by du Boulay, or of Rhodes studied by Herzfeld, had largely given up recourse to violence and feud, and pursued their quarrels vigorously in the courts of the local towns, or in less financially dangerous ways inside the community. In Greece too memories of their civil wars, and the increase in central authority, seem to have had important effects.[14] Tentative methodological conclusions might be that, first, emphasis on the values of honour, shame and dominant masculinity still has value in studies of the ancient and the modern Mediterranean, and it may be premature to replace it with 'hospitality', or reciprocity (as recommended by Herzfelt), equally important and related concepts though those are. Second, one cannot simply look at some modern Mediterranean societies and say that because Athens was seriously different in its attitudes to violence and the law, it should not be considered as an honour-based society – conceptions of what constitutes 'honour' and best displays masculinity vary widely, and each society has to be studied for itself and in relation to its own complex structures and history.[15] One must recognize further that many such societies also provide mechanisms and discourses where the dominant male ideologies, and the sufferings and contradictions they help to engender, can be acceptably challenged, often by those systematically oppressed by these structures and values.[16] But finally, of course, classical Athens must be seen as structurally different from all modern Mediterranean societies in many ways – one need mention only that it was neither Christian nor Islamic, it derived great confidence from its major role in having fought off the threat of Persian domination, rather than being obsessed by memories of the foreign rule, by Turks or others, it operated an advanced citizen democracy, it was a slave society, it was relatively unindustrialized, and, despite the existence of urban complexes, it lacked a sharp distinction between rural and urban institutions or cultures. Comparisons at various levels may still have heuristic or provocative value, in stimulating hypotheses for further analysis, but they need to be explored with the greatest possible precision and caution.

Types and levels of violence

The circumstances alleged in the speech against Konon with which I started do not stand alone as examples of fierce *macho* violence among members of the Athenian élite (as Osborne called it, 'a neglected feature of Athenian life').[17] The cock-crowing element is in itself, 'perhaps the most revealing such instance left in the records' (Winkler 1990a, 49) of such sensitivity to honour and insult among the wealthier citizens; and the further details of the behaviour of Konon and his friends, and their aristocratic and Lakonizing groups with their offensive self-chosen nicknames such as Ithyphalloi and Autolekythoi, their sacrilegious private acts, and their violence over *hetairai* and against enemies or passers-by, all make this speech, in Murray's words, 'the most revealing source for the less respectable side of sympotic behaviour'.[18] There are, however, several other instances, above all, the many cases mentioned in Demosthenes' prosecution of Meidias, which most explores issues of *hybris* and violence: in addition to Meidias' allegedly sober and deliberate assault on an old enemy at the very public ceremony of the Dionysia, there are the brawls at dinner-parties at which Euthynos killed Sophilos and Euaion killed Boiotos, and most intriguing, the killing of Nikodemos apparently by Demosthenes' young friend Aristarchos (Dem. 21. 72–110). The other speeches focused on violence, or where violence was a significant part of more complex disputes, mostly also concern the political or sub-political classes, as of course do most of our speeches: most important are Lysias 3 and 4, Isokrates 20, and much of Ps.-Demosthenes 47, and the many accusations of violence made against Alkibiades. Apart from the assassination of Ephialtes, however, it is notable how rare unambiguously political killings or woundings were during the nearly 200 years of the democracy.[19]

It is not easy to assess how prevalent such patterns of violence were in Athenian life. On the basis of the evidence of the sample of law court speeches which happen to have survived, or whose titles are recorded, obviously no sort of statistical analysis is possible. No useful conclusions can be drawn from the fact that we know of, or suspect the existence of, two certain and perhaps five probable lawsuits of *hybris*, ten or so of homicide, perhaps nine of *aikeia*, and similarly small numbers of slander or deliberate wounding.[20] We can have no idea at all of the rates of homicide, violent crime, theft or fraud per 30,000 citizens, or of the relative rates of the different charges brought (and the same acts may lead to different charges), nor of the proportion of crimes committed which led to no legal action at all, which were settled, or stopped, at arbitration, or which reached a lawcourt hearing; nor, of those, how many were followed by conviction or acquittal, nor how many convictions led to execution of judgment. Hence, if one wishes to know whether it is appropriate to classify Athens as a violent society, in comparison with other cities in Greece, elsewhere in the ancient world, such as Rome, or with other pre-industrial societies, all one can do is to look at the speeches and arguments we have, and other relevant evidence, to assess the perceptions and arguments we find there, to see, for example, how frequent fights were thought to be, how their causes and progression are discussed, what distinctions of seriousness are made and in what terms, and what sorts of responses were felt appropriate.

Here my aim is to justify four preliminary conclusions. First, that among the relatively leisured classes observable in the speeches, fighting arising from insults and rivalries, especially sexual rivalries, was reasonably common, if often without very serious consequences; very probably, though little evidence is available, this sort of honour-driven violence operated in similar ways among the poorer members of the citizen body. Second, on the other hand, general social protocols imposed or encouraged fairly strict limits on permissible violence of this sort, and those who went beyond such limits with inadequate provocation, either on the spot or later, and planned 'revenge', could arouse general public hostility and even effective resistance in some cases, from those believing themselves to represent the community's interests. Third, those being attacked had certain undeniable rights of self-defence, including in certain circumstances the right to kill, to protect both the person and honour of those directly attacked and the state's interest. Fourth, and contrastingly, in most cases the community expected victims not to escalate the violence at the time, or plot direct revenge later, but rather to seek legal recompense. I shall argue that this will have seemed a realistic strategy for many because of the widespread acceptability of litigation. This in turn was based on three beliefs: that the courts offered all at least a chance of a satisfactory result; that success in the courts gave victims revenge, that it satisfied their anger and sense of wounded honour, and might give them additional benefits, including financial rewards; and that at all events litigation gave their grievance a public hearing. Overall, I would argue that the political and legal system worked hard to achieve three broad and complex aims: to reconcile ideals of masculine self-expression and the defence of a citizen's honour with the ideals of conflict-resolution and community spirit – which was also the mark of the good citizen and hence a 'masculine' ideal; to combine the particular desire for extra (or 'vertical') honour (*philotimia*) of the élite, harnessed through the mechanisms of acceptable honorific returns (*charis*) for their public services, with the people's desire to use the élite's competitiveness and the institutions of the courts to control undue violence, luxury or ambition among this same élite; and third, to encourage the spread downwards to the majority of male citizens of many of the traditional leisure activities and values earlier associated with the élite.[21]

The 'acceptable face' of male violence?

Much evidence confirms that a level of violence or insult could be regarded by some at least as common, be accepted fairly casually, and was not necessarily expected to produce either serious injury or major legal problems. The main settings for such insults and acts of violence are naturally the *gymnasia* and shared meals/drinking parties, and the main stimuli the common factors of drink and sexual rivalries; there were also no doubt, frequently enough, brawls among the market-stalls, or scuffles over boundary disputes in the fields; and there were occasional spectacular public and violent expressions of hatred and self-confidence, such as Alkibiades' and Meidias' assaults on *chorēgoi*.[22] The most impressive text suggesting that socially contained fighting could be held to be a routine part of the leisured citizen's lifestyle is Aischines' admission that he has been, and still is, engaged in erotic activity with boys, has written poems, and has engaged in competitions (*philonikiai*) and fights (*machai*) of the sort that tend to occur in such affairs (1. 135–6). He is responding to the allegation expected to come from 'one of the Generals', in support of Timarchos, that Aischines is a notorious lover of many boys, and a 'pain at the *gymnasia*'; but in his admissions that he has indeed been involved in affairs, competitions and fights one can clearly hear the attempt to assert membership of a *macho* élite to which erotic competition and fighting was important (cf. also Fisher 1998). At the same time there is here, and elsewhere in the speech, a consciousness of an important distinction which we find regularly in these contexts, though doubtless there was much room for disagreement on where it exactly the distinction should be placed. Aischines' fights – he implies – were evidently swiftly over, of no lasting consequence, and no one was seriously hurt or humiliated; but the savage whipping, beating and would-be enslavement administered by Timarchos and Hegesippos to the state-slave (or ex-slave) and cockfighting expert Pittalakos, and indeed their sorts of *kōmoi* and fights generally, are (naturally) held to be much more serious, and to arouse the indignation of those who witness them or hear the cries. Equally naturally, Hegesandros and Timarchos claimed – allegedly when trying to persuade Pittalakos to leave the altar – that the whole affair was just a *paroinia*; similarly Konon and his sons claimed their fights were mere drunken, youthful pranks, whereas Ariston asserted it was a gratuitous, and serious, assault, that demanded legal retaliation.[23] Perhaps the most explicit statement that the city and the laws need not take such hot-blooded fights in drink, over sex-objects, as reasons for inflicting serious penalties, is in Lysias 3 (*Against Simon*). 43; here the defendant, ashamed at being involved in such a lawsuit at his age, is trying simultaneously to argue that Simon was throughout in the wrong, the aggressor in the fights, and an intruder into the house and on his delicate nieces, and that the whole series of events did not merit a case of deliberate wounding before the Areopagos (cf. especially Cohen 1995, 131–5):

> It would be dreadful if in cases where people fight and get wounds arising from drink and competitiveness, or gaming, or verbal insults, or over a *hetaira*, cases where the people regret what happened when they recover their senses, if you were to institute such dreadful and major retributions (*timōriai*) as to drive some people from their country.

Comedy offers much corroborating evidence. The inextricable connection between consumption of food and drink, consumption of women and casual, if limited, violence is held to be characteristic of the image of Attic male social life in old and middle comedy. A similarly relaxed attitude to that of Aischines is found, for example, in the anecdote with which Athenaios introduces his thirteenth book on women and *symposia*: Antiphanes the comic poet, finding his play-readings didn't go down well with Alexander the Great, allegedly responded by claiming that his play would be best appreciated by those who have often eaten shared dinners (*deipnoi apo symbolōn*) and have more often given and taken blows over a *hetaira*.[24] A well-known sequence of comic passages from Book I offers a more ambivalent picture, as they trace the typical degenerative development of *symposia* and *kōmoi*: one short sequence emphasizes the medical and social value of wine, and then suggests that excessive drinking brings first *hybris*, then madness, then paralysis (Athen. 36 B = *adespot.* 101 K-A); a longer one, from Euboulos, sees the progression from health, love and sleep to *hybris*, shouting, *kōmoi*, black eyes, summonses, nausea, madness and throwing things about.[25] Such fights at parties were especially appropriate for and tolerated among the young: we find, for example, the association of youth and drunken *hybris* in Alexis (Athen. 36 D–E = 46 K-A), and many similar passages are quoted, later in Athenaios, by his severe character Pontianos, in defence of his view that wine is the 'mothercity of terrible things' such as drunkenness (*methai*), madness, and *paroiniai* (443 C–D). The same assumption is made, and questioned, throughout Antiphon's

Third Tetralogy, where the prosecution alleges that drink contributed to a homicide. The emphasis on youthful punch-ups explains why the elderly Konon and the embarrassed middle-aged boy-lover for whom Lysias 3 was written may expect to find their behaviour considered the more reprehensible, and why the behaviour of the *opsimatheis* like Philokleon (Ar. *Vesp.* 1299–363), and Theophrastos' twenty-seventh character, reverse the norm to comic effect.[26]

There are other factors in Athenian society which may have tended to encourage this form of limited, allegedly acceptable, violence, especially between more or less consenting youths at play, in addition to the pressures of masculine competitiveness. First, there was little in the way of any regulatory or detecting police force (as in most pre-industrial cities, including Rome before Augustus, and indeed many in early modern Europe); hence limits to violence in the streets and in informal social settings were set rather by other citizens present at, or arriving on, the scene.[27] Second, young men were trained to be fit, and used to fighting with hands and weapons.[28] Third, they were used to some degree to watching – and in some cases to enjoy watching – acts of violence – of animals, in cockfights, or against them, in the ceaseless sacrifices; or violence inflicted on society's rejects, in public executions, or the exposition of *kakourgoi* in stocks.[29] It is hard to estimate the effect of all of this, and certainly one would not wish to suggest that toleration of spectacles of violence and savagery came near to matching the extremely popular gladiatorial combats and animal fights found in the Roman amphitheatres, and throughout the cities of the Roman Empire.[30]

Fourth, and finally, it should be emphasized that casual violence against dependants and slaves, and the beating of children, were all likely to have been common. Slaves, like children, were known as *paides*, and derivation of that from *paiein* is a casual joke in Aristophanes (*Vesp.* 1295–8); the picture is supported by very extensive evidence for slave-whipping and other painful and degrading punishments as the main means of control, and as a prime defining difference between free and slave adult males.[31] Frequent beating of children was evidently uncontroversial, and justified as a means of correction and education, for those who have yet to attain rationality (cf. Golden 1990). Rather less is heard explicitly of wife-beating as a regular practice, but it seems unlikely that it did not occur pretty routinely. It seems a plausible assumption that the relative reticence of the sources should be explained by ambiguities in the nature of male authority and women's nature; the standard ideological positions were probably that husbands should usually be able to persuade their wives to conform or obey, and that on the other hand women should not complain if failings were dealt with by physical punishment, provided it was not 'excessive'.[32] We may be sure at all events that Athenian men assumed widely different levels of what was acceptable violence or sexual compulsion according to civic status and to gender.

Unacceptable violence and the rhetoric of insult

Athenian law recognized the offence of 'wounding with intent' [to kill] (*trauma ek pronoias*), where the criterion indicating such a serious intent may well have been the use of an offensive weapon, such as a knife or piece of broken pottery (*ostrakon*);[33] and accounts of fights can naturally, where appropriate, emphasize the degrees of injuries caused.[34] But the offence of *hybris* was in theory available to victims of serious assault – or 'those who wished' to take up their case – and was treated as a major crime with implications for the whole community, as was indicated by the fact that the penalties, including the possibility of the death penalty, did not involve financial gain for the victim; and *hybris* is clearly defined and understood above all in terms of action deliberately intended to bring major and improper dishonour or shame on others.[35] Equally, the language of those complaining in the courts about assaults (usually in cases of *aikeia* rather than of *hybris*) make it clear that the most popular rhetorical device used to arouse the anger of the jury is through a description of the gross insult, the *hybris* and the consequent humiliation inflicted, whether through verbal insults, blows, especially with the fist and to the face (cf. Meidias' punch *kondulois*, *epi korrēs*), repeated blows or kicks when the victim is helpless (on the ground in the mud in the assault on Konon);[36] this line, depending, as Demosthenes acknowledges (21. 72), on the manner of speech and action, gestures, looks and so on, and hence on the strength of witnesses rather than reports of injuries, was no doubt especially open to rhetorical exaggeration, or, conversely, to stout denial. More grievous *hybris* may be the cases of savage whippings inflicted on victims tied to a pillar or post, where there is evidently an assimilation to the punishment of a slave (the Teisis case, and the assault on Pittalakos).[37] Also useful was serious infliction of injuries, supported by the best they could achieve by way of supporting medical evidence – even if no seriously offensive weapon was used as in the Konon case (Dem. 54. 10–12). Another factor which could help to guide opinion against one side in a fight, and be crucial should it come to court, is the question of aggression, who 'started the unjust hands'. Also relevant might be the numbers involved in both sides.[38] But the impression remains that emphasis on deliberate infliction of dishonour and shame in addition to actual violence was the most effective rhetorical means of arousing anger in an audience, for all that it could depend on the dubious testimony of eyewitnesses (see above all Dem. 21. 71–6).

Self-defence and self-help

In some circumstances, Athenians who found themselves victims of outrage could resort to direct action to preserve or restore their wounded masculinity and honour. Traditionally for many 'Mediterranean' societies, seduction or rape of wife or daughter has been held to be the most extreme and desperate 'dishonour' which demands a satisfactory response. In this area, Athenian law famously offered the wronged husband or father catching the *moichos* a variety of choices, as it did also for the householder catching a nocturnal housebreaker. He might kill him, but only under certain specific conditions, and there was a risk of subsequent prosecution for homicide, as Euphiletos, the speaker of Lysias 1, discovered. He might impose anal humiliations,[39] or exact money on the spot. Finally, he might bring a lawsuit and have him condemned by a court. Clearly in the operation of all these penalties the state is expressing its own interest in the preservation of households that make up the city, and the secure succession of sons, and, it may be, protecting the city's shrines from 'pollution' of impure sexual offenders. But if one asks why the laws offer the injured man such a choice of methods of self-help or of legal procedures, it can only be because of community-wide feeling that in Euphiletos' words 'all men think that this *hybris* is the most dreadful of all' (1. 2); nor should the belief that the woman was polluted be sharply distinguished from her condemnation as one who shamed her males and her family.[40] The protection allegedly offered by the law of self-help to the honour of the wronged citizen is best analysed through the arguments and sophistries of Lysias 1. Euphiletos, the defendant, in a rather implausible rhetorical trope, goes so far as to suggest that what he actually said to the adulterer was 'It's not me that's killing you but the law' (1. 26); and at the end of the speech he claims that he thinks that the revenge, or *timōria*, involved in his killing Eratosthenes was not a private revenge for his own sake, but was achieved for the whole city (1. 47). But there is no reason to suppose that in emphasizing the polis' interest in seeing adulterers receiving exemplary punishment Euphiletos is concerned in the slightest to deny or undermine the legitimacy of his own desire for revenge for the insult to his honour as a citizen householder.[41] It is true that Euphiletos is trying to fudge the legal issue by suggesting that the laws impose, rather than permit, such exactions of penalties,[42] and that he is of course seeking to deny any ulterior motives other than revenge for the wrong, as must be the basis of the accusation against him; he is wrapping himself as far as possible in the laws. But he also makes it clear that the purpose of such a severe law is precisely to protect the honour and vital interests of all other husbands and fathers, who therefore wish to see such offenders punished (1. 47–50) He also emphasizes that Eratosthenes 'corrupted my wife, shamed my children and committed *hybris* against me myself, entering my house' (1. 4; cf. 25); this repeated phrase 'entering my house' does not somehow remove attention from the sexual offence, as Herman argues, but rather enhances the heinousness of the insult to the husband and citizen's honour by focusing on the social setting of the crime at the heart of the household, in the bedroom. The honour-code and norms broken by Eratosthenes are emphasized, not underplayed (as much by the constant repetition of the terms *hybris* and *timōria* as by other means); the cautious and cunning response of the wronged man, gathering friends and moving in to the steady and well-explained kill, are – despite his equally careful presentation of himself as naive and a little foolish earlier – meant to characterize Euphiletos as a thoughtful, serious and deliberate defender of his own honour, his household, and the interests of all the male citizens as protected by the law. In fact in many societies where 'honour'-based violence is common, emotionally committed defenders of their honour do not have to act in hot blood, at the first opportunity, or at all rashly; after all an avenger may be supposed to harbour deep, controlled passion and act at his own time – and derive greater pleasure therefrom (cf. the proverb 'Revenge is a dish best tasted cold').[43] Such a deliberate vindictiveness, however, could be considered in some circumstances excessive or inappropriate, and lead to the avenger being labelled a bitter man (*pikros*); such was Konon's strategy in so characterizing his opponents for taking what was in reality a trivial little fight all the way to court.[44]

Retaliation and self-restraint

Such mechanisms of self-help, which might go as far as homicide, were available when dishonouring intruders broke or burst into the house, or when dealing with an assailant who was clearly trying to kill one, and who started the fight, if no plausible alternative existed.[45] But in other cases, where a man was physically assaulted, but his life was not obviously threatened, limits of self-defence were placed, designed, according to the important and largely plausible account of Dem. 54. 17–19, to impose immediate self-restraint in the hope of subsequent legal satisfaction. Instead of escalating any conflict, from verbal abuse to blows, from punches to a serious weapon, from wounding to homicide, the person attacked was encouraged to seek legal recourse, not resort to self-help. Can we say whether this encouragement, broadly speaking, produced the goods? Did enough Athenian victims survive assaults, seek legal help, and if so, did they retain a sense of their own masculine, free and independent identity, or did they do so only at the cost of suppressing their 'honour' and accepting a shameful second-best, in the interests of the wider community?[46]

Self-restraint for the greater good of the community was certain to produce tensions and contradictions in those whose honour was attacked; exploring the contradictions explicitly in the courts, and justifying the resolution allegedly adopted, was a necessary strategy for many litigants. Recent discussions of these issues have perhaps tended to polarize, and to (over)-emphasize either the restraint (Herman), or the defence of honour and masculinity whether by direct retaliation or through legal procedures (Cohen); of the two, Cohen's strategy seems to me far closer to the evidence.

One major text is Demosthenes' speech against Meidias.[47] Demosthenes claims credit for his own very considerable restraint when faced with Meidias' obstructions, hostilities, legal manoeuvres, and finally the public punch-up at the Dionysia (whatever may have been his real reasons for not retaliating). He compares other cases, both of proper restraint (including many others in the intense atmosphere of rivalry and *philotimia* between *chorēgoi*),[48] and of understandable strong retaliation: the precise language used in these cases needs attention. Both Euthynos, when yet a youthful wrestler, who killed the (presumably somewhat older) pancratiast Sophilos, and Euaion who killed Boiotos, retaliated with homicidal violence when seriously insulted at private parties. Euthynos survived to make his name as a wrestler,[49] whereas Euaion was condemned by only one vote, and Demosthenes claims to have strong sympathy with him or anyone driven to strong retaliation for the *hybris* against his body. But, he reports, the jurors condemned him by a majority of one; the conclusion Demosthenes draws is that those who voted against him did so on the grounds not merely that he had retaliated, but because he had caused death; whereas the other jurors thought that 'such an excess of *timōria*' should be conceded to a man suffering *hybris* to his person (21. 73–5). Demosthenes, even though faced with greater provocation himself, chose (allegedly) the legal recourse. His claim is then that:

> I exercised so much forethought (*pronoia*) to prevent anything irrevocable happening, that I did not even retaliate at all; from whom, then, should *timōria* be rendered to me for what I suffered? I think it has to be from you and the laws, and that this must be a signal (*paradeigma*) to all the rest, that one should not oneself retaliate in one's state of anger against all those who commit *hybris*, against the brutal men (*aselgeis*), but should bring them before you, because it is you who make secure and preserve the protection in the laws for the victims (*tas en tois nomois tois pathousi boētheias*).
>
> (21. 75–6)

It is clear that in making this choice between the legal or the extra-legal response to insulting aggression, one was not choosing between the satisfaction of regaining honour through revenge, and the acceptance of dishonour for the sake of community peace; it is between seeking a direct *timōria*, achieved in the heat of anger, which runs the risk being thought excessive and provoking further violent feuding or legal responses, and a slower *timōria* available through the courts: the clearest sign of this is that the laws are explicitly said also to offer *timōria* to the victims, and assistance to those who thus call out for help (*boētheia*). To claim as Herman does that self-restraint and recourse to appropriate legal procedures constitute a surrender of one's claim to honour and revenge is a fundamental error; it is significant that Herman, who expresses disdain for close attention to 'the analysis of

abstract concepts such as *hybris*', offers a paraphrase, not a precise translation, of this passage, and a paraphrase which ignores the clear implications
of *timōria* and *boētheia*.[50] Demosthenes' arguments here may be, as
MacDowell claims, an 'advance on old-style Greek morality'; but they are in
fact far removed from the considerably more 'advanced' view which placed
impersonal punishment above retaliation, found in Plato's Protagoras or
Plato's Socrates, or later in Musonius Rufus.[51] As the innumerable statements
in the law court speeches using this language of legal *timōria* and *boētheia*
show, litigants prosecuting their enemies for crimes of aggression, appropriation, fraud or whatever expected the jurors to respond with anger to their
tales of maltreatment, loss and dishonour, and with sympathy to the claim
that one function of the courts was to 'render *timōria*', and thus satisfy the
anger, of those judged to be the victims.[52] A different mistake is found, I
think, in an interesting discussion in Saunders' book on Plato's penality;
after citing some of the many examples of such appeals to anger among the
jurors, and some where the dangers of excessive or too hasty anger are
recognized, Saunders suggests that we have here a built-in tension between
two assumptions, one, that anger is legitimate, and second, that jurors
should be impartial and judge only on the facts (1991, 99–100). However,
this seems to conflate two different situations: one where a jury may form a
rash, emotional, judgment, based on an incomplete prior acquaintance with
the facts; and the other where a jury acts deliberately from a proper reaction
of anger, rationally based on the facts as established by the litigant.[53]
Litigants in the courts consistently hoped the court would be receptive to
claims that they should share the victims' anger, and offer them revenge; but
they had also, of course, to be mindful of the overall interests of the
community, and of the overall records of all parties, in reaching their
verdicts.[54]

But, as Demosthenes emphasizes, such restraint in the face of a public
insult came with difficulty. In addition to the cases that Demosthenes
describes, one can add further examples where it was to be expected that
Athenians would retaliate swiftly and 'like men' when faced with grievous
hybris: a striking instance is the argument that a supposed adulterer would
be mad, and would risk certain death, if he suggested to his mistress, at her
wedding, that she refrain from sleeping with her husband, when her brothers
– who happened to be wrestlers – were present.[55] But it is also noticeable
that in the philosophers, theoretical expressions of the view that a man must
retaliate against insult, if he is not to be a slave, envisage *timōria* achieved
through the courts as well as, or instead of, by direct action. For example,
Gorgias' assertion that it is the experience of a slave, not a man (*anēr*), to be
humiliated and to be unable to come to the aid (*boēthein*) either of himself
or of those he cares for, refers both to the slave's legal incapacities and his
general weakness (Plato, *Gorgias* 483). In many places, Aristotle treats
revenge as a necessary element in individual freedom, and of the well-

functioning society. In the discussion of the virtues in the *Nicomachean Ethics*, the deficiency in relation to anger leads its sufferers to be foolish, in not getting angry on the occasions when they should; to be inclined not to retaliate when humiliated, and allow oneself and one's *oikeioi* to be insulted, is slavish (4. 1126 a 2–8). The *megalopsychos* will not be moved to abuse or attack even his enemies, unless provoked by their *hybris* (4. 1125 a 5–9); or again *aretē* (virtue), with power, when treated with *hybris*, is to be feared (*Rh.* 2. 1382 b 1–2) because it will assuredly react. In all these cases proper and appropriate forms of retaliation and revenge are envisaged, and these must be essentially within the laws of the community; in the *EN* proportionate reciprocity maintains the polis, which includes the security that citizens can return harm for harm, or else it will seem to be a state of slavery (5. 1132 b 32–a 2), and in the *Rhetorica*, an *a fortiori* argument for learning forensic skills is that it is *aischron* to be unable to defend oneself physically, and hence it is even more so to be unable to defend oneself in argument (*logos*), since that is more characteristic of being human. Thus Aristotle clearly assumes that in a proper community all citizens expected to have some success in pursuing legitimate revenge through legal action.[56]

It appears then that the Athenian system encouraged its citizens in many cases to control their initial impulses to self-help, and to choose instead to have recourse to the law courts or legalized procedures. Some awareness of a slow historical movement in that direction may be discerned in the pattern of Aischylos' *Oresteia* (458 BC), where the community court instituted in Athens (the Areopagos) resolved the sequence of revenge killings, though only after a hearing where the decision was taken by the narrowest of margins, and in the light of many, often rather dubious, personal and political issues.[57] The sequel, the settlement between Athena and the Furies, makes it clear that wounded honour, anger and revenge are not superseded by the legal system and its supernatural backing, but incorporated within the system. But Athenian drama can also problematize the system of justice as a deliverer of revenge, especially in times of serious political corruption and civil war. Above all, Euripides' *Orestes* (408 BC), a deliberate, pessimistic reworking of the *Oresteia*, shows a trial at Argos, where the verdict to condemn Orestes is delivered after speeches by variously corrupt and factional politicians, whereupon he and his *philoi* (like a contemporary group of aristocratic *hetairoi* upset by a democratic decision) respond by attempting a further direct revenge killing of Helen. It turns out that here neither civic courts nor violent acts of extra-legal feuding offer any hope of just solutions in a corrupt world, and the attempt by Apollo at the end to sort things out seems perfunctory and unconvincing (cf. Hall 1993b).

In reality, and in times of relative stability such as most of the fourth century from which our law court speeches come, litigants seeking revenge through the law had to operate in complex situations, where there were many competing factors to be considered. Athenian law, with its 'open texture', offered litigants in many cases a choice of procedure, which might be exercised in a way which produced financial payments to the prosecutor, rather than the infliction of death, exile or physical penalties on the offender; or they might settle at arbitration, or informally out of court.[58] It seems clear that a number of Athenians who had been the victims of a humiliating assault chose a *dikē aikeias*, which produced a fine, in preference to a *graphē hybreōs*, where the public nature of the offence meant that if there was a fine it would go to the state.[59] It is at least possible that many who found their wives or daughters in adultery accepted a financial recompense, in or out of court, rather than insisting on the death or humiliation of the adulterer (Foxhall 1992b, 301–3). One might be tempted to suspect a trend among Athenian males from seeking rewards in terms of revenge and the restoration of honour towards the acceptance of cash settlements. Lawrence Stone has sought to identify a comparable switch in the handling of adultery in early modern England; whereas upper-/middle-class husbands used to prefer to assault or duel with their wives' seducers, they came to prefer to sue for trespass on their property and accept compensation. Stone (1987) describes this process as an important switch from 'feudal honour to bourgeois money', from 'violence to litigation', which displays the 'commercialization of values'. He also describes this with the phrase, 'Price-tags had been set on masculine honour and female shame', which gives a significantly different emphasis; the renegotiation, not the denial, of honour (Stone 1987, 303). If it is true (and there is little evidence either way) that Athenians tended less to humiliate or even kill adulterers (as Euphiletos had at least, at no little risk), and adopted procedures that would bring in money, it remained a means of recovering 'honour'; one should not conclude that 'honour' is no longer at issue in the calculation. A public conviction and financial payment diminished the status of the offender, and might in part restore some lost honour; the element of restoration of the cuckold's honour was actually recognized in court, in the provision permitting the wronged husband, falsely accused of illegal imprisonment of the alleged adulterer, to reassert his right for the personal infliction of pain and humiliation there and then in the court room, though not using a sword (but perhaps involving, one presumes, the anal penalties discussed above).[60] But of course there was also the contradiction here that any public hearing or public apology drew attention to the man's failure to control his woman. This desire for anonymity may have led many to resort to a private accommodation, or to inaction;[61] hence the safeguard, for the community, provided by the procedures of the *graphē moicheias*, enabling another to prosecute if the husband did not, and the requirement of a husband to divorce a wife caught in adultery, on pain of disenfranchisement (*atimia*), an alternative, more grievous, form of dishonour (cf., for instance, Harrison 1968, 35–6).

Equally, there could be a number of reasons to prefer to bring a *dikē aikeias* rather than a *graphē hybreōs*, even in cases of such insulting assaults as Konon's was alleged to be. In addition to the specific desire for cash, there might be the desire to adopt a quieter, less dangerous, procedure, and a greater chance of gaining a conviction; but it does not follow that a conviction for *aikeia* would not bring considerable emotional satisfaction of revenge for the victim and no little public humiliation for the assailant (cf. Cohen 1995, Ch. 5). On the other hand to 'sell' a strong case altogether for a cash settlement enabled one's opponents and gossiping outsiders to impugn one's courage and masculinity more effectively, as is revealed by Aischines' language (3. 51–3) on the Meidias case; he 'sold his *hybris* and the city's vote for a mere 30 minai'. If this did happen, Demosthenes may yet have got some satisfaction from whatever compromise he actually struck, and from Meidias' partial acceptance of culpability; he will also have had other political and non-political reasons for making such a settlement at that moment. Nonetheless, it was, or was later represented as, at least a partial compromise of his honour, and less than the ideal outcome of his long legal and extra-legal feud with Meidias.[62] The laws made efforts to restrict such settlements once the court cases had been accepted, by imposing some form of *atimia* and a 1000 drachma fine on those who failed to proceed with a *graphē*, but how far these laws were implemented is a question of some doubt, as is the question whether they would have applied in the Meidias *probolē* case.[63]

In practice, many Athenians, especially poorer ones, were doubtless forced by social pressures, intimidation, charm or fear of an expensive defeat in the courts, to accept some form of settlement, whether at an early stage, at arbitration or whenever, as the best they could get. Some of the problems and contradictions here are commonly explored in comedy, perhaps best and most relevantly in the later scenes in Aristophanes' *Wasps*. The violent and hybristic behaviour of the drunk and uncouth old man, and his pathetically inadequate attempts, following his instructions, to soothe and charm by witty anecdotes those he had beaten up and ripped off, might arouse complex and diverse reactions among the audience towards different forms of sympotic excess, and violent or litigious responses. Some might indeed bask in a sense of social superiority, identifying with the insulted upper class guests and confident that they too could indeed laugh off any trouble the drink might induce. Others might, as Dover suspects (1972, 125–7), relish the 'antinomian' vigour and energy of the rejuvenated Philokleon's excesses, and feel, with regret, that only in comic fantasy could the ordinary citizen get his personal, if violent, revenge both on his social superiors and on the laws of society, such as those against *hybris* and *aikeia*, which prevent a 'real man' from reacting as he wishes. Others again, I suspect, may have felt considerable distaste alike for the snobby guests at the party, and for the wild violence and abuse of the drunken old fool, and sympathize rather with his victims. It is not evident to me that the text enforces on us the view that the woman bread-seller or the beaten-up 'accuser' are excessively pompous or litigious; they could seem, rather, to be attempting, in a reasonable and correct manner, to recover their goods and win some redress, preferably by a quick settlement or, failing that, by legal process.[64]

Under the Athenian legal system, then, there was encouragement to settle disputes by a combination of the legitimate, but restrained, pursuit of the citizen's honour with the interests of the polis; the claim and emotional drive for revenge was not denied or undermined, but rather harnessed to the interests of the community. Preference for honour and revenge, over money, as motives for prosecutions in many contexts is very evident – and is part, perhaps a large part, of the hostility to 'sycophants'.[65] Further indications of the recognition that the victims' desire for revenge had to be publicly satisfied, but also kept under control, can be seen in the provisions that criminals might be exposed in the pillory or the stocks, that many penalties were carried out in public, and that the prosecutors were enabled to gloat as criminals were executed, or in other ways be involved in the execution of penalties.[66]

Confidence in legal processes

In further support of the view that many of those seeking revenge resorted to legal procedures to achieve some redress and restoration of their honour, one can mention that some factors which in other honour-sensitive societies encouraged males to find such an idea unacceptably unmanly, uncertain and slow seem to have been relatively absent in Athens. The following considerations also suggest that levels of *macho* violence in the streets were relatively low, and that many Athenians felt a fair degree of confidence in their courts, and shared the belief that self-help carried serious dangers both for households and for the community as a whole.

The abandonment of arms-carrying (sidērophoria)

Greek society knew no formalized duel procedures; and in classical Athens men no longer went about wearing swords or daggers. If they needed a weapon when out, our narratives suggest the usual practice was to pick up stones in the streets, or to find or create an *ostrakon* (the equivalent of the broken bottle).[67] Both Thukydides (1. 5–8), and Aristotle (*Politics* 2. 1268 b 40) saw this as a crucial sign of the development of a specifically Greek form of civilization, and a contrast with the contemporary habits of 'barbarians', or more backward parts of Greece. Thukydides argued that the development of the classical city saw a decline in piracy, greater protection of houses, as well as cities, and crucially the giving up of arms-carrying; he also thought that this occurred first in Athens.[68] Thukydides later displays his awareness of how the Peloponnesian War ('his war') disrupted this desirable state; describing the consequences of Dekeleia he emphasizes that the city had became a fortress, as men were constantly going about on duty (7. 28), presumably as a result of the need for hoplites to be constantly ready for action;[69] later, as a more serious sign of *stasis* and fighting inside the city, in the preliminaries to the oligarchic coup in 411 BC, the 400 and their body-guards appeared bearing daggers in the council chamber (8. 69).

Aristotle (*Pol.* 2. 1268 b 33–69 a 3) saw this as an example of a necessary element of progress produced by legislation, and there are many (probably later) traditions on the introduction of laws forbidding the carrying of arms in public by the famous lawgivers of Western Greek states.[70] There seems no evidence of a law against *siderophoria* in operation in our law court sources – if there had been a Solonian or pre-Solonian law, perhaps the custom had become so widely accepted by the classical period that it no longer needed to be mentioned in any of our sources. It is evident from the Thukydidean and Aristophanic passages cited above that citizens appearing in arms would arouse concern and alarm: a military need was the only acceptable excuse, and even that might arouse suspicion.[71] In any case, and in marked contrast, say, to seventeenth-century England, nineteenth-century Corsica or twen-tieth-century Cretan villages, brandishing or bearing arms in peace time was strongly deprecated; we have many narratives indeed where it seems remark-able that individuals going out facing the certainty or strong likelihood of a fight do not go well armed, though they may carry staffs.[72] One case is Eratosthenes on his dangerous adulterous expeditions (Lys. 1. 27, 42); Euphiletos claims he realized that Eratosthenes might well have had a dagger, but in fact he had not, though Euphiletos had evidently so equipped himself for his revenge. Similarly none of the various characters in the dispute described in Ps.-Demosthenes 47 (neither the trierarch collecting his gear, nor his enemies raiding his house) seem to have weapons at any stage, though there was a fight, and both parties then prosecuted each other for assault (*aikeia*); they engaged each other with fists or staffs, and the villains throttled and bashed the old freedwoman with their bare hands, or conceiv-ably with staffs.

This general picture seems to support the implications of the sophisti-cated arguments about the provision of carefully gradated charges depending on whether weapons were used (as in Dem. 54. 17–19). The evidence suggests that people would be cautious before taking the step of using a weapon (and cf. the legal restrictions on what one could use on an adulterer, or a proven adulteress appearing at a festival); hence in serious fights men would use an *ostrakon* or stones before a sword. Yet in Athens, most if not all citizens would own a sword or a dagger, and one was permitted to use them in specified occasions against *kakourgoi/moichoi*. This reticence does seem, as Herman argues, a highly significant indicator of a significantly non-violent society.[73]

Community action: help and witnesses at fights

If the dangers of uncontrollable fights, or savage beatings, perhaps then leading to further extra-legal revenge attacks, were to be resisted – as they seem on the whole to have been – some community mechanisms for the restraint of combatants, some preparedness for people to act as witnesses, and a reasonable level of confidence in the legal system would all be of considerable importance.

There was little help to be expected, if violence erupted, from intervention from the Eleven, the Scythian archers, or any other public officials broadly engaged in 'policing' activities (cf. Hunter 1994, 143–9). Hence a crucial role, in theory, was played by the traditions of neighbourly self-help, where cries for bystanders to run to help, *boēthein*, might induce parties to stop the fighting, act as witnesses, or help bring offenders to their senses. Several narratives allegedly display genuinely neutral passers-by intervening, remonstrating and subsequently giving evidence;[74] an opponent's witnesses were naturally derided as his friends and drinking companions (Dem. 54. 31–2). In general, the functions of witnesses in the Athenian courts, as Humphreys and Todd have argued, was as much to lend the support of their reputations and respectability to their side, or to persuade the jury by their expert local knowledge of the people and events, as to convince them of their precise testimony.[75] In practice one may doubt whether in the street-fighting cases all the witnesses were actually genuine bystanders, rather than committed friends of one or other litigant. Nonetheless in such cases, unlike other cases, genuinely neutral bystanders, provided they appeared respectable enough, would actually be preferred, as their evidence could testify both to the exceptional offensiveness of the aggressors and to the vigorous public spirit alive in the community; evidence from alleged friends of the accused, alienated by his offensiveness, was also highly desirable (cf. Lys. 3. 19). But of course in practice many bystanders might in fact be reluctant to be involved, unless really outraged, because of the feeling that many fights were relatively unserious and equally balanced, and of the contradictory value attached to minding one's own business; it is a mark of the overzealous (*periergos*) man that he attempts to break up fighters when he is not acquainted with either of them.[76] All in all, the forensic evidence suggests that the ideal attributed to Solon (?Arist. *Ath.Pol.* 9. 1, Plut. *Solon* 18) of the honest citizen prepared to intervene to defend the obvious victim of unjust violence did affect social practice to some extent. It cannot easily be assessed, however, how far it produced calming action in the streets, and assisted prosecutions and judgments later.[77] One can add that varied other evidence of cooperation in farming activities, or in the army, small-scale friendship groups and commensality, innumerable *deme*, *phratry* or other local festivals, mutual interest-free loans, and generous help by local rich men out of *philotimia*, all do no harm to the suggestion that members of

Attika's local communities could on occasions act in such a way against notable offenders. All these different aspects in which citizens demonstrated their desire to win honour by serving the collective acts and needs of their communities are equally to be seen as part of their ideals of masculinity.[78]

Arbitration

Local community action was also, and very importantly, involved in attempts to settle disputes before they reached the jury courts; a range of procedures, involving the Forty, the 'tribal' judges (successors of the thirty 'local justices'), and both voluntary and compulsory arbitration procedures, might allow disputes to be settled more amicably, with less publicity and at lesser expense. The effectiveness of these procedures is, in the nature of our evidence, very difficult to assess, since our evidence mostly concerns cases which did come to court; on occasions, such as the Demosthenes, Meidias and Straton affair, the arbitration could bring fresh feuding and personal disasters. But it seems likely that these mechanisms played a much greater role in the system than can now be recovered.[79] We may note, however, that the *dikē aikeias* seems to have been moved *c*.340 BC from the Forty, subject to arbitration, to the monthly courts (*emmēnoi dikai*), which appparently offered a swifter procedure, did not involve arbitration, and were supervised by the *eisagōgeis* (?Arist. *Ath.Pol.* 52). One would like to know why this happened in this case in addition to commercial, mining and tax-farming disputes. It seems possible that there was a sense that cases of *aikeia* were becoming more frequent or more serious, and rarely produced successful arbitration. The *graphē hybreōs* was already, it seems, a swift action which, unusually, needed to be brought within 30 days;[80] and the importance of expressing swift public outrage at certain types of publicly committed *hybris* at festivals was further recognized by the development of the *probolē* procedure to deal with them (MacDowell 1990, 13–17).

A number of general arguments can be adduced for the view that most Athenians felt remarkable confidence in their courts, and that this confidence increased over time. As Hansen above all has emphasized (for example, 1991, especially 178–80, 300–4), the major constitutional changes during the latter part of the fifth and through the fourth century BC consistently gave more final powers to the jury members, sitting as courts or as *nomothetai*. Comedy, above all the *Wasps*, assumes that the litigiousness of individual Athenians, and their collective delight in sitting on juries and earning their pay, were alike remarkable, and proverbial throughout Greece.[81] There exist unresolved debates among scholars on the composition of the juries. Were they mostly poor and elderly, as many ancient sources suggest, or were a large number of them comfortably off, even *eisphora*-payers? Were most farmers or urban-dwellers? Did they tend to react with class hostility and prejudice against the rich and the political élite, or did they often show lenience to their claims to special treatment because of their achievements or their expenditure on community services out of *philotimia*? Were prosecutors normally regarded as money-seeking sycophants or revenge-seeking and patriotic enemies of the guilty?[82] Whichever views one leans towards on these questions, and there are reasonable arguments on both sides, the composition of any individual jury was surely complex and hard to predict. One may add that jurors were given no guidance on matters of law or precedent, and that they evidently relished having control offered to them over the wealth, careers or lives of their fellow citizens, especially the most powerful among them. Hence litigants would be likely to approach a court full of uncertainty about what sort of jury, and what verdict, they would encounter, and sure only that much would depend on the effectiveness of their rhetoric on the day. Most of our evidence concerns the better-off citizens, and much of it confirms not only the readiness of so many of them to risk money and reputations by prosecutions before these courts, but even more their remarkable preparedness to go back time and again to pursue their enmities or their political goals further.[83] Poorer citizens will, as always, have found it harder to discover how the legal system worked, and to get cases to court themselves. But they were unlikely, if able or forced to appear before a jury, to find the jurors consistently biased by class composition and attitudes against them; and they might well have experience as jurors themselves, or at least have elder relatives who had. It seems true that prevailing attitudes shared something of a conservative consensus, for example in favour of the preservation of existing properties, even though the rich may have owned most of the land.[84] Attitudes to the various forms of thieves and muggers were solidly hostile, and retribution could be swift, while alleged jury-pay scroungers also might meet little mercy.[85]

Fundamentally, the demos knew it was their system, and they had the opportunities to operate within it and the power to change it. It seems likely, for example, that the democratic juries of Athens outdid the record of litigiousness found in Spanish cities during the sixteenth and seventeenth centuries, when there was a great increase in litigation because new styles of royal justice encouraged more confidence than had previous systems (Kagan 1983). Or again, there are grounds for arguing that much of early modern England was a remarkably peaceful society, in part because there was a strongly deferential culture and an emphasis on law-abiding behaviour, and in part because of the substantial roles played by self-appointed prosecutors and their associations.[86] One might well claim that in Athens the role given to individuals in the legal processes was markedly greater, and extended further down the social scale; hence the system worked because of the people's awareness that they themselves made and ran the legal system, and that their personal safety and their personal properties, however small, depended on their maintaining the laws in the interests of all, and on their preserving also some consent to the system among the rich.[87] Particularly striking here is the conclusion to Demosthenes' speech against Meidias: the argument is that if the jurymen are able to walk home free from fear of attack by their enemies, it is because the laws exist and are upheld by the juries; therefore they must convict Meidias, or their personal enemies will be emboldened to attack them.[88]

Other reasons for consensus and confidence in the system may arise, paradoxically enough, from the same sympotic and sexual activities that often produced more or less serious conflicts. It is true that the drinking group was seen as socially problematic at least from the time of Solon, and the goings-on of some of the more politically active of these groups during the Peloponnesian War will have made the tensions much worse, and left long memories (Murray 1990c). The most dangerous groups were thus seen to be those formed by self-selecting aristocrats with values alien to the democratic spirit (such as those of Andokides, Alkibiades, Kritias or Konon). But we should not, I suspect, see all *symposia* in that mode, nor exaggerate the general conflict between the people and the leisured classes; I discuss elsewhere ways in which increased participation by many ordinary Athenians in both gymnastic and sympotic activities may have contributed to the reduction of social tensions between the rich and the masses.[89]

Finally, yet another reason for a fair level of control of violent impulses, and conflict-avoidance in fourth-century BC Athens, may have derived from the recent political experiences. As adumbrated earlier, in the Andalusia studied by Gilmore, and in various Greek communities, memories of the civil wars before, or after, the Second World War appear to have acted as powerful restraining forces persuading members of small communities to seek settlements rather than to develop conflicts, or to resort to gossip and backbiting rather than to open violence (see above). Similar memories, after the Peloponnesian War and the periods of *stasis* at their worst in 411–10 and 404–3, may well have operated as inhibiting factors in fourth-century BC Athens. The amnesty, however much it may only have been accepted initially through fear of the Spartans, and however it operated in practice, seems to have had a lasting ideological effect.[90] The point was well put in the Platonic seventh letter.[91] After the somewhat grudging praise of the great moderation (mixed with some unsurprising acts of revenge) shown by the restored democracy (325 B), the author sees hope for the troubled Sicilian cities in the importation of people and *isonomia* from the rest of Sicily, the Peloponnese, and even from Athens. 'For there too there are people who are exceptional among men for their virtue (*arete*) and who hate men who kill *xenoi*'. What is needed in any community, he insists, after a period of serious *stasis* and killings, is a time when all individuals cease to harbour their memories (*mnesikakein*) and pursue revenges (*timoriai*) over their enemies, and instead establish fair laws and a guiding and enforcing spirit of respect and fear (*aidos* and *phobos*): only this will instil in all sides a willingness to restrain the impulse to revenge and to obey the laws (336 D–337 B).

In conclusion, it seems hard to believe that Athens was a seriously violent society, despite the persistence of a strong ideological commitment that citizens should prove their manhood, maintain their honour and avoid shame, and for all that much low-level fighting occurred. Perhaps the most important reason for this state of affairs was that prevailing civic values encouraged those who felt insulted and wronged to have recourse to the courts and the arbitration procedures, and to believe that thereby revenge was achieved, and honour and manhood could be satisfied. Thus restraint, with a view to later legal revenge, was a praised and common response; instant retaliation, though understandable, could easily, if felt to be at all excessive, involve the risk of a successful prosecution in turn. There were other related reasons. The state and its legal system enjoyed high levels of legitimacy among its citizens, and encouraged an endless play of hostilities before the popular juries; to strive to excel through the political and legal systems, and to win honour through service to the community, were important aspects of being a good or a distinguished citizen and thus a good man. Fears of *stasis* would arise in the community if too many citizens were thought to be prepared to indulge in retaliatory violence; and so local community spirit and neighbourhood protection, cooperative friendships and trust, were all widely found, and may have prevented many fights from dangerous escalation. The crimes of the very poor did not terrify the rest, nor win any sympathy; the ideology of the free citizen tended to unite them all against the non-citizens. Many less rich males may well have adopted or imitated aspects of the life-style of the rich, while the persistent democratic rhetoric of *hybris* and the threat of severe penalties, even if only occasionally inflicted, must also have had their effects in restraining serious exploitation of social inferiors by the élite.

Notes

1 Variant masculinities and identities in flux may be in question, rather than the problematic nature of an unquestioned masculinity: cf. e.g. Segal 1990, and Cornwall and Lindisfarne 1994. For ambiguities in Greek conceptions of the masculine and the feminine, cf. also Loraux 1989/1995. I am grateful for helpful comments to the participants in Leicester and elsewhere where versions of these ideas have been presented, to Lin Foxhall, John Salmon and an anonymous reader, for comments on the draft, and also for much discussion to Hans van Wees. None is to be blamed for the paper's deficiencies.
2 Geertz 1973; Hoffman 1974; Winkler 1990a, 49; Taplin 1987, 1993; Fowler 1989; most fully and illuminatingly, Csapo 1993: cf. especially 20–1 on Konon's hybristic cock-imitation. I strongly favour Taplin's and Csapo's identification of the Getty birds as the two *Logoi* from the first edition of Aristophanes' *Clouds*.
3 Gilmore 1982, 1987a and b, 1990; his approach is criticized for being over-abstract and spuriously coherent, and as accepting a universal and essential structure for masculinity, e.g. by Cornwall and Lindisfarne, and by Lindisfarne, in Cornwall and Lindisfarne 1994, 27–9, 82–3; cf. also analysis of the complexi-

ties of conflicting masculinities in modern Greece in Loizos and Parataxiarchis 1991.
4 For ideologies of male supremacy in Athens, and complexes of (often wildly erroneous) physiological and medical beliefs underpinning them, one need only refer to works such as Gould 1980, Just 1989, Foxhall 1989, Dean-Jones 1994. Cf., e.g., comparable ideologies among the Bedouin of the Western Desert in Egypt, analysed by Abu-Lughod 1986, 118–67; for even stronger ideologies, and wilder theories of male and female growth and physiology, cf. e.g. Herdt 1987, 1994a, on the Sambia of New Guinea.
5 Cf. especially Dover 1978, Winkler 1990a, Halperin 1990, Cohen 1991, Ogden 1996.
6 For the conceptualizing of masculinity and femininity among traditional New Guinea societies practising elaborate homosexual initiation rituals, cf. above all Herdt 1987, 1994a; for Athens, Vidal-Naquet 1981/1986, 1986; Winkler 1990b, 20–37, Secunda 1990; more sceptically on the phratries, Lambert 1993, 144–52.
7 For example, Bremmer 1980, Sargent 1984, 1986; against, Dover 1988, 115–34.
8 Cf. especially Bremmer 1990, Ridley 1979, Crowther 1985, Neils 1994: 151–9.
9 Cf. e.g. Cartledge 1997, Fisher 1993.
10 Cf. Loraux 1981/1986, 104–8, Whitehead 1993, Cartledge, above, 62.
11 Cf. e.g. Gilmore 1987b. A recent *mise en scène*, with bibliography, is provided by Cartledge 1995a; cf. also Cohen 1991, Hunter 1994; more sceptical, Herzfeld 1987, Stewart 1994, Herman 1996.
12 See e.g. Peters 1967, Black-Michaud 1975, Durham 1909, Wilson 1988 on Corsica; in his recent articles on these topics, Gabriel Herman repeatedly contrasts classical Athens specifically with those traditional (or in his terms 'tribal') societies with high rates of interpersonal violence driven by honour, or with early modern societies riven by duelling, and weak central governments (1993, 1994, 1995, 1996). But these are far from being the only relevant comparative societies which take honour and shame very seriously. Cf. also Cohen 1995, 19–25
13 Campbell 1964; cf. also the Bedouin in the Western desert in Egypt: Abu-Lughod 1986.
14 Du Boulay 1974, especially Ch. 8; Herzfeld 1987, 159–60; also Handman 1983, 154–9, on tendencies to violent fights, but diminishing rates of homicide and serious crime since 1950, among villages near Mt Pelion in Thessaly.
15 This is the prime methodological failing in Herman's recent articles, 1993, n. 36, 1994, 106–7, and 1995.
16 Cf. Abu-Lughod 1986, Part II on the roles of poetry among the Bedouin; Loizos and Parataxiarchis 1991, Ch. 10. For Athens, rituals such as the *Halōa* or the *Adōnia*, or ecstatic cults, tragedy, comedy, and what remains to us of women's poetry, popular song and mime, should all be considered in this light. Cf. Winkler 1990a, especially chapters 3, 6 and 7; Goldhill 1986; Bowie 1993; Taaffe 1993.
17 Osborne 1985, 50; less neglected now, with the works by Cohen, Fisher, Herman and Hunter cited elsewhere.
18 Winkler 1990a, 49; Murray 1990c, 157.
19 On Alkibiades, cf. Fisher 1992, 87–8, 97–8, 148–9; Ephialtes, ?Aristotle, *Ath. Pol.* 25. 4; cases of homicide are listed by Herman, 1994, 101; cf. also Herman 1995.
20 Cf. Osborne 1985; Fisher 1990; Herman 1994, 100–1; it may be noted that for the history of (e.g.) early modern England, where infinitely greater materials exist from which to produce crime statistics and other forms of analysis, historians engage in ferocious debates on how 'violent' England may have been, at different

times, and in which directions it may have been changing: cf. e.g. Stone 1985, 1987, Sharpe 1984, 1985, Cockburn 1977, 1991.

21 On the distinction between vertical and horizontal honour, cf. Stewart 1994, especially 59–63; cf. also Ober 1994, 97–101 for a comparable distinction between the basic dignity of the ordinary citizen, located in his citizen rights, political equality, personal security and bodily inviolability, and the competitive honour of the rich and the politically active. On the general aims of the liturgy-system, 'harnessing' the *philotimia* of the élite, cf. also Davies 1981; Ober 1989; Hunter 1994; Whitehead 1983, 1993; Gabrielsen 1994, 47–60.

22 For example, Ar. *Vespae* 1299–325, etc., and many comic fragments; assaults on *chorēgoi*: Dem. 21. 16–18, 147, [Andokides] 4. 20–1.

23 Aeschin. 1. 61; Dem. 54. 13–14.

24 Athen. 555 A. The anecdote was quoted in Lykophron's scholarly work in nine books *On Comedy*, apparently composed under Ptolemy Philadelphos; Lykophron was a Euboian poet who composed many tragedies and may (or may not) have composed the *Alexandra* (cf. Pfeiffer 1968, 119–20).

25 Athen. 36 B–C = 93 K–A; cf. the other passages cited there. There seem to be remarkably few pictures of sympotic fighting on Athenian vases; for one example, see the red-figure cup by Onesimos from Capua (Leningrad, Hermitage Museum, 651; illustrated in Vickers, *Greek Symposia*, 16 and Murray 1990a, 182 Fig. 16).

26 Cf. Dover 1974, 103; Murray 1983.

27 The role of the Scythian archers and later slave-'police', under the command of the Eleven, the *boulē* and other officials, have been studied most recently by Hunter 1994, 145–9. On bystanders, below, 88.

28 For example, Hanson 1989, Ridley 1979.

29 Cockfights, Aeschin. 1. 60–1, and n. 2 above; sacrifices: e.g. Burkert 1983, Rosivach 1994; public and humiliating punishments, Aeschin. 2. 181, Dem. 23. 69, Lys. 10. 16, Dem. 24. 105, and Saunders 1991, 293–4; Hunter 1994, 176–81.

30 Cf. e.g. Robert 1940; Hopkins 1983, Ch. 1; Toner 1995, Ch.5.

31 On physical punishment of slaves and its ideological significance, Garlan 1988, Fisher 1993, Hunter 1994; for Rome, now Saller 1994.

32 Cf. the clear and disquieting implications of Homer, *Iliad* 15. 16–33; Semonides 7; Ar. *Lysistrata* 510–21; Plato Comicus 105 K–A; Euripides, *Medea* 242; Plutarch, *Alkibiades* 8. Hunter 1994 and Just 1989 are oddly silent on this question. One might compare the public acceptance of such male 'assertiveness' in controlling wives among the Bedouin: Abu-Lughod 1986, 89. On other forms of sexual violence against women, cf. Winkler, 1990a. There remains a striking contrast between this reticence and Roman nostalgic praise for noble wife-beaters (Valerius Maximus 6. 3. 9–12) or the casual acceptance of regular wife-beating among the families with which Augustine's mother Monica was familiar in Thagaste (cf. *Confessions* 9. 9. 19, and Shaw 1987, 28–31). There seems even less evidence, not surprisingly, for sexual abuse within the family, in contrast to sexual abuse of young slaves; in part the ready availability of such sex-objects may have diminished levels of abuse of free children, but this is surely unlikely to have made, for example, father–daughter abuse a fairly infrequent problem (whether Ar. *Vesp.* 605–9 is relevant is disputed: cf. Dover 1972, 125–7, and MacDowell and Sommerstein *ad loc.*).

33 Lys. 3. 28, 4. 6–7; Fisher 1990, 133; Todd 1993, 269.

34 Cf. e.g. the Konon speech, Dem. 54.; contrast Isoc. 20 *Against Lochites*.

35 Fisher 1992, Ch. 2, 1990; MacDowell 1990, 23–8, Ober 1994, 89–91.

36 Dem. 21. 72 (and MacDowell, 1990, *ad loc.*), with Aeschin. 3. 52; Dem. 54. 8–9

37 Lys. fr. 17 (Gernet-Bizos); Aeschin. 1. 62; cf. also Dem. 21. 180: see Hunter 1994, 182; Cohen 1995, 137–9.
38 Cf. the insistence in Dem. 54 on the one-sidedness of the assault.
39 Ar. *Nubes* 1083–5; *Plutus* 168; Xenophon, *Memorabilia* 2. 1. 5; Isaios 8. 44. This has been properly, I think, brought back into the area of active options by Carey 1994, against Cohen 1985 and (less firmly) Roy 1991.
40 Cf. Parker 1983, 94–7; Fisher 1992, 78–9.
41 That he is so undermining the idea of revenge is a central argument of Herman 1994; 1995, 53–4
42 1. 28; cf. Foxhall 1992b, 302.
43 Herman's attempt to argue that a passionate avenger must act immediately, and immoderately, once any opportunity offers, rests on very selective use of ethnographic parallels, and ignores much more. For example, Herman (1995, 62) refers to Wilson's (1988) excellent analysis of feuding in nineteenth-century Corsican society; but Herman's claim that Corsicans, who were certainly much more likely to resort to extra-legal violence in defence of their honour than Athenians, knew no self-restraint, and operated with a dominant ideology of 'immediate, brutal and excessive retaliation', ignores very many instances, documented by Wilson, of moderate responses, of slow and delayed revenge, or of the use of the courts in preference to violence. Cf. also Cohen 1995, 65–7; and Herzfeld 1985, 76–82, 174–83, on Glendiots in Crete. One could compare the remark in J. L. Austin's 'Pleas for Excuses', from the early days of 'Oxford philosophy', that one must distinguish succumbing to temptation from losing self-control, as a man yielding to the temptation to eat an improper extra slice of high-table ice-cream may yet act with 'calm and finesse': Austin 1970, 198 n. 1.
44 Dem. 54. 14–16: cf. Aristotle, *Rhetorica* 1. 1368 b 24, *Ethica Nicomachea* 4. 1126 a 20–8. Similarly, the *opsimathēs* of Theophr. *Characteres* 27. 9 gets a deserved beating from his rival when he had assaulted his *hetaira's* door, but then goes to court.
45 For cases of theft, cf. Cohen 1983; Hunter 1994, 134–9; homicide in self-defence, MacDowell 1963, 75–81.
46 Recent discussions on these issues, reaching very different conclusions: Hunter 1994, Cohen 1995, and Herman 1993, 1994, 1995.
47 Among recent discussions, cf. Fisher 1992, Ch. 2, 1990; MacDowell 1990, 23–8; Wilson 1991; Ober 1994; Cohen 1995, 90–101; on the issue of whether the speech was delivered, or whether as Aischines alleged (3. 51–3), Demosthenes 'sold out' the case for thirty minai: Harris 1989; MacDowell 1990, 23–8; Fisher 1992, 38.
48 21. 58–69. Cf. Cohen 1995, 96–7, who emphasizes Demosthenes' recognition of intense rivalries at the festivals, but in referring to the 'normality of such conduct' does not perhaps do justice to the effectiveness of Demosthenes' rhetoric, which isolates Meidias' excessive direct action in such contexts as appalling, and virtually unique, with only the highly dubious, and slightly less serious, case of Alkibiades (21.147) as a precedent.
49 The fight took place on Samos, but whether Euthynos was put on trial, and if so, whether this took place there, or in Athens, and whether regulations concerned with the Athenian clerouchy on Samos may have been involved, are all questions which the text does not permit us to approach.
50 Herman 1995, 49–50, and n. 13; against this approach, cf. also Cohen 1995, 93–6; and on complex negotiations of manhood among the Glendiots, Herzfelt 1985, 72–91.
51 MacDowell 1990, 282; Herman 1995, 59–60. Musonius Rufus 10; cf. Lutz 1947.

52 Examples include Lys. 10. 3; 13. 1–3; 14. 3; 24. 2; Isocr. 20. 3, 5–6; [Dem]. 53. 1–3; Dem. 58. 1–2, 57–9; [Dem]. 59. 1, 11–12. Cf. also Hunter 1994, 127–9; Cohen 1995, 70–4.

53 Saunders quoted Humphreys 1983, 248; but her contrast was a different one again, between putting prior knowledge out of one's mind, and (as did Athenian jurors) acting as if it were the local community making full use of all local knowledge.

54 Cf. Todd 1993, 160–3; Cohen 1995, 181–6.

55 Hypereides For Lycophron 4–6. Cf. Just 1989, 119–20.

56 On the relevance of Aristotle's recognition of the importance of revenge, cf. also Cohen 1995, 65–70; Schütrumpf 1995, 65–6, responding to Herman's views. I would thus resist Herman's comment, ibid., that there is a significant contradiction between Aristotle's opinions and those typically expressed in the courts.

57 Cf. Goldhill 1992, 89–90; Cohen 1995, 16–18.

58 Cf. Osborne 1985; Todd 1993, 160–2.

59 Dem. 21. 47, with MacDowell ad loc.

60 79, with n. 39; Ps.Dem. 59. 66–7, cf. Carey ad loc.

61 Foxhall 1992b, 302–3; 1996; Aeschin. 1. 107 offers some support for the reluctance of wronged husbands to bring cases to court.

62 Cf. Fisher 1990; differently, Ober 1994, 90–2.

63 Cf. Harris 1989; Fisher 1992, 38; MacDowell 1990, 13–16; Wilson 1991, 164–5.

64 MacDowell 1995, 178–9 for their loss of sympathy through litigiousness; Bowie 1993, 96–101, for a more ambivalent reaction to Philokleon's autocracy and violence.

65 Hunter 1994, 125–29; Cohen 1995, 101–7; on sycophants, the contrasting views (both one-sided and overstated) of Osborne 1990 and Harvey 1990.

66 Lys. 10. 16; Dem. 24. 105; Aeschin. 2. 181; Dem. 23. 69. Cf. Gernet 1981, 252–6; Fisher 1992, 95; Hunter 1994, 176–81; Todd 1993, 144–5.

67 For example, the fights in Lys. 3 and 4 passim, Dem. 53. 17 and 54 passim. It is not clear to me whether the weapon in use on the Onesimos cup (above, n. 25) is an ostrakon, a stone, or a sandal: many other vases show men and boys carrying staffs, and a good few show sandals being used in sado-sexual contexts, cf. Kilmer 1993, 103–7, though he seems in serious danger of underestimating the amount of pain apparently being inflicted by the men.

68 What evidence he could have had is far from clear (as often with the generalizations contained in the 'Archaeology', 1. 1–21): cf. McDonnell 1991. The assimilation of earlier Greece to contemporary barbarism was a common ideological move, though Thukydides' own awareness of conditions in northern Greece, and general knowledge of how slaves got to Greece, may lie behind these judgments.

69 Cf. also Ar. Lys. 556–64, where men in armour in the agora doing their shopping are a sign of the disruption caused by the war.

70 Cf. Diod. 12. 19, 13. 33; Szegedy-Maszak 1978; Gröschel 1989; Herman 1994, 105; van Wees 1998.

71 On the date of the change in relation to the archaeological and iconographic evidence, cf. van Wees 1998.

72 Staffs were regularly carried by the elderly, and apparently by many adults as well; a disabled man might 'carry two where others carry one' (Lys. 24. 12), and vases show men carrying and using their staffs frequently. Even so, carrying a staff, allied to a fast walk and a loud voice, could be grounds for prejudice and hostility (Dem. 37. 52).

73 Herman 1994, 102–5; van Wees 1998.

74 Lys. 3. 14, fr. 75 Th.; Ps.-Dem. 53. 17–18; Dem. 54. 9.

75 Humphreys 1985; Todd 1990b, 23–31.
76 Theophr. *Char*. 13. 5. Cf. on *polypragmosyne* and 'minding one's own business' Dover 1974, 188–90; Adkins 1976; Carter 1986.
77 Cf. Solon fr. 4, Plut. *Sol*.18, Dem. 21. 45–6; Fisher 1992, 76–82.
78 For example, Hunter 1994; Millett 1991; Whitehead 1986, 234–52; on *philotimia* as explicitly a sign of masculinity, cf. Xen. *Hiero* 7. 3; as essentially civic, e.g. Dem. 21. 67–9; Whitehead, 1983, 1993.
79 ?Arist. *Ath.Pol*. 53; on Straton, Dem. 21. 83–101. On these procedures and their possible development, cf. Humphreys 1983, 1985; a good treatment of arbitration also in Hunter 1994, Ch. 2.
80 Dem. 21. 47, MacDowell 1990 *ad loc*.; but cf. Harris 1992 for doubts about the quotation of the law here.
81 Ar. *Vesp. passim*, *Nub*. 206–9; Thuc. 1. 77; and e.g. Cartledge 1990, 43–4; MacDowell 1978, 40.
82 Cf. Jones 1957, 35–7, 123–4; Sinclair 1988, 124–7; Markle 1985; Todd 1990a; Osborne 1990; Harvey 1990; Hunter 1994, 125–9.
83 This is a central theme of Cohen 1995; what matters for this argument is that it is so often through manipulation of all the resources of the law that these 'feuds' are carried on.
84 Cf. ?Arist. *Ath.Pol*. 56. 2; Osborne 1992, Foxhall 1992b.
85 Dem. 21. 182, though the actual case, Pyrrhos the Eteoboutad, does not sound like a typical destitute citizen; Cohen 1983, and Todd 1993, 283–4 for laws against theft.
86 Sharpe 1984, 1985, Macfarlane 1981, Cockburn 1991; restatements of the alternative view, Stone 1985, 1987; the introduction and various essays in Hay and Snyder (eds) 1989.
87 Cf. also the analyses of Ober 1989, and Hunter 1991, 143–51.
88 There is no little irony in a powerful figure like Demosthenes identifying with the poorer jurors in using such argument (cf. Wilson 1991), but this rhetoric pervades the speech and may yet have been highly effective (cf. Ober 1994, 100–4).
89 Pellizer 1990; Fisher 1998, 1999.
90 Cf. e.g. Ostwald 1986, Ch. 10; Todd 1993, 232–6, 285–9.
91 Whether or not this letter was actually written by Plato, it is evidently from a Platonic milieu, and an interesting comment on its period.

4

Sex and paternity: gendering the foundation of Kyrene

Eireann Marshall

Introduction

The foundation of Kyrene was represented both through 'historical' myths, which depicted the colonization of the city by Theran settlers guided by Battos, and through the hierogamy ('sacred marriage') between Apollo and the nymph Kyrene. In this paper, I show how the gender dynamics which are played out in these foundation narratives mirror each other (cf. Cartledge, this volume, 54–6). In both, the foundation of the city is described in sexual terms: Apollo and Battos are constructed as masculine begetters of the colony, while Kyrene, the nymph and the personification of Kyrenaian land, is constructed as the mother.

The hierogamy between Apollo and Kyrene

An examination of the hierogamy between Apollo and Kyrene reveals how this union was used as a metaphor for the foundation of the city.[1] The association between the sexual union and the foundation is made clear in Pindar's ninth *Pythian* (51–7), where Cheiron tells Apollo:

> You came to this glen [in Thessaly] to be her husband and you mean to carry her off over the sea to the excellent garden of Zeus. There you will make her queen of a city when you have assembled the island people around the plain-encircled hill. Soon the broad-meadowed queen, Libya, will earnestly welcome your noble bride in golden palaces. There that queen will immediately allot her a portion of the land to be her lawful domain . . .

In this passage, as in an earlier passage from the same epinician ode (lines 5–8), the foundation of the city and the hierogamy are intertwined. Apollo's act of sending forth the Therans ('the island people') to Kyrene ('the plain encircled hill') is conflated with his sexual act with the nymph (Dougherty 1993, 194). Diodoros associates the events in the same way when he describes Apollo sleeping with the nymph and subsequently colonizing the land where this union took place (4. 81). Kallimachos, in his *Hymn to Apollo*, similarly connects the city with the hierogamy when he describes Apollo as looking favourably on Kyrene because of his encounter with the nymph (line 95).

The 'historical' and 'hierogamy' myths are also linked by the fact that both foundation narratives centre around the same locus in Kyrene, near a sacred grove of myrtles which was known as the Myrtoussa.[2] A dedication to Apollo *Myrtōos*, dating from the first century AD, allows us to locate the Myrtoussa in the intramural Sanctuary of Apollo in Kyrene.[3] Since the Myrtoussa is associated with the hierogamy, myrtle itself can be seen to be connected with the hierogamy in some way. As Aphrodite is associated with myrtle, it is likely that she was seen to have encouraged the union with a myrtle branch.[4] Although there are no direct references to Aphrodite touching the divine couple with myrtle, she is connected to the hierogamy by several authors. Pindar includes Aphrodite at the union:

> Silver-footed Aphrodite welcomed the Delian guest, touching with a nimble hand the god-built chariot; and she shed a charming coyness (*aidōs*) on their sweet union, thus blending in bonds of mutual wedlock the god and the maiden-daughter of widely ruling Hypseus.
>
> (*Pyth.* 9. 9–17)

Although Aphrodite is not depicted as touching the chariot with myrtle, her action functions in a similar way. Her touch sheds an *aidōs* on the couple which encourages the hierogamy to take place.[5]

It is on this Myrtoussa that the Libyan King Eurypylos offered the city to the nymph Kyrene because she killed a lion which was ravaging the territory.[6] The act which allows Kyrene to gain control of the city, an act which serves as a metaphor for its foundation, is thus linked to the hierogamy because both occur in the same place. The union between Apollo and Kyrene is associated with the 'historical' foundation of the city since the Myrtoussa is the location in Kyrene where the Theran settlers are imagined to have arrived first. Kallimachos depicts Apollo and Kyrene standing on the Myrtoussa watching the colonists arriving in Kyrene and walking towards them (*Hymn* 2. 90–2). Furthermore, Herodotos describes the Therans arriving at the same location in Kyrene as Kallimachos, since he has them arrive at the *kyra*, or the Spring of Apollo, which is near the Myrtoussa (4. 158).

The hierogamy and the penetration of Greek colonists have further similarities. The nymph Kyrene, in Pindar, is taken by Apollo from Thessaly to Libya to be wed; although the colonizers of Kyrene come from Thera and not Thessaly, they are also brought by Apollo across the sea to Libya.[7] Furthermore, the advice which Cheiron gives to Apollo on how to woo the nymph (*Pyth.* 9. 39–66) is given in oracular form, and is reminiscent of the oracle which Apollo gives to Battos (Dougherty 1993, 148). Cheiron foretells that Apollo will colonize Libya, and the Pythia foretells that Battos will do the same.[8]

Gender dynamics in the hierogamy between Apollo and Kyrene

Gender dynamics can be embedded in foundation myths through hierogamies. An examination will show how masculinity was constructed through these foundation myths and, in turn, how the ancients gendered their collective identities.

The masculinity of Apollo is emphasized by the construction of the nymph Kyrene's femininity; but Kyrene is not typically feminine. She is set apart from typical Greek females by Pindar:

> She disliked the back and forth ways of the loom, and disliked festive dinners with inactive girls of her age; but, fighting with bronze spears and a sword, she killed wild animals, which ensured quiet peace for her father's cattle.
>
> (*Pyth.* 9. 18–23)

Kyrene shuns typically feminine activities such as weaving and partakes in activities which demonstrate that she has masculine bravery and physical strength.[9] Furthermore, the nymph is made *archepolis* by Apollo (*Pyth.* 9. 54) and is given the masculine role of ruling the city (Calame 1990, 301).

However, Kyrene is also described in feminine terms. She is a personification of the land of Kyrene.[10] The fruitfulness of Kyrene is emphasized by Pindar, who refers to Kyrenaian land as 'rich in flocks and fruit' (*Pyth.* 9. 7), and as 'not without tribute of all manner of fruits' (*Pyth.* 9. 58). Although Pindar emphasizes Kyrene's fertility because it was famous for its abundant crops, his depiction of the land's fecundity makes the land akin to the nymph: she, in her fecundity, gives birth to Aristaios.[11] Furthermore, Pindar uses adjectives such as 'blooming' (*Pyth.* 9. 8: *thalloisa*) which can describe either the land or the nymph (Dougherty 1993, 142). Kyrene, the nymph, and Kyrene, the land, undergo, in the ninth *Pythian*, similar transformations from an uncultivated, unsettled state to one which is cultivated and florescent. Thus nymph and the land are wild and untamed before the hierogamy, but are transformed into a mother and a civilized city respectively (Rubin 1978, 358–9) through the penetration of Greek influence, divine and human.

Since Kyrene personifies the land which feeds the Kyrenaians, she is constructed as the mother of the Kyrenaians. This is emphasized by Kallimachos, who refers to Kyrene as his 'fecund mother' (fr. 602) and in so doing uses the same adjective as Pindar: *thalloisan*. The way in which Kyrene is imagined as nourishing the Kyrenaians reveals how land and motherhood are conflated. Pindar describes the land on which the city is situated in an anatomical way: 'Battos will found a city on a white breast of the swelling earth (*en argennoenti mastōi*)' (*Pyth.* 4. 8).

The land of Kyrene is graphically constructed as a mother.[12] Since Pindar elsewhere describes Kyrene as the 'plain-encircled hill', he may, in part, liken Kyrene to a breast for topographical reasons. However, the contour of the land does not, by itself, explain why Pindar chooses to use the breast as a metaphor for Kyrenaian hills. A similar connection between maternity and land is made by Archestratos, according to whom the finest barley groats come from Lesbos, 'in the wave-surrounded breast of famous Eresos'.[13] As will be seen, Apollonios even more graphically describes the land as a breast feeding its population.[14] Kyrene and other personifications of land are therefore constructed as feeding their people like mothers feed their young. Kyrene feeds those who lived on her with the milk with which she would have fed her son, Aristaios, if he were mortal and were not fed on nectar and ambrosia (*Pyth.* 9. 63).

Kyrene's femininity reinforces Apollo's masculinity because it is through him that she becomes properly feminine. It is her marriage to Apollo that transforms Kyrene from a masculine huntress to a mother. Though she rejected feminine roles before her marriage with the god, afterwards she is tamed and is given the feminine, nurturing and civilized role of tending the Kyrenaians.[15]

Apollo is constructed as initiating the marriage. While Mnaseas says that Kyrene went to Libya of her own free will (ap. schol. Apollonios Rhodios 2. 498 = Wendel 168), Pindar, Apollonios Rhodios, Diodoros and Nonnos write that Apollo carried her off to Libya from Mt Pelion.[16] In fact, in these latter versions, Apollo seizes the nymph forcibly. Pindar says that Apollo snatched (*harpase*) the nymph (*Pyth.* 9. 6), and so represents the marriage as a violent abduction brought about through masculine initiative.[17] The implication is that masculine initiative brings the foundations of cities.

Apollo also transforms Kyrene into a personification of the land, in that he names the land on which the union takes place (Pind. *Pyth.* 9. 51–8; Diod. 4. 81. 1–3); the act of naming itself is a display of masculine power (see Foxhall, this volume). Here the story of Kyrene and Apollo follows a pattern typical of foundation myths: marriage between an Olympian god and a nymph who gives her name to the land, or who bears a son who does the same.[18] By being made personifications of the land, these nymphs are made the mothers of those who live on it. Therefore, the act of naming can be connected with sex in that both acts result in eponymous nymphs being made mothers. By sleeping with her and by making her a personification of the land, Apollo makes Kyrene the mother of both Aristaios and the Kyrenaians.[19] Apollo's naming the city can be seen as a metaphor for the foundation of the city as well as a metaphor for making the nymph the mother of the Kyrenaians.[20]

The way in which Kyrene's maternity of the Kyrenaians and Aristaios are linked shows how the birth of Aristaios is a metaphor for the birth of the city.[21] Foundation myths which are presented in the forms of hierogamies often conflate the births of the cities with the births of sons.[22] The similarity between the births of Aristaios and the city of Kyrene can be seen in the fact that Aristaios is born in the Myrtoussa, where the city can be said to have been born (Ap. Rhod. 2. 505–6).

The link between the birth of Aristaios and the foundation of the city suggests that Apollo was constructed as the father of the Kyrenaians in much the same way as he was the father of Aristaios. Since the city is founded as a result of the sexual union with the nymph, the city can be seen as being conceived through this union. Apollo's seed can be said metaphorically to generate the city in that it is planted in the land.

The myth of Euphemos and Kalliste is reminiscent of this conception. When the Argonauts were stranded in Libya, Euphemos is said to have been given a clod of Libyan earth by the Triton, Eurypylos, and told by him that his descendants would colonize Libya.[23] Apollonios describes a dream which Euphemos has when he is on board the Argo:

> It seemed to him that the divine clod of earth which he held in the flat of his hand close to his chest was being suckled by white springs of milk, and that from it, however small, a woman like a virgin drew near.[24]

At this point, Euphemos sleeps with the woman, but instantly repents because he fears he has committed incest with his daughter. The young woman tells him that she is Kalliste, the daughter of Triton and Libya, that the milk is hers, and that she will nurse his descendants. Euphemos throws the clod of earth into the sea and Kalliste becomes the island which will later be renamed Thera (Ap. Rhod. 4. 1755–8). Euphemos sleeps with the personification of the land which will be a mother to his descendants. While his union with Kalliste did not result in the generation of a city, the myths betray the same gender dynamics. Euphemos will father a race of men who will be fostered by the land with which he has slept.

It has been argued that, in the city's foundation myths, Apollo is the generating principle behind Kyrene. It is through Apollo's initiative that both the hierogamy and the foundation take place; he makes the nymph

Kyrene the mother of both Aristaios and the city, Kyrene. Likewise, Apollo is made a father by the same act: with the same seed he makes Kyrene fruitful. Through Kyrene, the nymph, he generates Aristaios, and through Kyrene, the personification of land, he generates the city which the land will feed and nurture. These foundation myths allowed the Kyrenaians to gender their identity, and to maintain a powerful masculinity at its core. Through the hierogamy, the Kyrenaians could construct their city as begotten by a god who was archetypally both male and Greek.

Battos the Founding Father

Apollo is also central in the 'historical' colonization legends: his oracle instructs Battos to lead the Therans to Libya (Hdt. 4. 150, 155). The god's impetus in the colonization of the city is stressed over and over again. Kallimachos writes: 'Apollo told Battos about the city and led his people as they entered Libya and swore he would vouchsafe a walled city to our kings' (*Hymn* 2. 63–8). Pindar also emphasizes Apollo's role in sending forth the Therans. He describes the Delphic oracle given to the Therans:

> With Apollo not far away, the Priestess proclaimed Battos the colo-
> nizer of fertile Libya, and that he would presently leave the holy
> island and found a city of noble chariots on a gleaming hill.[25]

Apollo's role in the colonization legends of the city closely parallels the hierogamy myths. It is through his initiative both that the consummation with Kyrene takes place and that the city is colonized. The gender dynamics played out in the two different legends reflect each other: Battos is constructed as a father in much the same way as Apollo is.

Like Apollo, Battos is the sole initiator of the colonization, the sole founder or *oikist* (Hdt. 4. 159). In Herodotos, the 'Theran account' some-what minimizes Battos' role: the Delphic oracle is given to Grinnos, not Battos.[26] However, once the Therans decide to colonize Libya Battos, even in this account, is the sole authority (Hdt. 4. 154). The 'Kyrenaian account' emphasizes Battos' role more strongly. His personal background and defects are relayed, and the calamities which befall Thera, mentioned by both accounts, are here attributed to his inactivity alone (Hdt. 4. 154–8). Pindar likewise emphasizes Battos' role: 'Aristoteles [Battos] led men with swift ships, opening up a deep path across the sea.'[27]

Like Apollo, Battos can be seen as metaphorically begetting Kyrene. This is brought out in a curious passage from Pindar, where Medea says:

> I foretell that from this sea-beaten land [Thera], the daughter of
> Epaphos [Libya], will at some time have planted in her a root of

cities (*asteōn rizan phuteusesthai*) cared for by men near the foundations of Zeus Ammon.[28]

The act of planting is connected to sex in that the same verb (*phuteuo*) is
used for both. Marriage is often described in ancient literature as the sowing
of fields, and children are seen as the produce, or offshoots from this
sowing.[29] In Aischylos' *Seven Against Thebes*, Oidipous is described as
inseminating his mother's furrow with a bloody root (*rhiza*).[30] The root is
used as a metaphor for offspring, just as the furrow is a metaphor for the
womb. Pindar uses similar sexual terms to represent the foundation of
Kyrene. The city, which is metaphorically represented as founded by the
planting of Libyan land with a root, can be seen to be founded by means of
a sexual act; the root, or the offspring produced from this act, is a metaphor
for the city.[31] Although Battos is not explicitly represented as carrying out
this planting, the implication is that he does so as the founder of Kyrene.[32]
Both Battos and Apollo beget the city by planting the earth with their seed.[33]

Battos can also be seen as the father of Kyrene in the sense that he is seen
as founding the *genos* of the city. Kyrene, in several different places, is
referred to as the city of the descendants of Battos. Pindar ends his Fifth
Pythian with the following prayer to Zeus (lines 124–5): 'I pray that he grant
the *genos* of Battos this new prize at Olympia.' Since the ode was written in
honour of the Battiad Arkesilas IV, the *genos* of Battos in this passage can
refer to the Battiads. However, an important purpose of epinician odes was
to reintegrate the victor, whose athletic success made him temporarily
greater than his fellow citizens, within his polis by exalting the polis' foundation (Dougherty 1994, 43). Pindar does not aim to glorify Battos purely in
order to glorify his descendant, Arkesilas IV, but also to glorify Kyrene;
Battos' *genos* can therefore be taken to refer to the city as well as to the
Battiads.[34]

The way in which Battos was seen as the metaphorical ancestor of all
Kyrenaians is evident in his title *archēgetēs*. Several inscriptions, including
the *Stele of the Founders*, a fourth-century BC decree including oaths which
purport to have been made at the time of the colonization of Kyrene, and a
fourth-century BC sacred law (*SEG* ix. 3, 72), demonstrate that Battos was
given the title *archēgetēs*, at least later. This title was given to founders of
genealogical lines and to founders of colonies.[35] Ephorus, for example,
writes that Eurysthenes and Prokles, because of their poor government,
were not given the honour usually bestowed upon *oikists* of founding lines
named after them, and hence were not given the titles of *archēgetai*.[36] As the
archēgetēs of Kyrene, Battos was honoured not only as the city's founder but
as its progenitor. In addition, Pindar writes that Battos was venerated as a
hero (*Pyth.* 5. 94–5). If hero cult developed from ancestor cult, the hero
could be, in a sense, the ancestor common to all the members of the polis.[37]
Battos was in any case its first king and the founder of a dynasty. Kings are

commonly seen in paternalistic terms, in that their subjects are likened to their offspring. For example, Sophokles emphasizes Oidipous' position as the monarch of Thebes when he has Oidipous refer to the Thebans as his children (*tekna*), at the beginning of *Oidipous Tyrannos*.[38]

The way in which Pindar describes Euphemos founding the *genos* which will colonize Libya is similar to the way in which Battos is described as fathering the Kyrenaian *genos*. He describes Euphemos begetting the race which will go to Thera: 'He [Euphemos] will find in the beds of foreign women an excellent race, which will come to this island [Thera]' (*Pyth*. 4. 50–1). In this passage, he is depicted as fathering the *genos* in graphic, sexual terms. Later in the same ode (lines 254–6), Pindar uses the same terminology to describe Euphemos begetting the *genos* as he uses to describe the way in which Kyrene was planted in Libya: 'The seed of your bright wealth was received in a foreign land (*arourais*: seed land) on the destined day or nights: for the race of Euphemos was planted there (*genos Euphamous phuteuthen*).' The terminology used in these two passages emphasizes how colonization can be described in sexual terms. The same verb (*phuteuo*) is used to describe the city being planted as that used to describe a *genos* being planted. Furthermore, the city and the *genos* are both produced from seed (Pind. *Pyth*. 4. 42–3, 254: *sperma*) and both kinds of seed are received in land. Thus the acts of founding a city and fathering a *genos* are conflated. Battos is the founding father of Kyrene because he 'begets' the city through founding it (planting cities) and through fathering its *genos* (planting seed). These two different forms of paternity parallel the two principal meanings of the title *archēgetēs*, namely, founder and progenitor.[39] The same conflation between planting a *genos* and planting a city is found in the hierogamy myths. As we have seen, in these myths Apollo's sleeping with the nymph Kyrene and begetting Aristaios parallels his sleeping with the personification of land and begetting the city.

Conclusion: the male as the generating principle behind the city

While, on the face of it, the Apollo–Kyrene nexus and the Battos story could be seen to offer competing aetiologies of the city, these different myths are intertwined and reinforce each other's claims. They are linked by Apollo, who is central to both mythical traditions and is represented as either founding Kyrene through his union with Kyrene or as initiating the foundation of Kyrene through his oracle. The way in which the two myths work together suggests that the Apollo–Kyrene nexus was constructed in response to the god's role in the 'historical' foundation of the city.

The gender dynamics in the 'historical' myths and the 'hierogamy' myths which recount the foundation of Kyrene parallel each other and are emphasized by the fact that the city is described as founded or born through sexual acts controlled by Greek, male power in divine form. One might compare the conception of the city in these myths with the theory of generation developed in Aristotle's *Generation of Animals*, notably in the first two books, in which the male is the efficient and formal cause of generation and the female the material cause.[40] In other words, the male provides movement and 'form', while the female provides 'matter' (1. 716 a 4–8, 730 a 25–30). Aristotle uses several examples to illustrate this theory of reproduction, including that of carpentry, in which the female 'matter' is likened to wood and the male 'movement' likened to form given to the wood by the carpenter (1. 729 b 17–19; 2. 730 b 12–21). He therefore sees the male as the generative principle and the female as that which provides the nourishment for the offspring and allows it to come into being (1. 716 a 20–4, 730 a 15). It is the *dynamis* of the male semen which causes the material and nourishment of the female to take on particular characteristics (1. 730 a 14–16). In other words, the male determines the nature of the offspring. Since the male is the generating principle, he is characterized as active, while the female is passive (1. 729 b 9–19).

The agricultural metaphors used in the foundation myths resemble this theory of generation. In these myths, a land-seed nexus appears repeatedly. Apollo sleeps with the personification of land and provides the seed from which the city is born. Battos plants his offspring/city in Libyan land, and Euphemos begets the Theran *genos* by planting his seed in land. In this nexus, the male is represented as the active, generating principle and the female the passive element out of which the city comes into being. The passivity of the female is evident in the metaphor used to describe her. She is land and as such only nourishes the seed planted by the male until it comes to fruition. In addition, the female feeds the offspring/city and, in the case of the eponymous nymph, protects it. The active role allotted to the male in the generation of the city is evident in that it is through his initiative that the hierogamy takes place and that the city is founded. This is reinforced by his acts of naming. It is through the male that the city is planted/generated since he provides the seed from which the city comes into being. Thus the female is represented as the receptacle of the male seed which generates the city. The titles given to Apollo and Battos reflect these gender dynamics. As *archēgetai*, they are constructed as the progenitors of Kyrene.[41] Urban civilization is generated through energetic masculinity.

The foundation of the city can also be attributed to masculine initiative in the sense that the Theran settlers may have been predominantly male, and developed sexual relationships with native women.[42] This is intimated by Kallimachos, who describes Libyan women watching the settlers performing the first Karneian festival (*Hymn* 2. 90–2). Pindar also weaves the intermarriage of Kyrenaians and Libyans into the fabric of the foundation myths when, towards the end of his ninth Pythian, he relates the story of the 'ancestral' Kyrenaians wooing the Libyan Antaios' daughter (105–25). Since the intermingling of the two populations in these passages is represented as the marriage between Kyrenaian males and Libyan females, it is possible that the colonizing element was identified as masculine.

The way in which urban civilization is generated through masculine impetus can be seen in the way Heracles is described by Diodoros as civilizing Libya by bringing its land under cultivation.[43] In order to make the land cultivable, he subdues its wild beasts, because land ruled by beasts is uninhabitable. He also destroys the Amazons and Gorgons who lived in Libya because, according to Diodoros, he is the benefactor of mankind and societies run by women are uncivilized (Diod. 3. 54). Domination by women is represented as uncivilized, rather as land ruled by beasts is not civilized. Apollo is constructed as taming beasts and feminine prowess in a similar way. According to Pindar, Apollo subdues lions so that civilization can flourish in Libya, and civilizes an otherwise masculine, lion-killing nymph through marriage (*Pyth.* 5. 62). In both myths, masculine intervention tames uncivilized elements. Cities are founded and civilization is achieved through masculine impetus. The male is the generating principle behind the city: Greek urban civilization is his preserve.

Notes

1 Hierogamy is used in other legends as a poetic metaphor for the foundation of cities. Pindar recounts the foundation of Rhodes as the marriage between the eponymous nymph and Helios (*Olympian* 7. 71–6), and depicts the foundations of Thebes and Aigina as the hierogamies of those nymphs and Zeus (*Isthmian* 8. 16–23). See also Diodoros Sikulos 3. 68, where Ammon sleeps with Amaltheia and then makes her the mistress of the region in Egypt in which their union was consummated; Nonnus 13. 363–5, where Cadmus builds one hundred cities in Libya where he consumates his love for Harmonia. See also Dougherty 1993 and 1994.
2 Chamoux 1953, 268; Calame (1990, 306) refers to the terrace as the Mount of Myrtes. See further below, n. 4.
3 *IGRR* i. 1035; see also *SEG* 9. 190: A fragmentary Hadrianic inscription from the sanctuary mentions the hierogamy. For the identification of the Myrtoussa in Kyrene see Chamoux 1953, 268; Stucchi 1975, 117; For a loggia enclosing a sacred myrtle bush, see Ensoli 1990, 157–76.
4 Kallimachos, *Hymn to Apollo* 90–2; Apollonios Rhodios 2. 505; Stephanos of Byzantium s.v. *Myrtoussa*. Also, myrtle is regularly used in garlands, including those worn by the nuptial couple in the wedding ceremony (Foxhall, pers. comm.).
5 Woodbury 1982, 248. This *aidōs* would not be the same as that felt by young, unmarried couples (e.g. Pind. *Pyth.* 9. 39–50 where Apollo feels shyness when he sets eyes on Kyrene) but would be adapted to marriage and thus act as a barrier against love with other partners; Gildersleeve 1885, 340; Carey 1981, 69; Dougherty 1993, 138: Aphrodite is seen as fitting the wedding together.
6 Callim. *Hymn* 2. 90–2; Akesandros of Kyrene and Phylarchos, *ap.* schol. Ap. Rhod. 4. 298.
7 *Pyth.* 9. 5. Dougherty 1993, 140, 144, 146, 148–9, for the similarity between hierogamy and colonization in general.

8 For the oracle given to Battos: Hdt. 4. 150–6; Callim. *Hymn* 2. 63–8; Pind. *Pyth.* 4. 5–8.

9 *Pyth.* 9. 32: Apollo admires her undaunted spirit and power; Dougherty 1993, 70–1 describes Kyrene as reared by a man to masculine arts and refers to Kyrene as the archetypal athlete.

10 The nymph is the personification of Kyrene in every sense; she personifies both the land and the city. Carey (1981, 81) shows how the nymph and the place are conflated in *Pyth.* 9. 57, 85; Dougherty 1993, 127, 139. For personifications, see Stafford in Foxhall and Salmon 1998.

11 Dougherty (1993, 145) writes that Kyrene imitates the land's fertility and will give birth.

12 See Farnell 1930, 150; Calame 1990, 289; Norwood 1945, 35: Norwood thought that Libya was being depicted as a mother, but *Pyth.* 9. 55, where Pindar describes Kyrene as a 'plain-encircled hill', shows that it is the city which is referred to.

13 Fr. 4 = Athenaios 3. 111 E, trans. Wilkins and Hill, 1994.

14 4. 1731–45; Isaiah 66. 10–14 describes Jerusalem in similar terms: 'That you may be suckled, filled from her consoling breast, that you may savour with delight her glorious breasts . . . . At her breast will her nursling be carried and fondled in her lap. Like a son comforted by his mother will I comfort you.'

15 Kyrene, even before her marriage, however, is depicted as guarding her father's cattle: *Pyth.* 9. 23. For transformation after the marriage, see Rubin 1978, 353–67.

16 For Apollo taking Kyrene over to Libya: Callim. *Hymn* 2. 95, (the hierogamy as a rape); Pind. *Pyth.* 9. 5; Ap. Rhod. 2. 502–5; Diod. 4.81ff; Nonnos 13. 302 (Apollo takes her off in a kidnapper's chariot).

17 Carey (1981, 69–70, 80) points out that the use of the word *harmozoisa* in line 13 indicates that some sort of a betrothal between Apollo and Kyrene was imagined and that they were, thus, depicted as legally married. Carey believes that Pindar, in aiming to flatter the Kyrenaians, depicts the hierogamy as an ideal marriage; Robbins (1978, 104) sees marriage and not rape as the basis of the sexual relationship; See also Woodbury 1982, 245, 247. For the violence in the union in Pindar see Dougherty 1993, 64, 141–4.

18 Above, n.1 (Zeus, Ammon). Pind. *Ol.* 7. 74–6: the sons of Helios and Rhodes, Kameiros, Ialysos and Lindos, give their names to the three cities on the island. Female deities and their sons, however, do not exclusively give their names to cities: for colonizing heroes, like Theras and Cecrops, see Dougherty 1993, 65–6; 146–7; Calame 1990, 292.

19 Diod. 18. 17. 1; Pind. *Isthm.* 8. 22–3: Kroton and Aigina are made mothers at the same time as being metamorphosed into personifications of land. Robbins 1978, 97: through marriage Kyrene becomes fruitful. Dougherty 1993, 142: Apollo causes the land to bloom just as he causes the nymph to bloom.

20 Pind. *Ol.* 10. 43–51: Herakles founds the sanctuary at Olympia by marking out its boundaries, putting a fence around the Altis and, lastly, giving a name to the sanctuary which had hitherto been nameless; Segal 1986, 97–8.

21 Ap. Rhod. 2. 505–6; Diod. 4. 81. 1–3; Nonnos 13. 299–301; Dougherty 1993, 145.

22 Pind. *Isthm.* 8. 21–3: the union of Zeus and Aigina produces not only the city but Aiakos. Helios and Rhodes: above, n.18.

23 Pind. *Pyth.* 4. 19–23; Hdt. 4. 179; Ap. Rhod. 4. 1551–63; 1731–64.

24 Ap. Rhod. 4. 1731–64 (quotation 1733–7); Fraenkel 1950, 132–3; Calame 1990, 295–7; Livrea 1987.

25 Pyth. 4. 5–8. See *Pyth.* 5. 62: Apollo put fear into lions who were threatening Battos so that 'his oracle might not be unaccomplished'.

26 Hdt. 4. 150–3; see Malkin 1987, 60–9.

27 *Pyth.* 5. 87–8. Cf. also *Pyth.* 4. 55–6. Diod. 8. 29 also concentrates on Battos, who goes to Delphi in order to cure his stammer and instead is ordered to found Kyrene. For similar concentrations on one individual, see Hdt. 5. 42: Dorieus, the younger brother of Kleomenes, unsuccessfully colonizes Libya in order to escape the prospect of being ruled by his brother. Hdt. 4. 149: Theras founds Thera on his own initiative because he cannot stomach being subordinated to his nephews. Pind. *Ol.* 7. 30; 1. 31: Tlepolemos and Hieron are described as the sole founders of Ialysos and Aitna respectively.

28 Calame (1990, 285, 289, 299) identifies this root as the clod of Libyan earth given by Eurypylos to Euphemos which is transplanted into Libya to produce cities. See also Segal 1986, 74. On the clod in general see Pind. *Pyth.* 4. 19–23; Hdt. 4. 179; Ap. Rhod. 4. 1551–63; 1731–64. Pind. *Pyth.* 4. 42–3 refers to the clod as the seed (*sperma*) of Libya.

29 Calame 1990, 288; Vernant 1977, ix: 'For the Greeks marriage is a form of ploughing, with the woman as the furrow and the husband as the labourer'; Dougherty 1993, 63–5: 'The husband is the one with the plough; he brings order and culture to the feminine land' (p.64); Segal 1986, 81. In the marriage formula, the father of the bride tells his son-in-law that he is giving him his daughter for the 'ploughing of legitimate children' (Menander, *Perikeiromenē* 1013–14; Seaford 1990, 152).

30 752–5; Calame 1990, 293 for the root as a metaphor.

31 Farnell 1930, 151: the root can be taken to refer to the city, Kyrene, which is a root because as the metropolis of the region it gave rise to other cities. Gildersleeve (1885, 283) interpreted Libya as conceiving and bringing forth Kyrene. Calame 1990, 289: 'the fecundation of the earth thus, simultaneously, results from and produces nurturing cities'.

32 Pind. *Pyth.* 5. 86–7: Battos is described opening a deep path across the sea. This motif is reminiscent of the ploughing motif in *Pyth.* 4. 14–15. Calame (1990, 289) also sees Battos as the force behind this planting.

33 Calame (1990, 289) interprets the gender dynamics in the passage from the Fourth *Pythian* in much the same way: the earth is feminine and Battos the masculine principle which colonizes it; see Dougherty (1993, 66) for gender dynamics in hierogamies where the land is female and the male supplies culture through his sexuality.

34 *SEG* ix. 63: A first century AD inscription commemorating the end of the Marmaric War also refers to Battos as Kyrene's ancestor.

35 Casewitz 1985, 246–8; Malkin 1987, 241–8.

36 Strabo 8. 366 = *FGrH* 70 F118. The ten Kleisthenic tribes were each given *archēgetai* who were seen as ancestors of the tribes (?Aristotle, *Ath. Pol.* 21. 5–6; Malkin 1987, 243–4)

37 Seaford 1994, 111; Malkin 1987, 243)

38 Battos is destined, through his genetic inheritance, to found Kyrene and beget its *genos* since he is descended from Euphemos (Hdt. 4. 150). In Pind. *Pyth.* 4. 50–3, Euphemos is described as begetting a *genos* which would, in turn, beget Battos.

39 Casewitz 1985, 246–8; Malkin 1987, 245.

40 I am indebted to S. M. Elliott for her work on the 'female principle' in Arist. *Gen. An.* His view of the female's role in generation is not uniform throughout the work. In book four, he assigns to females a more active role than he does in the first two books, in that he allows the female, to a certain extent, to provide movement and to influence in generation. See 4. 777 b 28–30, where the soul is

produced by a mixture of male heat and female coldness. See also the papers by Harlow and Foxhall in Foxhall and Salmon 1998.

41 Pind. *Pyth.* 5. 60: for Apollo as the *archēgetēs* of Kyrene; Callim. *Hymn* 2. 55–7: 'It is Apollo that men follow when they map out cities.'

42 Van Compernolle (1983, 1033–49), Braund (1994, 81–3), and Rougé (1970, 307–17) emphasize the necessity for intermarriage with native populations; Graham 1984, 294–314 believes that there must have been at least some Greek women who were included in the settlement process for cultic reasons. See also Dougherty 1993, 67–76, 151–2.

43 4. 17. Calame 1990, 288: agriculture is central to representation of ancient urban civilization.

5

The masculinity of the Hellenistic king

Jim Roy

The rulers who took control of the major fragments of Alexander's empire, and in time their heirs, had to legitimise their position, just as those subject to their power had to make that power tolerable to themselves, and so an idealised view of Hellenistic kingship emerged. It is the purpose of this paper to consider what part the masculinity of the king held in the public perception of kingship among Hellenistic kings and Hellenistic Greeks.

How kingship was perceived by Hellenistic Greeks[1] has received considerable attention, and in its broad outlines is well known: besides a lengthy analysis by Préaux, there are good recent summaries in English by Walbank and Smith.[2] The king held absolute power, and there was no constitutional body capable of imposing serious restraint on him.[3] Royal power was first established above all through military strength, and the king's role as military leader – by definition, victorious military leader – remained central.[4] Towards the gods the king was pious (even if, as often, he was himself worshipped as divine). The king was wealthy,[5] but not greedy. The king was kind and generous, using his power and wealth justly and magnanimously for the welfare and protection of those who could claim his favour; praise for kings as saviours and benefactors is common.[6] The perception of the king was furthered by royal cult (see Price 1984a, 25–50), and also by the physical images of the king presented to public view.[7] Cultural patronage was also used to create a favourable image of the king.[8] It is clear that a justificatory ideal of kingship emerged, and that each king in his own reign was – ideally – expected to live up to it, but at the same time could deploy some form of the ideal in his own interest.[9] The king made very considerable efforts to keep his image as charismatic ruler before the public.[10]

While in each generation the king could and should personally justify his exercise of power, it was obviously also desirable to give kingship a justification that endured across generations, and, for that reason (and because of Macedonian precedent, and also of obvious personal and family ambitions) Hellenistic kingship was from the outset, unsurprisingly, dynastic.[11] Very soon after the death of Alexander the Great, the leading figures in his empire clearly recognised that marriage to a daughter or other female relative of another leader was politically advantageous, so that, when the leading contenders for power assumed royal status towards the end of the fourth century, a pattern of politically motivated marriage was well established.[12] It was a natural step to promote the sons of these marriages as the next generation of rulers. Thus the king, identified as military leader and political ruler, was also seen as dynastic son (or heir), husband, and father. The king's place within a dynastic chain was reinforced by such titles as Philopator, Philometor, and Philadelphos[13], and in the case of the Ptolemies continuity was emphasized by the repeated use of the name Ptolemy itself. Statue-groups showing several generations of a royal family emphasized dynastic continuity.[14] Great store was put upon an appearance of royal love producing legitimate heirs: Theokritos, in a poem in praise of Ptolemy II, goes so far as to point out (17. 34–44) that, when husband and wife love each other as did the king's parents Ptolemy I and Berenike, then a man may safely entrust his estate to his children, but that less loving wives produce children who do not resemble their father.[15] Any claim or rumour that an heir to a throne was not a genuine member of his dynasty was a challenge to his right to succeed: that such challenges occurred[16] is simply another indication of how solidly established dynastic succession became as a legitimation of rule.

The common Hellenistic views of kingship are illustrated by many documents, particularly inscriptions, so many that here a very few examples will suffice. Ilion[17] expressed its goodwill and loyalty to Antiochos I in a text which makes clear his military success, gained with the support of the gods and his Friends (political advisers) and armed forces; the text also clearly located Antiochos within the Seleukid dynasty as son of King Seleukos and husband of Queen Stratonike; it went on to prescribe prayers for the King, the Queen, the Friends and the armed forces; and finally the city's ambassadors were instructed to express the city's good wishes for the health of the King, [the Queen, their children,] the Friends, and [the armed forces].[18] In this text the king's role as political and military leader is made clear, as are his services to Greek cities and his dynastic position, with recognition also of his wife's importance. Likewise Teos[19] recognised Antiochos III as benefactor and saviour, praising him for his ancestral goodwill; the text refers to the King's Friends and armed forces, and also pays great attention to Queen Laodike, who is praised as a benefactress in her own right and receives major honours alongside the king. Royal cult commonly associated the king with his ancestors[20] or with his present family and his ancestors,[21] emphasizing the dynastic nature of his rule. Such texts, in typical fashion, define the king's identity by reference to his Friends, his army, his dynasty and his queen.

In this projected image conventionally masculine functions are attributed to the king. Political and military activities were in the Greek world male activities, and the Hellenistic king is a supreme example of the male carrying out such activities with vigour and authority. A justification frequently offered for the king's right to rule was the right of conquest, expressed as the rule of 'spear-won' land;[22] it is not clear how vividly the phallocratic symbolism of the term was present in the minds of Hellenistic Greeks, though it was echoed in Theokritos' compliments to Ptolemy II – 'spearman' and 'skilled in wielding the spear'.[23] The king's dynastic role is obviously masculine, maintaining and transmitting the dynastic succession within which his ancestors, himself and his successors exercise their political and military functions. The king's masculinity was not intended to be seen as truculent or crudely pugnacious: militarism was tempered by a certain chivalry towards defeated opponents in clashes between rulers (Gehrke 1982, 262–3), and much military activity was presented as protection of those friendly to the king. Moreover, as outlined above, the virtues of the Hellenistic king included not only piety but generosity, and cultural patronage was regularly deployed as an instrument of royal policy; and cultural attainments were also emphasized when Attalos II praised his nephew's tutor, laying stress on literary skills and moral worth.[24] Nonetheless, even if such tendencies mellowed the king's masculine exercise of power, the masculine nature of his rule was still very clear.[25] That kingship was not however simply an implicitly masculine exercise of political and military activities traditional to Greek males, but was understood by Hellenistic Greeks as explicitly masculine, is shown by the public image of kingship, and in particular by royal iconography.

The public image of the king's masculinity was projected in various ways. In the age of the Diadochoi, for instance, Lysimachos made play with his image as lion-killer, exploiting a thoroughly masculine image of himself as a courageous huntsman. There were also similar stories about Krateros and Perdikkas, which may make the actual story of Lysimachos' lion-killing dubious; but the use of the story by Lysimachos, and his obvious expectation that such a masculine image would reinforce his position as ruler, are clear.[26] From the time of Alexander onwards Greek artists developed the motif of the royal hunt as an element of royal iconography, borrowing a subject already ancient in oriental and Egyptian art. Battle-scenes were also developed as a genre celebrating royal exploits.[27] More widespread, more important, and even more explicit, however, is the masculinity of the king projected by the physical portraits of Hellenistic rulers.

Our present understanding of the Hellenistic royal portrait is due above all to Smith.[28] While portraits on royal coinage were presumably subject to some form of direct or indirect royal control, it was not the rule that sculptural portraits of Hellenistic kings were made according to fixed official types – in which respect they differ from Roman imperial portraits (Smith 1988, 27–31). Nonetheless general conventions about the portrayal of the Hellenistic ruler developed.[29] The royal portrait drew on the earlier repertoire of Greek art, in sculpture drawing notably on representations of athletes and athletic gods, and an iconography of royal representation developed which used both royal and divinizing attributes but also relied on such characteristics as stylization of the facial features and a royal upward gaze. The faithfulness of the image as a recognizable portrait of the king varied; the aim was sometimes a strikingly handsome idealized appearance rather than an individual portrayal.[30] In any case the features were shown as smooth, without wrinkles, furrows or double chins, and the expression was impassive; royal portraits were thus distinguished from other genres of portrait such as the philosopher.[31] The portraits did not necessarily show the king's real age:[32] typically the king is shown as a youthful, vigorous, beardless man aged about twenty to thirty, and no king, except possibly Euthydemos I, looks more than about thirty-five to forty. Most striking of all is that, while kings were sometimes portrayed wearing armour – royal statues in civilian dress are not found[33] – and sometimes on horseback, by far the most common form of royal statue was the standing naked figure.[34] The iconography thus presents the Hellenistic king in idealized form, royal and serene, mature enough to rule whether in the vigour of young manhood or in the prime of life, and with his distinctive and consciously masculine place in the Greek plastic arts' repertoire of masculinity (see Figures 5.1 and 5.2) The use of such iconography for kings from a wide range of major and minor dynasties suggests that this masculine image of the king came to be universally recognised among Greeks. The king's image thus borrowed from traditional Greek iconography of masculinity, and redefined it for his own day. Such royal portraiture confirms, if confirmation were needed, that not only the obviously male king but Hellenistic kingship itself was to be seen as essentially masculine. Moreover, the masculine representation of kingship continued even as the king's power shrank: although royal benefactions, for instance, declined dramatically in number from about 150 BC,[35] and the military power and resources of Hellenistic kings also declined in the latter part of the second century BC,[36] examples of the king sculpted as a standing naked figure are still found in the later Hellenistic period.[37]

There are occasional hints that the exercise of the king's power could be represented in gendered form. Thus, in the great procession organized in Alexandria by Ptolemy II, behind a float on which stood statues of Alexander and Ptolemy I, walked women named after the Greek cities in Ionia and elsewhere in Asia Minor and the islands which had been subdued by the Persians. However, while it is likely that current Ptolemaic policy towards Greek cities was somehow symbolized, the precise meaning of this element of the procession is far from clear,[38] and it cannot be taken to suggest close political union between Ptolemy II and all of the cities represented. Even such a faint suggestion that Hellenistic kingship could be symbolized as sexual congress of masculine king and feminine kingdom is rare in Hellenistic Greek art and literature, perhaps because it did not sit well with the Hellenistic king's typical (if superficial) courtesy towards Greek cities.[39] It is also true that for Hellenistic Greeks (though not for

Figure 5.1 Seleukos I from the Villa of the Papyri at Herculaneum
Source: Museo Archeologico Nazionale di Napoli 5590, Smith (1988) Catalogue 21, Roman replica of a portrait of Seleukos I Nickator

Figure 5.2 Pyrrhos of Epiros from the Villa of the Papyri at Herculaneum
Source: Museo Archeologico Nazionale di Napoli 6150, Smith (1988) Catalogue 5, Roman-period copy of a portrait probably of Pyrrhos of Epiros

certain non-Greek cultures) the idea of kingship was not dependent on the king's possession of any particular piece of territory (see, for example, Walbank 1984, 65–6), which may have discouraged gendered representation of the king's possession of territory. Even if, however, the king was not normally projected as a male ruler possessing a female kingdom, Hellenistic royal iconography sought to make it abundantly clear that royal rule was essentially masculine.

Another major aspect of the king's perceived masculinity was his relationship to his queen.[40] The strong desire to use dynastic succession as a significant means (among others) of legitimizing Hellenistic kingship created a important role not only for the king as male heir-husband-father but also for the queen as consort-mother. Royal women might conceivably have fulfilled such a role without being given major public status, but in fact the Hellenistic dynasties chose to give their queens great prominence alongside the kings. One result of the queen's public role was that, paradoxically, the Hellenistic king, despite enjoying enormous personal power, had to define his public identity at least partly in terms of his wife, as few Greek men ever had to do.[41] Another result was that eventually, because the limits of the queen's role were not well-defined, she could take on enough of the king's masculine role to compromise the masculine definition of royal rule.

For the early Hellenistic kings, all from a Macedonian background, the most obvious model for the role of a royal wife was the pattern of behaviour (so far as it was thought acceptable) shown in recent generations by the women of the Argead dynasty; and indeed the Argead model was at first followed, though major change soon took place. Philip II and Alexander the Great had certainly been polygamous, and polygamy may well have been normal for Argead kings throughout the classical period.[42] Consequently there were often several Argead royal wives at any one time, and none held a uniquely privileged position as royal consort (though some wives enjoyed higher status than others). The role of at least the more prominent Argead royal wives changed from the time of Philip II,[43] and some were given much greater public prominence, typified by the chryselephantine statues of Philip's mother Eurydike and wife Olympias in the Philippeum at Olympia alongside those of his father Amyntas, Philip himself and his son Alexander.[44] Some Argead women of the late period also played a part in the political life of the dynasty: their activity was often condemned as improper interference in political affairs, but the condemnation came largely from political opponents (see Carney 1995, 377–80). Then after the death of Alexander the lack of effective male Argeads allowed some Argead women to play a leading part in the competition for power which followed.[45] Argead women thus had 'a political role which in ordinary circumstances was modest, but which could become important, even decisive, when dynastic succession was at issue' (Carney 1995, 391).

This Argead pattern is found repeated at the courts of the first Hellenistic kings. Polygamy was common: clear examples are the several wives of Demetrios Poliorketes and of Pyrrhos of Epiros.[46] In other cases royal polygamy would explain relationships which ancient writers and some modern scholars have seen as that of king and mistress rather than wife, notably the relationship between Ptolemy I and Berenike. As is well known Berenike accompanied her aunt Eurydike when the latter travelled to Egypt to marry Ptolemy I, but herself formed a relationship with Ptolemy and bore him both Ptolemy II (who eventually succeeded at the expense of Eurydike's son) and Arsinoë (full sister and eventual wife of Ptolemy II). Berenike certainly married Ptolemy I at some time and finally became his official consort: there is a good case for the view that the marriage was early and polygamous, alongside that of Ptolemy and Eurydike.[47]

There were however rapid and important departures from Argead practice. Once Hellenistic rulers adopted the title 'king' (*basileus*) from 306/5 BC, the corresponding 'queen' (*basilissa*) was soon adopted for royal wives.[48] Much more significantly, the practice of polygamy was dropped in the early third century BC,[49] and monogamy became the rule for Hellenistic kings. From then on official documents consistently refer to a single queen as the king's consort.[50] At about the same time queens began to wear the diadem, the symbol of the Hellenistic ruler.[51] This change from polygamy to monogamy was of enormous importance, shifting markedly the equilibrium within the royal marriage: instead of dominating a group of clearly subordinate wives, the monogamous king had to redefine his own identity in relation to that of his single queen.

The public prominence given to some late Argead women became the norm for Hellenistic queens. Alongside the public image of the king was projected to the world at large the image of the queen as consort-mother, and it was from the outset normal practice to make the Hellenistic queen's role a very public one.[52] When sibling marriage was practised (see Carney 1987c), then obviously the queen was also joint descendant, with her husband, from his ancestors; but the political importance of the king's choice of consort meant that the queen was in any case chosen from a family of standing and often from a royal house,[53] in other words she had a certain status in her own right even before the marriage. After her marriage she was made a focus of public attention, in several ways.[54] Queens were elevated to divine status and shared in the royal cult.[55] Cities were named after queens.[56] It is notable that the Hellenistic queen's physical image was very often displayed in the Hellenistic world, whether alongside that of her king-husband or on its own. Teos, for instance, voted to set up statues of both Antiochos III and his queen Laodike;[57] and, when Antiochos III set up a cult of his wife Laodike throughout his kingdom, he ordered that her chief priestesses wear gold crowns bearing her image.[58] It is less easy than in the case of the kings to generalise about how Hellenistic queens were portrayed, because there are difficulties in distinguishing surviving portraits of queens from those of goddesses;[59] but it is clear that the queen's image, prominently displayed, was to be identified as such.[60] Hellenistic dynasties made their queens into well-known and readily identified figures.[61]

The official image of the king's masculinity was thus defined in public not by effacing his queen but by using her as an equally prominent feminine counterpart. Court poets emphasized the mutual devotion of king and queen, as Theokritos *Idyll* 17 (referring both to Ptolemy I and Berenike I, and to Ptolemy II and Arsinoë II) and Kallimachos *Lock of Berenike* (referring to Ptolemy III and Berenike II). It became common, at least in the Ptolemaic and Seleukid dynasties, to emphasize 'the mutual collaboration and devotion' of the royal couple by referring to them in official documents as 'brother' and 'sister'.[62] Highly selected aspects of the private life of the ruling family, and above all the married love of the king and queen, were presented to the public: the closeness of the royal couple assured the future of the dynasty, and so the future prosperity of the kingdom and its subjects. Because the public image of the king was closely associated with that of the queen there developed a public role for the queen, and the feminine and masculine aspects of Hellenistic royalty had to be related to each other.

What was at stake was the official public image of the queen, not the personal and private relations between queen and king. The highly personal nature of the Hellenistic king's power meant that those in personal contact with him could hope to affect political decisions by exercising informal influence over him in private, and some queens and other royal women did so. When, for instance, Pyrrhos arrived at the Ptolemaic court as a hostage for Demetrios Poliorketes, he saw, according to Plutarch, that Berenike I was the most influential among the womenfolk of Ptolemy I;[63] the story implies that Berenike in particular, and other royal womenfolk to a lesser extent, had influence – in the context necessarily political influence – over Ptolemy. Even earlier the Diadochos Antipater reputedly consulted his daughter Phila on political matters (Diodoros 19. 54. 4–5). Such private influence, probably much more common than the surviving evidence shows, was however a different matter from the public presentation of the queen's role.

It is also obvious that the official image of the royal couple was an artificial construct, and often bore little resemblance to the actual conduct of those concerned. Nonetheless, however much human frailty intruded in various ways on the private life of the royal couple, it did not diminish the official standing of their public image.[64] (Unofficial opinion, expressed sometimes in criticism, was another matter.[65]) The official importance of the royal couple as upholders of the dynastic succession did not prevent rapid changes of marriage-partner when political circumstances, or even personal preference, made that desirable. For instance, when the end of the Second Syrian War brought peace between the Ptolemies and the Seleukids, Antiochos II repudiated his wife Laodike and married the Ptolemaic princess Berenike, daughter of Ptolemy II.[66] Political duty made the

Ptolemaic princess Kleopatra Selene wife in turn of Ptolemy IX, Antiochos VIII, Antiochos IX, and Antiochos X (Will 1982, ii 447–8). Occasionally a change of wife was due to an emotional entanglement: Philip V was evidently attracted to the wife of the younger Aratos, Polykrateia, whom he seduced and subsequently married;[67] Antiochos III was equally attracted by the much younger Euboia whom he married in 191 BC;[68] and the curious marriage between Seleukos I's son and heir Antiochos I and Stratonike, previously married to Seleukos himself, may also have been due to personal attraction.[69] But such switches of spouse did not change the fundamental pattern of royal couple, king and consort, projected to the world at large.

The necessary dynastic image also did not prevent kings from practising the sexual freedom which was a common prerogative of the male in the classical world and was even more readily available to an autocrat. Many kings – too many for more than a few examples to be mentioned here – are known to have had affairs, casual or more durable, and it can probably be assumed that more or less all kings had mistresses. (Kings also occasionally had homosexual affairs, but these are not generally represented in ancient literature as of major importance.[70]) The subject of royal mistresses obviously lent itself to gossip, and it attracted a certain amount of interest in antiquity.[71] Theokritos (14. 57–68) makes one character, who is praising Ptolemy II's qualities as an employer of mercenaries, include among Ptolemy's good points the fact that he is sexually active (*erōtikos*). Even when monogamy had become the norm for Hellenistic kings, some royal mistresses were well-known to the world at large. When carried to excess such masculine pursuits drew criticism. Philip V, for example, behaved disgracefully at the Argive Nemea, and the number of women whom he seduced was a matter of scandal.[72] Polybios, by implication, attacked Ptolemy II Philadelphos for excessive generosity to mistresses:[73] the rewards for one mistress, Bilistiche, included temples and shrines dedicated to Aphrodite-Bilistiche.[74] Antiochos IV had to suppress a revolt in Tarsos and Mallos provoked by his gift of the cities as a *dōrea* to his mistress Antiochis.[75] The cases of Bilistiche and Antiochis show that some royal mistresses were accorded very public recognition. Nonetheless officially the Hellenistic king was a monogamous husband, and, just as sculptural images of the king ignored both age and ageing, so the official projection of the royal couple ignored the king's publicly acknowledged mistresses.

It was the public relationship between the king and the queen that had to be officially defined, and with it the masculine and feminine roles in the exercise of power. The relationship could be defined in various ways. A very simple solution was to project the queen as exemplifying the conventional virtues of a Greek wife and mother. Such virtues are set out in a decree of Hierapolis in Phrygia[76] in honour of Apollonis, wife of Attalos I and mother of Eumenes II: in the text she is praised for piety to the gods, respect for her parents, a distinguished life with her husband, success in rearing her children and harmonious relations with them, and goodwill towards her daughter-in-law Queen Stratonike. These virtues, although given very public prominence, are appropriate to a wholly subordinate feminine role, with no activity in political affairs. Such a retiring role was not, however, typical of the Hellenistic queen, because from very early in the Hellenistic period queens had a formally acknowledged share in managing the business of state.[77]

Examples of state business handled by the queen are easy to find from the early Hellenistic period onwards. Ephesos in honouring a Boiotian described him as resident at the court of (*diatribōn para*) Phila, wife of Demetrios Poliorketes, rather than with the king himself, and Samos used the same language in honouring for his help for Samians in exile a guard-commander at the court of Phila.[78] (It is notable that Phila also received cult honours at Athens.[79]) Miletos honoured Apame, wife of Seleukos I, for the concern she had shown for Milesians fighting for Seleukos, and also over an embassy about building work at the temple in Didyma (*Inschriften von Didyma* 480). The queen might herself write on state business, as illustrated by two letters of Laodike III, wife of Antiochos III. In one letter (*SEG* 39. 1284) Laodike wrote to Sardes, acknowledging the visit of Sardian ambassadors who reported to her the city's decision to dedicate to her an enclosure and altar and to hold in her honour a festival called the Laodikea; the (fragmentary) end of the text shows that the king himself, having also received a Sardian embassy, also wrote to Sardes. In another letter[80] Laodike wrote to Iasos, saying explicitly that she was acting in accordance with the policy of her husband but also claiming that she had been kept informed of his benefactions to friends and allies; she went on to say that she had given orders to a *dioiketes* to convey 1,000 *medimnoi* of corn to Iasos each year for ten years,[81] and then, while reminding the polis of the king's hopes for it, hinted that she might herself offer further benefactions if it proved loyal to the Seleukids. When various foreign states helped Rhodes after an earthquake, Antigonos Doson gave silver, timber and pitch, and his queen Chryseis gave corn and lead.[82] From the time of Kleopatra II Ptolemaic queens are seen to be associated with their husbands in the issuing of royal ordinances.[83] In all these examples the queen is seen doing things that might be supposed to belong to the masculine competence of the king. The question therefore arises of how the queen could be seen to perform such activities without compromising the king's masculine rule.

One solution was for the queen to direct her activities principally towards a specifically feminine sphere within the general business of royal rule. Here it is sufficient to point to the excellent recent analysis of the queen's role by Savalli-Lestrade, who draws attention to the importance of the queen as protectress within the kingdom of fecundity within marriage, of agricultural work, of crops and of peace.[84] The queen could thus enjoy an active role, complementary to that of her husband and much more positive than the dutiful virtue for which Hierapolis praised Apollonis.[85]

Yet queens did not confine their activities to such a sphere, and it was clearly felt that the queen could be seen to play an even greater part in the business of state without overstepping her feminine role. There were of course limits to a queen's proper exercise of power, and Arsinoë I, wife of Ptolemy II Philadelphos, was obviously judged to have exceeded them, since her husband exiled her to the Thebaid for conspiracy (the details of which are wholly obscure) and executed her fellow conspirators.[86] Other queens, however, were acknowledged to have an important but acceptable share in determining the policy of their kingdom. Ptolemy II claimed to be acting, in no less a matter than the common freedom of the Greeks, in accordance with the policy of his ancestors and of his sister:[87] the ancestors in question were his parents Ptolemy I and Berenike, and his sister was his sister-queen Arsinoë II, who was, like his parents, already dead at the time. Ptolemy's claim projects dynastic solidarity, and acknowledges the importance of both his mother Berenike and his wife Arsinoë: the extent of Arsinoë's real influence over Ptolemaic foreign policy has been disputed,[88] but what is striking is that Ptolemy II evidently had no qualms about saying in public that in his kingdom the queen had a part in the formulation of major policy. Sherwin-White and Kuhrt (1993), commenting on the letter of Laodike III to Iasos, offer this generalized judgment:

> From the start of the Seleucid dynasty, the queen had won public recognition and honours, such as honorific statues, from Greek cities in and outside the empire, which can express the influence of a queen over the king's policy-making, though that is disguised by the public emphasis that the queen's actions are in line with the king's policy . . . [89]

Their view supposes that the queen typically had positive influence over policy, rather than merely offering a limited and acquiescent supplement to the king's decision. A remarkable text from Telmessos, published by Wörrle,[90] shows that Greeks understood how important a part a queen might play in deciding policy. Having received from Ptolemy II a letter confirming that their city would not be given as a grant (*dōrea*), the Telmessians sought to ensure (lines 25–32) that no-one would ask for their polis or its villages or any of its territory in a *dōrea* 'from any king or queen or other dynast': as Wörrle pointed out, the reference to a queen must reflect a recognition that a queen could exert effective influence over her husband-king, and it is striking that the Telmessians made that recognition clearly apparent in an official document. Even in military matters a queen could have a public role to play. As noted above, the vigorous and capable Phila, admittedly a loyal supporter of her husband Demetrios Poliorketes (despite his continuing marriages to other women[91]), was mistress on occasion not only of her own court but even apparently of her own guard. More strikingly Arsinoë III, who was a full sister of Ptolemy IV Philopator and was to become his wife within a few months, accompanied her brother and his senior commanders as they rode along the battle-line before the battle of Raphia in 217 BC;[92] it is notable that when Polybios reports the fact he is not moved to offer any particular comment on Arsinoë's presence on the battle-field.[93] By such actions queens were involved directly in political business at the highest level, precisely the business which it was the king's duty and privilege to deal with.

Thus the king projected an explicitly masculine image of himself as a ruler, expressed through royal iconography, and linked with that image of himself as male ruler the intimately associated image of his female consort; but he did not define the limits of his consort's public activities in such a way as to separate clearly in the public perception her feminine activities from his own masculine ones. When there was no clash (or at least no publicly admitted clash) between the king's policies and the activities of his queen, public prominence, and even an important share in state business, could apparently be accorded to the queen without making her in any way a challenge to her male partner's power, or to his public image as an explicitly masculine ruler. The proper limits of a queen's activities seem, however, to have been very loosely defined, and situations arose in which – often for want of a dominant male ruler – a queen took on the traditionally masculine role. A greater political role for a queen is usually represented by ancient writers as behaviour that was to some degree shocking,[94] the more so because queens were generally able to play a major independent role only in times of difficulty or uncertainty which called for radical and often violent action. The record of the Hellenistic queen as an independent political agent is therefore a colourful one, as the following examples, chosen from significantly more, clearly show.

At Kyrene in the mid-third century BC after the ruler Magas' death his widow Apame and his daughter Berenike both behaved remarkably. Apame broke off her daughter's engagement to the future Ptolemy III and summoned to Kyrene Demetrios, brother of Antigonos Gonatas, thereby seeking to alter radically the political alignment of Kyrene; when, however, Apame herself began an affair with Demetrios, Berenike had Demetrios killed in her mother's bed and went on to marry Ptolemy.[95] On that occasion there was no male member of the dynasty in control, since Magas was dead and had left no sons, but the episode shows strikingly what the women of a Hellenistic royal family might be capable of. Similarly, when the death of Antiochos II created some uncertainty about the Seleukid succession, his estranged (but reconciled?) wife Laodike intervened vigorously to promote the claims of her son Seleukos II against the infant son of Antiochos' second wife Berenike, and contemporaries, in calling the ensuing conflict between the Seleukid and Ptolemaic empires the Laodikean War, clearly saw Laodike as largely responsible for its outbreak.[96] In time a queen might assume open power: Kleopatra I, for instance, on the death of her husband Ptolemy V in 180, governed as regent and her name appeared before that of the king, her son Ptolemy VI, on official documents.[97] The notoriously bitter conflict between Ptolemy VIII and his sister-wife Kleopatra II, exacerbated by Ptolemy's further marriage to her daughter Kleopatra III, included open civil war. Ptolemy even murdered Ptolemy Memphites, his son by Kleopatra II, and sent the dismembered corpse to her. At one point Kleopatra II proclaimed herself sole ruler, as Kleopatra Philometor Soteira, though she was unable to maintain sole rule.[98] When Ptolemy VIII finally died in 116 BC he bequeathed power to his widow Kleopatra III and whichever of their two sons (Ptolemy IX and Ptolemy X) she might prefer: in fact she shared power now with one son and now with another until Ptolemy X murdered her in 101.[99] The Ptolemaic princess Kleopatra Thea, having been wife in turn of the Seleukid kings Alexander Balas, Demetrios II, and Antiochos VII, then sought greater personal power once Alexander and Antiochos were dead; when Demetrios emerged from Parthian captivity, she rejected him and reputedly ordered his death, and then killed her son Seleukos, but finally another son, Antiochos VIII Grypos, obliged her to drink the poisoned wine which she had intended for him.[100] Ultimately there arrived the most famous example of the Hellenistic queen's open exercise of supreme political power, Kleopatra VII, with her celebrated career in both Ptolemaic and Roman politics.[101] To generalise, some Hellenistic queens – notably but not only Ptolemaic wives – did not merely encroach upon but actually took over the functions of the Hellenistic king, exercising what had been an inherently masculine authority.

The increasing power of the queen is at least hinted at in later Hellenistic royal iconography. From the second century BC there appear portraits of queens with a masculine tinge. Smith, discussing second-century BC Ptolemaic queens' portraits, writes:

> Besides the continuing use of the familiar female ideal, there was a new option – an older, harder-looking queen, not merely more individual, but also somewhat 'masculinized'. These portraits are naturally more easy to recognize (though one has been perversely taken for a man (*the papyri Kleopatra*). They are surely to be interpreted in the light of the Ptolemaic queen's more 'male' role in the second century. In place of passive divinized beauty they seem designed to express a new female executive determination.

(See Figure 5.3 – *the papyri Kleopatra*.) Of the *Vienna Queen* in particular Smith says: 'The head is most easily understood if we imagine that the model was a Greek portrait type similar to the Louvre Kleopatra, ... the Egyptian sculptor has somewhat traduced a subtly masculine female image'; the result, as the plate shows, is a very harsh-featured portrait.[102] Contrarily

Figure 5.3 A Kleopatra from the Villa of the Papyri at Herculaneum
Source: Museo Archeologico Nazionale di Napoli 5598, Smith (1988) Catalogue 24, Roman-period copy of a second-century Ptolemaic queen, probably Kleopatra I or II or III.

there is evidence from the *Sibylline Oracles* that in the late Hellenistic period Greek-speaking Jews in Egypt, thinking of Kleopatra, personified political power as feminine[103] (though no evidence of such a tendency survives from Greeks of the day). Both tendencies – representing the queen as masculine, or royal power as feminine – challenged the masculinity of the Hellenistic king.

A paradoxical situation thus arose. Royal rule in the Hellenistic Greek world had been identified as explicitly masculine in contemporary iconography, and this masculine image continued to be projected into the late Hellenistic period, as is shown by the late statues of kings portrayed as nude males. An important part of the king's masculine image was his close association with his queen, who had a major public role in collaboration with the king. In most such royal marriages the king was projected in public as the dominant partner, secure enough in his masculine power to admit to the world that his wife had a share in the running of the kingdom. In time, however, it emerged that a queen could exercise the rule that had been so confidently represented as masculine: for the first time in the historical record of the Greek world women held major – on rare occasions supreme – political power.[104] The Hellenistic king's masculinity, though still proclaimed in the now traditional iconography, was clearly compromised by the demonstration that royal rule was not exercised only by men.[105]

Notes

1 Some kings, of course, had many non-Greek subjects to whom kingship had to be projected in different terms, a particular problem for the Ptolemies in Egypt where – not to mention other ethnic categories – the native Egyptians maintained their culture alongside that of the Greeks; this paper will however concentrate on Greek views of kingship. See Herz 1992 and Koenen 1993 for valuable analyses of how the Ptolemies responded to the differing needs of Greeks and Egyptians in Egypt. Lévêque 1991 examines how, particularly in matters of religion, Graeco-Bactrian and Graeco-Indian kings responded to the interests of certain social groups among their non-Greek subjects. Herz 1996 compares the methods by which dynasties, notably Ptolemies and Seleukids, sought legitimation among Greek subjects with the methods adopted towards a range of other ethnic and cultural groups; and Laubscher 1991 argues that an equestrian statue of a Ptolemy (probably Ptolemy II) exploits both Greek and Egyptian ideology.

2 Préaux 1978, 1. 181–388; Walbank 1984, especially 81–4, and Walbank 1992, 74–7; Smith 1988. See also the brief but useful observations on the subject's bonding to the Hellenistic king, or the lack of it, in Dihle 1993. Hellenistic kingship is also discussed, with special reference to the Seleukid empire, by Sherwin-White and Kuhrt 1993, 114–40 (especially 129–132). Le Bohec 1991 explores the royal ideology of the Hellenistic kings of Macedon. Hatzopoulos 1996 shows the role of the king within Macedonian government.

3 Even in Antigonid Macedonia the king's power was in effect absolute despite 'certain vestigial popular rights' (Walbank 1984, 225–6). Sherwin-White and Kuhrt 1993, 118–19 stress the autocratic power of the king. Occasional instances of joint kingship, when one king was more senior than the other (Walbank 1984,

66–7), may well have strengthened rather than weakened the power of the senior king.

4 See Gehrke 1982 on the fundamental importance of military success to the public image of the Hellenistic king. Gehrke also makes interesting points (262–5) about the limits of the king's militarism. Austin 1986 also brings out the military role of the king, stressing the need for success: he notes (458) that Hellenistic kings, apart from the Ptolemies after Ptolemy IV, fought personally at the head of their troops. In criticizing the failure of Ptolemy IV to pay proper attention to the business of state Polybios (5. 34) stresses two consequences: one was conspiracies against the king, and the other a military weakening of the Ptolemaic empire such that it could not so effectively menace the Seleukid empire or safeguard its own territorial possessions.

5 Austin 1986, 459–61 discusses the importance of wealth for the Hellenistic king.

6 See Bringmann 1993a on the king as benefactor, with the comments of Walbank 1993; and Bringmann 1995. (Bringmann 1993b is a briefer version, in German, of 1993a). See Erskine 1994 on the notion of the common benefactor, especially 71–7 on Hellenistic precedents.

7 See Smith 1988 and 1993, with the comments of Ridgway 1993.

8 See Weber 1993 on the use of patronage of poets by the first three Ptolemies, and on the poetry produced as a result: his study also (18–32) illuminates the development of the Ptolemaic royal court. Weber 1995 offers a comparable but briefer analysis of the efforts of the first three Antigonids. Von Hesberg 1989 discusses the use of lavish displays by early Hellenistic kings on public occasions such as festivals as a means of affirming and legitimizing their status. Nielsen 1994 discusses the nature and function of Hellenistic royal palaces.

9 See notably Bringmann 1993a on the king as benefactor.

10 See Gehrke 1982 on the charismatic (in the Weberian sense) nature of Hellenistic kingship and on the ways in which the king's status was displayed.

11 There is recent discussion of the dynastic factor in Hellenistic kingship by Sherwin-White and Kuhrt (1993, 125–9).

12 On the marriages of Hellenistic rulers see Seibert 1967: the early marriages of contenders for power in Alexander's former empire are discussed at 11–26. Cohen 1974 analyses the patterns apparent in these early marriages: first, attempts to marry into the family of Alexander the Great; then, after the death in 309/8 of Alexander's sister Kleopatra, marriages between contenders for power (Diadochi) and non-diadochan families; and finally, after the battle of Ipsos in 301, marriages between diadochan families (which implied a mutual recognition of royal status and set the pattern for the inter-dynastic marriages common in the Hellenistic kingdoms).

13 On the complex nuances of the title Philadelphos, see Muccioli 1994.

14 Hintzen-Bohlen 1990, who points out that such groups were set up by the rulers themselves: when a Greek city or other such body dedicated a royal statue-group, emphasis switched from dynastic continuity to the unity and goodwill of the current ruling family.

15 See Schmitt 1991 on the highly selective presentation to the public of aspects of Hellenistic royal family life, especially the married love of king and queen.

16 During the very bitter struggle which developed at the end of Philip V's reign between his sons Perseus and Demetrios, rumours circulated that Perseus was not a true son of Philip (and in some versions not even of Philip's wife Polykrateia), clearly as a threat to Perseus' chances of succeeding his father. On this episode see Walbank 1967, 241 (with references) and Will 1982, ii 253–5: note particularly in Livy 39. 53. 3 the rumour that Perseus did not physically resemble Philip, and the use of the fact that Perseus' mother was Polykrateia,

whom Philip had seduced and taken from her first husband. Again, behind the struggle between Ariarathes V of Kappadokia and his brother Orophernes was, reputedly, the confession by their mother Antiochis, wife of Ariarathes IV, that, while initially childless before giving birth to Ariarathes, she had falsely passed off Orophernes and another son (also called Ariarathes) as children of herself and Ariarathes IV: again the rumour that he was not the king's son was used against a claimant to the throne. See Will 1982, ii 371–3, with references.

17 *Inschriften von Ilion* 32 (English translations in Austin 1981, no. 139, Burstein 1985, no. 15, Bagnall and Derow 1981, no. 16).

18 The text at this point is not well preserved, and the items in square brackets, though probable, cannot be read with certainty.

19 *SEG* 41. 1003 (English translations of an earlier edition of the text in Austin 1981, no. 151, and Burstein 1985, no. 33).

20 For example, in the Alexandrian cults referred to in the elaborate dating formula at Xanthos under Ptolemy V (*SEG* 36. 1218) the reigning king is associated with his ancestors, male and female.

21 For example, at Kyrene (*SEG* 9. 5) the Ptolemaic cult of the King, the Queen, their son, and their parents and ancestors.

22 Walbank 1984, 66; Davies 1984, 296.

23 17. 56 (*aikhmēta*), 103 (*epistamenos doru pallein*).

24 *Inschriften von Ephesos* no. 202 (English translation in Burstein 1985, no. 90). Note also the association of two Ptolemaic royal statues with statues of poets and philosophers in the sanctuary of Serapis at Memphis (Zanker 1995, 172–3): 'Beyond the immediate historical or political circumstances this is clearly a celebration of universal learning as a quality of the good ruler.'

25 There was a literary convention that any king forced to give up the diadem (symbol of his rule) would weep (Ritter 1965, 67–8); on men and weeping, see van Wees, this volume.

26 See Lund 1992, 6–8 on Lysimachos the lion-killer, and 153–93 on how Lysimachos projected himself as king.

27 See Pollitt 1986, 38–41 (hunts), 41–6 (battle-scenes). Cf. however Rice 1993, 231–2 on the limited surviving evidence for memorials of royal success in war.

28 See Smith 1988 and 1993, with the comments of Ridgway 1993. See also Fleischer 1991 on Seleukid portraits, with closer concentration than Smith on chronological developments, and comment on iconographic expression of dynastic links (especially 116–37). There were of course not only individual portraits but also statue-groups: see Hintzen-Bohlen 1990 on royal family-groups (and 1992 on various forms of memorial set up by Hellenistic ruling powers, including kings).

29 What follows on royal portraiture relies very heavily on Smith 1988, especially 32–48. See also Smith 1993, particularly on the differences between royal portraits and other contemporary forms of portraiture, such as the athlete and the philosopher.

30 Note the comment of Green 1995 on Smith 1993: 'Smith also points out that the visual stereotypes employed make it impossible to confuse a king with a philosopher and he highlights some of the more subtle varieties with these categories. This is a good account. What he perhaps does not stress enough for a general audience, even if he does acknowledge it, is the absence of any search for photographic likeness: these so-called portraits are artificially constructed statements about the individuals concerned, and individuality takes very much second place to the construction of the public statement. One might dare to say that one should not take images at face value.' See also Fleischer 1991, 3.

31 On the iconography of the philosopher see Zanker 1995.

32 Smith 1988, 47 cites, among other examples, Antiochos I and Antiochos III, who both ruled for more than twenty years, but do not grow visibly older in their portraits; and Antiochos V who, when aged about nine, looks roughly the same age as his father Antiochos IV, then aged about fifty. See also Fleischer 1991, 123 and 131.

33 In real life 'the wearing of Macedonian military dress remained normal practice with all kings till the last of the Ptolemies' (Austin 1986, 458).

34 Ridgway 1993, 240 suggests that statues of the king in armour may have been commoner than is indicated by the number of examples surviving as originals or copies, because some such statues were executed in bronze (as is known from certain examples now lost), and such bronze statues, being difficult to copy in marble, are less likely to be represented by surviving copies. See also Rice 1993, 231–2, Fleischer 1991, 135–6, and Laubscher 1991, 223–4 (drawing attention to reproductions in smaller format). The particular statue discussed by Laubscher showed – unusually – a king on horseback but naked except for a chlamys (which does not hide his body) and elephant-scalp headgear.

35 Bringmann 1993a, 11, and 1995, 102.

36 The point is evident from the general course of Hellenistic history, though kings of course continued to wage war in the first century BC. It is notable that the examples cited by Gehrke 1982 in his study of the 'victorious king' are drawn from the period down the middle of the second century BC. Note too the evidence adduced by Bringmann 1995 that royal benefactions ceased to promote the king's military prestige after the Roman defeat of Philip V.

37 Examples are Smith 1988 Catalogue (155–180) nos. 61 and 125.

38 The scene is described by Kallixenos, quoted by Athenaios 5. 201 D–E: its significance is analysed by Rice 1983, 102–10. On the float were also figures of Priapos, Arete, and Corinth.

39 See Kallimachos *Hymns* 1. 78–89 as an example of how deeply the notion of the king as a ruler of Greek cities had penetrated contemporary Greek literature. On earlier Greek gendered images of colonial conquest, cf. Cartledge, this volume, and Marshall, this volume.

40 The main general work on Hellenistic queens remains Macurdy 1932 – still a valuable book, though subsequently discovered inscriptions and papyri, as well as subsequent scholarship on Hellenistic history, now allow revision of Macurdy's views, as recent work by several scholars has shown. In several articles Carney (see especially 1988a, 1991, 1994b and 1995) has analysed the role of early Hellenistic queens, with special emphasis on queens of Macedon; Le Bohec 1993 offers a review of the evidence now available on queens of Macedon and its implications; Wyke 1992, 100–3 briefly reviews the official image of the Ptolemaic queen as beneficent ruler, drawing on both Greek and Egyptian evidence. On Hellenistic queens generally the most important recent contribution is by Savalli-Lestrade 1994.

41 Obviously in many periods of Greek history the choice of wife was important to a man's status, but what commonly mattered in the choice was the status of the wife's original family, not her own status as an individual. The point is clearly illustrated by Herodotos' account (6. 126–31) of how the archaic tyrant Kleisthenes of Sikyon married off his daughter Agariste: marriage to Agariste was a prize for which numerous prominent suitors competed, but Agariste herself barely appears in the story, whereas the Hellenistic queen was a prominent and important individual in her own right. The closest parallel to the Hellenistic queen's importance for her husband's public identity seems to be the public prominence achieved by women members of the wealthy élite in Hellenistic Greek cities because of the dynastic nature of their families' status (van Bremen

129

1983): but prominence for such women seems not to be attested before the second century BC, and did not challenge the authority of male members of the families, as the prominence of the Hellenistic queen eventually challenged the masculine authority of the king.

42 Greenwalt 1989: see also Carney 1992.

43 Carney 1991, 162: see also Carney 1993b and 1995. See also Mortensen 1992, especially 163–5 on Eurydike, mother of Philip II.

44 See Carney 1995, 380–1; Le Bohec 1993, 238–9.

45 Carney 1987a, 1987b, 1988b, cf. 1994a; Heckel 1983/4; Le Bohec 1993, 235–6.

46 On the marriages of Demetrios Poliorketes see Seibert 1967, 27–33 and Le Bohec 1993, 232–3; and on those of Pyrrhos Seibert 1967, 100–3. See also in general Macurdy 1932, 106 and Savalli-Lestrade 1994, 418 with n. 15.

47 On Berenike see RE 3. 282–3 art. Berenike (9), and Peremans and van't Dack 1968, vi no. 14497. In both of these accounts Berenike's marriage to Ptolemy is dated c.317; but she is often regarded as not yet married to Ptolemy when her daughter married Lysimachos (e.g. Seibert 1967, 72, 74; Will 1979, i 88; Will 1984, 103). See also Heckel 1989, 33–5. (The view that Berenike was also Ptolemy's half-sister, as a daughter of Lagos, has been refuted: see Macurdy 1932, 104; Heckel 1989, 33–4.) Carney 1994b, 123–4 presents a strong case for seeing the marriage of Ptolemy and Berenike as polygamous in the Argead tradition. Carney 1995, 382–3 points out that Argead polygamy will have seemed strange to contemporary Greeks, and a tendency to dismiss polygamous wives as mistresses would be understandable. One might speculate, for instance, about the status of the *hetaira* Thais by whom Ptolemy I had children, marrying one of them, Eirene, to King Eunostos of Soloi (for the marriage see Seibert 1967, 77–8, with references): Ellis 1994, 87 n. 57, following Borza, envisages the possibility that Ptolemy married Thais.

48 Carney 1991; Le Bohec 1993, 237–8. The title was first used soon after 306 for Phila, polygamous wife of Demetrios Poliorketes (Carney 1991, 161 with n. 44). Seibert 1967, 95 n. 14 states, without argument, that if a king had a principal wife (Hauptfrau) and a subsidiary wife (Nebenfrau) the distinction between the two was clear because the principal wife bore the title *basilissa*: this seems far from certain. In the Ptolemaic kingdom alone the title *basilissa* was eventually given to female members of the royal family other than the king's wife or regent, i.e. to 'princesses' (see Müller 1991, 396 with n. 22, giving further references): this practice does not appear to have caused confusion about the status of the king's wife. See also Savalli-Lestrade 1994, 417–18.

49 Le Bohec 1993, 233 argues that after Demetrios Poliorketes no king of Macedon was polygamous. Carney 1994b, 125–6, 130–1 suggests that competition to be seen as heir among sons by different wives at the court of Lysimachos may have shown the dangers of royal polygamy and hastened its end, but also (n. 28) points to Demetrios Poliorketes' attempts to avoid having two wives around at the same time, and to Lysimachos' sending away Amastris when he married Arsinoë, as signs of a change in attitude to polygamy. Justin 24. 2. 9 reports that, in order to persuade Arsinoë to marry him, Ptolemy Keraunos promised to have no other wife: if reliable, this report would suggest that queens may occasionally have played a part in bringing about the shift to monogamy. However, while particular circumstances may well have affected the attitude to marriage of individual rulers, the striking and important fact is the rapid and universal adoption of monogamy by the kings.

50 In the second century BC the situation of Ptolemy VIII, married simultaneously to his sister Kleopatra II and to her daughter Kleopatra III, was clearly anomalous and produced an anomalous formula in official documents: 'King Ptolemy

and Queen Kleopatra the Sister and Queen Kleopatra the Wife'. See Macurdy 1932, 157–8, where the anomalous official formula is noted: the formula is found, for instance, perfectly preserved in an ordinance of *c*.124–116 (Lenger 1980, 124–8 and 380, no. 52 (= Lenger 1990, 15)).

51 Ritter 1965, 114–9. The first attested case of a queen wearing the diadem is Arsinoë as wife of Ptolemy Keraunos: she also wore it later as wife of her brother Ptolemy II. Ritter argues that in Arsinoë's day other queens probably also wore the diadem.

52 The evidence for the public role of the queen, much of it epigraphic, is set out and analysed thoroughly by Savalli-Lestrade 1994.

53 On the social status of queens before marriage see Seibert 1967, especially 122–3.

54 See Carney 1991, 162 with the references in n. 49, and, on Macedonian queens, Le Bohec 1993.

55 See Weber 1993, 251–70 on the deification of early Ptolemaic queens; and, for the Roman period, Fischler, this volume.

56 See Carney 1988a, with reflections on the significance of the practice. It is seen at work in *SEG* 39. 1426, which records the foundation in Kilikia of a city named after Arsinoë, wife and queen of Ptolemy II and mother of Ptolemy III.

57 *SEG* 41. 1003 (English translations of an earlier edition of the text in Austin 1981, no. 151, and Burstein 1985, no. 33).

58 Pouilloux *Choix d'inscriptions grecques* 30 (with references to the two other surviving inscriptions on the same matter). There is an English translation of the text in Austin 1981, no. 158.

59 Smith 1988, 48: cf. 43 on the limited use of specific divinizing attributes in portraits of queens. It is only from Ptolemaic Egypt that any quantity of female royal portraits survives (Smith 1988, 89–90): see also Thompson 1973, 1980.

60 On two statues of the Attalid queen Stratonike, for instance, set up by Pergamon at Pergamon and by Athens at Delos, the accompanying inscriptions, worded very similarly, identified her not as wife of Eumenes II or her later husband Attalos II but as daughter of Ariarathes IV of Kappadokia: the wording might suggest that, at least occasionally, the queen's role as royal spouse was not given prominence, but, as Müller has recently shown, that particular form of identification was used in this case to demonstrate Attalid support for Ariarathes V, and supposed that viewers would in any case identify Stratonike as the current Attalid queen. The case of Stratonike shows that even a queen whose political role was only a passive one was expected to be known and recognised by Greeks at large. See Müller 1991, superseding previous attempts to explain the texts (e.g. Allen 1983, 200–6).

61 Van Bremen 1983 argues that the euergetism practised by a wealthy élite in Hellenistic Greek urban society led to a blurring of public and private life for the élite, whose prominence had a strongly dynastic element, and that these developments led to a much greater public role for female members of the élite. Van Bremen finds evidence for such a female role from the second century BC onwards: by that time the prominence of the Hellenistic queen could have provided a model for women of the élite (though van Bremen does not consider the possibility). These wealthy women, as van Bremen shows, frequently received honours, including statues, from their cities.

62 See Jones 1993, 81–6: quotation, 85. Jones, 82, points out that in the Ptolemaic dynasty, after Ptolemy II and Arsinoë who were by birth full brother and sister, the practice of referring to the king's consort as 'sister and wife' is found from the time of Berenike II, cousin and wife of Ptolemy III. He also argues (*passim*) that the practice is found among the Seleukids from the 270s.

63 *Pyrrhos* 4. 4 (the text refers to *gynaikōn* of Ptolemy, presumably meaning either womenfolk closely attached to the king or plural wives).

64 Similarly, political conflict within the dynasty (discussed later) did not generally disturb the official image.

65 The poet Sotades offers a colourful example of criticism, attacking Ptolemy II both on his mistresses and on his official marriage: after earlier episodes of disapproval, he condemned Ptolemy's marriage to his sister Arsinoë ('You thrust your prick into an unholy opening') and fled from Egypt, but was caught and drowned by the Ptolemaic admiral Patroklos (Fraser 1972, 117–18, with notes giving references). Cameron 1990, 295–304 suggests reasons for thinking that *Anthologia Palatina* 5. 202 is a lampoon by Posidippos on Bilistiche, mistress of Ptolemy II.

66 Seibert 1967, 79–80; Will 1982, ii 239–42. The subsequent conflicts in the Seleukid empire are notorious: Will 1982, ii 249–61, 294–6.

67 Seibert 1967, 39; Walbank 1967, 261 with n. 3.

68 Seibert 1967, 61–2; Will 1982, ii 204–26. Despite ancient criticisms, the marriage demonstrably did not hinder Antiochos' military activity.

69 Seibert 1967, 50–1. See Brodersen 1985 on the limitations of the source-material for this episode (though the marriage clearly took place), and the comments of Schmitt 1991, 81–2.

70 Examples of such homosexual affairs include the following. An Aristokles is attested as a lover of King Antigonos (Ath. 13. 603 D–E), and Agathokles, later politically prominent, was reputedly as a boy the lover of Ptolemy III (Polyb. 15. 25. 32, scholia Aristophanes *Thesmophoriazousai* 1059: Pomeroy 1984, 186 n. 51). The younger Aratos, whose wife Polykrateia Philip V seduced and then married, may have been a lover of Philip (Walbank 1967, 73 n. 5): Aratos, who was sent as ambassador in 226 BC (Polyb. 2. 51. 5, Plut. *Aratos* 42), is likely to have been older than Philip, who was born in 238 BC (Polyb. 4. 5. 3, 4. 24. 1), and so to have been the senior partner (*erastēs*) in the relationship.

71 Athenaios in Book 13 refers to several royal mistresses of the Hellenistic period (13. 576 E–577 A, 577 F–578 B, 589 F–590 A, 593 D–E, 596 E), and notes (13. 577 F–578 A) that Ptolemy son of Agesarchos gave a list of kings' mistresses in his work on Philopator.

72 Walbank 1967, 91, with references.

73 Polyb. 14. 11. 2–4. Ath. 13. 576 E–F quotes both Polybios (this fragment) and Ptolemy Euergetes (with more names) on Philadelphos' mistresses. See Pomeroy 1984, 53.

74 See Pomeroy 1984, 54–5, with references: it is notable that Plut. *Amatorius* 753 E–F suggests that the cult of Aphrodite-Bilistiche still existed in Alexandria in his day. Weber 1993 discusses the cult of Bilistiche and literary references to her: Cameron 1990 suggests reasons for believing that *Anth. Pal.* 5. 202 is a lampoon, probably by Posidippos, on Bilistiche, referring both to her status as the king's mistress and to her victories in equestrian events at the Olympic Games (and Cameron also suggests that *Anth. Pal.* 5. 210 is a tribute by Asklepiades to Didyme, another mistress of Ptolemy II).

75 2 *Maccabees* 4. 30–1, discussed by Wörrle 1978, 207–12.

76 *OGIS* 308 (English translation in Austin 1981, no. 204). It is noteworthy that in the Athenian decree praising Eumenes II for his part in restoring Antiochos IV to the Seleukid throne Apollonis, as Eumenes' mother, is mentioned as prominently as his father Attalos I (*OGIS* 248, English translation in Burstein 1985, no. 38). Polybios 22. 20. 1–4 praises Apollonis in terms comparable to those used in *OGIS* 308: see on this passage Walbank 1957–1979, iii 211, also giving details of various honours accorded to Apollonis. See also Le Bohec 1993, 241 on the

qualities expected of Macedonian queens. Texts honouring women members of the wealthy élite in Hellenistic Greek cities laid very heavy stress on such traditional feminine virtues (van Bremen 1983, 233–5).

77 Savalli-Lestrade 1994 reviews the evidence for the public role of the Hellenistic queen much more fully than is possible here.

78 See Wehrli 1964, 142, with references. Wehrli concludes that Phila had not only her own court but also her own guard, and discusses the historical context, including notably Demetrios' campaigns, which may have led to Phila residing for a time apart from Demetrios. On the courtiers and 'Friends' surrounding the Hellenistic queen see Savalli-Lestrade 1994, 429–31.

79 See Wehrli 1964, 142, with references.

80 *Inschriften von Iasos* 4 (English translations in Austin 1981, no. 156, and Burstein 1985, no. 36).

81 See Savalli-Lestrade 1994, 428–9 on the likelihood that the corn was to be provided from estates belonging to Laodike herself, and generally 424–9 on the euergetism and on the personal resources of Hellenistic queens.

82 Polyb. 5. 89. 6–7. While other rulers, including Ptolemy III and Seleukos II, also made gifts, Polybios makes no mention of any other contribution from a queen. See Le Bohec 1993, 244.

83 The corpus of ordinances is in Lenger 1980, complemented by Lenger 1990. What might have seemed to be the earliest example of a Ptolemaic queen associated with her husband in issuing a royal ordinance has been redated from the third-century reign of Ptolemy IV Philopator and Arsinoë III to the first-century reign of Ptolemy XIV and Kleopatra VII (Lenger 1980, 222–6, 382, no. 82 (= Lenger 1990, 19)). Lenger noted (1980, 225) that the association of the queen with power was only attested in royal ordinances from the reign of Ptolemy VI Philometor, husband of Kleopatra II: at the time the earliest known example was an ordinance of Ptolemy VI and Kleopatra II dated to 163 (Lenger 1980, 90–1 no.36), but a slightly earlier ordinance in the names of Ptolemy VI, Ptolemy VIII, and Kleopatra II dated to 165 is now known (Lenger 1990, 13 no. 32*). In the first century one ordinance was issued in the name of Berenike IV alone (Lenger 1980, 202–4 no.72 with Lenger 1990, 18).

84 Savalli-Lestrade 1994, especially 426. Wyke 1992, 100–3 reviews the image of the Ptolemaic queen as beneficent ruler, drawing on both Greek and non-Greek evidence.

85 Van Bremen 1983 addresses a comparable question of how women members of the wealthy élite in Hellenistic Greek cities could play a major public role without compromising the authority of the male members of their dynasties, and argues that the public role of these women was confined to safe activities which reinforced the authority and standing of their male relatives.

86 Schol. Theoc. 17. 128; Diogenes Laertios 7. 186. See Fraser 1972, i 347, quoting the sources in nn. 46–7. Arsinoë II has been suspected of having engineered the downfall of Arsinoë I, but there is no evidence to give the suspicion plausibility, let alone proof: see Burstein 1982, 204.

87 H. H. Schmitt *Staatsverträge des Altertums* iii 476 ('The Chremonides Decree') lines 16–18. There are English translations of the text by Austin 1981, no. 49 (but with the mistranslation 'of his ancestor and of his sister' for 'of his ancestors etc.'), Bagnall and Derow 1981, no. 19, and Burstein 1985, no. 56. The document is an Athenian decree, but it seems most unlikely that the Athenians would have originated the view that Ptolemy II was acting in accordance with the policy of his ancestors and sister: the relevant section of the text is beyond doubt a paraphrase or resumé of part of an official Ptolemaic communication to Athens. Neither the king's parents nor his sister-wife are named, which suggests that the

Athenians did not quote the original wording in full: the phrase used in the Athenian decree assigns no more importance to Arsinoë than to the king's parents. However Habicht 1995, 147 points out that, thanks to the work of Grzybek, the death of Arsinoë is now dated not to 270 but to 1st or 2nd July 268, and so only about two months before the Athenian decree was passed: but see also Koenen 1993, 51 n. 61 (and 66 n. 96, 71 n. 110) for a date slightly different from that of Grzybek.

88 Some earlier scholars had seen Arsinoë II as a dominant force in shaping Ptolemaic policy. Burstein 1982, however, after reviewing earlier work, comes to the conclusion that, while Arsinoë played a prominent and popular role as Ptolemy II's queen, the available evidence does not show that her influence in Ptolemaic government was greater than that of other third-century BC queens. Hauben 1983 seeks to strengthen the case for attributing to Arsinoë significant influence over the development of Ptolemaic maritime strength. See also Heckel 1989, 34–6.

89 Sherwin-White and Kuhrt, 1993, 127–8 commenting on *SEG* 26. 1226 (= *Inschriften von Iasos* 4); they give a translation of the text (which is also translated by Austin 1981, no. 156, and Burstein 1985, no. 36).

90 Wörrle 1978. He discusses the reference to queens at 231–2.

91 See Wehrli 1964 for Phila's career.

92 Polyb. 5. 83. 1–84. 1 with Walbank 1957–1979 *ad loc.* (giving references for the evidence on the date of the marriage between the battle in June 217 and the Pithom decree in November 217).

93 The actual participation of Kleopatra VII in the battle of Actium did attract attention and comment, coloured by the various Roman or pro-Roman judgments of Kleopatra: see Becher 1966, 182–3. Images of Kleopatra, favourable and unfavourable, are subjected to detailed and subtle analysis by Wyke 1992: the 'militant woman' is discussed at 108–12, but cf. – among much else – 'the validating fictions created by Kleopatra herself' (100–3). See also Kleiner 1992. On the much earlier military activities of the Argead women Kynnane and her daughter Adea/Eurydike see Carney 1995, 389–90.

94 Cf. Carney 1993a on hostile judgments of the political activities of Alexander's mother Olympias, whose behaviour was broadly comparable to that of men of her day.

95 See Will 1979, i 245–6, with references. On the career of Berenike generally see Fantham *et al.* 1994, 144–51.

96 Laodike also later supported her second son Antiochos Hierax against the interests of Seleukos II. See Will 1979, i 249–50, 254–5.

97 Whitehorne 1994, 86–7, with references.

98 See Will 1982, ii 429–39; Whitehorne 1994, 103–31.

99 See Will 1982, ii 440–5; Whitehorne 1994, 132–48.

100 See Will 1982, ii 435–6, 445–8; Macurdy 1932, 93–100; Whitehorne 1994, 149–63.

101 See Kleiner 1992 on how Kleopatra's political importance received public acknowledgement on Roman coinage struck by Antony.

102 Smith 1988, 94–5. The *Vienna Queen* is no. 74 in Smith's Catalogue (and Plate 48. 1–2).

103 Wyke 1992, 103 draws attention to *Oracula Sibyllina* 3. 75–92, 350–80, in which power is personified as a woman, commonly identified by modern scholars with Kleopatra VII: this important evidence for the personification and gendering of royal power in the Hellenistic world is almost certainly derived from Jewish circles in Egypt (Collins 1983, 354–61, and 1987, 430–6; and cf. Parke 1988, 2, 6–8).

104 Savalli-Lestrade (1994, 431–2), summing up the role of the Hellenistic queen, presents the queen's position as essentially dependent on the ability of the king to maintain his position: while broadly true, that summary understates the ability of some queens to pursue a personal career with changes of royal husband or co-ruler.

105 This paper was written without an opportunity to consult Wikander 1996, which looks particularly at Berenice I, offers very interesting comments on how dynastic demands led to the public visibility of Hellenistic royal women and on change in gender roles in Hellenistic society, and reaches conclusions close to those offered here.

6

Sexing a Roman: imperfect men in Roman law

Jane F. Gardner

What is a man? In any society, determining the sex of individuals is a legal, as well as a social necessity. The legal capacities, and the gender roles, of the two sexes vary from one society to another, but in Rome, the determination of masculinity was especially important because of the peculiar authority given in Roman law to the male in his gender role as *paterfamilias*; he could exercise *potestas* over other free persons within the *familia* of which he was head, and, unlike women, he had no restrictions on his legal capacity to engage in transactions with other heads of household (Gardner 1993, chapter 4).

The basic classification as men or women was biological, but it produced a sharp distinction between the gender roles of the two. This applied only within certain areas of the law, mainly family law (though Roman lawyers tend also to use terminology appropriate to males in reference to activities which are not in themselves gender-specific). There is little room within the rules of Roman law for the kind of explicit gender-stereotyping, reflecting ordinary social attitudes, found in literary sources; where it does occur, it is usually in a jurist's comment on a legal rule, or his definition of the content of a non-legal term. So, for instance, the exclusion of women from some legal activities open to men, as well as the requirement that women have male tutors to authorize certain property transactions, is ascribed to their supposed mental or physical inferiority to men; the concept of psychological femininity or masculinity appears here in classical law as, later, it does in the Christian period in relation to homosexual activity. Similarly, lawyers' definitions of what comprise legacies of 'men's clothing' and 'women's clothing' refer to social assumptions about appropriate 'masculine' behaviour.[1]

Perceptions of 'masculinity' therefore are rarely relevant in Roman law, since it was not in itself a source of legal problems; the difficulties arose rather with the ascription of distinctive legal capacities on the basis of biological maleness. This paper will be concerned mainly with such legal problems as were held to arise for Romans when someone classified as legally male was nevertheless for certain physical reasons unable to function fully as a physiological male. First, however, the initial classification is considered.

An infant is assigned a sex at birth. In modern societies, this sex is recorded on a birth certificate when the birth is registered. Modern medical science knows three methods of determining sex, visual, gonadal (which usually becomes available only after surgery), and, a recent development, chromosomal (some would add a fourth, hormonal).[2] The only one used also in the ancient world was the visual – simply looking at the external appearance of the genitalia. The others have become particularly important in the last twenty-five years or so, because of the legal questions arising out of various cases involving transsexuals – that is people, usually men, who have had surgical intervention to change their apparent sex and wish also to have their original sex assignment, made at birth, altered – something that in the past has been permitted only when mistake in the original assignment has been proved. Questions have been raised of the purpose of marriage, of the psychological welfare of the individual and of human rights. The concept of 'psychological gender' has begun to gain ground.[3]

The Romans did not pose themselves the question in these terms. Nero's 'marriage' with his catamite Sporus, whom he had had castrated, was nothing more than a charade.[4] Roman lawyers did not even consider the possibility of regarding *castrati* as females. Once a man, always a man. What concerned lawyers was the ways in which a dysfunctioning penis, or complete or partial removal of the genitals, might affect the legal capacity of impotent men and *castrati* in their gender role as males.

Not everyone, however, is positively assignable to one or other sex on visual inspection alone. The gender roles and legal capacity of the two sexes in adulthood differed in a major way, though this did not start to become important until the approach of legal adulthood; for most purposes of Roman law, the sex of a Roman child was irrelevant. However, where initial sex determination is based on visual inspection of the external genitalia of a young child, abnormalities can give rise to erroneous classification. Appearances may be ambiguous. The Romans had the concept of hermaphroditism. In cases of true hermaphroditism, the individual's sexual organs are partly male and partly female, but the external genitals do not necessarily present an ambiguous appearance. One or two legal cases involving true hermaphrodites have arisen in modern times, but there has been no consistency in their handling. An Australian court in 1979 ruled that a hermaphrodite was neither male nor female, and therefore incapable of marrying; a Scottish judge in another case decided that public feeling and the law compelled him to decide for one sex or the other, and allowed a hermaphrodite to have the original birth registration as female changed.[5] In the Republic and early Empire, there are numerous reports of hermaphrodites among prodigies and omens and, during the Republic at least, these appear normally to have been killed at birth. Under the Empire, when these persons were apparently no longer routinely killed,[6] it was necessary to assign them to a sex, but Roman law admitted of no third sex. The matter appears to have remained unresolved for a considerable time – possibly a reflection of the rarity of the phenomenon. At any rate, Ulpian expresses only as an opinion (*puto*) what essentially was a rule of thumb for treating each case as it presented itself. A hermaphrodite should be classified, he said,[7] as belonging to that sex of which the apparent characteristics prevailed. That person would then have the legal capacity of a member of that sex.

The more relaxed view of hermaphrodites in the Empire, compared with the Republic, is seen in the elder Pliny's remark, 'Persons are also born of both sexes combined – what we call hermaphrodites, once called *androgyni* and classed as prodigies, but now as entertainments'.[8] However, he gives no details.[9] Just after his initial definition of hermaphrodites as of combined sex, he gives four examples of what he calls transformations of females into males:

> In the *Annales* for 171 BC we find that at Casinum a girl still with her parents became a boy, and the augurs ordered his deportation to a desert island. Licinius Mucianus reported that he saw at Argos a man called Arescon whose name had been Arescusa, who had even married (as a woman), but presently he developed a beard and masculine characteristics and took a wife; he also saw a boy at Smyrna to whom the same thing had happened. I myself saw in Africa a L. Constitius, a citizen of Thysdris, who changed into a man on the wedding day.[10]

These people were evidently not regarded at birth as prodigious abnormalities, like hermaphrodites, but were accepted as females. Initial mistakes in assigned sex may have been made because of the ambiguous appearance presented by undeveloped pre-pubertal male genitals. The true sex did not become apparent until the individual reached puberty, when other sexual characteristics asserted themselves. Instead of initial error being suspected, however, the later physical changes were ascribed to marvellous transformation and became the stuff of stories, which lost nothing in the telling (as in the last example, where we are expected to believe that the physical change was instantaneous).[11]

In the last three of Pliny's examples, the re-assignment is associated with marriage, and so with arrival at the appropriate age for puberty, and in the first also it is evident that the passage of time revealed an error in original sex-assignment, as male sexual characteristics became more evident. Pliny provides no examples of genuine hermaphroditism.

There are two references in the *Digest* to specific aspects of the legal rights of hermaphrodites. Only men could witness wills; a hermaphrodite could do so, if of the appropriate apparent sex.[12] Men could witness wills; women could not, because they were not in the fullest sense heads of *familiae*.

Actual sexual capacity, as well as gender roles, appears to be involved when Ulpian says: 'A hermaphrodite, obviously, if male characteristics prevail in him, will be capable of instituting a posthumous heir'.[13] However, this appearance is misleading. Ulpian here is providing a rule to be applied should the case arise; it is doubtful whether his opinion is based on any actual examples of true, that is gonadal, hermaphrodites, or even of apparent hermaphrodites. Again, it is a question of gender roles; what matters in this context is not actual male physical potency, but simply classification as male of someone who has what passes for a penis. The subject under discussion is the institution of posthumous heirs. This is something which under Roman law only males could do, or were required to do, because only men had *sui heredes*. *Sui heredes* were those people in a man's *potestas* who became legally independent at his death (namely, his legitimate children, both sons and daughters, including posthumous children, and his sons' children). They must be either instituted as heirs in the will, or expressly not instituted, otherwise the will was invalid[14] – so it was sensible, and legally acceptable, to include putative future posthumous children in the will, even in one made by a bachelor. 'It is agreed', says Ulpian, 'that every male can write in a posthumous heir, whether he is already married or not yet'.[15]

'Every male', however, was a problematic term for lawyers, since the whole point was that these *postumi* were the man's own biological children, not adopted children. This brings us to the main subject of this paper, that is, what legal problems, if any, arose in consequence of physiological deficiency in persons legally classified as biologically male and therefore eligible to fulfil male gender roles.

Ulpian reports an active juristic debate in the first century AD and later:

> The question is raised, whether someone who cannot easily beget can institute a posthumous heir. Cassius and Iavolenus write that he can; for he can also marry and adopt. Both Labeo and Cassius write that a *spado*[16] can also institute a posthumous heir, since neither age nor sterility is an impediment to him. But if he has been castrated, then Julian agrees with the opinion of Proculus that he cannot institute a posthumous heir, and that is the principle we follow. Clearly a hermaphrodite, if male characteristics are prevalent in him, will be able to institute a posthumous heir.[17]

One might wonder why, in some of these instances, the question should be discussed at all, but this is not just legal nit-picking – important matters were at stake. The validity of the institution of the heir had to be established, whether or not the testator appeared physically capable of begetting such an heir, since a will validly instituting a posthumous heir had the effect of invalidating any previous will. Moreover, if the testator's wife alleged that she was pregnant at the time of his death, the assignment of the estate had to wait until the posthumous child (whether it was in the will or not) appeared in the world. Procreative capacity was important; some *postumi* could not be created by adoption (Gai. *Inst.* 2. 138, 140; *Dig.* 28. 2. 27). Paulus firmly dismisses possible doubt in the first case: 'If someone who for reasons of age and health is perhaps incapable of having them institutes posthumous heirs, a previous will is broken, because regard must be had to the nature, and customary capacity of generating, in a man, rather than to a temporary defect or ill-health on account of which the man is deprived of the faculty of generating'.[18]

However, what about men constitutionally incapable of generating? The various physical conditions involved are described and discussed in Dalla 1978, chapter III. 1. *Spado* was a term which could be used generally, to refer to men whose testicles had in various ways been destroyed or damaged[19] and even to *castrati* (*Dig.* 23. 3. 39. 1), as well as to those naturally impotent; in *Dig.* 28. 2. 6, Ulpian apparently uses *spado* to refer to those permanently impotent, whom he distinguishes from those temporarily so.

What is interesting is the arguments used by jurists to justify their opinion that males who are impotent can validly institute posthumous heirs. A biological argument is used by both Labeo and Cassius, who draw a contrast with factors such as age and sterility – understandably, because the terms in which, according to Ulpian, the initial question is posed (an is, qui generare facile non possit, postumum heredem facere possit, 'whether someone who cannot easily beget can institute a posthumous heir') allow at least a theoretical possibility of generative capacity, and so the *spado* also could be held to be included.

The wider definition of *spado*, including both the naturally impotent and men with damaged or destroyed testicles, is used by Ulpian in his commentary on the *lex Iulia et Papia* (*Dig.* 50. 16. 128). Unfortunately, we do not have the context, but the likelihood is that lawyers were prepared to interpret the Augustan marriage laws to give *spadones* some relief or exemption from the penalties of childlessness; it would be helpful to know how much concession they were willing to allow.[20] The *sine qua non*, however, as far as potential *postumi heredes* are concerned, is, obviously, in the view of Labeo and Cassius, the possession of a penis.[21]

Ulpian concurs with the opinion of Julian and Proculus that the institution of a posthumous heir by a *castratus* has no legal effect. This is merely a recognition of the obvious fact that the *castratus* is not going to be able to generate any children in the future[22] and settles the technical question of whether the institution invalidates a previous will. It does not imply any other limitation on his gender role as a male.

Cassius and Iavolenus, on the other hand, base their opinion on the male's gender role – his legal capacity both to marry a wife and to adopt. Anyone who had a penis, even if not in full working order, or who used to have one, was classified as a man, and therefore, once recognized as legally adult, had the legal capacity of a man. Only a *paterfamilias* could adopt, and only a *paterfamilias* could have *sui heredes*, posthumous or otherwise, who were his children born of lawful marriage.

So it seems, in principle at least, as if both *spadones* and *castrati* should have been held legally capable of marrying and adopting. Concerning *spadones*, the sources are in agreement at all periods that they have the full legal capacity of males. However, certain limitations are recognized to the capacity of *castrati*. Besides marriage and adoption, to which I shall return presently, the third principal matter which lawyers feel it necessary to discuss is the question of determining when a biologically disadvantaged male may be held to have reached legal adulthood.

In calling someone a *paterfamilias*, Ulpian explains we are not designating only a person, but also a legal right:

> We call the person who has mastery in a house a father of *familia*, and he is correctly called by this name, even though he has no son; for we are referring not only to him as a person, but to his legal status; in fact, we call even a minor a *paterfamilias*.[23]

In other words, being a *paterfamilias* is gender-specific. Only biological males can have *potestas*, and this is what is indicated by the term *paterfamilias*; actual paternity is not implied. Therefore, the term *paterfamilias* can be used also of someone who has not yet reached puberty. An *impubes*, however, is not yet legally an adult, and so is incapable of any legal action. There is an obvious problem with someone constitutionally impotent, and *a fortiori* with someone castrated before reaching puberty, in determining when they become adult.

Legal adulthood for women was, at least from the time of Augustus, and probably earlier, determined not by actual attainment of puberty, but by age. A girl was legally adult, and marriageable, at the age of 12, whether or not she had in fact reached puberty. For males, opinion was divided among the jurists of the first century AD, and Gaius reports the division as still apparently unresolved in his own day, namely, about the middle of the second century AD:

> Sabinus, Cassius and the rest of our teachers consider that a boy reaches puberty when he shows the fact by his physical development, that is, when he is capable of procreation, but in the case of

those who cannot so develop, such as the naturally impotent, they hold that the normal age of puberty must be taken. The authorities of the other school consider that puberty must be judged simply by age, that is, they hold a boy to have reached puberty when he has reached the age of 14.[24]

The 'other school' was that founded by Antistius Labeo and headed later in the first century by Julius Proculus.[25] On their interpretation of what constituted legal adulthood, impotence was no problem, as it obviously would be if puberty was taken as the criterion. However, the 'Sabinians', as the former school were known in the post-classical period, also sensibly accepted age as the criterion for *spadones*.

As to what happened in practice, whatever the followers of particular legal schools might recommend, the question of adulthood became a legal issue for the most part only in one of two situations: if the young man in question was already out of *potestas* – that is, either his father had died or he had been emancipated – and for some reason he or the tutor administering his property wanted to terminate *tutela*; or if it was intended to arrange his marriage at rather an earlier age than seems to have been common among Roman men. In the symbolic marking of adulthood by the assumption of the *toga virilis*, no special preference was shown for the age of 14, or for the fourteenth birthday. Coming-of-age parties were customarily tied to one day in the year, the festival of the Liberalia on March 17th. Cicero could have given his son Marcus the *toga virilis* at the age of 14, when the boy was with him in Cilicia, but he did not do so until the end of March 49 BC, when he was nearly 16; his cousin Quintus received the toga a year earlier, at about the same age.[26] Both would then be regarded as legally eligible for marriage, although it is some years before Cicero's correspondence raises the subject concerning either boy.[27]

Sometimes, however, it was necessary for practical reasons to define 'puberty' in terms of a specific age. When a legacy of *alimenta* was left to children until they reached puberty, a fixed age had to be specified, so that the cost to the estate could be calculated. Hadrian issued an instruction, later reiterated in a rescript of Septimius Severus, that this should be taken to mean up to the eighteenth year for boys and the fourteenth for girls – not, Ulpian says (*Dig.* 34. 1. 14. 1), that that was the usual definition of puberty, but, from considerations of *pietas*, for this one purpose alone it was thought public-spirited (*non incivile*). By that time, one might suppose, even the late developers would normally have reached puberty.

One situation when the attainment of adulthood obviously became an issue was when the young person died, having made a will. Was it valid? The general rule was stated in terms of age – 12 for girls, 14 for boys,[28] but a qualification is found in Paulus' *Sententiae* (3. 4a. 2): *spadones* can make a will from the age by which most people reach puberty, namely the eighteenth year.[29] This is a very odd way of putting it. If the age rule of 14, rather than the requirement of puberty, was meant to be the criterion of capacity to make a will, presumably a will made by a 17-year-old would be held valid if he died at that age, whether or not there were signs of physical puberty. It would surely not then become invalid if he lived to 18.[30]

I think we have to supply the relevant situation which is envisaged here; Paulus' remark makes sense only if we take it to mean, not that a *spado* could not make a will until he was 18, but that he could not be prevented from making a will once he had reached 18, because he would then automatically be considered legally adult. If a recalcitrant tutor was refusing to resign his charge and acknowledge his ward's adulthood on the excuse that the latter had not reached puberty, this could be spun out only until the ward reached the age of 18, when he could represent himself as *spado*, and claim the right to be regarded as legally adult.

Sexual potency was not a legal prerequisite for lawful marriage either. Marriage (*matrimonium*) as the union of male and female, was for the Romans, like the procreation and rearing of offspring, an institution of *ius naturale* (natural law) (*Dig.* 1. 1. 1. 3), and not exclusive to humans. Marriage as recognized in civil law, however, was merely a private contract between individuals, and it was required only that the partners (who, it was taken for granted, were of different sexes) were legally adult, had *conubium* (appropriate civil status), and that they or their *patres* consented. Failure to generate children did not invalidate a marriage, and it made no difference whether the husband was temporarily or permanently impotent, so long as his assigned sex was male. Non-consummation was irrelevant to the validity of the marriage: non enim coitus matrimonium facit, sed maritalis affectio, 'For it is not coition, but marital intent, that makes matrimony'.[31]

This is in contrast with the present law of England and Wales and also of Scotland.[32] In both English and Scottish law, consent alone is not enough; sexual incapacity can be grounds for voiding a valid marriage. In Scotland (Marriage (Scotland) Act 1977), marriage is voidable on grounds of the husband's impotence, as it is in the law of England and Wales (Marriage Acts 1949–83) if the marriage is not consummated on grounds of the incapacity of either party.[33] It probably would never have occurred to Romans to use such an argument, because it simply was not necessary. Marriages could be terminated at any time by a simple declaration of repudiation, on either side, and no causes need be alleged. It is not until Constantine that specific causes are required for divorce, and impotence is not included among these until the reign of Justinian.[34]

If consummation was irrelevant to the validity of a marriage in Roman law, then there was no reason why impotent men could not lawfully marry. They could also adopt. To be able to adopt, it was not necessary, in Roman law, to be married (*Dig.* 1. 7. 30 Paulus), any more than it was necessary to be married, or to have a son, in order to be a *paterfamilias*. In order to adopt, one had to have *potestas*, and so only adult males could adopt.[35]

The capacities to adopt and to contract marriage with women were part of male gender roles, and men's actual biological capacity was not an issue. This is true, at least, of the legal attitude to impotence. *Castrati* were problematic, but only in so far as the removal of their genitals meant that certain specific events with legal consequences either could not occur, or could not be presumed to have been intended; this is true, at least, of texts concerning marriage.

Adoption by *castrati* is an issue, so far as our texts go, only with Justinian.[36] Gaius (*Inst.* 1. 103; cf. *Dig.* 1. 7. 2. 1) said that *spadones* could adopt by both methods (i.e. adrogation and adoption); Justinian's *Institutiones* add that *castrati* could not. There is no obvious legal reason for the distinction, if meant to apply to both methods, since after Justinian's change of the law of adoption in AD 530, ordinary adoption by someone not a male ascendant (which obviously neither a *spado* or *castratus* was) did not confer *potestas*, and the adoptee's inheritance rights in his natal family were unaffected. *Adrogatio* did confer *potestas*, and was, moreover, normally allowed, as in classical law, only after enquiry, and to those who had not, or could not have, children of their own. Dalla's discussion (1978, 163–89) of sexual incapacity and the law of adoption does not help to clarify this puzzle. As far as the legal sources go, there is no reason to believe that *castrati* in classical Roman society could not perpetuate their names and families, if they wished, by adopting – after all, bachelors could adopt.

As for marriage, Ulpian's opinion, cited above, that *castrati* could not validly institute posthumous heirs is merely a necessary acknowledgment of their physical incapacity, not in itself a statement that they could not validly marry. When Marcianus says that a *spado* could manumit a female slave (sc. one not otherwise eligible for manumission, under the *lex Aelia Sentia*) for the purpose of matrimony, whereas a *castratus* could not[37], the reason for the distinction is clearly that in the latter case, since there was no physical possibility of consummation, this marriage was never intended to be a genuine physical union but was merely an attempt to circumvent the *lex*. This decision does not presuppose that a *castratus* was in general unable to contract a valid marriage.

However, if a marriage is defined as a union which has certain legal consequences, then it appears that the legal point of view was that *castrati* could not marry. Certainly, it was physically impossible for them to father legitimate children.[38] The legal consequences of marriage for property also had to be considered. Dowry was the legal property of the husband during marriage, and in certain circumstances some or all of it could be retained by him at the end of the marriage.[39] Legal interpretation held that a union between a *castratus* and a woman was not to be considered marriage, and the property was not therefore dotal.[40] This again is merely a recognition of the physical fact that the *familia* of the *castratus* must end with himself.

These hesitations about marriage apart, *castrati* had the same legal rights as any other Roman and, what is more important, they had the rights of men.

Dalla's discussion of marriage (1978, 267–9) rather confuses the issue by introducing the idea that these distinctions may be attributed to general social disesteem of the class of individuals from whom *castrati* in the main came – disgraced, half-men, usually foreign and of slave origin. These ideas are certainly present in literature, but they are not found in law. Ulpian's interpretation, over the matter of dowry, that there is no *matrimonium* between a woman and a *castratus*, is no more a moral condemnation of such unions than is implied by the prefect of Egypt's refusal in AD 117 of a woman's claim to some money deposited with a soldier, now deceased, on the grounds that it could not constitute a dowry, since soldiers were not able to marry.[41] Certainly castration, whether of slaves or free men, was strongly disapproved of in Roman law, and was repeatedly prohibited, with ferocious penalties for breach, from the time of Sulla (*lex Cornelia de sicariis et veneficiis*) onwards,[42] the repetition of the bans perhaps indicating their lack of effect. There was clearly a market for *castrati*, and the trade in imported *castrati* was not stopped. Indeed, they were a source of revenue.[43]

Most free *castrati* will have entered Roman society from slavery; to that extent Dalla's remark about them being slaves and foreigners is true. Nevertheless, their emasculated state, however much it may have resulted in their social disesteem, was not by itself a ground for any curtailment of their legal rights as citizens.

The only evidence which might *prima facie* be taken to suggest otherwise is a well-known story in Valerius Maximus (7. 7. 6). In 77 BC the urban praetor, Cn. Orestes, granted possession of the estate of a freedman, Naevius Anius, to a certain Genucius, who was a Gallus, a castrated priest of the Magna Mater, and had been made heir by Naevius. However, Naevius' patron appealed to the consul Mamercus Aemilius Lepidus, who overturned the award. According to Valerius, Aemilius gave as reason for his judgment that Genucius, having castrated himself, could be regarded as neither male nor female, and he added a decree that Genucius was not to 'pollute the tribunals of the magistrates by his obscene presence and corrupted voice, on pretext of seeking his right'.[44]

The value that should be put on this story is shown by the one with which Valerius explicitly pairs it. Another urban praetor refused to allow a certain Vecillus possession of the estate of Vibienus, as provided in the latter's will, on the grounds of the man's disreputable way of life – he was a *leno*, a pimp. In both cases, the magistrate was exercising arbitrary personal judgment, not implementing existing law. *Lenones* were certainly, in legal terms, *infames*, 'infamous, disgraced', and therefore subject to certain restrictions on their legal capacity[45], but the effects of *infamia* did not include inability to receive under a will. *Castrati* were not, simply as *castrati*, *infames*, though they might be for other reasons; besides, even the *infames* were not prohibited from speaking in court in their own behalf. What was really going on is fairly clear. Naevius' patron, who as the law then stood could have claimed half the estate, wanted it all, and appealed against the praetor's decision; the consul sided with him against Genucius.

Some doubt is shed on the genuineness of the whole incident, however, by the fact that Roman citizens were not permitted to be Galli (Dionysios of Halikarnassos 2. 19. 4). Either Genucius had been a Gallus while a slave, and subsequently been manumitted and given up the priesthood, or – more likely perhaps – there was a good legal reason for Aemilius' judgment, that Genucius was not in fact a Roman citizen and therefore not entitled to receive under the will. The rhetoric about his polluting presence was just that.

Either way, the story does not show that *castrati*, simply as such, incurred legal disability. However, it is not unlikely that many of the citizen *castrati* were freedmen, who had been prostitutes or catamites as slaves, and continued as free men to earn their living in that way, and that was certainly an activity which would cause them to incur legal penalty as *infames*. Male prostitutes are listed in the *lex Iulia municipalis* among those who are not to be admitted to membership of local councils. Among those banned in the praetor's edict, on the grounds of the disgracefulness of their way of life, from representing others in court (*Dig.* 3. 1. 1. 6) are catamites, whether professionals or enthusiastic amateurs (the phrase used is 'qui corpore suo muliebria passus est' ('someone who has been physically treated like a woman')). They were more severely treated in the praetor's edict than practitioners of other forms of what was regarded as socially deviant sex. Pimps and female prostitutes (and, probably, though not mentioned, male heterosexual prostitutes also) were allowed to go to law at least on behalf of close relatives; catamites were denied this. In later law, a man who voluntarily submitted to a homosexual act lost half his property and the capacity to make a will (Paulus, *Sent.* 2. 26. 13 = *Coll.* 5. 2. 2). In the Christian empire, the penalty for catamites was death by burning.[46]

This sexual context is one of the very few in which the words 'manly' (*virilis*) and 'womanly', or 'womanish' (*muliebris*) occur in Roman legal writings. *Virilis* occurs in a few references to particular duties and functions, deriving from capacity to have *patria potestas*, which are described as 'men's work' – being tutors, standing surety for others or representing them in court, banking; since *spadones* and *castrati* were classified as men, they would have the right to perform them.[47] Otherwise, *virilis* and *muliebris* occur in two types of context. One concerns homosexual acts – the other, clothing. Lawyers are concerned to define men's clothing and women's clothing, in order to determine the contents of legacies. Women's clothes are 'those obtained for the *materfamilias*, which a man cannot readily use without incurring censure (*sine vituperatione*)', while unisex garments are those 'which without reproach (*sine reprehensione*) either a man or a woman may use' (*Dig.* 34. 2. 23. 2 Ulpianus *xliv ad Sabinum*). Paulus writes in similar vein (*Sent.* 3. 6. 80): 'When a legacy is left of men's clothing, only those are included which are appropriate for a man's use without shaming his masculinity (*salvo pudore virilitatis*)'.

There is clearly a dress code. Behaviour and appearances are important and there is an image of 'masculinity' to be guarded, that is, of psychological masculinity. It is not enough merely to be biologically male, one must give out the appropriate signals and play the expected gender role. Although the aim in the context is merely descriptive, namely, to specify the contents of legacies, lawyers in the phraseology of the definitions are reproducing the prejudices of lay society. For a man deliberately to imitate the behaviour of the opposite sex was not merely unbecoming, it was self-degradation. Transvestism as such, however, was no crime; it formed the subject of a joke by the Republican jurist Quintus Mucius Scaevola.[48] This sort of symbolic inversion of gender roles was not taken very seriously.

The other context is sexual, and there the important word is *muliebris*. I have already mentioned the exclusion under the praetor's edict of the person *qui corpore suo muliebria passus est*. The reference is not to womanly emotionalism or effeminate behaviour, but simply to taking the female part in the sexual act. *Virilis*, as it happens, does not occur in this citation of a classical legal text. In the text of AD 390 (above, n. 46), it occurs twice, first in a phrase whose meaning is obscured by the convolutions of late rhetoric,[49] but which apparently is intended to refer to passive homosexuals, and perhaps to *castrati*. There *virile*, in the phrase *virile corpus*, is equivalent to *masculum*, meaning simply biologically male; the fuller text of the *Collatio*, however, going on to justify the punishment of catamites[50] (and expecially, perhaps, of *castrati*), uses the phrase *virilis anima*, 'a man's mind', clearly denoting psychological masculinity.

This added emphasis in later law on psychological masculinity perhaps reflects the Christian rationalization of gender differences as not merely what Peter Brown (1988, 432) has called a 'civic hierarchy' of the sexes, but as a divinely ordained, spiritual one. In classical law, though active homosexuals were penalized, nothing is known about the details of the law. Passive homosexuality was, it seems, more severely treated in the praetor's edict than other forms of socially deviant sex, since in inverting the biological roles of men and women, it also ran counter to the necessary role in society of man as *paterfamilias*, which combined sex and gender. The Church added the extra element of divine authority.

To sum up: legal capacity and gender role in Roman society depended upon assigned sex at birth. Males were those who had what passed for male genitals (even if dysfunctional or later removed), and they had public and private rights, including *potestas*, which were denied to biological females. Sexual ambiguity was recognized only in the case of hermaphrodites and was resolved in a rough and ready way by assigning them the gender role of what appeared to be the prevailing sex. The legal problems raised by impotence or genital loss were few in number, though important for the life of the person affected, and concerned mainly technicalities arising from the biological implications of the gender role of a *pater*. Male gender rights were curtailed only for those *castrati* whose sexual behaviour inverted biological roles.

Notes

1 See below, 146–7; Gardner 1993, ch. 4; Gardner 1995.
2 I am leaving out of account recent, and controversial, developments in genetics which make it possible to determine sex before birth.
3 Bradney 1987; Finlay and Walters 1988; Meyers 1990, 219–38.
4 Suetonius, *Nero* 28; Juvenal 2. 117; Martial 12. 42.
5 The case in the Family Court of Australia in 1979 (Finlay and Walters 1988, 74 n. 95) was brought concerning a true hermaphrodite, who had undergone surgical treatment to remove his 'female' anatomy, and had contracted marriage as a male; the court gave the ruling, since regarded as controversial, that the marriage was null, since 'he' was neither male nor female – a decision which entailed in effect that 'he' was incapable of marriage. A sensible decision was reached in the Scottish case (Meyers 1990, 232), in which it was ordered that a birth registration as female should be changed to male in the Register of corrected entries. The individual in person presented a predominantly female appearance, and had female chromosomes, but both ovarian and testicular tissue and male psychosexual attitudes – that is, his psychological gender was male. The judge ruled that the person was neither male nor female, but that public feeling and the law required him to hold that all persons were one or the other; in this case, the male was held to prevail, though psychological gender does not appear to have been a major consideration.
6 I owe information on this change in Roman practice to Alex Nice; the main ancient sources for the Republic are Livy and Julius Obsequens, *liber de prodigiis*; see, e.g. Livy 27. 11, 37; 31. 12; 39. 22; Obsequens 22, 25, 27a, 32, 34, 36, 47, 48, 50, 53. At 57, Obsequens reports the birth to a woman, in 83 BC, of a snake, which was disposed of in the same way as a hermaphrodite.
7 *Quaeritur: hermaphroditum cui comparamus? et magis puto eius sexus aestimandum qui in eo praevalet* (*Dig*.1. 5. 10).
8 *Gignuntur et utriusque sexus quos Hermaphroditos vocamus, olim androgynos vocatos et in prodigiis habitos, nunc vero in deliciis* (*Naturalis Historia* 7. 3. 34).
9 A few women, he remarks (*HN* 11. 109. 262), have an abnormal (*prodigiosa*) resemblance (*sc.* to males), just as hermaphrodites do to either sex.

10 *Invenimus in annalibus P. Licinio Crasso C. Crasso Longino coss. Casini puerum factum ex virgine sub parentibus, iussuque haruspicum deportatum in insulam desertam. Licinius Mucianus prodidit visum a se Argis Arescontem, cui nomen Arescusae fuisset, nupsisse etiam, mox barbam et virilitatem provenisse uxoremque duxisse; eiusdem sortis et Zmyrnae puerum a se visum. Ipse in Africa vidi mutatum in marem nuptiarum die L. Constitium civem Thysdritanum.*

(*HN* 7. 4. 36)

11 Diodoros Sikulos 32. 10–11 describes two Hellenistic examples where the testicles were overgrown by membrane and surgery was necessary at puberty to allow their emergence (I owe this reference to Duncan Cloud).

12 Hermaphroditus an ad testamentum adhiberi possit, qualitas sexus incalescentis ostendit (*Dig*. 22. 5. 15. 1 (Paulus *iii sententiarum*)). Paulus' colourful language (incalescentis) suggests not, perhaps, that a prospective witness challenged as hermaphrodite might be asked on the spot to demonstrate his essential physical virility by achieving erection, but perhaps that that criterion was used where sexual re-assignment of a grown person was being considered.

13 Hermaphroditus plane, si in eo virilia praevalebunt, postumum heredem instituere poterit (*Dig*. 28. 2. 6. 2).

14 Gaius, *Institutiones* 2. 123, 183. A woman's *postumi* could bring a querela inofficiosi testamenti ('complaint of unduteous will'), the success of which did not necessarily render the will totally invalid (Buckland 1966, 330).

15 Placet omnem masculum posse postumum heredem scribere, sive iam maritus sit sive nondum uxorem duxerit (*Dig*. 28. 2. 4).

16 That is, someone incapable of penile erection – for applications of the term, see further below.

17 Sed est quaesitum an is, qui generare facile non possit, postumum heredem facere possit. et scribit Cassius et Iavolenus posse: nam et uxorem ducere et adoptare potest. spadonem quoque posse postumum heredem scribere et Labeo et Cassius scribunt: quoniam nec aetas nec sterilitas ei rei impedimento est. Sed si castratus sit, Iulianus Proculi opinionem secutus non putat postumum heredem posse instituere, quo iure utimur. Hermaphroditus plane, si in eo virilia praevalebunt, postumum heredem instituere poterit (*Dig*. 28. 2. 6. pr.,1).

18 Si quis postumos, quos per aetatem aut valetudinem habere forte non potest, heredes instituit, superius testamentum rumpitur, quod natura magis in homine generandi et consuetudo spectanda est, quam temporale vitium aut valetudo, propter quam abducatur homo a generandi facultate (*Dig*. 28. 2. 9).

19 *Dig*. 50. 16. 128: *thlibiae, thliasiae*. Dalla 1978, 125 observes that Theophilus *Par*. 1. 11. 9 speaks of *spadones* in the narrower, pathological, sense, i.e. those impotent from natural causes, as theoretically capable of recovery and cure; this, Dalla thinks, it was necessary to specify because of the expectation that adoption would follow nature. However, the Roman law of adoption does not make any requirement of potency in the adopter.

20 So Dalla 1978, 255. At 269 he suggests that women had been marrying *spadones* (in the widest sense, including *castrati*) as an attempt to evade the penalties of the Julian laws on celibates without the risk of having sons, and that the distinction in *Dig*. 28. 2. 6 reflects an attempt, in the third century AD, to deal with the case of such marriages being used to circumvent the law, *in fraudem legis*. However, the former supposition, even if true, is not substantiated in the sources, and, in any case, as shown above, the question of the institution of posthumous heirs is raised for other reasons, and what is relevant is the procreative capacity of the male testator, not the validity of any present or future marriage. In *Dig*. 40. 2. 14. 1 Marcianus says that a *castratus* cannot manumit *matrimonii causa*; however, the issue is not the validity of the intended marriage but the evident fraudulent intent of a manumission contrary to the conditions of the *lex Aelia Sentia*.

21 In the widest sense, *spadones* may include even *castrati*: Dig. 21. 1. 6. 2 (Ulpian), 7 (Paulus); 23. 3. 39. 1 (Paulus). This is found in discussion of the aedile's edict, as to what does or does not constitute a physical defect in slaves, horses and mules. Ulpian thinks that a slave who is *spado* is sound, as is one with defective testicles but still capable of generating – but, Paulus adds, if so necessary a part

149

of his body is totally missing, he is *morbosus* (*Dig.* 21. 1. 6. 2, 7). Mules, however, are by definition incapable of procreation, so castration is irrelevant to their soundness, unless their work capacity is affected. The case is less clear with horses; Ulpian cites the opinion of Ofilius that a buyer can sue if he was not informed that a horse had been castrated (*Dig.* 21. 1. 38. 7). Their breeding capacity does not affect their physical sturdiness, but could be held to affect their value. However, as far as Roman law is concerned, slaves and mules may be regarded as having sex roles, but no gender roles.

22 Compare *Dig.* 37. 14. 6. 2 (Paulus). Patrons who made it a condition of manumission that ex-slaves should swear an oath not to acknowledge and rear legitimate children (who would have a claim to part of the freedman's estate) were apparently penalized under the *lex Aelia Sentia* (presumably by loss of patronal rights); this did not apply if the freedman was a *castratus* (Dalla 1978, 263).

23 pater autem familias appellatur, qui in domo dominium habet, recteque hoc nomine appellatur, quamvis filium non habeat: non enim solam personam eius, sed et ius demonstramus: denique et pupillum patrem familias appellamus. (*Dig.* 50. 16. 195. 2).

24 puberem autem Sabinus quidem et Cassius ceterique nostri praeceptores eum esse putant qui habitu corporis pubertatem ostendit, id est, eum qui generare potest; sed in his qui pubescere non possunt, quales sunt spadones, eam aetatem esse spectandam cuius aetatis puberes fiunt. sed diversae scholae auctores annis putant pubertatem esse aestimandam, id est, eum puberem esse existimant qui xiiii annis explevit (Gai. *Inst.* 1. 196). For the date of Gaius' *Institutes*, see Honoré 1962, 69. Later jurists add no further information.

25 Cassius and Iavolenus were successors of Sabinus; Schulz 1946, 119.

26 *Epistulae ad Atticum* 6. 1. 12; 9. 19. 1; Ovid, *Fasti* 3. 771–6.

27 *Att.* 15. 29. 2; 16. 1. 5 (6th and 8th July 44 BC).

28 Gai. *Inst.* 1. 40, 2. 113; *Dig.* 8. 1. 5; Paulus, *Sententiae* 3. 4a. 1.

29 Eighteen years is also, as Dalla 1978, 193 notes, the age difference which Modestinus (*Dig.* 1. 7. 40. 1), possibly interpolated, and Justinian (*Institutiones* 1. 11. 4) say should exist between adopter and adoptee, a period defined as *plena pubertas*. Adoption should imitate nature. This, however, applies to all adoption, not only those by *spadones* or *castrati*, and affords a comfortable margin; we may compare the lower age limits for manumission set by the *lex Aelia Sentia* (20) and for procreation set by the Augustan marriage laws (20 for women, 25 for men), which were set some years later than even late developers would normally reach puberty.

30 The expression of the *Sententiae* as a whole is very compressed. Schulz 1946, 176 remarks that the work was 'so short relatively to the matter treated of that . . . it was necessarily elementary'.

31 *Dig.* 24. 1. 32. 13; cf. 35. 1. 15; 50. 17. 30.

32 In both, as in Roman law, and in the law of most countries (Sweden and Denmark are exceptions), same-sex marriage is not legally recognized; a marriage is void unless it is between a male and a female. Cases of 'marriages' involving transsexuals have been decided differently in different courts. The decision in the notorious Corbett *v.* Corbett case (1971) was that the marriage was void because it was held that the transsexual 'wife' remained a man. Chromosomal evidence was what finally determined the case and the judge commented: 'Having regard to the essentially heterosexual character of . . . marriage the criteria must . . . be biological'. In contrast, more weight was given to the harmonization of physical and psychological gender by the superior court

of New Jersey, which upheld (1976) a claim for marital support made by a transsexual 'wife' (Finlay and Walters 1988, 50–8).
33 Mason 1990, 4–9; Cretney 1984, 63–7.
34 Corbett 1930, 243–8; *Codex Iustinianus* 5. 17. 10 (AD 528).
35 With the separation of *potestas* from succession rights by Justinian (*Cod. Iust.* 8.
47 (48) 10), a distinction was made between 'full' adoption and 'less full', which
involved succession only, something which was allowable also to women, in
certain circumstances, by imperial grant from the time of Diocletian (*Cod. Iust.*
8. 47 (48) 5); 'less full' adoption was not entirely gender-specific. 'Full' adoption,
however, remained the prerogative of men. In 'full' adoption only, the person
adopting acquired *potestas* over the one adopted. Adoption was 'full' only if the
adopter was a paternal or maternal ascendant of the adopted, or if the adoption
was an adrogation, that is, the adoptee was already out of *potestas*. Obviously,
this meant that, after Justinian, an impotent man adopting could acquire
potestas only if the adoption was an adrogation.
36 *Inst.* 1. 11. 9. Sed et illud utriusque adoptionis commune est, quod et hi, qui
generare non possunt, quales sunt spadones, adoptare possunt, castrati autem
non possunt (AD 533).
37 Et si spado velit matrimonii causa manumittere, potest: non idem est in castrato
(*Dig.* 40. 2. 14. 1).
38 Although Paulus remarks (*Dig.* 2 .4. 5) pater is est quem nuptiae demonstrant,
'the father is the person identified by a marriage', lawyers were not necessarily
prepared to accept the legitimacy of a child born to a married woman, if, for
instance, there was a year-old-baby in the home of a husband who had been
absent for ten years or if it was known that for ill-health or some other reason
the husband had not had intercourse with his wife for a long time (*Dig.* 1. 6. 6).
39 Some of the dowry could be retained for the children after divorce initiated by
the wife, all of it if the marriage was ended by the wife's death; there could also,
after divorce, be retentions under various headings. See Gardner 1986, 104–9,
112–14.
40 Si spadoni mulier nupserit, distinguendum arbitror, castratus fuerit necne, ut in
castrato dicas dotem non esse: in eo qui castratus non est, quia est matrimonium,
et dos et dotis actio est (*Dig.* 23. 3. 39. 1 Ulpianus *xxxiii ad edictum*).
41 Riccobono, *FIRA* III.19a; contrast the specific exclusion of women of immoral
life from receiving bequests under soldier's wills: *Dig.* 29. 1. 41. 1; 34. 9. 14.
42 References in Dalla 1978, ch. 2, especially 78–116. The use of violence appears to
be what is objected to: cf. Dalla 1987, chapter 5, on legal and social attitudes to
homosexual violence against free men. The scantiness of the evidence does not,
however, permit evaluation of the attitude of public law to homosexuality
between consenting adults, especially to the behaviour of the active partner. The
tolerance alleged by Peter Brown (1988, 29–30) rests on literary evidence.
43 Among the luxury goods pertaining to *vectigal* (tax) listed by Marcianus (*Dig.*
39. 4. 16. 7) are *Spadones Indici*, presumably castrated somewhere outside
Roman jurisdiction.
44 ne obscena Genucii praesentia inquinataque voce tribunalia magistratuum sub
specie petiti iuris polluerentur.
45 On the legal consequences of *infamia*, and the persons it affected, see Gardner
1993, chapter 5.
46 Laudanda igitur experientia tua omnes, quibus flagitiosus luxus est virile corpus
muliebriter constitutum alieni sexus damnare patientia, nihilque discretum
habere cum feminis occupatos, ut flagitii poscit immanitas atque [odium]
omnibus eductos, pudet dicere, virorum lupanaribus, spectante populo flammis
vindicibus expiabit: ut universi intellegant, sacrosanctum cunctis esse debere

hospitium virilis animae, nec sine summo supplicio alienum expetisse sexum, qui suum turpiter perdidisset.

'Your excellency will therefore enquire after those who have the disgraceful self-indulgence to condemn a masculine body adapted to female mode to undergo the experience of the other sex, and to make no distinction between themselves and women who ply, and will punish them in avenging flames before the eyes of the populace as the hateful enormity of their offence deserves, dragging them out from (shameful to say) all the brothels – so that all may understand that the host of a man's mind ought to be sacrosanct to all, and not without the supreme penalty has someone sought after an alien sex, who shamefully lost his own' (*Coll.* 5. 3. 2 = *Codex Theodosianus* 9. 7. 6 (AD 390), with additions).

47 'Men's work': Gardner 1993, 97–101. Although we hear quite a lot, in this legal context, about the supposed mental weakness of women as a sex as a ground for these distinctions of gender role, in most texts the use of *virilis* is merely biologically descriptive – certain gender roles are reserved for biological males. In just one text (*Dig.* 26. 6. 4. 4) Tryphoninus (active under Severus) uses *virilis animus* as the other side of the coin from weak female mentality – single-parent mothers are not expected to undertake the responsibility for prosecuting dishonest guardians of their children 'since forming a judgment on such deed and assessing them takes a male mind (*virilis animus*)'.

48 *Dig.* 34. 2. 33 (Pomponius). Mucius said that he knew a certain man who habitually wore women's dresses at dinner. If that man left a legacy of women's clothing, said Mucius, these dinner-dresses should not be included since they were being treated as menswear. On transvestism in Roman law, see Manfredini 1985.

49 Schulz 1946, 328 says of the chancery style: 'It is a labour to extract the sense from the flowery verbiage'.

50 Catamites are probably also referred to in the opening of a constitution of Constantius and Constans (*Cod. Iust.* 9. 9. 30 = *Cod. Theod.* 9. 7. 3: AD 342), *cum vir nubit in feminam*; the immediately following words (*femina viros proiectura*, etc., Krüger followed by Mommsen) are corrupt and ambiguous. *Nubere* 'to marry' is used where the subject is a woman (with the bridegroom in the dative), whereas a man 'takes' (*ducit*) a wife.

7

Experiencing the male body in Roman Egypt

Dominic Montserrat

There can be little doubt that in antiquity, the male body provided an important symbolic gauge of discourses about power, identity and social position (see Gardner, this volume). The male body was a surface upon which power relations were mapped, and which could be exploited as a forum for the display of these dynamics. According to ancient physiology, the unmarked, unspecified and unqualified human body was male, providing the yardstick by which other kinds of bodies were measured and defined. A man's physical characteristics were explained in terms of his innate male claim to physical superiority; his body hair, for instance, was a visible sign of the internal heat which placed him at the top of the ascending scale of body supremacies concocted by ancient physiologists. Wearing a beard enabled the man to face the world with confidence, knowing that he was displaying a sign of his masculinity and his position at the top of the somatic hierarchy.[1]

But it is important to remember that in the ancient world, not all men possessed the same category of body. The body of a Roman emperor, with its potential for divinity, is different from that of a male citizen or a male slave; and a slave can acquire the body of a citizen or an emperor as his status changes (see Dupont 1989). The ways that ancient people inhabited and experienced their bodies were inseparable from their social and economic position. Slaves were *no more* than bodies, the passive human property of their owners. The most common Greek terms for slaves underscore this powerlessness and passivity: *sōma*, literally 'body', and *pais* 'infant'.[2] Yet in spite of the otherness of the physical body of the slave to that of the free person, at the same time it was potentially the same, because of the possibility of manumission, when the slave was freed and renounced his slavish body along with his slavish status.

My focus in this paper is the male body in Roman Egypt as evidenced in the documentary papyri of the first three centuries AD. I will examine what information the papyri offer for how the male body functioned as social/cultural index and for internal hierarchies of the body within the wider category of 'male'. Also, I intend to consider the question of recovering the experience of the male body: what was it like to inhabit such a body in Roman Egypt?

From the outset, I have to admit that this is a contentious project. The extent to which one can use papyrus documents – by and large formulaic records of economic transactions or bureaucratic processes – to write this kind of *Annales* school history, has often been questioned.[3] I would argue that this is a viable project, but before it can be done the status of papyri as archaeological artefacts as well as written documents has to be acknowledged. Here I have been influenced by the so-called post-processual school of archaeologists, who seek to reinstate the emotional, the experiential and diverse aspects of ancient life, rather than interpreting archaeological remains via Foucauldian notions of power and control.[4] This approach counters that of classicists concerned with literary evidence for the body, who are preoccupied with embodiments of sexuality and representation, or the body as a locus for theorization, in preference to the (re)construction of individual identities and bodily experiences in any lived or corporeal sense.[5] I think that the former approach is potentially dangerous. Some of the assumptions underlying recent studies of the human body in antiquity still imply binary and dichotomous (one might say Foucauldian) notions of sex-typing, with masculinity located in the ascendancy of the mind over bodily or emotional experience. There is a danger that current work on the body in antiquity will maintain this typically androcentric, externalized separation of mind, body and emotions. Within the field of classics and ancient history, the current scholarly interest in mapped and elaborated treatments of the body may reflect the post-modern aesthetic of surface, while perpetuating a separation from the body and the identity of the individual.

The papyri from Roman Egypt are a useful corpus of data for avoiding this perpetuation of binarism and duality. Papyri are uniquely informative in locating human bodies, because they are about real people in real environments, about real bodies moving through space, growing, touching, eating, having sex: a panorama of the diversity of bodily experience. Papyri provide plenty of evidence for the experiential, inhabited dimension of the body. For instance, they document the range of practices involving cultural work on the male body available in Roman Egypt, such as circumcision, hair-cutting and shaving during *rites de passage* (see Montserrat 1996, 36–41). At their best, they can enable the historian to construct personal narratives about the male body. To explore the usefulness of this data for my project, I will concentrate here on two types of male body in the papyrus texts: the slave and the free.

Slavish male bodies

At the provincial town of Oxyrhynchos in middle Egypt sometime in the first century AD, two men called Apion and Epimachos procured a little slip

154

of papyrus only ten centimetres square and wrote, in very bad Greek, a curious letter to a third man, Epaphroditos. Presumably they knew him quite well, because Epimachos used the familiar short form of his name, Epimas, in the greeting. They peppered their letter with the phraseology of an official edict, giving a flavour of satire to their words, but also an air of portentousness and command. In the margin, they added a rough drawing, which they labelled. Then they blotted the letter, folded it up into a tiny packet and addressed it: 'deliver to the best beloved Epaphroditos'. One can only guess at the reaction of Epaphroditos when he opened the letter and read (or had read to him) the following proposition:

Apion and Epimas proclaim to their best beloved Epaphroditos that if you allow us to bugger (*pugizein*) you it will go well for you, and we will not thrash you any longer if you allow us to bugger you. Farewell.

(P. Oxy. XLII 3070)

After reading this, maybe Epaphroditos glanced at the cartoon in the margin – and then looked again (see Fig. 7.1).

It is easy to imagine him turning the letter round in an effort to make it out. The original editor of this text, in 1972, noted that 'a primitive drawing in the margin clarifies (without real necessity) their intentions'. In fact, the drawing seems to contain a deliberate ambiguity, which the label reflects. The upper word reads *psōle*, 'hard-on', and the lower two words *kai phikis*, 'and arse'. There are several ways of interpreting the drawing. Maybe it is supposed to represent both these foci of male homosexual desire at once. If one examines the drawing closely, it would be difficult to say whether one is looking at the exposed glans of an erect penis with an exaggerated meatus seen from above, or a pair of schematized buttocks with an exaggerated anus. Alternatively, a more spatial reading is possible. The words 'hard-on' and 'arse' taken in conjunction with the drawing in between them, may be an attempt to represent Epimachos' and Apion's fantasy of taking Epaphroditos orally and rectally.

Why Apion and Epimachos decided to write down in this way their desire for Epaphroditos is puzzling. On the surface their letter would seem to be little more than a piece of more-or-less playful fantasizing, on a level with the sexual graffiti on the wall of a public lavatory. Other vernacular homosexual texts from elsewhere in the Roman world play around with image and text in a similar way to the letter. 'Here I fucked my sea-going chum up the mouth and arse', wrote a man on the wall of a building thought to be a male brothel at Ostia. He emphasized what he had done in bed with the man by drawing a puckered anus in the u of 'fucked' (Latin *futui*). In the Roman world, as now, a *ménage à trois* was a regular male homosexual fantasy. Another graffito scrawled on the walls of the same building in Ostia even

Figure 7.1 P. Oxy. 3070
Source: Reproduced by courtesy of the Committee of the Egypt Exploration Society

records a threesome with another man called Epaphroditos.[6] It is possible that the Epaphroditos from Oxyrhynchos was a prostitute; it is also possible that the letter is meant somehow to injure him, in the same way that graffiti say 'so-and-so is gay' with an intent to hurt. However, I believe that this letter is an expression of private desire, and that if it is considered in more detail, this ephemeral wish caught on papyrus speaks eloquently about some aspects of the construction and experience of the male body in Græco-Roman Egypt.

One of the most illuminating features about the papyrus is the name of the recipient, Epaphroditos ('charming'), which is almost invariably a slave name in Egypt.[7] Ancient slave names sometimes tend towards the cute, especially if the slave turns out to be physically attractive. Apion and Epimachos, on the other hand, are never attested as the names of slaves. The circumstantial evidence suggests that Epaphroditos was, or had been, a slave; and this is important for decoding the ancient sexual protocols which underlie this letter. For much of antiquity, sanctionable homosexual acts were usually based on inequality: you are not supposed to desire somebody of the same age and status category as yourself. Therefore younger men and slaves are fair game, particularly your own slaves, who are your passive human property. This disparity of power is acted out in the sexual roles played. Within such a system, 'real' men are defined as impenetrable penetrators, and therefore the only role suitable for an adult male is to be active: to be the passive partner would be womanish and inferior. Free men sacrifice their 'real' man status if they submit to penetration, for instance if they prostitute themselves. It seems to me that the sexual scenario conjured up by the letter and the drawing fits this model of relationships well. Epimachos and Apion seek to dominate sexually the socially subordinate Epaphroditos by penetrating him, whether singly or both at the same time. Their power over him is underscored by the juxtaposition of beating and buggery. Beating is almost an analogue to penetration, because it is invasive and therefore demeaning, and thus it also enforces the distinction between slave and free. The original editor of the papyrus assigned it the title of an 'indecent proposal', but in fact the letter contains little in the way of a proposal, which implies some element of mutuality and consent. Although Apion and Epimachos may have phrased their sexual needs jocularly, their desire for Epaphroditos is not a proposal between equals for mutual pleasure, but a demand for the use of a subject body backed up by the threat of violence and degradation.

So much for the usage of the slave body: what about its physical appearance?[8] The bodies of slaves are described in several papyrus documents,[9] which illustrate two general points about these documentary bodies. First, as a rule the only detailed descriptions of bodies in the papyri are of either slaves or people who have been the victims of violence (the latter discussed below). This suggests to me that the only time it was appropriate to talk about a body in its entirety was when it was a passive object: i.e. either somebody who had been assaulted and needed to have their injuries assessed to get appropriate reparation, or a slave, who somatically is in a permanent and given state of passivity and subjection.

Second, the papyri describe free and slave bodies differently when functioning in the same situations, thus emphasizing their qualitative difference. This is illustrated by a type of document usually known to papyrologists as 'orders to arrest'.[10] These are brief chits requesting local policemen to arrest an individual who has been accused of some crime and take him to be questioned, often from a village to a provincial capital. I quote a couple of representative examples:

To the chief policeman (*archephodos*) of the village of Theadelphia. Send up immediately Sarapion son of Sabinos and Harphaisis his brother on the accusation of Diodoros Didas.

(SB XVIII 14014)

To the archephodos of Mermertha. Send Eros the wine-merchant on the accusation of Dioskoros.

(P. Oxy. XXXI 2576)

The free people being arrested here are passive objects, to be taken away, deprived of their freedom and perhaps punished: in a sense, they manifest slavish traits. Yet the arrest warrants give no physical descriptions of these individuals at all, merely stating their names, patronyms and sometimes occupations without mentioning their bodies. Documents which aim to apprehend fugitive slaves, however, go into much more detail about the appearance of the runaways. Apart from their very vividness and poignancy about how these subject individuals wore their own bodies, they are informative about some perceived somatic norms and the differences between the slavish and the free body. In a sense, they can be read as another form of the ancient interest in self-definition through opposition. I have already mentioned how the physical body of the slave was radically other to that of the free person, while at the same time being potentially the same. The unflattering descriptions of runaway slaves seem to express the tension implicit in this paradoxical somatic difference.

The most detailed of these word portraits is found in a third century AD document from Oxyrhynchos, which may be the actual notice which was publicly posted. The fugitive, whose name is lost, is described as

an Egyptian from the village of Chenres in the Arthribite nome, utterly ignorant of Greek, tall, skinny, clean-shaven, with a [small] wound on the left side of the head, honey-complexioned, rather pale, with a wispy beard – in fact, with no hair at all to his beard – smooth-skinned, narrow in the jaws, long-nosed. By trade a weaver, he swaggers around as if he were someone of note, chattering in a shrill voice. He is about 32 years old.

(P. Oxy. LI 3617)

Naturally some of the bodily details are included here for entirely practical purposes, but there may be a sub-text to their inclusion. Because he is a slave, this anonymous slave cannot be a 'real man', and the adjectives applied to his body serve both to set him physically apart and render him ridiculous. He is ugly and beardless. His beardlessness perhaps marks him out as potentially penetrable, since the visible growth of facial hair is one of the demarcators in the ancient world of being masculine and unavailable for penetration. His lack of beard also renders him infantile, although 32 years old; and like a child he goes around jabbering away as though he has delusions of grandeur. This is a very common collocation in the ancient world – free children lose their infantile status with maturation, but slaves do not, at least as long as they remain slaves, hence the designation *pais*.[11]

Similarly conceived but less extreme descriptions are found in other 'wanted' notices:

> If any person has found a slave called Philippos . . . about 14 years old, pale-skinned, badly-spoken (*psellon*) . . . wearing a thick woollen tunic and a used shoulder-belt, he should [deliver him] at army HQ and receive [. . .].
>
> (P. Oxy. LI 3616)

Psellon may mean again that Philippos cannot speak Greek very well, or that he has a speech impediment. The fact that he is pale-skinned (*leukochrōs*), a rare descriptor in the papyri, may indicate that he is of foreign origin. Another document, registering the sale of the slave Prokopton also known as Aptos, gives an idea of his appearance on the day that he was sold at Oxyrhynchos in June 265 AD. He was 'aged about 42, white-skinned, slightly flat-faced, with scanty eyebrows, short-nosed, scars on the left forehead and eyebrow and jawbone, slight squint' (P. Oxy. XLII 3054). Prokopton is less unflatteringly described than Philippos and the man from Arthribis, perhaps because he is not a runaway; and the mention of his numerous scars evokes a real man's body after a lifetime of hard work and probably hard knocks.

I read these detailed, objectifying descriptions of male slaves as concomitants of their servile status: they are passive objects that can be enumerated in the same intimate terms as a piece of property, terms that would be inappropriately objectifying for a free person. Furthermore, these word-portraits are couched in the language of passivity, subjection and infantilization, traits which mark the men out as slaves and therefore potential victims of violence, of whatever sort. They are all part of an ancient visual rhetoric of slavery which, however illogically, assumed a physical difference between the free and the servile.

Free bodies

The bodies of free men receive a very different treatment in the documentary papyri. The only men whose bodies are the subject of descriptions are those who have been subjected to violence. The context is usually a report written by the public physician (*dēmosios iatros*) ordered by a civic official to examine the injuries of somebody who has been beaten up and has lodged an official complaint against the attacker.[12] Thus on 14 June AD 331, the public doctors Theoninos, Heron, Silvanos and Didymos reported to Flavius Julianus, the *logistēs* (= *curator*) of Oxyrhynchos:

> We were instructed . . . in response to a petition handed in by Aurelios Paesios, son of Senenuphis, of the village of Pela, to examine his condition and make a written report. Whereupon we examined the man on a bunk in the public office building; he had gashes on the right side of his head [. . .] of the membrane and a swelling on the right side of his forehead and a contusion with a skin wound on his left fore-arm, and a slight contusion on the right forearm.
>
> (P. Oxy. XLIV 3195.31–49)

Another doctor's report from Oxyrhynchos, dated AD 316, describes a similar train of events. This papyrus is unfortunately too damaged to give a consecutive translation, but its general gist is clear. The *dēmosios iatros* Aurelios Apion son of Herodotos was summoned by the *logistēs* to examine the injuries of the guard Moueis. He found him bedridden (*klinērēs*) with, among many other injuries, two wounds on his crown, others to the right side of his head and the left temple, swellings and bruises on his left ear, a wound on the right shoulder-blade, his right hand crushed and swollen as far as the middle finger, swellings and contusions on his left hand, and wounds from blows (*trōseis*) to other parts of his body (P. Oxy. VI 983 = SB III 6003).

Here the emphasis lies on one aspect of the man's body – the wounds that rendered him passive and vulnerable, only able to fight back bureaucratically. The image of the doctors finding the injured men Paesios and Moueis lying prostrate and helpless on a bed, and the enumeration of the defence wounds inflicted on their arms and hands as they tried to ward off blows to the head, stress the passivity and powerlessness of the victims' bodies. Beating was degrading, as was the inability to repulse an attacker, and the wounded male body in these contexts seems almost to be deprived of its masculinity, if that was defined in terms of activity rather than passivity. The ministrations of the doctors perhaps underscored the feelings of disempowerment the men were already experiencing. As well as general physical examinations, the medical reports describe the doctors probing individual wounds, penetrating the body. One report details how the doctor Gaius Menecius Valerianus found fragments of the missile that had caused a patient's injury embedded in a deep head wound.[13]

Such detailed evocations of the male body, with their sharp focus on body parts, are responses to exceptional circumstances. Elsewhere in the documentary papyri, virtually the only pictures of men's bodies that occur are in the subscriptions to official documents by the male witnesses.[14] These men are usually summed up by a series of stock epithets focusing on particular physical features, usually facial, while ignoring others. Presumably, these fragmented descriptors would have been enough to conjure up rough pictures of standard types, in the same sort of somatic shorthand that is used in contemporary 'lonely hearts' advertisements. This very general evocation is then personalized by listing identifying marks, almost always scars on parts of the body that are visible when clothed, especially the facial features.[15] Scars do not seem to have had any semiotic charge other than as functional markers of individuality.[16] They certainly do not carry the same sort of high-status connotations as, for example, duelling scars did in nineteenth century Germany. Typical are the subscriptions to a will witnessed at Oxyrhynchos in AD 130. These give the names of the male witnesses and the locations of their scars, and state, as further proof of identity, the image engraved on their personal seal-stones:

> I, Apion son of Zoilos, have witnessed . . . I am aged 44, with a scar under the chin, and my seal-stone is an image of Sarapis . . . I, Apollonios son of Asklepiades, from the same city, have witnessed . . . I am aged 70, with a scar by the outside corner of the right eye, and my seal-stone is an image of Hermes.
>
> (P. Oxy. III 492.18–24, excerpted)

In other texts the images of the signatories become standardized to the extent that the scar becomes the only signifier of individuality: for example, the scribe of a manumission document written in AD 86 described all the parties to it as having the routine honey-coloured complexion and long face and being of medium height, but left gaps to fill in the details of their scars (P. Oxy. XXXVIII 2843). Here the scar has become a sort of mnemonic for the individual.

Ptolemaic period documents in Greek tend to go into greater detail and employ multiple body descriptors more than Roman texts. These adjectives occur in a regular order of height, complexion, hair, shape of face, followed by any other distinguishing features, usually scars or peculiarities of the eyes, so that one moves in on the subject gradually, from far away to close up. For instance, Panas son of Pates appears in a document of 100 BC as 'aged 45, medium height, honey-coloured, straight-haired, broad-faced, straight-nosed, with a scar under the right eye, and sparsely bearded'. (P. Adl. G 13. 2. 5) A description of this complexity would be unusual later on, when people are generally reduced to a more or less standard combination of complexion with head shape. In contrast, documents in the indigenous Egyptian language, Demotic, very rarely delineate the parties at all, perhaps through traditional usage rather than because the participants were less 'body aware'.

These physical designations were probably applied by the scribe writing the text as the parties sat in front of him, rather than by the individuals themselves. Therefore how somebody is imaged would have depended on how a scribe interpreted the stock descriptive epithets in terms of the man before him, rather than giving any idea of how that person conceptualized his own body. However, these standard epithets do provide an idea of the hierarchy of body parts and features, with eyes, hair and cranial shape each conveying differing amounts of information about the person.

Apart from those referring to beards, the same set of adjectives is applied to women and men. Hair colour is rarely alluded to, unless gray; presumably most people had various shades of dark hair which was not distinctive enough to be a useful determinant in itself (as the Roman mummy portraits suggest). Instead, the extent of hair or its texture is remarked upon. Men are 'straight-haired' (*tetanos*),[17] 'curly-haired' (*klastos* or *klastothrix*),[18] 'with balding forehead' (*anaphalontos* or *anaphalakros*)[19] and 'wispy-bearded' (*spanopōgōn* or *kakopōgōn*) (e.g. P. Tebt. III 814. 27). Even more important are the eyes, and the rich vocabulary used to describe them indicates their symbolic importance in 'a world in which the scrutiny of one's fellow man was not an idle pastime but an essential survival skill' (Gleason 1990, 389). As with hair, their colour does not seem to have been very important, although some people are referred to as being 'light-eyed' (*glaukos* or *charopos*). Instead, adjectives referring to the eyebrows,[20] the shape of the eyes or eye defects are much more common – the last an uncomfortable reminder of how prevalent eye diseases were (and still are) in a climate like that of Egypt. There are individuals who are 'rather short-sighted' (*hyposkniphos*) (e.g. SB XII 10859), 'one-eyed' (*monophthalmos*) (e.g. P. Brux. I 10. 21), with squints (e.g. PSI XIV 1402. 16) and cataracts,[21] and many who are blind (*typhlos*).[22] Other than the hair and eyes, the main general foci are the head and face, concentrating on the shade of the complexion and the shape of face. Two sets of adjectives are frequently juxtaposed to describe people. A person can be 'honey-coloured' and 'long-faced', or 'round-faced' (*strongyloprosōpon*) and *melanchrōs*, probably meaning 'dark-skinned' or 'swarthy': one is reminded of the 'brown and blue' collocation of the modern lonely hearts column. The extent to which 'the Egyptians carefully distinguished themselves from their darker Nubian and Ethiopian neighbours' (Cameron 1990, 288) is not easy to assess. The documents use a restricted range of complexion vocabulary, but then one might not expect there to be many southerners among the document-writing classes in the provincial cities. By the same token, pale individuals are not often encountered, and are usually foreigners or slaves. Other people have various degrees of ruddiness, denoted by the adjectives *pyrrhakēs*, *hypopyrrhos* and *epipyrrhos*. There are occasional face-shape variants such as *koilogeneios*, 'with a receding chin'. Noses are usually straight (*euthyrin*) or snub (*simos*).

The rest of the body does not really come into these descriptions other than as a locus for scars. A vague indication of height is given, usually that the person is middle-sized (*mesos*), and occasionally men are said to be well-proportioned (*eumegethos*). Pleasing body proportions were an important preoccupation of ancient physiognomic writers (Evans 1969, 40). There are some instances in a related group of documents of the adjective *hypoklastos* (e.g. P. Adl. Gl. 1. 9), possibly to be translated as 'somewhat stooping', but more probably meaning 'wavy-haired'. Sensory abnormalities are occasionally referred tó, including people who are deaf (*anaudos*) and dumb. Aberrant whole bodies, such as dwarves, do not appear, though this should not necessarily be read as revulsion towards the imperfectly formed.[23]

Conclusion

The male body in the papyrus texts, whether slavish or free, is a fragmented one. For the purpose of documentary descriptions, it is broken up into parts; but it is unclear what overall body picture, if any, the parts would have evoked to the readers of those documents. And would a description of a document witness as being *melichrōs* and *makroprosōpos* and wearing a seal-ring of Sarapis, really have been helpful if it was necessary to track him down when the document he had witnessed was disputed? Perhaps standard collocations like *melichrōs* and *makroprosōpos* were enough to evoke a mental picture of a prevalent physical type, which was then individualized by noting details like scarring. By contrast, male slave bodies receive very much closer attention to their constitutent parts, and these physical details could be utilized if the slaves became fugitives. Overall, the papyrus documentation recalls the paradoxical pairs of Bryan Turner's description of the social body as 'at once the most solid, the most elusive, illusory, concrete, metaphorical, ever present and ever distant thing . . . a site, an instrument, an environment, a singularity and a multiplicity' (Turner 1984, 8). The male body in Roman Egypt, free or slavish, determined the social self and social location; it formed male identity within the world beyond.

Acknowledgements

I would like to thank Lin Foxall and John Salmon for their great editorial patience; Terry Wilfong, who first suggested to me the idea of the documentary body; and Mike Davis, Lynn Meskell and Jonathan Walters, who all suggested interesting approaches to the papyrological data. All references to papyrological publications follow the abbreviations suggested by Oates 1992.

Notes

1 On masculinity and body hair, see Gleason 1990.
2 On *pais* as a slave designation at Athens, see below, n. 11.
3 See for instance Keith Hopkins in the *Times Literary Supplement*, 18 October 1996, 6, who calls them 'dead documents' which give only the illusion of dealing

with real individuals. For a discussion of what kind of history to write with documentary papyri, see Bagnall 1995, 2–8, 108–17.

4 For bibliography, and an excellent summary of post-processual archaeological theory's relevance to the ancient body, see Meskell 1996.

5 The essays by Holt Parker and Sandra Joshel in Richlin 1992, 90–111 and 112–30 are good examples of this genre.

6 See Clarke 1991, 93 and nn. 17 and 19: 'All three of us, Agathopus and Primus and Epaphroditus, came at the same time'. All-male threesomes also figure in erotic epigrams, such as *Palatine Anthology* 12. 155, 210.

7 For Epaphroditos as slave name, see BGU II 493 ii.6; BGU IV 1112.5; O. Wilck. 1482.1; P. Gen. II 62.32; P. Hamb. I 4.16; P. Lond. II 261.56 (p. 55), re-edited with a new fragment in SPP IV pp. 63–78, lines 56, 178, 300, 306, 315, 329, 361; P. Lond. II 280 (p. 193); P. Oslo III 111a.25; P. Oxy. III 475.21 *et seq.*; P. Ross. Georg. II 26.2; P. Sarap. 79e 2.2; SB VI 9017 nr. 30. Nero also had a freedman called Epaphroditos (Suetonius, *Nero* 49. 3. 10; Tacitus, *Annals* 15. 55. 4).

8 On this question generally in the Roman world, see Bradley 1994, 141–4.

9 See P. Paris 10 (= UPZ 121 = Sel. Pap. II 243) and P. Lond. VII 2052 for some interesting Ptolemaic descriptions of slaves, unfortunately beyond the time range of this paper.

10 For discussion and bibliography of these texts, see the introduction to P. Oxy. LXI 4114.

11 Golden 1984, 309–11 and nn. 7–13. The description of the slave in P. Oxy. LI 3617 is reminiscent of the descriptions of Egyptians in Juvenal 1. 26–9; 15. 31–2, 124–8.

12 For doctors' official reports on injured people, see P. Oxy. XXXI 2563, n. 27: add P. Oxy XLIV 3195; P. Oxy. XLV 3245 and the references given there; P. Oxy. LIV 3729; P. Athen. 34. For injured women, see P. Mich. V 228 and P. Oxy. LI 3620.

13 BGU II 647.21–6 from Karanis in the Fayyum, dated 22 August AD 130.

14 On these descriptions, see Hasebroek 1921; Caldara 1924; Evans 1969, 39–40.

15 Instead of scars, the marks of voluntary bodily modification are occasionally used, such as pierced ears on men (e.g. BGU X 1971; P. Adl. 5, 12, 15, 17; P. Ryl. IV 581; PSI IX 1016; P. Strass. II 87) or tattoos (e.g. BGU VI 1258, P. Lond. VII 2052), perhaps indicating cultic affiliation. The rarity of references to such permanent modifications suggests that they must have been quite unusual and were perhaps culturally problematic, since pierced ears for men were an indication of foreignness, and tattoos usually indicated slavish status, for which see Jones 1987.

16 Elsewhere in the Roman world, scars could have quite different connotations: see Leigh 1995, 200–2. Bagnall 1993, 187 suggests that by the late antique period scars may have acquired connotations of lower status.

17 For example, BGU VI 1258 passim; P. Koln I 50. 20; P. Ryl. IV 586. 31.

18 For example, P. Ryl. IV 581. 7; PSI IX 1018. 10.

19 For example, BGU X 1971; SB XII 10859.

20 For example, P. Lond. VII 2052, SB III 7169. 21 and P. Fuad I Univ. App. II 120, where the individuals have eyebrows that meet in the middle (*sunophrun*).

21 For example, SB X 10571. 4; P. Berl. Frisk. I 22. 17; P. Ant. III 187 fr. a. 11.

22 For example, P. Corn. 22. 3. 73; P. Köln IV 198. 7; P. Mich IV 223–5 passim.

23 Dwarves in Egypt had positive religious connotations: see Dasen 1993, 145–59. Physical disability does not seem to have limited induction into élite civic groups for males: see Tod 1951, 95–6 and Montserrat 1996, 39 for discussion.

8

Imperial cult: engendering the cosmos

Susan Fischler

Following Octavian's success in 31 BC against M. Antonius and Cleopatra at Actium, cities throughout the Greek East commemorated the first Roman emperor with divine honours. He was recognized as a god, and the Greeks set up fully functioning cults, with priesthoods and festivals conducted in his name. By 29 BC, that is, within a two year period, large numbers of Greek cities had instituted some form of imperial cult, while the Roman provinces of Asia and Bithynia had established provincial cults with associated temples, priesthoods and games.[1] The implementation was so rapid that there are few doubts of the willing participation of the Greeks in its conception. Some scholars have even suggested quite plausibly that the main impetus for instituting such honours came from the cities themselves, not from the imperial authorities.[2]

The best analysis of the development of the imperial cult in the Greek world is undoubtedly Price's work (1984a) on the functioning of the cult in Asia Minor. He postulates that by deifying emperors and members of the imperial family the Greek cities made Roman power comprehensible in their own terms: they incorporated a foreign emperor into their power structures by making him a part of the main symbolic system of the city. Thus, imperial cult was about the nature of power, and to reword shamelessly Nicole Loraux's observation (1990, 25), 'in the Greek world of war [and politics], power is in essence and by definition virility'.[3] Masculine power lay at the core of imperial ideology, and hence notions of masculinity were fundamental to the way in which the power of the emperor was understood.

Yet even a brief review of the extensive epigraphic and archaeological remains for the cult in the East attests vividly to the widespread deification of the women of the imperial family, in ways which unite these women with some of the most powerful images in Graeco–Roman culture. Only by defining ancient ideas of masculinity more precisely can we explain this phenomenon, and begin to understand how representations of women can help to construct and enhance images of men, even those who rule a vast empire.

Price (1984a, 162) briefly acknowledges the centrality of the imperial family to the operation of the cults:

The stability of imperial rule was perceived to lie in the transmission of power within the imperial family and, in consequence, considerable importance was attached to the whole imperial house. . . . The empire was in the hands of the family.

This would account for some consideration being paid to the female members of the family, but not necessarily for the frequency and authority of the portrayal.[4] Price's analysis provides an essential understanding of the function of these cults in Greek society, but does not directly address these issues.

The extent and nature of the problem can easily be illustrated with three sets of related evidence which will be referred to again later in the discussion.

First: at Ankyra in Phrygia, there is evidence of a cult established to the divine Augusti (*theoi Sebastoi*) who are altarsharers (*homobōmioi*) and whose cult is tended by a priest and priestess appointed from amongst the local élite:

[The *boulē* and the *dēmos* of Ankyra honour] . . . the crownbearer and president of the games and priest for ten years of the altar-sharing divine Augusti . . . [5]

Further epigraphic evidence attests that these deities were the emperor Augustus and his wife Livia.[6] Ankyra was not alone in pairing these two under the umbrella title of *theoi Sebastoi*: throughout Asia Minor, inscriptions and coins often refer specifically to either Livia and Augustus or the later emperor Claudius and his wife Agrippina in this way.[7] There was also a cult of the *homobōmioi theoi Sebastoi* at nearby Aizanoi. Significantly, this cult was probably established when Aizanoi was granted an official neocorate by the *koinon* of Asia, suggesting the cult had received the support of the *koinon*.[8] Furthermore, such 'official' cults were normally approved by the Senate and the emperor at Rome, and to some extent were overseen by the governor of Asia (Price 1984a, 66–7). Although the institution of equal honours to both the emperor and his wife was unusual (and, it should be noted, was probably created after the emperor's death), it was clearly not regarded as an extreme or unacceptable form of worship.

Second: the island of Lesbos was particularly fulsome in its honours to imperial women, some of whom, unusually, had established personal ties with the *koinon* of Lesbos during extended stays on the island.[9] The city of Mytilene identified many imperial women with the cult of a leading mother goddess of the region, a deity called *thea Aiolis karpophoros* (the divine Aeolian fruitbearer).[10] For example, one inscription refers to M. Granius

Carbo as 'the *hypogymnasiarch* of the divine Sebasta Aeolian fruitbearing Agrippina [the Younger]' (*IG* xii. 2. 258 = *IGR* iv. 100). Other examples have been found of divine dedications including inscriptions to 'Julia, daughter of Caesar, Venus Genetrix' (*IGR* iv. 9) and to 'Julia Agrippina, wife of Augustus, the new goddess Augusta of the Council, eternal gynasiarch'.[11] As the administrative centre for the *koinon*, Mytilene also celebrated cultic rites in honour of Livia in her guise as Sebasta Hera (found on an altar in the gymnasium), and included both Livia and Octavia, Octavian/Augustus' sister and M. Antonius' wife, in the local festival of Hestia.[12] Flowing tributes to the imperial women as mother goddesses were an established norm throughout the Greek East. Moreover, it was not uncommon for them to receive individual cultic honours at the same time as the emperor. Although Mytilene was unusually generous in its granting of divine honours, the city's commemorative acts remain illustrative of the practice in general.[13]

Third: at Aphrodisias, at the Sebasteion or temple dedicated to the Augusti, a series of relief panels along the south portico illustrate the perceived relationship between the imperial family and the Greek world.[14] The temple complex, started under Tiberius, was mainly constructed under Claudius and finished during the early years of Nero's reign. Two panels include the empress Agrippina the Younger. One which includes the emperor Claudius will be discussed below. The second (Fig. 8.1) depicts the young Nero in military uniform being crowned with a civica corona by his mother Agrippina.[15] As the wife of the (dead) divine Augustus, she is apparently seen here as passing on the authority of the state.[16]

In some ways these examples are unusual, as there is more evidence for cult practices surviving from these sites than many others, but they do illustrate the type and range of practices which were typical in this period before cult honours became more standardised.[17] All three of these sites demonstrate the centrality of the women to the imagery and practice of imperial cult in the Greek East. In fact, Price's work carries as its appendix a catalogue of sites containing evidence for imperial cult in Asia Minor (1984a, 249–74), and fully two-thirds of the sites that he notes also contain evidence for deification of female family members.[18] This significantly outweighs the evidence for male members of the family besides the emperor, including that for a cult to the established heirs (although ascertaining exact numbers is somewhat problematic). It is evident that the image of imperial women was central to the way in which the Greeks thought about the emperor himself.

At first, this may not even seem problematical, but if masculinity was a key component in the Greeks' understanding of power, the image presented by the women in these cults is at least curious, if not contradictory. One thing remains clearly consistent: the emperor was presented as the ultimate patriarchal figure. Within the cities, he is most frequently identified as Zeus Sebastos, the Augustan father of the gods (Price 1984b, 85–6). In inscriptions, his control of the state is seen as essential to the maintenance of order,

Figure 8.1 Agrippina crowns Nero
Source: Photo: New York University Excavations at Aphrodisias

and his actions as well as his inclusion in civic cults make him the leading citizen of all cities. Thus we have inscriptions such as the first decree issued by the *koinon* of Asia in 9 BC:

168

Whereas Providence which divinely ordered our lives has, with zeal and munificence, arranged the most perfect good for life by producing Augustus, whom she has filled with virtue for mankind's benefit, sending us and our descendants a saviour who brought war to an end and set all things in order; and since Caesar [Augustus], with his appearance, exceeded the hopes of all those who had anticipated good tidings before us, not only surpassing those who had been benefactors before him, but not even leaving any hope of surpassing him for those who are to come in the future . . .

(*TDGR* iv. 101. vi)

The characteristics depicted in this description are essentially those of the outstanding male authority figure: militarily dominant, benevolent ruler and the supreme benefactor of the state. Augustus had become the ultimate father and the ultimate citizen of every city.

It is exactly this core image of the patriarchal ruler which appears threatened by the image of the imperial women seen above. Within Graeco–Roman ideology, a male citizen's authority rested in his dominance over his extended household. Female relatives who acted with restraint and respect were an essential part of a leader's public persona (even if only because their passivity ensured that their names were not mentioned in public).[19] Those (male) citizens who could not control their women risked losing their control over the state, i.e. they lose one of the elements essential for their masculinity. Thus, Aristotle, for example, postulates that the Spartan constitution was fatally weak because it allowed women too much influence in public affairs (*Politics* 2. 1269 b 12). To maintain a patriarchal image, the emperor had to appear firmly in control of his household, and thus fit and able to rule the empire.

Yet the examples cited above show the leading female figure in the state sharing divine honours with the emperor (admittedly, while the wife or mother often did share honours, usually there are indications that she was the lesser god).[20] In the case of the relief panel from Aphrodisias, we have what seems to be a representation of the imperial mother transmitting power to her son. If any of these images were indeed revolutionary or simply threatened to embarrass the régime, they would not have been chosen by the cities as a means of honouring the emperor. Both the male and female images must have been deemed by the Greeks to have been a desirable way of characterizing the régime and they would have believed them to be acceptable to the Romans.[21] So what accounts for the prominence of the imperial women and these powerful images of female authority?[22]

The Hellenistic cities did commemorate women from within their own cities: there are some well known examples of élite women holding civic offices and performing acts of civic euergetism, who also received public recognition.[23] Van Bremen (1983) notes that civic benefactions were

169

associated with male members of the élite and were normally calculated to maintain male élite authority and privilege within the polis. She suggests that, rather than being a sign of independent authority, the patronal acts of these women were seen as being a part of the extended activities of their male family members, and thus did not violate gender roles or social institutions.

This practice provides a possible model for interpreting the honours granted to imperial women. However, the circumstances were profoundly different. The élite women were themselves citizens of the communities which commemorated them. In contrast, the imperial women rarely made any direct or indirect contact with most of these cities. The vast majority of evidence for commemoration comes from areas far removed even from the path which imperial family members took when traversing the East on diplomatic missions. Therefore, these women as individuals were by and large unknown to the communities that so honoured them (Lesbos can be seen as the exception that proves the rule).[24] Furthermore, it is clear from the nature of imperial honours that the *exempla* which the Greeks must have been drawing on were divine in nature and based on local religious practices. So, the role of élite women in civic euergetism might well provide some insight into the activities of imperial women, but it does little to account for their incorporation into the symbolic language of the polis through the implementation of the imperial cult.[25]

The obvious precursors to the imperial cult were the Hellenistic ruler cults which were established throughout the region, and which were also predominantly introduced from below, i.e. by the cities themselves. Yet many scholars have argued that the imperial cult cannot be regarded as simply an extension of this earlier form of worship. The limitations of this argument have been set out succinctly by Price in his study of the imperial cult (1984a, 25–40) and more briefly by Millar (1984b, especially 53–4), who emphasizes the greater scale of the imperial cult in contrast to the earlier ruler cults. Moreover, although the cities were themselves the main instigators in establishing these cults, as they were with the later imperial cult, they usually commemorated the divinity of their ruler only after that king had provided some specific service to the community. Royal intervention could come in the form of, say, financial or military assistance to the city in question.[26]

Hellenistic queens were often included in the commemorative honours accorded by the cities in a way quite similar to the imperial women, that is, they received epithets associated with local deities, festivals and statues. However, there are still major differences: they, too, often appear to have been involved in some specific act of euergetism that was being recognized with gratitude by the community.[27] Moreover, the range, number and frequency of honours is not generally as great as those accorded to the Roman empresses. So, although there are recognizable similarities between the cults, earlier practice alone cannot account for the ways in which the Roman women were included in cult worship.[28] Furthermore, it must be remembered that, in general, precedents are not an explanation of a social practice. Continuity does, however, suggest that the practice performed a significant function within society and that the activity is an inherent part of the collective ideology.

Another approach to the problem would be to accept at face value the evidence for the extraordinary status of the imperial women, and, using Price's work as an analogy, to analyse this evidence as if these women were themselves equivalent in status, importance and power to the emperors. One could argue that given, say, Livia's predominance within the imperial family, it is perhaps not surprising that she should receive full cultic honours, as cities attempted to come to terms with her place in civic power structures.[29] This interpretation is too simplistic: there is little evidence at any time that the women were seen as equal in authority to the emperors, either at Rome or in the provinces. Although the Julio–Claudian princesses could be seen as powerful figures who were active in the régime, this would only have a strong impact on those who were aware of the ins and outs of political events and power plays at Rome. In general, there is little indication that contemporary Roman events or gossip had any effect on the system of divine honours in the East.[30] Nothing accounts for such extraordinary honours being awarded to women whom people rarely, if ever, saw or contacted, and who held no individual significance for these cities, except and unless their inclusion in the cult was somehow essential to the depiction of the Roman emperor.[31]

In order to assess the significance of the imperial women for the Greeks, I examine (briefly) Roman Athens' representations of the imperial women, and the relief panels at Aphrodisias.

Roman Athens

Roman Athens was the most imperial of cities, both because the memory of the Athenian empire and Athenian supremacy was still alive in the first century, and also because the language of its civic space changed dramatically in this period as a result of Roman domination. The economy of the city had suffered greatly in the first century and this led to an increasing reliance on Roman money for new buildings and civic amenities. The resulting architecture throughout the city can be seen as a symbolic expression of Roman military, economic and political supremacy. The nature of the imperial cult in the city was a visible extension of this domination.[32]

The evidence for the cult at Athens ranges from a temple and stoa to public decrees and private dedications. Despite the unusual quantity of evidence for divine honours to the imperial family, scholars can still only speculate as to the nature, practice and various locations of the cult at Athens.[33] Not only is it unclear if there was a separate Sebasteion; it must be highly questionable whether the extant material presents a coherent or complete account of the function and provisions of the cult here. With these caveats in mind, a brief overview of the relevant evidence for the early years of the Principate allows some conclusions to be drawn about the extent to which the deified imperial women were an essential feature of imperial worship, and how they were represented.

The Athenians had granted divine status to Roman leaders before the onset of the Principate. They had previously recognized the divinity of Julius Caesar, as well as M. Antonius, and even Octavia.[34] As early as 102/1 BC, a cult to the goddess *Rhōmē* existed in the city (Graindor 1927, 149–50). However, under Augustus, this worship expanded into a systematic ritualization of the relationship between the polis and the imperial family in Rome. Soon after 27 BC, a temple to *Rhōmē* and Augustus was erected on the Acropolis, to the east of the principal façade of the Parthenon, in accordance with Augustus' express wish that his cult be associated with that of Roma.[35] The cultic rituals of the city were altered over time: a Caesarea was instituted at an early date, while the great Augustan Panathenaia was probably introduced about the time of Claudius.[36]

As Shear describes, the open space of the ancient agora was slowly being filled by the expansion and adaptation of old buildings, and the construction of new ones associated with imperial rule (Shear 1981, 360–1). For example, an annex with two altars was added to the stoa which housed the cult of Zeus Eleutherios in the ancient Agora: evidence suggests the cult itself may have been altered to include the emperor Augustus and some of his family members (in such a case, it would be highly unusual if Livia were not included, at least after Augustus' death).[37] C. Caesar received a dedication as the new Ares, the temple of Ares having been moved to the agora in this period. Drusus Caesar, or possibly Augustus himself, was also a part of this cult.[38] Later, Claudius was worshipped here as Apollo Patrōos, another important deity of the agora (*IG* ii² 3274).

The political hierarchy was thus replayed in the divine order, with the unchallenged superiority of the emperor as Zeus the patriarch, supported by an heir represented as Ares. His almighty power and domination was again represented and reinforced visibly by the temple on the Acropolis. Not unexpectedly, the male rulers are depicted throughout the city in many guises, but the dominant images are of conquerors and protectors. Thus the changes in the power structures in the city are mapped onto a changed symbolic order.

The image of the imperial women was superimposed onto this evolving landscape through their incorporation into the city's religious structures. Their inclusion in the divine honours granted to the dynasty occurred at an early date, even excepting the divine epithets given to Octavia. Livia also was acknowledged as *euergetis*, and her divinity was recognized in at least one private dedication to her.[39] She and Julia, her stepdaughter, were represented as deities associated with the goddess Hestia, with whom they shared a priestess.[40] Graindor suggests that architecturally the round tholos-style temple of Rome and Augustus on the Acropolis was deliberately evocative of the temple of Vesta (i.e. the Roman Hestia) in Rome. He adds that Hestia may have been worshipped in this temple as well. If so, it would have further emphasized the link between the imperial family and the goddess, and between the imperial capital and Athens (Graindor 1927, 153–5).

Given the women's identification with the goddess Hestia, they too might well have been included in the cult on the Acropolis, but it would be unusual for women not deified at Rome to be included in a temple to *Rhōmē kai Sebastos*.[41] If they too were worshipped on the Acropolis, then they were elevated to great heights within the civic pantheon, and thus would have had a highly visible and significant role in bonding the Athenians with the new imperial order. Even if this was not the case, the connection between the tholos temple, the goddess Hestia, and the combined priesthood of Hestia and the imperial women would have created a symbolic unity in which the imperial women were a crucial element. The emperors were represented as protectors of the city, but the women as Hestia were the guardians of the hearth, both of the city and of the individual *oikos*.

Other evidence also suggests that there was no simple correlation between emperors and state, imperial women and the *oikos*. A simple paradigm of male = public/female = private obscures many of the complexities and interactive elements of the divine order of the ancient Greek pantheon, let alone the altered system established with the imperial cult. Like Augustus, Livia was also worshipped in the agora. Evidence of her cult is provided by the following inscription found near the Bouleuterion: 'The *dēmos* and the *boulē* dedicate this to Julia Sebaste Artemis Boulaia, mother of Tiberius Caesar Sebastos'.[42]

Here Livia is assimilated into the cult of one of the major deities of the agora, Artemis Boulaia, closely associated with the council of the Areopagus. The cult was instituted sometime after AD 14, and, by implication, it was probably maintained in the Bouleuterion. The importance of the emperor, and by extension his family, being seen in many guises, mortal and immortal, throughout the city, has been stressed by Price (1984a, 170–207). Julia Sebaste Artemis Boulaia is probably yet another example of the imperial *mater familias* being linked with an important local female deity, as seen at Mytilene. But the fact that Artemis is female and therefore bound to be associated with a female imperial family member does not diminish the significance of the presence of the divine Livia in the council chamber.[43]

Inevitably, the imperial family was connected with the Roman agora, the new commercial centre of the city, donated to the city by Caesar, and financially supported by Augustus.[44] According to Hoff (1996), recent excavations adjacent to the Roman marketplace may have located the Sebasteion, thus accounting for the unusual quantity of evidence found there. For example, a statue base was found near the entry of the market dedicated to Livia as *Ioulia thea Sebastē Pronoia*.[45] This suggests that Livia may have had an official cult as Julia Pronoia, an epithet used of Athena,

173

both here and in her great cult at Delphi (*SEG* 27. 485). While her divine role was as a protector, in this case of financial transactions, here again she can not be seen as solely looking after the concerns of affairs in the *oikos*. In their divine aspects, the imperial women transcend any social codes or limitations which may have restricted the lives of ordinary women. Thus, we have further evidence of their powerful personae within Athenian society, and the Greek world at large.

Less evidence has survived for individual honours to imperial women after the Augustan period.[46] Of that which has, the most significant is for the development of the cult of the emperor Claudius' mother, Antonia. One inscription shows that a Tiberius Claudius Novius, son of Philinus, besides being the general of the hoplites four times, priest of Delian Apollo and president of the Augustan Panathenaia and Caesarea, was honoured as well with the distinction of being the high priest of Antonia Augusta. Antonia may also have had a priest to her as *thea Antonia*, who held a special seat in the Theatre of Dionysos, or possibly this is another reference to the priesthood Novius held (*IG* iii. 315, cf. 316). Either way, the importance of her priesthood can be judged by the eminence of the man who held it.

The imperial women were an integral part of Athens' dynastic worship and the city's evolving belief system. Yet no evidence suggests the possibility that any woman, even Livia, was worshipped for her own sake, independently of the rest of the ruling family, within the civic cult. As in the case of the inscription found outside the Bouleuterion, most dedications make explicit her relationship to the emperors: 'To the mother of Tiberius Caesar Sebastos' (see n. 42). In their various divine guises, these female deities present a powerful, but supporting cast, helping to link the divine emperor and patriarch with the most important aspects of civic and family life. Enough evidence survives to postulate that the general structure of the imperial cult at Athens fits, and helps to clarify, the pattern seen elsewhere.

Imperial women and the mother goddesses

At Athens, a major cult for the women was the one they shared with Hestia, goddess of the hearth.[47] For the image of the emperor as divine patriarch, this cult provided a necessary link between the imperial state and the *oikos*. Elsewhere in the East, this connection was strengthened by the identification of the imperial women with local mother goddesses, as at Mytilene. Most commonly, they were either acknowledged as having the attributes of specific mother goddesses or had their worship combined with the local cults of these deities. Imperial woman and goddess was a potent and popular combination, resulting in some very powerful representations of divine empresses.[48]

Although few individual sites produce as much evidence for the cult as Athens, there is a vast amount of evidence from the whole of the eastern empire, making it possible to draw some general conclusions about imperial cult practices within these communities. The most common assimilation for the early imperial women was with the goddess Demeter; the second most common was with Hera.[49] As Hera, the Julio–Claudian women obviously complemented the emperor's Zeus, and with later dynasties, it was this assimilation which became standard. The next most usual form of worship was to include the women in the cult of any female chief deity of the locality, e.g. under Nero, Agrippina the Younger was quite suitably identified with the great cult of Rhea, mother of Zeus, at Kos.[50] On the whole, these local deities also tend to be mother goddesses.

By pairing a deified mother with a divine patriarch, the Greeks added the key element of fertility to the imperial image. Here the women are not only protectors of the *oikos*, but also symbolic of all female bodies, representing fertility and the bearing of heirs. But the fertility represented would have been not just that of the partnership, the male and female deities, but also that of their empire. Thus the women were seen as depicting the prosperity of the Roman world. The image is also one of a reassuring stability: of the emperor's marriage and hence of the dynasty and the realm. Despite the real problem back at Rome of finding heirs and ensuring the succession of them, Hera and Demeter project an image that implies heirs will always be provided.

This depiction of the women as the protectors and perpetuators of both their own home and family, and the homes and families of the Greeks throughout the empire would have complemented and added an important dimension to the image of the emperor as citizen–god.[51] This helps to explain why the two most honoured women of the first Roman dynasty were Livia and Agrippina the Younger. Although both were prominent members of the imperial family for much longer than any other woman, longevity alone cannot account for this phenomenon, as it does not explain their increasing popularity over time.

Unusually, Livia's appeal outlasted her lifetime, with her prominence ensured by her inclusion in cults to her and Augustus as the founders of the dynasty (as in the case of Ankyra and Aizanoi in Phrygia, described above).[52] Also, her cult may have been re-invigorated at provincial level by her deification at Rome in AD 42.[53] Agrippina received few honours in the East during her brother's reign, although she was amply honoured as the emperor Claudius' wife.[54] However, after the accession of her son, when she too was the widow of one god and the mother of another, her place within the cult centres is much more frequently attested and her status is often greater than before.[55]

Thus the reason for their high profile relates to this key image of the women as mothers: no other women of the dynasty managed the double success of being not only the wife of the emperor but also the mother of an heir who successfully claimed the Principate. As a Lykian decree found at Tlos records:

[Livia] created the race of the Sebastoi in accordance with the most sacred succession of the *epiphaneis theoi*, a house incorruptible and immortal for all time . . . [56]

Just as her divine attributes were most often those of the fertility goddess, so this decree shows that Livia's greatest significance in the minds of provincial leaders was in her role as mother and founder of the house of the Caesars. Interestingly, the Roman authorities are known to have particularly promoted the commemoration of these two women as well, and I would like to suggest it was very likely for the same reason: both Greeks and Romans needed these characteristics to be attributed to an emperor's reign. Male power and male heirs alone failed to convey a complete picture of the perfect emperor and of everlasting and benevolent rule.

Aphrodisias

The Greek world was permeated with these images of powerful, deified living women, but always in a way that was subordinate to and, most clearly, supportive of the emperor himself. It is in this context that the relief panels at Aphrodisias of Agrippina the Younger mentioned above must be set for that very powerful image of an imperial woman to be understood. The panels are part of a series which decorates the south portico of the so-called Sebasteion, and illustrate the perceived relationship between the imperial state and the Greek world (Smith 1987, 88–138). The temple complex was built over a period lasting from the time of Tiberius until early in Nero's reign. Many of the panels depict Rome's victories over the peoples and tribes of the empire, e.g. in Britain, Gaul, etc., while other panels present the allegorical benefits of Roman rule, e.g. *pax*, *concordia*, etc. With these reliefs are the two which depict the empress, including the one described at the outset of the paper (Fig 8.1) which seemed to undermine the authority of the emperor Nero.

Before further analysis of that panel is presented, the other, (possibly) earlier depiction of the empress with her husband Claudius (Fig. 8.2) needs to be discussed (Smith 1987, 106–10, plates viii–ix).

Here the couple stand in that familiar pose seen on funerary monuments throughout the empire: their clasped hands indicate the harmony of their marriage and, because of who they were and the location of the sculpture, of the empire. His divinity is indicated by his heroic nudity, but she is depicted in a mortal guise (perhaps this is an indication that he is dead, which would make this panel contemporaneous with the second). This relief makes an overt statement about the nature of the imperial marriage: its harmony was essential to the maintenance of order and stability within the empire and amongst the gods. The image had many resonances, and for contemporaries, it must have evoked memories of the empress in her other

Figure 8.2 Agrippina and Claudius
Source: Photo: New York University excavations at Aphrodisias

guise, as a fertility goddess. The ideology was made explicit at nearby Ephesus where coins were minted directly to the divine marriage of Claudius and Agrippina the Younger. Some of these coins with the legend '*Theogamia*' depict the emperor and his wife, but others portray Agrippina and her son Nero instead: an obvious allusion to the outcome of a successful dynastic marriage, namely, an heir.[57]

The second panel must be seen in the light of this first one, which clearly emphasizes the attributes of a devoted wife. As described above, this relief (Fig. 8.1) shows Nero in military uniform being crowned by his mother Agrippina with a *civica corona* (Smith 1987, 127–32, plates xxiv–xxvi). A closer look at the iconography of the sculpture greatly diminishes any perception of female authority, while also revealing that, contrary to initial modern reactions, Agrippina is subtly enhancing the emperor's image. The first misconception is in the interpretation of the *civica corona*. This was not the Roman equivalent of a gold crown, but a symbol of military victory, consistent with the emperor's dress. Second, although Agrippina is of a similar stature to Nero, he stands slightly to the forefront, indicating his superiority. She looks directly at him, making him the focus of the portrait, while he gazes off into the middle distance. No eye contact is established, no indication of equal status given. Nero is clearly the focal point of the sculpture, while Agrippina's role is limited to presenting the young, military emperor. Nero had yet to prove that he had that essential ingredient of military prowess in his makeup, but here he is commemorated as the successful general. Agrippina appears as the ideal mother, who has performed her duty and produced an heir who has successfully achieved military dominance.

So again, these images can be read as a portrayal of women as beings whose maternal presence ensures the inner stability and continuity of the imperial household, and thus of the Greek city and the empire at large. The emperor stands at the centre of a complex of images, both military and familial, designed to reinforce his strength, leadership and masculinity.

From Livia to Agrippina II and later, this symbolism underlies much of the imagery discussed and suggests a highly developed discourse about the nature of imperial power and its masculine and feminine elements. On the one level, empresses as wives and potential or actual mothers signified the continuation of the dynasty, while imperial fertility goddesses were reassuringly powerful symbols (and divine agents) for a higher order of stability and prosperity. But there was another level: these cults related the imperial household to civic power structures through its incorporation with the local gods. The inclusion of the women helped to define the various facets of divine imperial power, from the feminine element of fecundity to the more prosaic quality of protecting the hearth.

Finally, as in the case of élite women celebrated for their acts of euergetism, the imperial women were honoured in ways which enhanced not only the glory of the emperor, but also the prestige of the city. Cities stood to gain a competitive edge with their neighbours and approval from the emperor by instituting cults to the divine wives or mothers (whereas deification of male imperial family members might have been seen as promoting a rival claimant to power). Thus, both in terms of making the new order explicable and of benefits to be gained (through popularity with the emperor and increased status in their communities), the Greek cities had enormous encouragement to promote cults of imperial (female) divinities.

As the Principate became more firmly established, so too did imperial cult practices. Honours became more standardized as cities established accepted means of honouring the imperial régime and bringing the emperor into the world of the polis. The empress, be she wife or mother, was generally depicted in her guise as Hera, the divine consort. Thus the variety of images were brought together in a way which satisfied the need for a divine imperial female to enhance the nature of the régime. Livia and Augustus were routinely depicted as the divine founding couple of the dynasty and hence also of the Principate. The two were frequently paired as *Theoi Sebastoi* and often given priesthoods and honours separate from those of the reigning emperor and family.[58] The constancy of the image suggests that it provided a key element in imperial ideology.

But what element? Simone de Beauvoir in *The Second Sex* (1949 [1987]) famously postulates that man created the image of Woman as the Other, the uncivilized being who, more closely akin to the natural, helped to protect him from the uncultured elements of himself. Of the Greeks and their gods, she wrote,

> Aeschylus, Aristotle, Hippocrates proclaimed that on earth as on Olympus it is the male principle that is truly creative: from it came form, number, movement; grain grows and multiplies through Demeter's care, but the origin of grain and its verity lies with Zeus; *woman's fecundity is regarded only as a passive element.*
>
> (1949 [1987], 176 [italics added])

Woman, according to de Beauvoir, is essential to the construct of man: every élite needs its Other.

To this end, I would like to suggest that, on a basic level, the image of the mother goddess was a natural addition to imperial iconography, not because it was *de rigueur* that these women be honoured, but because their inclusion in the cult completed the image of the patriarchal emperor. It was more a part of the discourse about masculine power and the patriarchal ideal, than about an individual woman's power within the imperial state. As male authority figures, the emperors and their heirs were displayed as revealing the prowess of the heroes and the stately attributes of the first citizens of the empire. But to complete the image of the patriarch, the emperors also needed to display control over their household. They needed a wife or other female authority figure who was restrained and maternal, whose body was seen as fertile and thus symbolic of the continuity of the dynasty.

Yet there can be no denying that these divine female forms were almost frighteningly powerful: they were associated with the strongest, most potent goddesses known to the Greeks. It only served to reinforce the strength of the emperor that he could have the strongest goddesses within his family, and yet still subjugate them to his will and order. Thus the portrayal of his womenfolk enhanced the image of the emperor as a masculine leader, one who could be sure of exercising control over an immortal household and, by extension, the empire.

Acknowledgements

Many thanks to all those who granted me the benefit of their criticism and insight, especially Lin Foxhall, John Salmon, Barbara Levick and Fergus Millar. Also thanks to Richard Burgess for his help and guidance in interpreting the epigraphic evidence. Needless to say, any mistakes or misinterpretations are all my own.

Notes

1 Dio 51. 20. 6–9; cf. Millar 1984b, 53–5, for discussion of the rapid spread of the cult.
2 Although the Romans of course nurtured its development. See Price 1984a, especially 78–100, for a more detailed account of the process by which the practice of instituting cult honours spread.
3 'In the Greek world of war and adventure, power is in essence and by definition virility.'
4 See discussion of frequency below, 167.
5 *IGR* iv. 556. For the priestess, *IGR* iv. 555.
6 *IGR* iv. 582–4. For further discussion of the evidence for this site, see Vermeule 1968, 470.
7 For example, Mostene in Lydia: *IGR* iv. 1349; *BMC Lydia* 162, numbers 7–8; Price 1984a, 259. Apollonia Mordiaeum in Pisidia: *MAMA* iv. 142–3 = *IGR* iii. 312; Price 1984a, 270. For more detailed analysis and further evidence, see Fischler 1989, 125–7 (available in the Bodleian Library, Oxford).
8 For Augustus and Livia as 'altarsharers' at Aizanoi, *IGR* iv. 582–4. For its neocorate (probably dated to the reign of Tiberius), e.g. *IGR* iv. 584 = Smallwood (1967) no. 134.
9 For full discussion of the evidence for cult worship of the imperial princesses on Mytilene, see Fischler 1989, 143–6. Both Julia the Elder (Dio 54. 24. 6; Josephus, *Antiquitates Judaicae* 16. 20, 62) and her daughter Agrippina (Tacitus, *Annales* 2. 53–4) spent extended periods of time on the island. For more detailed discussion of Agrippina's itinerary, see Kokkinos 1992, 17–24; for the travels of both women, see Fischler 1989, 48, 52.
10 Identified as such by Robert 1960.
11 *IG* xii. 2. 211 = *IGR* iv. 81: probably a reference to the younger Agrippina.
12 *IG* xii, suppl. 50, cf. Riewald 1912, 302.
13 Although Price 1984a, 56 has referred to the Mytilenean honours as 'some of the most explicitly divine . . . found anywhere', they nonetheless conform to an established pattern; see Fischler 1989, 144.
14 Smith 1987, 90. For a recent review of evidence for ruler-cult from this site, see Reynolds 1996. For publication of the bulk of inscriptions relating to Roman interaction with Aphrodisias, see Reynolds 1982.
15 Smith 1987, 127–32, no. 11.
16 An analysis asserted by Smith 1987, 129.
17 Price 1984a, 57–9, for the effects of the standardization of cultic honours.
18 See Fischler 1989, 74–163 for in depth presentation of evidence for divine commemoration of the imperial women in the Julio–Claudian period.
19 Famously, Thukydides 2. 45: 'Not to show more weakness than is natural to her sex, and not to be talked about for good or evil among men, is a great glory to a woman'. Many of these attitudes are implicit within the texts, although seldom

addressed directly. For analysis of male attitudes toward Greek women, see especially Just 1989.

20 Fischler 1989, 98–163; Price 1984a, 172–88 on images and subtle distinctions in presentation between mortals, divine rulers and gods. For more on Greek cult statues in general, see the excellent analysis by Gordon 1979.

21 See Price 1984a, 65–77, for presentation of cult as a form of gift exchange, which would necessitate that both giver and recipient recognize the worth of honours being offered.

22 See Stafford in Foxhall and Salmon 1998.

23 For example, Euxenia of Megalopolis (second century BC) and Menodora, daughter of Megakles from Sillyon, as discussed by Van Bremen 1983, 223. Her more recent views can be found in Van Bremen 1996. Many such élite women were also involved as priestesses in the imperial cult, e.g. Claudia Hedea of Chios, *SEG* 15. 532; Caristania Frontina Iulia of Pisidian Antioch, *Ann. Ep.* 1941: no. 142, cf. Levick 1964, 99 for family background.

24 Only three, or possibly four, of the Julio–Claudian women travelled throughout the East as adults: Livia (20–19 BC, Dio 54. 7. 4–6), Julia the Elder (16–13 BC, Dio 54. 19. 6; Joseph. *AJ* 16. 12) and Agrippina the Elder (AD 18–19, Tac. *Ann.* 2. 53–79) travelled with their husbands; Antonia perhaps joined her son Germanicus and Agrippina on their eastern journey in AD 18 (see Kokkinos 1992, 17–24). Of these, only Livia received extensive amounts of commemoration throughout the region.

25 But it does help to account for the more rare instances where imperial women were elected to local offices, usually the gymnasiarchy, or were recognized as *euergetai*. These circumstances may well arise after some direct contact has been made, as at Mytilene, Fischler 1989, 65–71.

26 Many examples: e.g. Antiochus III and his wife Laodice were honoured as benefactors by Teos in 204/3 BC after staying in the city and, among other 'good deeds', exempting the city from tribute (Austin 1981, no. 151); Scepsis honoured Antigonus in 311 BC after receiving 'great benefits' and freedom and autonomy from the king (Austin 1981, no. 32).

27 For a more detailed discussion of the range of activities of Hellenistic kings, and the disjunction between the ideology of the masculine ruler and the practices of their wives, see Roy, this volume.

28 For recent analysis of the development of Hellenistic ruler cult, see Herz 1996.

29 For an unfortunate example of this approach, see Fischler, 1989, 98–163, especially 136.

30 Which accounts for why Livia, for example, was often deified during her lifetime outside Rome, both in the east and the west. An exception to this rule was the deification of Drusilla, sister of Gaius Caligula, in AD 38, when the emperor decreed that she was to be worshipped throughout the empire: Dio 59. 11. 3.

31 For an explanation of the use of women as symbols, particularly of abstract concepts, see Stafford in Foxhall and Salmon 1998.

32 Shear 1981, 356–77; Geagan 1979, 378–82, for a list of buildings and renovations attributed to Augustan benefactions.

33 See Graindor 1927, Geagan 1979, 382–5, Shear 1981; and Hoff 1996, on a new possibility for the location of a Sebasteion in the Roman agora.

34 Julius Caesar, e.g. as *sōtēr* and *euergetēs*, *CIA* iii. 428; colossal statue, Raubitschek 1954, 68, cf. Weinstock 1971, 166 n. 2. In the manner of Hellenistic rulers, Octavia and Antonius were honoured as *theoi euergetai* during Antonius' stay there in 39–7 BC; Raubitschek 1946, 146–50.

35 Dio 51. 20. 6–8. See Hänlein-Schäfer 1985, 157–9; Shear 1981, 363; Graindor 1927, 150–1.

36 Augustan Panathenaia, *IG* ii² 3270, lines 4–5, cf. *IG* iii 652.
37 Thompson 1966, 180–1; Hänlein-Schäfer 1985, 160, A21; Shear 1981, 364. The pedestal in the south room might have been supplied for statues of the imperial family, as, for example, at Olympia (see Price 1984a, 160–1; Thompson cites other examples of such groupings of imperial family statues). Generally, as cultic honours became more standardized throughout the East after the death of Augustus, Livia and Augustus were presented as a unified pair (this practice was unrelated to her death and subsequent deification at Rome); see Price 1984a, and n. 14 above.
38 C. Caesar: *IG* ii² 3250. For discussion, see Levensohn 1947, 68–9; Thompson 1966, 181–7. Drusus: *IG* ii² 3257. See also Shear 1981, 361–2.
39 Graindor 1927, 256, no. 20. Dedication: *IG* ii² 3239.
40 Seat to 'priestess of Hestia and Livia and Julia' at Theatre of Dionysus: *CIA* iii. 316, cf. Graindor 1927, 153–4. The inclusion of Julia indicates a date sometime before her *relegatio* in AD 2.
41 It is, however, attested elsewhere after the death of Augustus; Ankyra in Galatia, when granted a neocorate, created a priesthood of the divine *Sebastoi* and the divine *Rhōmē* in a temple which included likenesses of Augustus and Livia together (*OGIS* 533 = *IGR* iii. 157, probably early Tiberian).
42 Crosby 1937, 464–5, no. 12 = *SEG* 22. 152 = *EJ* 89. For restoration and discussion, Oliver 1965, 179; cf. *Agora* iii, *Testimonia*, no. 427. Shear 1981, 364, suggests that the southwest temple may have been dedicated to Livia as Artemis Boulaia, since the statue base was found near the site; cf. *Agora* xiv, 166.
43 Contrary to general practice (see next section), Artemis was also a virgin goddess, suggesting that a significant factor in determining syncretism was simply importance within the civic pantheon.
44 *IG* ii² 3175; Graindor 1927, 32.
45 *IG* iii. 461; Graindor 1927, 155. Given the use of the name Julia, the inscription probably dates to after Augustus' death. For speculation on the location of the Sebasteion, see Hoff 1996, 185–200.
46 For an inscription to Julia Livilla as *nea Nikēphoros*, Riewald 1912, no. 127.
47 Although uncommon, collocation of imperial cult with the cult of Hestia was not unique to Athens; compare e.g. Agrippina the Elder at Thera: *Hestia Boulaia Agrippina* (*ILS* 8790b).
48 As will be discussed further in the case of Aphrodisias. For more on imperial images, see Hänlein-Schäfer 1985.
49 The examples are too numerous to cite, although Riewald 1912 gives lengthy lists for e.g. Julio–Claudian women (302–3) and later imperial women (303–5) as Hera. As Demeter: e.g. Livia, at Lampsakos (*CIG* 3642 = *IGR* iv. 180) and Aphrodisias (*CIG* ii. 2815 = Robert 1960, 261); Agrippina II on Kos, *IGR* iv. 1104 (Isthmos).
50 Temple of *Sebastai Rheai*, Paton-Hicks 147. 119 =*IGR* iv. 1062. Colossal head of an imperial woman (Agrippina?) as Rhea found here: Laurenzi 1955–6, 124. 142.
51 The inclusion of the imperial family in household cult is certainly indicated by evidence such as the inscribed stones found on Mytilene, which appear to be private altars dedicated (in the dative) to members of M. Agrippa's family. For Agrippina the Younger, Drusilla, Nero and Drusus Caesar, IG xii. 2. 172b = *IGR* iv. 78b. For Drusilla, *IG* xii. 2. 482 = *IGR* iv. 114. Hanson and Johnson 1946, 398–9; Vermeule 1968, 204.
52 There are numerous cases throughout the East of joint cults continuing into Tiberius' reign and possibly later. Some examples: at Gytheion in Lakonia, a decree institutes elaborate honours to Augustus, Julia Augusta (i.e. Livia) and Imperator Tiberius Caesar Augustus, *SEG* 11. 923; at Ephesos, the mysteries

continued to be celebrated with the divine Augusti, *Syll.*[3] 655. As late as Hadrian, the temple of Augustus and Roma at Pergamum commemorated her birthday with that of Augustus, *IGR* iv. 353.

53 Deification at Rome, Suetonius, *Claudius* 11. 2; Dio 60. 5. 2; Seneca, *Apocolocyntosis* 9. 5. For provincial level response, see e.g. the edict of the proconsul of Asia, granting her cultic rites special dispensation, when she had been recognized as divine at Rome: Smallwood (1967) no. 380.

54 Relatively commonly found throughout the east, e.g. *P. Lond.* 1912 (Alexandria); *Eph. Epigr.* 7, 1242 (Ephesos); *CIG* 3858 (Akmonia in Phrygia).

55 For example, her priestess at Magnesia on the Menander is also 'priestess of Asia, crown-bearer, gymnasiarch, priestess of Aphrodite and even priestess of Demeter at Ephesos for life', Kern *I. Magn.* 158. At Ephesos, the dedication of the fish market honours first Nero, then Agrippina and lastly Nero's wife, Octavia (although she is the daughter of the previous emperor), *Ann. Ep.* 1930, 85.

56 *SEG* 28. 1227 = *IGR* iii. 547 (tr. Price): festival established by the *koinon* of Lykia; Magie 1950, 534. See Price 1984a, 216 for discussion of the Lykian decision and direct sacrifice to Livia.

57 Claudius and Agrippina, *BMC Ionia*, 73. 203–6 (plate xiii. 3); *BMC* I (Claudius), no. 231–3 (plate 34. 2). Agrippina and Nero , *BMC Ionia*, 73. 207–8 (dated to the reign of Claudius).

58 For example, at Ankyra, as shown above.

9

The cube and the square

Masculinity and male social roles in Roman Boiotia

Jill Harries

> A man should be four-square, perfect, like an odd number, while a woman should resemble a cube, loving the home, hard to shift.
>
> (Plutarch, *Roman Questions*, 102)

Historians are rightly cautious in using literary extracts, even from a range of authors, as evidence for intellectual and social trends. Still less plausibly can it be claimed for one author that he, individually, is representative of the opinion of 'society' as a whole, especially when that one author lived under the Roman Empire, the multi-cultural nature of which should preclude attempts at any 'synchronic, cross-cultural account' (Clark 1993, 2). Despite these *caveats*, however, the opinions of a single author with a known, if regionally and intellectually limited, context can provide significant insights into the terms of discourse on contentious issues in use in a given place at a given time. The witness of such an author may be the more impressive if he appears, in the main, a judicious exponent of a range of ideas and opinions, rather than an idiosyncratic polemicist, perhaps out of step with his time.

Such a one was Plutarch of Chaironea, arguably one of the most important and, until recently,[1] most neglected exponents of the gender debate in antiquity. Exceptionally well-read and open-minded, with an insatiable penchant for the citation of *exempla* from the Graeco-Roman past, Plutarch, a communicator rather than an analyst, preferred to regurgitate received ideas rather than to engage with the higher (and less generally accessible) reaches of philosophical speculation (Stadter 1992). It is true, however, that habitual adherence to *idées reçues* on the part of an author brings its own dangers for the historian; arguments advanced by a man conditioned by the rhetorical training of the early decades of the second Sophistic movement may express rhetorical *topoi*, not genuine belief. Yet, paradoxically, this risk also brings rewards: *topoi* themselves are a form of discourse reflecting the terms of debate and may be of wider significance than the 'real' opinions of a writer. Moreover, Plutarch goes further, in that he exploited the dialogue form, as we shall see, to engage, not always conclusively, with issues that concerned his contemporaries on the role of men and women in his native Boiotia and beyond.

Plutarch was not, of course, unusual in being a family man. Married to Timoxena, herself the author of a treatise, addressed to another woman, on that traditionally feminine preoccupation, *Love of Ornament* (*Moralia* 145 A), Plutarch recorded his affection for his wife and children in his writings. Another female influence was Klea, priestess at Delphi and recipient of the dedications of Plutarch's essays *On Isis and Osiris* and *On the Virtues of Women*. In the latter, Plutarch demonstrated, by means of historical *exempla*, that 'goodness in a man and a woman were one and the same thing', an idea even more forcibly expressed by the Stoic Musonius, whose writings were known to Plutarch (453 D, 830 B) and who had gone so far as to assert that 'a woman too must be manly (*andrizesthai*)' (Goldhill 1995, 137–8). Plutarch was also used to sharing his reading with women, as he recalled with regard to Eurydike, whose education became the responsibility of her husband, when she married (*Mor.* 145 B).

Clever women in philosophical families were not unprecedented (Hawley 1994). The fourth-century Cynic Hipparchia scandalized her relations by publicly adopting the 'masculine' dress and lifestyle of her husband, Krates, but her son by him was more conventionally named after Krates' brother, and their (probably fictitious) correspondence may have been in circulation under the Empire (Russell 1973, 90). Female Pythagoreans existed as honoured members of philosophical families in Southern Italy and other philosophers accepted that their women could make a positive contribution (Diogenes Laertios, *Lives* 8. 42–3). Yet for women to emerge as intellectuals at all, support must have been forthcoming from their family group; few, if any, hopeful women philosophers could have escaped the stranglehold of families with more restricted expectations. Such was the milieu in which Plutarch shared his life and thoughts with women and set down his reflections on their role and their relationship to men.

Remarks by men about women are as revealing about concepts of masculinity as they are about expected female roles (Goldhill 1995, 112). Definitions in terms of opposites – hot–cold, dry–moist, odd–even, male–female – were familiar in ancient thought (Lovibond 1994). What women were was, by definition, what men were not, and for either sex to take on the characteristics of the other was a matter for often adverse comment. The same emphasis on opposites justified expectations of separate social roles. 'War', as Hektor observed to Andromache, 'is the business of men' (Homer, *Iliad* 6. 492–3), as was government, and the idea that women could attend the Assembly or form a Senate was as ridiculous to the author of the *Historia Augusta* in the fourth century AD (Scriptores

Historiae Augustae *Heliogabalus* 3. 3–4; *Aurelian* 49. 6) as it had been to Aristophanes at Athens in the fourth century BC (Dover 1974, 96). Home, and the running of the household, were, *pace* Xenophon's Ischomachos (who treated his young wife to a course in household management), inevitably and securely the female sphere, as was the bearing (although not necessarily the rearing) of children.

Modern scholars, conditioned by the cultural assumptions of twentieth-century Western society, and distanced from the ancient Mediterranean world by two millenia, have been reluctant to give credence to this allocation of roles as an expression of complementarity, rather than of male chauvinist condescension. Countless references to female 'weakness' in the literary sources are read as reflecting popular prejudices derived from centuries of warfare, in which physical strength was at a premium; consequently, women were also debarred from 'political' life, the stuff of which traditional history is made, and confined to 'a woman's place', namely the home. Such references however, are often separated from their contexts and may therefore mislead (Zweig 1993). Plutarch himself, in his *Advice on Marriage*, reflects the accepted values of Mediterranean society when he stipulates that the husband should always have the guiding role in a partnership and should make all the important decisions about money. Yet elsewhere he also accepts the importance of both sexes to a partnership: in answering the first of his *Roman Questions* (*Mor.* 263 D–F), as to why does a bride touch fire and water, his response is that fire and water cannot flourish apart and 'so male and female apart from each other are ineffectual, but their joining in marriage produces the perfect shared life'. Even numerology is imported into the gender debate. In the third of four possible answers to the *Roman Question* 'why were male children given their names on the ninth day and females on the eighth day from birth?', Plutarch observed that nine is the first square number to be derived from the odd-number perfect triad (i.e. three-squared), while eight is the first cube from the first even number, two. Thus, as quoted above, a man, like an odd number, should be four-square, while a woman should resemble the solid and immovable cube (*Quaest. Rom.* 102). Such expressions of complementarity, however, while reflecting one view of gender roles, cannot be assumed to be Plutarch's own opinions. The *Roman Questions* are supplied with multiple-choice answers, many of which were still based on more negative attitudes, such as the origins of the *ius osculandi* as a family check on female drunkenness (*Quaest. Rom.* 6, *Mor.* 265 B).

Complementarity can also entail exclusion of one party from the sphere of the other and a sense, on the part of both, that the 'other' could not participate fully in their own experience. While much anti-feminine rhetoric can be put down to a male urge to express distrust of female 'otherness', women in the ancient sources are largely silent on the exclusivity of their own experience. Plutarch gave women, briefly, a distinctive voice, when he drew attention to their opinion on literary descriptions (by men) of child-birth. Male Greek tragedians had described through their female characters the agonies of giving birth,[2] but it was the opinion of Plutarch's women friends that men could not know what was really involved: three lines in the *Iliad* describing birth-pangs must, they said, have been written by a Homeric bard, who was also a woman: she (they said) either had just given birth or was in the process of doing so, as a male Homer, not having had the experi-ence, could not have so described it (*Mor.* 496 D, citing *Il.* 269–71). The notion of a 'female Homer' was thus exploited to reveal a conscious sepa-rateness in (Plutarch's) women's perception of themselves as childbearers: theirs alone was both the pain and the achievement, in which men, as the 'other', could not share.

Thus far, Plutarch's opinions on the nature of the male in relation to the female appear straightforward, even derivative. The equality of female virtue to that of men had been accepted (in theory) by Plato, and others had ques-tioned, or would question, from both philosophical and legal standpoints, popular prejudices on the intellectual inferiority of women. Where Plutarch advanced the debate, and is uniquely informative about contemporary terms of discourse, was in his ability to report male contemporaries' anxieties about women and, by inference, their own identities as men. For this purpose he exploited the dramatic potential of the dialogue form, as Plato had done, allowing the characters and concomitant prejudices of his speakers to emerge from what they said, and affording space for the expres-sion of conflicting viewpoints. Differing ideas, then, on masculinity and what should be expected of men, could be set out, analysed and, where appropriate, reinforced through the moralist's portrayal of character through dialogue.

A number of Plutarch's conversations on philosophy take place in the context of the symposion, traditionally an all-male institution. Women might attend for the preliminary dining, but would leave before serious drinking (and, by implication, conversation) began. In the second century AD, Athenaios reported the diatribes of the Greek historian Theopompos against the Etruscans, whose laxity in allowing their wives and daughters to be present at symposia proved their lack of culture and general immorality; Etruscan women, claimed Theopompos, were immodest, publicly promis-cuous, and drank with whomsoever they chose, while the symposia themselves were occasions for men to fornicate with prostitutes, young boys – and even their wives.[3] This Greek social convention, that women were barred from social drinking parties, although it could be modified in some limited religious contexts (Bookidis 1990), had its inevitable literary impact. Guests and speakers at Plutarch's symposiastic dialogues would therefore inevitably be men, not because Plutarch consciously sought to play down the role of women but because their presence at symposia would be a violation of both literary and social convention.

Guests at Plutarch's literary symposia consisted either of friends or relatives of Plutarch, or of great figures from the past. Women could, as stated above, be present for the first part of the evening. One such, introduced into the *Dinner of the Seven Sages* (*Mor.* 146 B–164 D), was Eumetis, also known as Kleobulina, whose father was the ruler of Rhodes in the sixth century BC. She became the object of private discussion between two other guests (*Mor.* 148 C). One, the less well-informed but aptly named Neiloxenos, from Naukratis, identified her as a lady famous for her riddles, questions and answers, which were known about even in Egypt. The other speaker, Thales, vigorously objected to this trivializing of Eumetis' abilities, pointing out that she had an amazing intellect (*phronēma*), the mind of a statesman (*nous politikos*) and a kindly disposition (*philanthrōpon ēthos*), and that she was thus able to influence her father, so that his government was more pleasing to the demos of Rhodes. This exchange – and in particular the ascription to Eumetis of a statesman's intellect – takes us beyond the mere restatement of the equality of virtue between men and women. The author appears to have identified in Neiloxenos the existence of an unacknowledged prejudice, which, through the medium of Thales, he was able to expose. Neiloxenos was not hostile to Eumetis and admired her riddles, but was unable to progress beyond that point to ask himself whether she might also possess 'understanding' and 'intellect'. It is a tribute to Plutarch's subtlety of understanding that he recognized that ignorance and indifference could be as damaging to the realization of women's potential as outright hostility.

More overt contempt for women's aspirations was expressed later in the dialogue by the physician, Kleodoros (*Mor.* 154 B). Impatient with a conversation consisting entirely of asking and answering obscure questions, he demanded to know how these trivial pursuits differed from Eumetis' riddles, which were the kind of thing one would expect her to weave together 'as other girls weave garlands' and ask to other women, but were entirely inappropriate for 'men of sense' (*nous*), the very quality Plutarch, through Thales, had claimed as the preserve of women as well as men. Naturally, such boorish opinions required refutation, and Plutarch brought in Aesop as Eumetis' champion: he proved the superior cleverness of Eumetis by asking Kleodoros one of her riddles, relating to medical matters – and the physician was unable to answer.

Taken together, these exchanges reveal a complex set of male attitudes both towards women and to their own prerogatives and identity as men. Consciously (Kleodoros) or unconsciously (Neiloxenos), men still perceived themselves as being superior in *nous*, in comparison with female *levitas* (cf. Gaius, *Institutes* 1. 189), but these were assumptions that Plutarch was prepared both to identify and refute. Yet even Plutarch could not – or would not – bend the literary constraints of the symposion to enable Eumetis to speak for herself or do anything to demonstrate directly her 'statesmanlike' qualities. Instead, we are presented with a young girl who knows her place, who is pictured as coyly learning wisdom from her elders and who blushes modestly and remains silent when attacked, leaving her defence to others. Thus, while using the symposiastic form to refute popular prejudices about male superiority, Plutarch simultaneously perpetuated the values of the symposion as an all-male institution, with all its implications for male bonding and the consequent reinforcing of male political, social and cultural cohesiveness. Assertions of equality in intellect or virtue coexisted with the fact of the exclusion by one sex of the other from activities it still regarded as peculiarly its own.

Thus far, we have remained in the territory of an élite with the leisure to engage in philosophical discourse about the possession of 'nous', a subject alien to the mundane existence of less privileged households. Of far wider interest was the theme of courtship and marriage. In this area, the conventions governing the behaviour of the sexes were clear. The bridegroom should be older and richer than the bride, as he would be in charge of her, once married, and he, or his family, should take the initiative in courtship and the setting up of the wedding arrangements. Role-reversal of any kind was liable to pose threats to male identities, and role-reversal in this all-important matter was likely to crystallize male phobias of threats to their masculine identity, as expressed in the social role of the dominant partner in courtship and marriage.

In his (all-male) dialogue, the *Erōtikos* (or *Amatorius, Mor.* 748 E–771 E), Plutarch built a discussion on love, with echoes of Plato's *Symposium*, round a (real or imagined) incident at the small Boiotian town of Thespiai in the third quarter of the first century AD. The young Plutarch, represented as visiting the shrine of Eros at the town with his wife, is engaged in philosophical debate with his cronies on Mount Helikon on the nature of love, while receiving regular reports as events unfold in the town below. The focus of the drama, which framed and determined the course of the debate, was a rich young widow of Thespiai, Ismenodora,[4] a lady of good family and exemplary life. She fell in love with a young man called Bacchon, the son of a friend. Her affection posed a challenge to young Bacchon's male world. He had male lovers, who did not want to let him go; he was subject to peer pressure from his companions in the hunt, another exclusively male activity; and he had reservations of his own, on grounds of his youth, about setting up house with a widow. Moreover, Bacchon was not only considerably younger than his female suitor, he was also less rich. Ismenodora's principal critic in the dialogue, Pisias, observed that Bacchon would be intimidated by her money, and thus dominated by her, as was doubtless her intention in wooing a young man, still in a boy's tunic. This traditionalist standpoint was backed up by another speaker, who made the issue of role reversal explicit in remarking that Ismenodora was older than Bacchon by as much as the bridegroom should be older than the bride. Younger and poorer than his wooer, vulnerable to the jibes of his peers and pressurized by social conventions on the relationship expected between husband and wife, Bacchon hesitated, unsurprisingly, to commit himself to that apparent contradiction in terms, a female *erastēs* (Goldhill 1995, 151–2).

These objections were promptly dismissed by the more reasonable participants, including the young Plutarch himself. If wealth, they argued, could be combined with virtue and breeding, it was foolish to reject it. On the score of age, Ismenodora was younger than some of Bacchon's male admirers and was capable of having children. The lady's supporters were even prepared to put forward the highly contentious notion that there was nothing in itself wrong with an older woman of sense governing a younger man and helping him with her experience and her affection: 'the nurse rules the baby, the teacher the child, the gymnasiarch the youth, the lover his younger beloved, the law and his general the mature man. No-one is without a ruler or able to act on his own. So is it so dreadful that an older woman of sense should guide a younger man?' (*Mor.* 754 D). This radical repudiation of the conventional balance of power in a marriage appears to conflict with opinions expressed elsewhere by Plutarch, notably in his *Advice on Marriage*, which argued that a husband should dominate his wife 'not as a master rules a slave but as the soul rules the body' (*Mor.* 142 D–E), and that this should apply to the husbands of rich wives as well, although some tact might be required: 'as with the horse, it is the curb you need to use, paying due heed to the greatness and prestige of the lady' (*Mor.* 139 B), while, despite being intertwined like ropes, 'the property and the house shall be called the possession of the husband, even if the wife contributes the larger share' (*Mor.* 140 F).

This apparent contradiction provides a salutary reminder that Plutarch's 'real' views should not be inferred from isolated citations (any more than those of anyone else). An obvious reason for caution is that his writings were influenced by rhetorical conventions which influenced the forms of argument employed, the purpose of the genres in which he wrote and the arguments he wished to employ. Thus the *Advice on Marriage* conforms to the conventions of treatises on that subject, while the more complex *Erōtikos* may be expected to contain special pleading in support of its advocacy of the overwhelming power of Eros. In fact, his technique in the dialogues of advancing contradictory viewpoints make it virtually impossible to pin down Plutarch's 'real' views on the relationship of men to women in detail, – although, as we shall see, his qualified support of Ismenodora in the *Erōtikos*, being both controversial and, probably, unconventional, may well accurately reflect his personal standpoint. What is significant for us is not Plutarch's personal beliefs but that he was interested enough in contemporary discourse on male and female roles to record (and perhaps expand) for posterity the terms in which it was conducted.

As the *Erōtikos* unfolded, Ismenodora encroached further on traditional male preserves. In the defining moment of the piece, the tolerance of the party on Mount Helikon was tested to its limits by the news that

Ismenodora had taken on the role of the, usually male, abductor, by kidnapping Bacchon, whom she believed to be really in favour of the match, and dressing him up for the wedding ceremony. This had precipitated a public disturbance in Thespiai, a crowd had gathered and the two gymnasiarchs were divided about what to do. This, predictably, was the last straw for the choleric misogynist, Pisias, who announced that the whole order of his (male) world was under threat, claiming that it was absurd to bother complaining about the destruction of law and justice, when 'rule by women' was an offence against nature itself. Indeed, he said, the public places of the polis, the gymnasia and Bouleuterion, should be handed over to women, 'now that the polis was totally emasculated'.

Not even Ismenodora's supporters could manage immediately to shrug off this yet more extreme example of female self-assertion. By extending the limits of a woman's ability to behave like a man, Ismenodora had put her own supporters on the defensive. Yet, once again, the arguments of the chauvinists were to be undermined, if not refuted, by Plutarch's deployment of four literary devices. One is Pisias' consistently brash and extreme over-statement of his case, which is designed to alienate the sympathy of the reader. The second is the exploitation of the ambiguity of myth: while Pisias expatiates on the murderous behaviour of the Lemnian women, who killed their husbands, Anthemion, the moderate and sympathetic speaker who follows, immediately twists the reference to recall the loving relationships of the Lemnian widows with the Argonauts, a *'truly* Lemnian action' (*contra* Goldhill 1995, 155). Third, Ismenodora's extreme behaviour is assimilated into an extended discussion on the divine nature of Eros. And, finally, Ismenodora's action is rendered socially (if not philosophically) acceptable by the outcome: further tidings arrive from the city that the marriage has been accepted by the community and that even Pisias has given in and was to join in the celebrations. That there may have persisted in the minds of his readership a sense of disjunction between the theoretical framework and the actual operation of desire need not have troubled Plutarch unduly: to have posed the question was more important than finding the answer.[5]

Whether or not Ismenodora and her marriage ever existed is irrelevant to Plutarch's philosophical and literary purposes, yet we may pause here and ask whether Plutarch invented this episode in order to make a point about women and love, or whether he based his dialogue on something that really happened. Ismenodora is a distinctively Boiotian name (above, 189 n. 4) and only two other uses of it are known. A flute-girl in Lucian, who gossips to her friend about the Theban prophet Teiresias' sex change (*Dialogi Meretricii* 5. 4) is an unlikely connection for a rich Thespiaian lady, but more may be inferred from the presence of another Ismenodora of Thespiai at the head of an inscription from the first century AD set up by the archons of Thespiai, M. Antonius Primus, M. Antonius Zosimus and P. Castricius Alcimus, commemorating fifty-three benefactors of the 'upper gymnasium'.

(*IG* vii. 1777). The date of this cannot be fixed with any certainty, but the rarity of the name and its occurence again at Thespiai strongly suggest a family connection between the gymnasium benefactress and the Plutarchean heroine.

It is the bigoted Pisias, rather than the reasonable 'Plutarch', who echoes the fears that recur in Graeco-Roman literary sources that over-assertive female behaviour was 'against nature'. The gymnasia and the Bouleuterion, areas for exercise and socializing, were traditionally male citizen preserves (although, as we have seen, an Ismenodora of Thespiai was epigraphically recorded as a patroness of one of the two gymnasia of the city); they were thus, conventionally, the pillars of the polis,[6] here pictured as a male construct, liable to 'emasculation', if Plutarch's Ismenodora's challenge to male notions of marital dominance was successful. Pisias thus assimilated the male citizens and their public role in the polis to the polis itself, hence his contention that the polis was indeed 'masculine' and therefore vulnerable to 'emasculation' by a woman, whose abduction and marriage to a notionally weaker man posed both a political and a sexual threat to Pisias' male world.

In his own terms, Pisias' insecurities with regard to female dominance were well-founded, and would have been exacerbated by the presence of more than one Ismenodora in the public life of the Greek cities of his day. Even before the first century AD, Boiotia had seen its women display leadership and strength of character: in the third century BC, one Nikareta of Thespiai had struggled for three years with the polis of Orchomenos to recover debts due to her, which arose out of transactions conducted by her late father.[7] Under the Early Empire, women in Boiotia, in company with others in the Greek world, emerged as active patrons, honoured by their poleis:[8] Flavia Zoila of Hyettos, for example, was voted a statue by the Council (for which she paid herself) as a public honour (*IG* vii. 2836); while Plutarch must certainly have been acquainted with Caecilia Lampris of Chaironea, who put up a statue to Vespasian at her own expense and on behalf of the polis (*IG* vii. 2418).

It may also be suggested, however, that the challenge to traditional male roles came primarily not from assertive women but from the undermining of masculine identities and expectations of their public role, especially among the élite, brought about by the permanent subjection of the Greek polis to Rome and the replacement of an independent élite with an aristocracy of service (Veyne 1978, 37). In the primitive, tiny, archaic polis, men had been required to use their physical strength to defend their communities and from this derived their right also to govern. The independence of the polis in Greece, especially in relations with other poleis and peoples, had been severely eroded with the coming of Philip II and Alexander of Macedon, but the expectation of honour and power from participation in public life was slower to die and found new, if in historical terms more limited, expression under the Roman Empire. In Plutarch's time, emperors and governors made no moves against the continuance of competitive rivalry among members of the local upper classes, on whose support the Romans depended for the proper management of finance and public order; only when economic problems and corruption due to excessive competition became apparent, did the central administration actively intervene – as, for example when Pliny was sent out to Bithynia by Trajan in AD 110.

Although, then, honourable outlets for civic ambitions remained, Plutarch's feeling for the past made him, along with many contemporaries, ambivalent about the benefits of Roman rule (Swain 1996) and acutely conscious of the limitations placed on the aspirations of his class. For the biographer of the great Greeks and Romans of the past, the essence of a free polis was the chance to engage in leadership in war, the overthrow of tyrannies and the formation of alliances; yet a precondition for all these activities was independence both in external policy and the choice of a polis constitution, and Plutarch, in his *Precepts of Statecraft*, was aware that war, revolution and serious diplomacy were no longer options for aspiring polis statesmen of his own day (*Mor.* 805 A). The would-be careerist in the late first century AD was obliged to remember that 'you who rule are a subject, ruling a state controlled by proconsuls, the representatives of Caesar' (*Mor.* 813 E), whose briefest edict could shift such power as was available from one person to another (*Mor.* 824 F). Caution was the order of the day: 'do not have too much pride or confidence in your crown, for you see the boots of Roman soldiers just above your head' (*Mor.* 813 E), but rather follow the Roman lead, like the actor follows the prompter. What remained for the leaders of poleis, then, was conciliation, both of the Romans, 'who are most eager to promote the political interests of their friends' (*Mor.* 814 C), and of their fellow-citizens, among whom they should aim 'always to instil concord and friendship' (*Mor.* 824 D). This pursuit of 'harmony and quiet' by the wise was, in Plutarch's opinion, the only choice left, 'since fortune has left us no prize open for competition' (*Mor.* 824 E).

This prudent advice amounted to a comprehensive repudiation of the ethos which had prevailed in the independent polis, and which determined social values long after political independence was no more. Not only was the all-male business of warfare prohibited, but the power of the free male citizen to declare and wage it had passed elsewhere, to the omnipresent wearer of the Roman soldier's boot. While, as Plutarch was careful to observe, service to the polis still brought honour and therefore status, power was not really worth having and therefore not worth competing for: the ethos of the *agōn* was no more. Violence and competition had been superseded by the rhetoric of arbitration, conciliation and co-operation with the conqueror. It is clear from the continued liveliness of city politics in the Greek world that Plutarch overstated the decline in the openings for power, status and honour still available to politicians of his day. Nevertheless, the removal of the exclusively male activity of war and the partial removal of government as all-important occupations made 'masculinity' and male social values harder to define.[9] This subversion of masculinity in turn rendered less clear-cut the relationship of the traditional 'opposites', male and female, masculine and feminine, man and woman. Men continued to dominate in the worlds of literature and patronage, as well as politics, and the inroads made by women on public polis life, although sometimes spectacular, were also limited; the monumental self-commemoration of a Plancia of Perge, 'daughter of the city' and responsible, *inter alia*, for the renovation of the city's southern gate (Boatwright 1991), or the marital self-assertiveness of an Ismenodora were still the exception, not the rule. Confronted by what could be termed political emasculation, men's formulation of what was distinctively 'masculine' became more subtle. Plutarch admired the heroines of history – especially those, like the courageous and devious Aretaphila of Kyrene in his *On the Virtues of Women*, who asserted 'masculine' virtue in polis life by overthrowing two tyrants, and then returned to her wool-working (*Mor.* 255 E–257 E). He respected the female intellect, but expected that intellect to take second place and refrained from giving women a voice in his dialogues; the all-important symposion, and the intellectual exchanges thereat, remained the preserve of men. Though more sympathetic to the aspirations of women than some, such as Pisias or Kleodoros, to whom he gave a voice, only to reject it, Plutarch paradoxically reveals how notions of male dominance could be redefined and modified, challenged, but then sustained, in the worlds of both the polis and the household. Then, as now, men deployed more insidious – and perhaps more effective – forms of self-assertion than force.

Notes

1 Foucault 1984, 1986; Goldhill 1995.
2 For example, Sophokles, *Electra* 532; Euripides, *Medea* 250–1.
3 Theopompos, *FGrH* 115 F204 = Athenaios 517–18; cf. Cicero, *Verrine* 2. 1. 26. 56)
4 The archaic form for the name is Hismenodora, not Ismenodora, as names with this root occur in the archaic period with the rough breathing. Names based on Hismen-/Hismein- are very strongly Boiotian and occur hardly anywhere else. The editors of the *Lexicon of Greek Personal Names* identify one in Phokis, three in Euboia, one on Paros, one in Thrace and two unassignable. My thanks to Elaine Matthews for this information.
5 Goldhill 1995, 154–60; Cooper 1992, 154.
6 cf. Diog. Laert. 7. 33; Schofield 1991, 12.
7 *IG* vii. 3172; Roesch 1965, 147–52, 166–70.
8 Van Bremen 1983, Boatwright 1991.
9 Compare Alston, this volume, on the masculinity of the Roman élite under the emperor.

10

'All that may become a man': the bandit in the ancient novel

Keith Hopwood

Simon Goldhill has recently drawn attention to the erotic *paideia* inherent in the Greek novels written during the period of the Second Sophistic.[1] The educative function of these works extends well beyond the erotic. Characters interact in situations drawn from many areas of society which must strike the reader as plausible, and, like scenes in the popular television 'soaps' of today, present real dilemmas and possible answers to them. In this paper, I want to discuss the appearances of bandits (*lēistai/latrones*) and consider them as undesirable role models for those wishing to construct a socially sanctioned masculine identity.

The ideal role for the successful aristocrat in the Roman world was that of victorious warrior (Harris 1979, Chapter 1), and the importance of martial excellence is further emphasized by the gradual appropriation of military honours by the emperors under the Principate.[2] Banditry, in contrast, is defined by the legal texts in opposition to the laudable exploits of the true Roman: 'Those are enemies against whom the Roman People has declared war. The rest are *praedones* or *latrones*'.[3] This negative definition has important consequences for the ancient conception of bandits: despite their superficial resemblance to soldiers in their carrying of arms,[4] they were everything a soldier was not. They were not authorized by the state, but by acting in accordance with their own perverse desires[5] they were arrogantly challenging the state's monopoly of violence.[6]

Livy has a story about an officer who by defying orders won a notable victory for Rome.[7] The Consul, Papirius, instead of honouring him, asks that he should be condemned to death, for:

> When military discipline has been defiled even once, the soldier will not obey his centurion, nor the centurion his tribune, nor the tribune his legate, nor the legate his consul, nor the master of horse his dictator. No-one would have respect for men or for Gods; neither commands of generals nor the auspices would be heeded;

soldiers would wander about without leave in peace and in war; careless of their military status they would go wherever they wished, by their own whim; the scattered standards would be abandoned, and soldiers would not muster to commands, nor would they distinguish day from night, favourable or unfavourable terrain, but they would fight whether ordered or not ordered by their general and they would not respect standards or positions: it would be blind and by chance like banditry, not like the solemn and sacred rites of war.

(8. 34. 7–11)

Banditry here is explicitly opposed to the correct way of waging Roman war. There must be rules, hierarchy and a system of command. Banditry confounds all these hugger-mugger, and represents that chaos which ensues when violence breaks its societally sanctioned bounds.[8]

Disorder is a theme in the novels' accounts of bandits. In Chariton's *Chaireas and Kallirhoe*, the bandit chief Theron ('The Beast') has heard about the pickings to be had from robbing a rich grave and seeks to reunite his gang for the task: 'So at dawn he hurried to the harbour and began looking them out one by one; some of them he found in brothels, others in taverns – an army fit for such a commander' (1. 3: trans. Reardon). Theron's troops were wandering at whim in places unsuitable for a Roman soldier. The Consul Papirius' warnings had been fulfilled: indeed, Theron is the commander of an anti-army, recruited from those places which good Roman commanders denied to their troops (Vegetius 3. 4; 26). Luxurious and licentious living was a habit typically associated with demoralized troops who might turn to banditry. One need only think of Corbulo's measures on taking up his command in Armenia.[9] The good Roman soldier must not be 'soft'; bandits, paradoxically, are expected to be. If Roman troops soften up, the gap between order and chaos narrows. The image of the bandit, the antipode of the soldier, exists to police the divide and define acceptable behaviour by its opposite. Luxury is, therefore, an inherent sign of disorder. Later in Chariton's novel, we hear of the misfortunes of a group of slaves who

> were left without any supervision: with abundant money at their disposal, they embarked on a bout of dissolute living. In a small town, where in true Greek fashion everybody was inquisitive, this extravagance on the part of visitors attracted general attention; a group of unknown fellows, living luxuriously, they struck people as probably robbers and at least runaway slaves.
>
> (4. 5: trans. Reardon)

Only bandits could behave in such a degenerate fashion. In fact, the slaves were themselves engaged in the nefarious and lecherous schemes of their master. Luxury and disorder are intimately connected as effect and cause. We must now consider the consumption of drink by bandits.

It is hard to believe that any army has not had to construct a framework whereby its troops might relax or obtain 'Dutch' courage by means of alcohol. Even Ottoman armies, servants of an Islamic state and themselves converts, had institutionalized consumption of alcoholic beverages through the tolerance of heterodox dervish lodges such as the Bektaşi order, patronized by the Janissaries.[10] Greek and Roman armies were supplied with both coarse and fine wine.[11]

Bandits, however, drink to incapacity. They not only 'roister',[12] but also drink while on duty to the extent of allowing their captives to slip away.[13] At crucial moments in his narrative, Xenophon of Ephesos depicts his bandits as helpless. As a similar story pattern occurs in Apuleius also, it is likely that this is a generally held view of bandits, not a foible of one particular author. Apuleius' bandits drink unmixed wine[14] which they have previously offered as a libation to the spirits of their 'commilites'.[15] Bandits recognize the military ethos, they honour their fallen companions just like real soldiers, but in parodic imitation. Apuleius gives details of their rituals to convince us of their verisimilitude by the historically appropriate trope of providing 'ethnographic' information.[16] In antiquity, the drinking habits of outsiders exercised fascination (Hartog 1980, 180–2). The drinking habits of bandits, which most closely resemble those of specialist esoteric groups like soldiers, convince us of the alterity of the bandit bands. If a 'sympotic' history of the ancient world, as proposed by Oswyn Murray (1990b, 3), is one which truly yet charmingly reveals the basic social institution of that world, then on 'sympotic' grounds, the bandits are seen to be outsiders within such a system.

The drinking habits of bandits not only characterize them but also fulfil a striking function in the narrative structure of the novels: bandits drink before their ultimate annihilation. Even as Apuleius' bandits enjoy their unmixed wine, their colleagues arrive, bringing in Charite, a beautiful and noble captive. The middle books of the *Metamorphoses* are then beguiled by the story of Cupid and Psyche, told to the noble prisoner by the wine-soaked bandits' moll. In the course of this narrative, Charite's equally noble fiancé, Tlepolemus, appears in disguise as the bandit Haemus, and carouses with the bandits. Soon the unmixed wine (here, fatally mulled) takes its effects: Tlepolemus leads them home 'colligatos vino magis quam vinculis' (Apul. *Met.* 7. 13) – a satisfying pseudo-etymology emphasizing the controlling aspect of the wine they drank to excess – or the binding effects of Dionysos the looser.

From Dionysos to Aphrodite: let us pass, like Chariton's bandits, from the tavern to the brothel. Here, the military norm and the bandits' transgressions come dangerously close. Serving Roman soldiers were not allowed to marry until the reign of Septimius Severus, and so, naturally,[17] associated in illegitimate liaisons that on discharge were considered as marriages – as long as they had only one partner each![18] Other outlets for the sexual drives of the Roman soldier are attested from military rosters. At Dura Europos on the Euphrates an *optio* took charge of billeting a troupe of female mime artists and actresses, suggesting that their entertainment function was officially sanctioned (Davies 1989, 67). In Germany, we hear of the *danseuse*, Polla Matidia (Davies 1989, 67 n. 27). Such *déclassées* (Leppin 1992, chapter 14) were available for the delectation of the Roman army: ideally, women of status were secure.

Bandits, by definition, did not respect status. This is clearly expressed in Thersander's outburst in Achilles Tatios' witty *Leukippe and Kleitophon*. Finding himself Leukippe's master, he takes the opportunity to indulge his own lust for Leukippe. Her protestation of virginity arouses the following expostulation:

> A virgin?! What daring and foolishness! Did a virgin pass the night with pirates like these? Did the bandits become eunuchs for you? Was the piratery one of philosophers?
>
> (6. 21: my translation)

As Leukippe points out, Thersander's own desires are no less culpable than those of bandits:

> Look at what you're doing; you are the real pirates! Aren't you ashamed to do what even brigands have not dared? You may not realize it, but your shameless behaviour is giving me even greater glory: even if you kill me in your senseless rage, someone will say, 'Leucippe was a virgin after the Rangers [*Boukoloi*], a virgin after Chaireas, a virgin even after Sosthenes'. These are modest claims; the greater encomium is 'a virgin even after Thersander, a more wanton sinner than any cutthroat. Whom he cannot rape he kills'.
>
> (6. 22: trans. Winkler)

When a respectable citizen stoops to such behaviour, how different is he from bandits? For bandits' passions, being directed against noble captive maidens, are always illegitimate. They are also obsessive, a failing generally ascribed to women in antiquity.[19] The original 'Egyptian thief at point of death' who *does* 'kill what he loves' appears in Heliodoros' *Ethiopika*.[20] He is Thyamis who, after defeat by the forces of law and order, kills (as he thinks) the heroine Charikleia. Further erotic obsession can be observed in Xenophon of Ephesos' Anchialos. His obsession is an inversion of the main theme of the novels: passionate chastity (Anderson 1984, 115). All the couples – Anthia and Habrokomes, Leukippe and Kleitophon, Chaireas and Kallirhoe – are wildly in love, but chaste.[21] Anchialos' threat to Anthia is the antithesis of this theme: the no longer to be deferred, here-and-now desire of unaccommo-dated man. As Xenophon makes clear, Anchialos is more inflamed by Anthia's protestations of love for Habrokomes. Anthia's own protestations verge on the masochistic: 'I pray that I may remain the wife of Habrokomes, even if I have to die or suffer still more than I have already.[22] Like the 'good girl', Justine, in de Sade, Anthia and the other heroines pay the price for being 'good women in a men's world' (Carter 1979, 38). As Justine's purity constantly excites her persecutors, so Anthia's protestations of fidelity arouse Anchialos. As he looms over her, Anthia defends herself with a sword, and the prospective rapist/penetrator falls victim to his victim, penetrated by his sword. Anthia then passively awaits her fate, to which we shall return later.

Throughout Xenophon's novel, Anthia is desired for her beauty. She had earlier attracted a pirate *praefectus castrorum*, Euxinos. He and his companion Korymbos plotted to seduce both Anthia and Habrokomes, until the arrival of the bandit chief Apsyrtos put an end to their designs (2. 1–3). Bandits are just as much prey to homosexual desires as heterosexual desires. Simon Goldhill (1995, chapter 2) has recently analysed the homo-sexual liaisons in these texts, drawing particular attention to the debate in Achilles Tatios as to whether homosexual or heterosexual intercourse is more satisfying for a man (2. 35–end). For our purposes, we need only consider the narrative accounts of bandits' homosexual relationships. Survivors of tragically-crossed homosexual love affairs appear as assistants to the heroes in the course of the narratives. Overwhelmingly, however, despairing lovers from such relationships appear among the bandits, in a strikingly similar manner to the rejected heterosexual lovers of Romantic literature.[23] The classic case is that Robin Hood among thieves, Hippothoos, in Xenophon of Ephesos' novel, who, since the death of his beloved, leads a bandit group in Kilikia. He later renounces his life of outlawry and returns with Anthia and Habrokomes to Ephesos where he erects a huge monument for his beloved Hyperanthes before retiring with our heroes.[24]

Homosexual *erōs*, then, is problematized within the texts. It is banished to the context of outlawry which it may well provoke, but it may also redeem the bandit from his deviant life. The equivocal attitudes of the Second Sophistic to homosexual *erōs* (Goldhill 1995, chapter 2) are reflected in the novels' bandit episodes also.

The major cult practice attributed to bandits is human sacrifice. Such practices were considered shocking in the Roman Empire and were generally eliminated by the Romans wherever they were encountered.[25] Human sacri-fice, by its very outrageousness, defines the bandits as 'other': outsiders, beyond the bounds of normal human behaviour (see Winkler 1980). Hippothoos' band decide to sacrifice Anthia to Ares. Ancient ethnographers were particularly interested in the outlandish rituals of foreigners;[26] here the custom is particularly remarkable: they hang the victim from a tree and throw javelins at her: 'the god was considered to accept the sacrifices of all who hit: those who missed tried to appease him a second time' (2. 2: trans. Anderson). The association of sacrifice to Ares and javelin throwing irresistibly reminds us of Herodotos' account of the Skythian sacrifices to Ares.[27] In this case, the victim is tossed in the air and caught on the spearpoints of the celebrants. Hartog has shown (1980, *passim*) that the discourse of Herodotos' Book 4 principally establishes the Skythians as utterly distinct from the Greeks. In Xenophon of Ephesos' account, the Skythian practice is deliberately inverted: the victim is a woman, not a man; spears are thrown at her instead of the victim being tossed onto spears; in Herodotos if the victim evades the spears he is considered unworthy, in Xenophon of Ephesos the bandits, if unsuccessful, are encouraged to try again. Here, explicitly, bandits are represented as topsy-turvy outsiders: a fine statement of the nature of an enemy within.

Sacrifice usually involves joining in a communal feast (Easterling and Muir 1985, 17). Mention of human sacrifice in ancient literature always hints at the possible horrors of cannibalism. Achilles Tatios confronts the problem directly. Leukippe has been captured by the Egyptian bandits known as Boukoloi; and her lover, Kleitophon, is just arriving with the rescue party. Kleitophon takes up the story:

> I recognised that the maiden was Leukippe. They poured a libation over her head and led her round the altar to the accompaniment of a flute and a priest intoning what I guessed was an Egyptian hymn . . . At a signal, they all moved far away from the altar. One of the attendants laid her on her back and tied her to stakes fixed in the ground, as sculptors picture Marsyas bound to the tree. He next raised a sword and plunged it into her heart and then sawed all the way down to her abdomen. Her viscera leaped out. The attendants pulled out her entrails and carried them in their hands to the altar. When it was well cooked, they carved the whole lot up, and the bandits shared the meal.
>
> (3. 15: trans. Winkler)

This passage has attracted much comment recently because of its apparent relevance to charges of cannibalism directed at early Christians,[28] and our modern fascination with cannibalism.[29] Leukippe is treated as a sacrificial victim: she receives the preliminary libation (like the sprinkling of water on the bullock's forehead in the *bouphonia* to make him nod assent),[30] then, unlike an animal sacrifice, she is tied down before she is struck. After the initial incision, her entrails (*splanchna*) are extracted and grilled. These would normally be eaten by only a select few, then the flesh would be divided among the congregation. Here, the *splanchna* are tasted by all and Leukippe's body receives burial. After the ritual, she is treated as a dead human, not divided as a dead victim. However, to cull the sources for exact parallels in attested cults is surely to miss the mark. This act is a bestial parody of an everyday religious act, made more frightening by its generalized similarity to any ritual. Its very frightfulness labels it as an act of creatures opposed to the order of their society. A parallel is the oath taken by those definitive subversives, the Catilinarian conspirators. Sallust states that they swore an oath over wine mixed with blood (*Bellum Catilinae* 22); Plutarch (*Cicero* 10. 4) states that the blood was human blood, and Dio Cassius (37. 30. 3) that it was the blood of a slaughtered child: clearly the story grew in the telling. Bandits were seen as similarly vicious subversives. Habitually steeped in human blood, they are the outsiders whose actions obscenely parody those of everyday decent society.

As a society within society,[31] bandits had not only their own rituals, but also their own rules and punishments. Poor Anthia's trials were not over when she killed her assailant Anchialos. On the return of the band, she was condemned (even by the 'noble' robber Hippothoos)[32] to be buried alive with two large dogs. The punishment recalls the fate of Roman parricides.[33] Anthia had offended against the form of patriarchy represented by the topsy-turvy world of the bandits: the 'protection' of the predatory male. She had resisted the desires of Anchialos, who, by possessing her, might well have become her protector within the bandit community.[34] The anti-society judged the virgin avoiding violation guilty of parricide: the penalty that in an ordered society ensured the dominance of the senior male member here reinforces the right of the outlaw to enjoy the woman at his mercy.

Bandits live well away from the haunts of normal men: in mountain caves or marshes near the sea, on the frontiers of the polis. In antiquity, these frontiers were patrolled by ephebes, young men temporarily withdrawn from society to experience a coming of age ritual before final reintegration.[35] Bandits never reintegrated. Perpetual anti-ephebes on the frontiers of society, they never crossed the threshold into respectable adult male citizenship[36]. Normally, young men learning toughness will grow out of their rowdiness and may be indulged (cf. Fisher, this volume): hardened outsiders overturning the values of the polis could not. Only Hippothoos finds a niche for himself as a kindly uncle in Ephesian society and, instead of founding a household, the ex-bandit consoled himself by erecting a monument for Hyperanthes, the lover of his youth, and settling down with his new partner, Kleisthenes.

Like the 'herds'[37] of ephebes, the bandits cultivate a distinctive appearance. Heliodoros' Boukoloi

> cultivate an alarming appearance, particularly as regards their hair, which they pull forward to meet their eyebrows and toss violently as it falls over their shoulders, for they are well aware that long hair makes lovers seem more alluring but robbers more alarming.
>
> (2. 20: trans. Morgan)

The hairstyle which is appropriate to youth is a mark of the 'otherness' of the mature bandit. Young men, however, mature; bandits do not. They are insurgents, not police, on the frontiers; rapists not lovers, gluttons not civilized feeders. Problematically they share the position of ephebes, yet do so for all time to display to ephebes and mature men the dangers of remaining in a state of transition: they are lost in a *rite de passage.*

My paper began with the tale of the bandit Theron ('The Beast'); I want to end with Apuleius' tale of Thrasyleon ('Bold-Lion'). Their names recall the beasts with which Roman law equated them.[38] Theron's men were bestially employed, Thrasyleon dies as a man among beasts.

In an attempt to rob a town-councillor's house in Plataia, Thrasyleon disguises himself as a bear that is to fight in the morrow's bear hunt. The disguised bandits easily gain access to the house, but Thrasyleon is too successful as a bear; he deceives the dogs into believing that he really is a bear and they attack him, worrying him until he is finished off by the boar spears of the tardily aroused attendants:

> Thrasyleon's spirit, which deserved immortality, was finally overcome, but not his endurance. That illustrious pride of our band never betrayed his soldier's oath by crying out or even screaming. Though torn by teeth and ripped with steel, he continued to growl and roar like an animal, as he bore his present misfortune with noble consistency. He won eternal glory for himself, although he surrendered his life to fate.
>
> (*Met.* 4. 21: trans. Hanson)

'Bold-Lion' is a fine soldier, never betraying his *sacramentum*, but dying game. Like Caesar, he kept his habit decorously about him.[39] Yet we remember that he is a bandit, in bestial disguise, dying among dogs. Papirius' warnings are illustrated by his fate. His is a perverse *sacramentum*, he is in 'our faction', not a military unit, his life as a man was perversely spent in the mountains; it was lost in the city as he played the part of a beast brought in for the town games.

Civilization is founded on the oath taken legally and duly, not one taken in a haunt of miscreants. Echoing Papirius, Libanios in the fourth century AD speculates on the nature of human life if the menfolk abandoned their duties as town councillors:

> Why don't we follow the lead of the bandits who have closed the highways by the murders they commit . . . ? We ought to allow them to increase their possessions in this way, for it is their daggers that rescue them from their oxen, their plough, the seed time and all the labours of the land and quickly bring them wealth.
>
> (48. 35: trans. Norman)

Just so. The ideology of banditry in the Second Sophistic is crisp: once responsibility has been removed, men revert to their bestial nature as semi-culturated ephebes, always in the wild, their tastes uncultured, like the Cyclops in their love of drink, so unlike the heroes and heroines of the novels who value chastity. Once order has been removed, life in the mountains is cheap and bestial. We, Jove be praised, are returned ephebes: we have grown up.

Notes

1 Goldhill 1995. For the Second Sophistic, when the Greeks experienced a rebirth of self-confidence under Roman rule, see Anderson 1993, Bowersock 1969, Bowie 1970, Jones 1978 .
2 Eck 1984, 131; Syme 1979, 308–29; Campbell 1984.
3 *Digest* 50. 16. 118; cf. 49. 15. 24.
4 The *locus classicus* is Dio Cassius 52. 3–5; cf. 75. 2. 5.
5 Contrast the position of Octavian/Augustus as conceived in *Res Gestae* 1: 'At the age of nineteen on my own responsibility and at my own expense I raised an army, with which I successfully championed the liberty of the republic when it was oppressed by the tyranny of a faction.' Subsequent success proved the justice of his cause, and the public spirit in which he acted. Compare St Augustine's comments (below, n. 31).
6 On bandits as an ideological threat to the Roman state, see Shaw 1984.
7 I emphasize the narratological aspects of this account, at the expense of the historical, because Livy seems to have used the few sources available for the period of Books 5–10 with a great deal of inventiveness. This practice has recently been drawn to our attention by Wiseman 1979, 3–56, and Woodman 1988.
8 On the psychological importance of this, see Girard 1977; Burkert 1983.
9 Tacitus, *Annales* 13. 35, with the comments of Isaac 1990, 23–5.
10 See now Goodwin 1994, 148–51. For a fictional evocation of their ceremonies, see the opening chapter of Y. Kadri Karaosmanoğlu's *Nur Baba*.
11 Davies 1989, 188; cf. Fink 1971, no.78, line 18.
12 Xenophon of Ephesos, *Ephesiaca* 2. 13.
13 Xenophon of Ephesos, *Ephesiaca* 3. 10.
14 A dangerous sign: compare Herodotos 6. 84 on Kleomenes' self-destructive drinking.
15 For discussion of 'commiles' in Roman ideology, see Williams 1990, 90; Campbell 1984, 37–8.
16 Thomas 1982, 1–7; Woodman 1988, 188.
17 Brownmiller 1975, 92–8, would criticize my easy appropriation of the adverb. I must appeal to the customary use of such 'chauvinist' seizure of nature when reconstructing the ideology of patriarchal societies.
18 For example, le Bohec 1994, 222.
19 The stories of Kirke and Kalypso are primal examples of possessive women. In Euripides' *Medea* (569–73), Jason comments on the feminine addiction to sex. Such a stereotype provides much of the comedy in *Lysistrata* also. On female lust, see Carson 1990.
20 Shakespeare, *Twelfth Night*, 5. 1. 112–3.
21 With the exception of Kleitophon in Achilles Tatios' adventurous novel.
22 4. 5 (trans. G. Anderson). Compare Leukippe's outburst cited above.

23 The *locus classicus* is the case of Valentine in Shakespeare's *Two Gentlemen of Verona* Act 4, Scene 1. Compare also Don José in Prosper Mérimée and Bizet, (H)ernani in Victor Hugo and Verdi (interestingly transformed into a real soldier in Shaw's *Arms and the Man*), the robber leaders in Schiller and Verdi, etc.
24 Very much as Newman Noggs retires with Nicholas and Madeleine at the end of *Nicholas Nickleby*.
25 Tac. *Ann.* 14. 30; Webster 1980, 74–5.
26 The point is well made by Hartog 1980 in his discussion of Herodotos' account of Skythian customs.
27 4. 62.
28 See, for example, Henrichs 1970.
29 Winkler 1980. Compare Arens 1979, Sanday 1986.
30 Easterling and Muir 1985, 17.
31 If not an 'imperium in imperio'. Compare Augustine's comments on banditry: 'When justice is removed, what are kingdoms, but large bandit bands; and what are bandit bands but small kingdoms?' (*De Civitate Dei* 4. 4).
32 On the concept 'noble robber', see Hobsbawm 1972, Chapter 3.
33 For an explicit statement of the punishment, see Paulus, *Sententiae*, 5. 21.
34 Brownmiller 1975 suggests that monogamy was instituted as a contractual protection against rape for women: the woman surrendered her sexual autonomy in return for guaranteed possession by one partner only.
35 There is now an extensive literature on the *ephēbeia*. See Brelich 1969, Tazelaar 1967, Vidal-Naquet 1981/1986.
36 Unlike the successful reintegration into society of Daphnis and Chloe (Longus 4. 36–40).
37 Spartan youths were grouped in *agelai* (herds).
38 For example, *Codex Theodosianus* 1. 29. 8.
39 On Caesar's decorous death see Suetonius, *Iulius* 82. 2; Plut. *Caesar* 66.

11

Arms and the man

Soldiers, masculinity and power in Republican and Imperial Rome

Richard Alston

In many Western societies, the male is seen as powerful, sometimes all-powerful, and is defined by his ability to wield power. In many cases, the power that is wielded is violent. Violence has been seen as a particularly male attribute and the usually legitimated violence offered by the soldier has often meant that soldiers have been represented as ideals of manhood. In modern Western society the role of the soldier has been somewhat marginalized, but violence has remained important in asserting masculinity in both public and private spheres, and a linkage between the male capacity for violence and capability of exercising other forms of social power is common. Women's access to social power, either violent or non-violent, has often been systematically restricted and women who have come to exercise any kind of social power have been seen as masculinized.[1] In British society and in many other Western societies, femininity has been associated with a lack of power, either physical or social, or at least an avoidance of obvious manipulation of power and a deference to male authority. Men, conversely, have been seen as temperamentally and physically suited to wield power.

Each society defines legitimate power, and the debate over the precise definitions and boundaries of legitimate authority is the essence of political discourse. In many societies these are matters of continual dispute and are therefore in continuous but varying degrees of flux. Since definitions of masculinity are so involved with power in many societies – and Roman society is no exception – it follows that there may be debate about and concerning the masculine (Brittan 1989, 3). It also follows that societies undergoing political or social change are likely to undergo a re-evaluation of masculinity. Tosh (1991) demonstrates, using the Benson family, how middle class views of masculinity in the late Victorian era changed in a generation, so that instead of asserting one's masculinity in the domestic environment, more and more the home became associated with the feminine and masculinity was affirmed away from the family.

Notions of masculinity are, of course, normative and, like notions of the feminine, often highly oppressive. Any disruption or change in notions of masculinity may be very personally disruptive and, if replicated across a considerable swathe of society, could produce political strains (Clarke, N. 1991). Attempts to define masculinity in times of social and political change can be seen as part of a discourse redefining social patterns and asserting a particular political and social ideology. Such a context could make discussions of masculinity highly personally and politically charged. Images of the masculine may reflect political struggles and attempts by various groups to assert their interpretation of correct male behaviour. In a complex and changing society, there may be several competing strands in the discourse on masculinity, and although we may be able to identify dominant strands, contrary views may never completely be suppressed.

This paper seeks to examine conceptions of masculinity, and in particular the relationship between soldiers and masculinity, in just such a society: Rome in the period around the so-called Augustan revolution. This was a period when Rome's political and social structures were affected by her military success in conquering the Mediterranean lands. The benefits of empire and its costs had a considerable impact on many sectors of Roman society. This period also saw a political revolution in that the oligarchy that controlled Rome became increasingly threatened. The result of the political turmoil at the end of the Republic was the eventual ascendancy of the generals and the reintroduction of monarchy into Rome under Augustus. In such a period of transformation, we see a certain questioning of traditional values and some changes in the dominant ideology of masculinity.

Conceptions of man

Latin has two entirely different nouns which are both normally translated into English as 'man'. Santoro L'Hoir's analysis (1992, 1–22, 63) of the usage of '*vir*' and '*homo*' in Latin prose points to rather significant Republican distinctions between the two concepts. Both '*homo*' and '*vir*' may be ideologically neutral in certain contexts but, in general, '*vir*' appears to have been used for more aristocratic men, or men worthy of praise, while '*homo*' seems to be used more often as the generic term or in hostile contexts.[2] '*Vir*' is the root of the abstract noun '*virtus*', a term overworked in Augustan literature, which ancient historians and Latinists struggle to translate, using words such as 'virtue' or 'manliness'. The *vir* is of higher status than the *homo* and it is the *vir* with whom we should identify the ideal man.

The concept of a *vir* appears, as we should expect, to be related to power (*potestas*). The man who wielded legitimate power was a *vir*. The *vir* was also to be as far as possible independent of the power of others. The ideal man should be legally, financially and personally autonomous.[3] Once that autonomy was threatened, either through incurring debts (a serious problem for the political classes of the late Republic), or by loss of the means for economic survival, or by loss of political freedom, one's status as a *vir* was also threatened. In a slave society, it is perhaps unsurprising that stress was laid on autonomy as a defining characteristic of masculinity, and many have seen the fundamental division in Roman society, and in other ancient societies, as being between the free and the servile.[4] The characteristics of the ideal man were not, however, simply negative: a freedom from subjection to the power of others. They also relate to the demonstration of autonomy through the exercise of power over others. Most notably, the head of a Roman household, the *pater*, had, originally at least, sweeping legal powers over his dependants, his children and his slaves, though not normally his wife. In his own house, even if nowhere else, the Roman man was a *vir*, a status reflected in the use of '*vir*' rather than '*homo*' by wives to refer to their husbands.

The normal workings of social and political life in this highly stratified society in which patronage was socially and politically important, meant that even the Roman élite contracted financial and political obligations. Ideally, however, these obligations were not to interfere with their freedoms. The line over which a patron could not cross in his treatment of a client is obscure, but there were limits on patronal authority and, as Millar points out (1984a, 1986, 1989), patrons could not depend on the complete and loyal support of their clients. The Romans appear to have been sensitive to the relationship between obligation and independence, and the literature of the end of the first century AD abounds with discussion of the correct treatment of clients by patrons. Discussions of dinner parties and Martial's descriptions of and complaints about the ritual morning salutation, a ceremony which needed particularly careful handling as it dramatized social inequalities and obligations, are the most obvious examples.[5] That such relationships were expressed in the language of friendship rather than through clearer expressions of status inequality reflects pre-eminent Roman aristocratic concerns with *libertas*, another term overworked in the Triumviral and Augustan periods.

For the non-élite, it was probably much more difficult to preserve even the illusion of independence, especially after the much debated decline of the free rural peasantry in the second century BC.[6] *Libertas* was, however, an important rallying cry for popular agitators in the city of Rome. *Libertas*, as defended through the *ius provocationis* by which the tribunes were called on to defend a citizen and prevent magisterial action against him, was a privilege that the Roman mob and, in fact, the Roman élite could be mobilized to defend. Thus, Cicero (*In Verrem* 2. 5. 160–73) alienated support from the corrupt governor Verres by stressing his breach of *libertas* in the public beating of the Roman *eques*, Gavisa, in Sicily; while Catiline and later Clodius were able to call on popular support against Cicero for threatened and previous breaches of the rights of citizens. Examples could easily be multiplied from the tribunician disputes of the last century of the Republic and, of course, in the quasi-historical accounts of the development of tribunician power during 'the struggle of the orders' in the fifth and fourth centuries BC. The politicians of the late Republic justified their actions in terms of *libertas*, and as Caesar's assassins celebrated their role as restorers of freedom, so Octavian presented his campaign against Antony as an attempt to free the state 'oppressed by the tyranny of a faction'.[7] In the end, the triumphant Octavian annexed to himself the role of defender of liberty through his acquisition of tribunician power, and he and subsequent emperors made use of their status as guarantors of individual freedom both to monitor their governors by providing individual citizens in the provinces, such as Paul, with a final court of appeal, and to override the rights of individuals.[8]

It is difficult to over-emphasize the importance of *libertas* in the last two centuries BC, though the importance of the concept in the earlier period is less than certain. Nicolet (1980, 38) points to a great strengthening of the guarantees affecting the individual citizen in 'a series of laws which soon came to be regarded as the essential core of Roman *libertas* and the keystone of the constitution'. For Nicolet (1980, 320) *libertas* 'is perhaps the key concept of the Roman civic and political vocabulary'. *Libertas* came to define Roman citizenship, regulating the relationship between a Roman citizen and the sovereign authority (*imperium*) of a Roman magistrate. The absolute *imperium* of Roman magistrates continued to be exercised over non-Romans, allies and enemies alike, and it is no coincidence that the rights of Romans and the differentials between Romans and allies increased at the very moment when Rome's empire was decisively extended beyond Italy and Rome's armies began to direct the wealth of the Mediterranean towards Italy. The political superiority of Rome's citizens was seen not just in the conquest of East and West, but also in several well-publicized violent exercises of authority by magistrates in the towns of allies. The public beating of magistrates of politically friendly states for not providing adequate facilities for visiting Romans was a demonstration of the legal superiority of Roman citizens, defended as they were from these abuses by the bundle of privileges of *libertas*. Beating, especially public beating, was a dramatic demonstration of the subjugation of the person to the power of another and an important symbol of the servility of the victim and his community.[9]

In the second century, *libertas* was becoming a defining characteristic of the Roman *vir*.[10] Social, political and economic changes probably further enhanced the importance of *libertas*. The growing wealth of the Roman aristocracy and changes in the organization of agriculture labour may have exacerbated tensions between upper and lower orders. Political disruption and the active use of the tribunate to mobilize political support probably focused attention on issues such as *libertas*. The violence that resulted from these political disputes, the driving of political groups from public areas by violence and the deaths of several prominent political figures, including tribunes, brought into the open the issue of political representation in the Roman state. The aristocracy could defend *libertas* against the threat of popular tyranny, especially as the Roman political élite became more conversant with Greek political history and theory, and popular leaders defended *libertas* against the threats posed to the traditional guarantors of *libertas* by magistrates and the oligarchy. It was over this ideological ground that the civil wars that brought the Republic to an end were fought.

There were two possible exceptions to this association of the *vir* with freedom from the *potestas* of another and freedom to wield *potestas*: an adult son in the *potestas* of his father, and a soldier.[11] The former is something of a non-problem. A son was clearly not independent and could be subject to outrages of his person, such as being beaten.[12] With a young son, this demonstrated his current standing, but, after all, he was yet to become a man.[13] On reaching adulthood, when a son might be expected to assume the status of a *vir*, paternal authority became a potential problem.[14] Rates of mortality, however, reduced the significance of this potential difficulty. According to Saller (1994, 58, table 3. 2e) only 54 per cent of 20-year-old males would have had a living father.[15] Ten years later, when aristocratic males would be entering magisterial posts, only 32 per cent would have had a living father, and towards the pinnacle of their careers, at aged 40, only 13 per cent would potentially have been under the authority of their fathers. Few sons would be in the position of the Prince Regent, waiting for his father to die before he could assume his rightful place in society. Even for this minority, potential problems could be avoided by formal manumission of the son or, as seems to be the more normal pattern, the creation of a separate, independent household for the son who would be given either an allowance or a portion of his inheritance (Gardner 1993, 55–72). Even if formally under the control of his father, a son could lead a largely independent life in which he could assert his status and exercise *de facto* authority over his own slaves and children.

Soldiers, freedom and manhood

Soldiers are a far more complex case. Military service was part of the duty of a male citizen, and a large proportion of male citizens in the early and mid-Republican periods will have served in the army.[16] Technically, the citizen under arms appears to have had very similar rights to the civilian, but in fact the soldier was subject to a whole range of more severe penalties for misconduct, and his right of appeal, and therefore his *libertas*, was limited (Nicolet 1980, 108–9). Bound by an oath, the soldiers were subject to greater authority and seem to have been in practice unable to call on the tribunes for support. Generals could, therefore, carry out exemplary punishments and even randomized punishments, such as decimation, without fear of tribunician interference or any legal consequences (political consequences were a different matter) on laying down their powers. Such an abdication of legal and personal autonomy is difficult to reconcile with a view of the ideal man which emphasizes just such qualities.

In the early Republican period, when the army served to face threats real or imagined against the safety of Rome itself, the defence of the city and the citizens could be seen as collective action to preserve communal and individual freedom. The threats were always that the political power of Rome would be flouted or that Rome would be subject to the authority of another state or that the citizens would be enslaved and lose their freedom. In such a case, a compromising of the liberty of the individual through military service in order to ensure the freedom of the community was both reasonable and to be expected. Indeed, failure to ensure order or to serve loyally could endanger the *libertas* of the individual and the community, justifying savage punishments. Our first-century BC sources on the 'struggle of the orders' represent the various factions as manipulating this tension: in some cases, the invasion of Roman territory encouraged enlistment and the subsequent reduction in political strife, while in others the citizens show a marked reluctance to enlist.[17]

The potential anomalies of the soldiers' situation probably only gradually came to the fore in the second century BC and later, when it was no longer credible to represent Rome's campaigns as being in defence of the freedoms of the citizens, and soldiers came to serve further from their homes and probably for longer periods. It was also the period in which an increasing emphasis came to be placed on *libertas* as a political concept and as a mark of individual status. Livy's Spurius Ligustinus (42. 34), a soldier who intervened in a dispute between former centurions and the enlisting magistrate over the rank proper to their status, can be seen as a symbol of the old world. His extended service over many years, in many different campaigns, was selfless devotion to the state. He would enlist again in any rank the general thought fit to assign him, and his intervention prompted the other former centurions to do likewise. Ligustinus, with his small peasant homestead, was even in 171 BC a throwback to a mythic past. The future and, in fact, Ligustinus' present lay with those centurions who thought more of their honour and status than selfless devotion to the community. Sallust's similar, but non-specific, portrayal of the soldier of a previous age in *Bellum Catilinae* 7 depicts the heroic soldiers' selfless devotion in highly rhetorical terms, in contrast to his portrayal of contemporary soldiers and society.[18]

The increasing polarization of political debate in the second century BC may have increased and made more obvious tensions between free status and service, especially when magistrates attempted to conscript troops for unpopular campaigns. By the first century BC, the soldiers were becoming increasingly professionalized and the military increasingly separate from the rest of the population. In the last years of the Republic, the military had a distinct political agenda. The soldiers increasingly threatened the political establishment and the constitution in pursuit of their own political and financial interests. The ideal of service to the wider community and the idea that the soldiers were simply citizens under arms with identical political interests to civilians were parts of a mythic past. Sallust, Livy and possibly Livy's source, writing in the first century BC, painted an ideal of military manhood which had, according to them, long departed.

Increasing social stratification and structural differentiation must also have had an impact. Politicians such as Cicero were men of letters and rhetoric, not primarily military leaders, though they may have held military appointments at various points in their careers. These men asserted their status and power in non-military areas, through culture, through civil politics and through their wealth. Command of troops was no longer the main area in which political reputations were made, and political careers did not necessarily culminate in military expeditions.

From the end of the second century BC, soldiers without property had been admitted into the army, but even before this the property qualification had ceased to have much significance. The army could be represented as being, and to a large extent probably was, composed of the poorer elements of society. The wealthy and largely hereditary oligarchy sought to legitimate and justify its power and the origins and trappings of its wealth. Birth and culture, notably Greek culture, were seen as markers of suitability to wield power.[19] This gradual redefinition of masculinity would progressively exclude the ordinary soldiers from the status of paragons of masculinity. The very poverty of the soldiers increased their dependence on military service and their generals, and so reduced their autonomy. Their loyalty to the general in civil disturbances suggested a loss of political liberty. For Sallust, the soldiers had degenerated to become men of corrupted morals (*Cat.* 11. 7) and he could describe with horror soldiers elevated from 'the flock' to become senators (*Cat.* 37. 6; cf. Cicero, *Pro Plancio* 72), an alteration in status which threatened civic order. The soldiers were not of sufficient status to be capable of exercising control and power. For Cicero, they were rustics, unadorned by the civilized values and culture that became a man, and, in stronger moments, he could even describe them as beasts.[20]

While there was probably no incompatibility between masculine respectability and service as a soldier in the third century BC and earlier, the increasing emphasis on *libertas* encouraged a growing disjunction between military service, especially among 'the herd', and the status of *vir*. The decline in the social status of soldiers in the last centuries of the Republic made it increasingly difficult for the ordinary soldier to be seen as a *vir*. Our sources are, on the whole, hostile towards soldiers whose power as non-*viri* threatened the whole fabric of society. In spite of the crucial role of military success in generating the prosperity and power of members of the élite, the soldiers did not conform to ideals of manhood.

Augustan masculinities: old men in a new world?

This tension between the socio-economic impact of the soldiers and their social status comes to the fore in the Augustan period. The confusion of ideals in the evidence from this period suggests that there was no agreed or dominant view of the *vir* or of the soldier. Augustus established the institutional framework for the professional army. After Augustus, most soldiers would have been away from Italy for their full term of service. That term was itself extended: Augustan troops could be expected to serve twenty years in the provinces, and many were even then unable to obtain discharge at the proper time, and a significant proportion of them would have died in service, even discounting the losses caused by enemy action. This geographical separation was enhanced by legal separation: soldiers were not allowed to marry, presuming that this was an Augustan regulation; their camp property was regarded as separate from any property held in civilian life; they were able to make wills to dispose of that property even if their fathers were still alive and they had not been legally manumitted.[21] The latter may mark some recognition that it was improper for a soldier to be within the *potestas* of another apart from his general. The marriage ban, however, prevented the soldiers from forming separate households, an area crucial to the exercise of *potestas*. So, although none but the commander was able to exercise authority over them, the soldiers' own *potestas* was limited. This separation of soldiers completed their emergence as a distinct status group; but the limitations on their *potestas* and the authority exercised over them reduced their status in the eyes of aristocratic writers.

In contrast to the gradual professionalization and social segregation of the ordinary soldiers, there was an attempt to inculcate a military ideology in the Roman aristocratic youth. The addition to the *cursus honorum* of junior military posts in charge of cavalry units and in the legions and the development of vigorous military exercises for aristocratic youths demonstrate Augustus' policy of generating an aristocracy fit to campaign. Yet, in attempting to spread military experience among the élite, Augustus created the paradoxical situation by which a professional soldiery was commanded by a largely amateur officer corps, which further enhanced the division of the *viri* from the soldiers. The debate over whether generals should be allowed to take their wives with them on campaign in Tacitus (*Annales* 3. 33–4) shows that the aristocratic man should be able to exercise his authority over both the troops and his wife.[22]

By his reforms, Augustus may have been trying to create in the aristocracy an ideology of service and duty, an echo of the attitude of Spurius Ligustinus, which would override concerns over their status and encourage service in a state in which all freedom had been lost. As the men of his family laboured under his auspices, so the aristocracy also had its duties to fulfil. This Augustan concern with devotion to the state may be reflected in the emphasis placed in Augustan literature on *pietas*, another concept which Latinists and historians struggle to translate. The great Augustan epic, the *Aeneid*, presents a *pius vir*, a hero who was devoted to his people and followed his disciplined fate through the disasters and wars to an ultimate triumph. *Pietas*, meaning something like duty to the gods, to the people and to the family, defines Aeneas' character.[23] Although he is far from being a mirror image of Augustus, the hero's moral character has implications for that of his descendant. *Pietas* defined Virgil's Augustan *vir* and became one of the conspicuous virtues of the emperor himself (*RG* 34). Other concerns, personal concerns, were to be put to one side in devotion to the nation as Augustus put his private welfare to one side when he sought to fulfil his manifest duty, first to avenge his father and second to govern the state. Suetonius (*Divus Augustus* 28) represents Augustus as having twice wished to lay aside the burdens of power for personal reasons; but, on both occasions, he was persuaded to return to the task for the good of the state. So Aeneas had to gather his future Romans and leave Carthage and Dido. Aeneas' rejection of the alluring Dido and her expanding city to face his destiny was an act of *pietas* and *virtus*. He was a man governed by his duty, not his passions.

The elegiac lovers also become voluntarily subservient to an ideal, their lover. Whatever one makes of the conventions of the genre, the stress on loss of liberty on the part of the elegiac lover is remarkable.[24] The very first line of the Propertian corpus (1. 1. 1) has Cynthia capturing the lover, and in the capturing Propertius loses his freedom. With remarkable frequency the elegiac poets return to the theme of their powerlessness in the face of the woman. In nearly all cases, it is the woman who has power to grant her favours to the man. The man is dependent, a slave to the woman. Propertius represents himself as struck, in a very physical metaphor, by Love who tramples him underfoot (1. 1. 3–4). Again, the lover is habitually betrayed by his woman who, like the traditional Roman male, is allowed free licence in her partners. Propertius is even assaulted by Cynthia herself, who storms Propertius' house in her chariot and breaks up a private party, driving away his two prostitutes and leaving him to beg for mercy (4. 8). In another standard poetic scene, the lover is excluded from the woman's house. He must beg entrance as a client. The client came to the house where his patron's power and authority were displayed. In Propertius, Cynthia exercises power by excluding the lover from her house. Propertius is unable to exclude Cynthia from his house and, on his own territory, is displayed as servile through the beating that Cynthia inflicts on him. The traditional, engendered exercise of power is reversed. Cynthia controls the house. Cynthia exercises power. Cynthia has adopted the role of a *vir*.

It is, of course, to be accepted that these events are elaborate fictions, and their relationship to any historical truth may be remote (Wyke 1987, 1989), but in Augustan propaganda, Antony's involvement with Cleopatra was represented as a form of devotion in which Antony was enslaved. It is not impossible that this was believed by some in Rome. Even if the social situation depicted by the elegists could not be replicated exactly, the image of the man enslaved to the romantic ideal that was the elegiac woman, certainly a non-traditional role for the *vir*, may have had a certain appeal for Roman men in the changed political circumstances of the very late Republic and Augustan period.

This new masculinity carried certain political implications. At face value, the elegiac lover rejects a military career and is bemused by others who follow the military path. Devotion to the lover could lead to a withdrawal from public life, and this could be seen as anti-Augustan, though in life the first of the four Augustan elegists, Gallus, reconciled the demands of governmental and poetic careers. The lover is, however, happy to experience and even celebrate the triumphs of the emperor, even if such celebrations are sometimes ironic (Prop. 3. 4). Nevertheless, there is in both Propertius and Ovid a remarkable abstraction from military matters. War is carried out by others, in districts remote from Rome, against tribes and peoples who are merely names on placards and exotica to be processed before the people of Rome. This abstraction parallels what must have been the real situation for very many of the Roman people. Although the amount of conflict in the early principate is frequently underestimated, even the officially active may have either avoided involvement in warfare or been involved in active warfare for only very brief periods. After the civil wars, in spite of the continual campaigning of the Augustan period, the age was one of relative peace for the majority of the population.

Given the increasing remoteness of warfare, the extensive use of military language by the elegists is surprising. The lover continually uses the language of camps, sieges and capture, and sometimes uses military imagery for more explicit purposes.[25] There is an element of violence in the depiction of sexual activity: battles are fought on the couch. The language of military activity and capture may have been part of popular parlance in discussing sexual activity, but the metaphor is extended beyond what could reasonably be regarded as popular usage. For the lover, his devotion to the loved one, his camping outside the door, and his besieging of her affections are similar devotions to that of military service. The soldier serves by conquering the Parthian; the lover serves by conquering his mistress. In this way, the devotion to one service automatically excludes participation in the other. Military duty took lovers away from their women and the two are depicted as incompatible.[26] The activities are only opposed to this limited extent. In fact, the activities are paralleled. Both require the man to abandon his independence and allow another to have power over him. Both can lead to physical suffering. Both visions of the masculine role would seem to have had only limited appeal for the *libertas*-loving Roman aristocracy in the longer term.

The developing autocracy in Rome presented the Roman aristocracy with a considerable problem: how was a *vir* to behave if the state was controlled by a single man and the only politically free man was the emperor himself? Not all *viri* could hope to become emperors. Political circumstances forced a limited adjustment in the concept of a *vir*, an adjustment which took the Roman aristocracy some considerable time to accomplish. Correct behaviour under a tyrannical ruler is a major theme of the historical writings of Tacitus, who traced the relationship between aristocracy and emperor from AD 14 to 96. He emphasizes his view that freedom, in the old Republican sense, disappeared in the Augustan period. He suggests that there was a thin line that a *vir* could tread between insubordination and servility. Few managed this honourable middle course, notably M. Lepidus (*Ann.* 4. 20), L. Piso (*Ann.* 6. 10) and his own father-in-law, Agricola.[27] Some preserved their freedom and their status as *viri* at the cost of their lives.[28] The majority never achieved this status, as Tiberius made clear by calling them 'men ready for slavery'. The phrase was supposedly delivered in Greek, but Tacitus renders it in Latin as '*o homines ad servitutem paratos*' (*Ann.* 3. 65). In the difficult conditions of the reign of Domitian, Agricola remained a *vir* by following his duty towards the state meekly and neither threatening nor praising the emperor (Tac. *Agr.* 1, 40–1, 44–5). Virility was preserved by a withdrawal into silence, a silence in public, among friends and even in the intimacies of the house where the *potestas* of the *vir* was threatened by informers even among his own slaves (Pliny, *Ep.* 1. 12. 7–8). Under a tyrant, the *vir* could no longer control even his own household. His only freedom was in silence. The restoration of liberty, as both Tacitus and the Younger Pliny emphasize, was a restoration of the voice of the aristocratic male.[29]

The imperial period saw an increasing internalization of *potestas*, which adapted ideas current in Greek philosophy (Foucault 1986, 45). Power was to be exercised on one's own person. Those who sought to sate hedonistic desires in sexual or other activities were scorned by the conservative élite (Brown 1988, 18–19). This abandonment of the person to desire was a form of slavery. A man who could not control himself was not capable of controlling others and certainly not suitable to control an empire (Dio Chrys. *Or.* 3. 34). Emperors such as Nero and Gaius were not, therefore, *viri*, in spite of their power, as can be seen through their 'effeminate' behaviour, but were slaves to their own passions (Suet. *Gaius* 52; *Nero* 29, 51). The lover of wisdom was the man who sought to control his emotions and his body. It is often noted that members of the élite appear increasingly concerned with their bodily weaknesses and with illness in the second century AD and later, but it is notable that the weakened bodies were forced to perform feats of endurance and work.[30] This exercise of *potestas* over the body, aided by philosophers, doctors and athletic trainers, became an aim and a distinguishing characteristic of the élite, an aim replicated in Christian ascetic attitudes.[31] The new man of the empire compensated for his loss of political freedom by extending his *potestas* over his own person. Virility became domesticated.

Tacitus' account (*Ann.* 1. 16–49) of the mutinies on the Rhine and Danube that followed Augustus' death in AD 14 provides us with an opportunity to assess the soldiers of the new imperial army against the ideals of masculinity. Tacitus displays a limited fellow-feeling with the soldiers, who clearly had legitimate grievances and were subject to flagrant abuses; but his narrative, editorial voice is hostile to the mutineers. They were led by men of low status, trouble-makers and rabble-rousers. They were men who were subject to beatings and who were unfree. Interestingly, Tacitus emphasizes their physical imperfections by noting how their general was forced to touch their toothless gums and to observe their scarred bodies. Scars from battle were marks of honour in the republican period, but these were scars from beatings administered by the centurions. The impact of Greek ideas of the perfection of the physical form, so obvious from Augustan statuary, must also have affected attitudes towards the body and disfigurement. Toothlessness, with its associations with old age, symbolized the natural loss of physical power. Their wild swings of mood, their violence towards social superiors, and their lack of a coherent policy suggest a further lack of personal control. The soldiers were enslaved to their officers and to their emotions. True, they were slaves in a world becoming enslaved to the emperor, but the soldiers were no more *viri* than those senatorial *homines* ready to be slaves. Thus, their show of independence, especially in the presence of a real *vir* (Germanicus, the hero of the early books of the *Annales*), was to be scorned.

Contrasting masculinities

For Dio Chrysostom, soldiers were a useful way of focusing attention on the problem of freedom, since although they were certainly not slaves, they were not completely free either, being subject to the power of their generals.[32] They were subject to military discipline, but famously could not discipline themselves. Writers frequently complain of the ill-discipline of the soldiers and of generals and emperors pandering to their needs. Since they were not capable of exercising control for themselves, they needed to be controlled by others; and those generals and emperors who used archaic and very firm disciplinary measures against the soldiers are usually praised. Corbulo's savage disciplining of the soldiers of the East apparently cost the lives of several of his soldiers, but he is not condemned for these actions (Tac. *Ann.* 13. 35). The introduction of a strict disciplinary régime became a *topos* associated with the actions of a good general.[33] Emperors who looked primarily to the troops for support or attempted to buy their support, such as Domitian and the Severans, are subject to scathing attacks. Dio Cassius (75. 2. 5–6) seems to speak from the heart when describing the soldiers who formed Severus' new praetorian guard.[34] They were boorish and bestial. Soldiers did not have the power and the control that came with being a man (Brown 1988, 9–12). They did not have the culture which allowed the *vir* to exercise self-control. Examples could be multiplied without difficulty. Juvenal's *Satire* 16 is an indictment of the privileges granted to soldiers. The soldiers were brutal and violent, attacking men in the street and then using violence to deny their victims justice. Apuleius (*Metamorphoses* 9. 39–42) shows the soldier attacking a gardener and then, his assault having surprisingly failed, using the full force of the state against his victim. Petronius gives us two stories of the brutality of soldiers. A soldier robs one of the main characters (*Sat.* 82). More dramatically, a man is accompanied on a journey by a soldier who, among the tombs outside the city, turns into a wolf (*Sat.* 62). Once again the soldier is associated with the inhuman.

By the end of the second century, the army had been transformed and bore little relationship to its mid-Republican forbear. The soldiers were mostly recruited from the frontier provinces, not from the heartlands of Greek and Roman culture from which most of the senators came (Mann 1983). Most of the aristocracy would have had little experience of warfare and few dealings with troops. The troops were a remote and threatening group. They were seen as cultural and moral inferiors, one step above the barbarians, and antithetical to the aristocratic *vir*.

Others could choose to represent the soldiers in different ways and thus offer competing views of the role and status of soldiers, and possibly of masculinity. The low status of soldiers in literary representations contrasts with imperial representations of soldiers. Augustus chose to distance himself from soldiers by dropping the term 'comrades' (*commilitones*) in favour of 'soldiers' (*milites*) in addresses to the troops (Suet. *Aug.* 25). But this habit was not universally followed: Trajan, an emperor who is idolized by our literary sources, referred to the troops as *commilitones*.[35] In the Severan period, Septimius Severus raised the status of soldiers and famously advised his sons to look to the support of the soldiers before all others (Dio Cass. 76. 15). Soldiers enjoyed an elevated legal status in the provinces as Roman citizens, and then as *honestiores*, a status which placed them on a par with the local élites of the empire. Yet the history of the legal status of soldiers is complex, and is certainly not one of straightforward aggrandizing of the position of soldiers (Alston 1995, 53–68). One of the most distinctive aspects of the legal status of the soldiers, the inability to contract a legal marriage, may have been ameliorated by various measures, but was not disposed of until AD 197 (Garnsey 1970; Campbell 1978). Similarly, although soldiers and veterans received significant privileges from the time of Augustus, there was continual pressure on those privileges from local and government officials, and several supposed grants of privileges in the second century may be simple restatements of rights obtained in earlier reigns; some privileges, such as rights of children of veteran auxiliary men, were reduced in the second century. The emperors had an obvious interest in securing the loyalty of the troops, and granting privileges was a comparatively cheap way of showing their regard for soldiers' interests, but convincing those who had to abide by those privileges, government officials and local élites, that the soldiers deserved to be treated as high status individuals was an entirely different matter (Alston 1995, 64-8).

Popular images of soldiers are more difficult to obtain. In Jewish sources, the soldiers were not only representatives of an alien and hostile power, but were also gentiles and could not, therefore, be represented as ideal men. In Christian sources, soldiers were most often associated with persecutions, and by the fourth century both the army and the dominant ideology had undergone significant change. Documentary material, inscriptions and papyri, present significant problems to the historian of *mentalité*. Soldiers' letters preserved on papyrus do not appear to show any consciousness that military service was a loss of independence and therefore posed a threat to the autonomy and masculinity of the recruit. On the whole, in the first two centuries AD, military service appears to have been a desirable alternative to working the land. The economic rewards were certainly sufficient inducement for the non-élite of Roman Egypt. Military service also brought some local status. Soldiers were representatives of the Roman state and were, therefore, people of some influence (Alston 1995). The loss of independence that came with military service appears not to have led to a reduction in status; rather individual power, and hence status, was enhanced.

Soldiers themselves appear to have been proud of their status. We cannot, of course, know how many soldiers and veterans avoided commemorating their military careers on tombstones, and the use of the designation '*veteranus*' by former soldiers in the communities of Roman Egypt is certainly not systematic. Nevertheless, we have a considerable number of military tombstones from many provinces of the empire giving the particular soldier's name, age, length of service and sometimes unit. The inscriptions also often note who erected the inscription: the soldier's heirs, freed or relatives. These individuals chose to be commemorated as soldiers. Frequently, these tombstones carry a rather formulaic depiction of the soldier. One of the most interesting and common of these depictions is of a cavalryman, frequently himself of barbarian stock, riding down a crudely portrayed and often naked, sometimes animalistic, barbarian warrior (*RIB* 109, 121, 159, 201). Military service was for these men a self-defining role. Service differentiated them from barbarians. It made them men.

Military service also gave soldiers increased power to inflict violence. 'Thuggery' is a characteristic of soldiers in élite depictions in this period. But violence is intimately associated with *potestas*. The élite exercised violence within their own homes. Their ability to inflict beatings and their immunity from such physical chastisement was a marker of the free man, but the soldiers, though liable to be beaten by their superiors, were also empowered to act violently towards provincials. This can be seen not only in warfare or the suppression of rebellion, but also in the actions of soldiers as police. Another of the stereotypical images of the soldier on tombstones shows him carrying not a sword but a stick; he also sometimes writes tablets. These soldiers were policing officers who, acting with centurions, dealt with many local disputes (Millar 1981; Šašel Kos 1978). The sticks were to chastise. They were as much a symbol of their superiority as the riding down of the barbarian.

This violence was not confined to the provinces, and the soldiers were in a position to exercise their authority in Rome itself. The praetorian guard provided the emperor with a ready means of dealing with his opponents which could be used against non-élite and élite. The élite had no answer to this physical violence. Soldiers could penetrate even within the household, either secretly as spies or openly as representatives of imperial power. By the imperial period, the élite had lost control over violence in the public sphere. Violence could be exercised in the home, in a controlled fashion, without anger, but not elsewhere. Dio Chrysostom (*Or.* 29) tells us of a boxer who won all his fights. The man showed such exemplary control of his body that he was able to win all his fights without recourse to the crudity of actually hitting anybody. He would dodge and weave all day until his opponent was worn down. Uncontrolled violence was savage and no part of the aristocratic image of the *vir*. Yet at the heart of Rome was the arena, the theatre of violence. The role of games in the presentation and enactment of power in Roman society has been thoroughly explored.[36] Here, the Roman people assembled under the control of the magistrate or emperor. As suppliers of the venue, as patrons of the games, and often as the ultimate arbiter of the fates of the performers, the emperors dominated the event. It was not just the emperor and those few aristocrats who participated who displayed their power in the arena; gladiators also publicly demonstrated *potestas* by successfully using violence to overcome opponents. Men of the lowest social status graphically demonstrated their virility before the Roman population. As a result, gladiators and others who took part in games developed considerable followings. Understandably, such men came also to be associated with magic, another form of illegitimate power. Such power, so publicly displayed, had obvious attractions for certain members of the élite, and it should come as no surprise that some emperors and aristocrats demeaned themselves in the eyes of many of their social equals by participating in the arena.[37]

Soldiers and gladiators did not conform to aristocratic ideals of virility. They were not free, even in the limited sense of the imperial period, and were not in control of their own bodies. They were unsuited by education and temperament to hold power, and any power they did have was illegitimate and a danger to the social fabric. Soldiers were more often described by members of the élite as beasts than as *viri*. Nevertheless, the power of soldiers and gladiators, though limited, was real and publicly displayed. As wielders of *potestas*, soldiers qualified as *viri*.

Conclusions

This rapid survey of attitudes to masculinity and soldiers over approximately four centuries around the Augustan revolution has touched on the various, multiple images of masculinity in the period. With the aristocracy, soldiers and gladiators we have different, competing, but closely related ideologies of masculinity. Most views of the *vir* emphasized *potestas* as a characteristic. The *vir*, as in so many other cultures, was a man of power. Yet it is unsurprising that in four centuries of cultural and political change the nuances of this definition were competed over and reordered. The transformation of Rome from a powerful city state ruled by an oligarchy to a world empire ruled by a monarch was bound to affect all aspects of Roman society, including masculinity. In the new climate generated by the loss of *libertas* and the impact of new ideas from the East, there appears to have been a questioning of traditional masculine roles. Characteristically, the response of the Augustan circle was to look back and found their new image of the *vir* in their vision of the past. The later elegists looked elsewhere and produced an alternative. These two new mythic discourses both dealt with traditional issues of *virtus* and *potestas*, but the political *rapprochement* between élite and emperor, the ultimate triumph of the early emperors, allowed the élite to adopt a course less radical than that of the elegists.

In writings which consider the correct behaviour for a man and the role of soldiers, we are looking at what is essentially a political discourse. The élite justified their power by representing themselves as *viri*, men suitable to hold power; they thus defined the characteristics of the *vir* by the characteristics that defined the élite themselves (Veyne 1987, 119). The shifts of political power at the end of the Republic led to shifts in the characteristics of the élite *vir* as the élite itself changed. As the political power of the élite became less central, so their ideological hegemony may have been questioned. Alternative centres of power emerged and, inevitably, alternative views of the *vir*. Masculinity, power and politics were inextricably intertwined.

Perhaps in some societies, some comparatively stable societies, ideas of masculinity remain stable. A boy learns how to behave from watching the men who surround him. He copies his father's walk, gestures, and demeanour. Bourdieu's notion (1977) of the *habitus* shows how such social structures can be generated and perpetuated.[38] Rome, however, was undergoing rapid and radical change in this period. The society of the city was large. The society of the empire was immense. There was more than enough scope for variation. In the circles of the élite, the soldiers had no claim to be *viri*, for they did not behave as *viri* should, but the circles of the élite were but a small part of the Roman Empire. In some parts and among the soldiers themselves, the soldiers' control over violence and their relatively high status as representatives of the empire qualified them as *viri*. Political events in the first two centuries AD demonstrated forcibly to the élite that the ultimate arbiters of empire were not the élite themselves but the soldiers. The emperor could use his troops to rob them of their wealth, their homes and ultimately their lives. The hostility of the élite towards soldiers stems from this threat to their political power and to their definition of and status as *viri*.

Notes

1 Examples are easily found: Elizabeth I claimed in her finest hour (an occasion when her courtier compared her to an Amazonian Queen) that she had risen above her 'weak and feeble body of a woman' and developed the stomach of a King (Neale 1979, 302); cartoon and puppet depictions of Mrs Thatcher were often in male dress; allegedly domestically powerful women were colloquially described 'as wearing the trousers' in particular households.

2 There is a problem of terminology in what follows. As L'Hoir's analysis makes clear, the Romans were far from consistent in their use of these terms, and although we may say that '*vir*' is generally used of aristocratic men who may be taken to be ideals of manhood, it is sometimes used in other contexts as '*homo*' is sometimes used in contexts in which we would expect '*vir*'. For instance, as I shall argue below, soldiers of the late republican and early imperial periods are not generally recognized in our literary sources as men worthy of respect, yet '*viri*' is commonly placed in the mouths of generals who wish to emphasize the strength of their forces. We should beware of an over-mechanical interpretation of Latin usage. For the purposes of this essay, '*vir*' is used to refer to an 'ideal of manhood' and I have attempted to make clear those occasions on which '*vir*' appears in the texts to be discussed.

3 Petronius, *Satyricon*, 57. This is a long and comic passage in which a freedman asserts his masculinity: 'I am a man amongst men. I walk bare-headed' (i.e. without the freedman's cap or, more freely, 'with head held high'). 'I owe no-one a bronze ass . . . ' (the lowest denomination coin). The joke lies in the parallel with 39. 4, where the same words are used by the gauche freedman host of the dinner party, and in the pretensions of this freedman who presumably behaves in the same servile manner as the other guests at the dinner party.

4 Fisher 1993, 1, 'the consciousness of the division between slaves and free men was one of Greek society's most fundamental and determining ideas'; Wiedemann 1987, 5, 'an Athenian or a Roman saw society primarily in terms of the polarity between slaves and free citizens.'; Wiedemann 1981, 1; Finley 1985a, 62–94; Herbert 1993.

5 There are many examples; a rapidly gathered selection: Martial, 1. 20, 43, 80, 108; 2. 5, 18, 68; 3. 82; 5. 22; 6. 88; 9. 100; 10. 10, 74; Pliny, *Epistles* 2. 6; Juvenal, *Satires* 1. 95–103; 5.

6 Even if there was no decline in absolute numbers of free men on the land, the rapid growth of the urban population and especially the population of Rome suggests a fundamental shift in the distribution of the free population towards the city.

7 *Res Gestae* 1. It is possible that the designation of Antony as 'a faction' was deliberately ambiguous and may have been intended to refer to his campaigns against the conspirators as well.

8 See Lintott 1993, 116–18 and Garnsey 1966 for general discussions of the emperor's control over rights to punish.

9 Nicolet 1980, 39; Saller 1994, 139.

10 For *libertas* as a political concept see Wirszubski 1950, especially 2–4, and Brunt 1988, 281–350. The latter quotes Ennius fr. 300–3 V, which links *libertas* with maculinity: 'It is proper for a man to be inspired by true manliness (sed virum virtute vera animatum addecet) and strongly stand blameless against adversaries; this is freedom, when he carries a heart pure and steadfast, all else is shameful and lies in the shadow of night' (my translation).

11 Lacey 1986 argues that there was an equivalence between the family and the state, so that a son was in the same position with regard to a father as a citizen to the state. This, he argues, does not compromise individual freedom. It seems to me, however, that such power structures must limit personal freedom.

12 Dio Chrysostom, *Oratio* 15. 18–19.

13 It is notable that the word for boy was used in both Greek and Latin to mean 'slave', suggesting a certain equivalence in relationship to the *pater*: Finley 1980, 96.

14 This is dramatized by Livy 24. 44, where a consul is met by his own father who is to serve as his deputy. The lictors fail to tell the father to dismount when he approaches his son until ordered to do so by the son. In so doing, the son demonstrates that his consular authority overrode his father's paternal authority, an action applauded by the father.

15 It is probable that those whose father was dead but whose paternal grandfather still lived would amount to less than 2 per cent and were even less significant in later age groups.

16 Hopkins 1978, 31–6, reckons that an average of 30–60 per cent of male citizens between 225 and 23 BC had served in the army.

17 In books 2, 3 and 4 of Livy, the normal account for each year commences with a discussion of political disturbances in which the people oppose conscription. The problems are settled or put off and then troops are raised to meet the foreign enemy. There are numerous examples; see, for instance, Livy, 2. 23, 32, 42–4; 3. 10, 42, 66; 4. 4.

18 *Cat.* 7–11 describes the moral decline of Rome in masculine/feminine terms as a softening of the Roman people, which is partly a result of the *luxuria* introduced to Rome by Sulla's soldiers.

19 Momigliano 1975, 1–21 details the relationship between Hellenization and ability to wield imperial power. Rawson 1985 shows the growing interest in intellectualism in the late Republic, but cautiously notes (38) that intellectual attainment was not in itself regarded as justification for political authority. Suetonius' biographies of the Caesars devote chapters to the intellectual attainments of the emperors; and by the time of Pliny the younger and Fronto, the display of culture was an important claim to social respectability.

20 *Ad Familiares* 11. 7; *Pro Archia* 24; *Orationes Philippicae* 8. 9; 10. 22.

21 Campbell 1978; 1984, 207–29; Alston 1995, 53–68.

22 The issue had been raised because of several cases in which wives of provincial governors were seen to be exercising improper authority; it may also be related to the role of women of the imperial household who had accompanied their husbands to the provinces and there wielded some ill-defined authority.

23 One may note the emphasis placed on *virtus* in the *Aeneid*. The famous first three words 'Arma virumque cano' (I sing of arms and a man) establish the main

themes. Compare the echoing of this in the first phrase of Tacitus' *Agricola*, a work also concerned with the relationship of the individual and duty: 'Clarorum virorum facta moresque posteris tradere' (to transmit the deeds and customs of famous men to posterity). See below, 215.

24 Propertius 1. 4. 3–4; 5. 19–20; 2. 23. 23–4; 3. 11; Ovid, *Amores* 1. 2; 2. 3, 4.
25 Prop. 1. 5. 21; 2. 1. 13–14, 45–6; 2. 8. 39–40; 12–15; 25. 5–10; 3. 3, 5–6, 8, 20, 25; 4. 1. 131–50; Ov. *Am.* 1. 2; 6. 35–40; 9; 2. 1. 21; 6. 13–14; 12. See Gale 1997.
26 Prop. 2. 7; 3. 12, 20; 4. 3, 5; Ov. *Am.* 1. 8. 41–2; 2. 9. 19–24; 10. 31–8.
27 For other examples see Cluvius Rufus (*Historiae* 1. 8), a *vir* experienced in the arts of peace, and Arulenius Rusticanus (*Hist.* 3. 80), whose wounding in a riot was made more shameful because of his status as a *vir*.
28 *Ann.* 16. 25 describes how Thrasea Paetus was urged by his closest friends to provide the Roman people with an example of a *vir* by facing up to Nero. Similarly, *Ann.* 3. 44 describes Sacrovir's rebellious followers in Gaul as *viri* who will depose the tyrannical Tiberius. Note also Boudicca's speech to her British rebels (*Ann.* 14. 35), in which Tacitus exploits the paradox of a woman leading men to freedom: 'id mulieri destinatum: viverent viri et servirent' ('that is the destiny of a woman: let the men live and slave'). The alliteration emphasizes 'vir'.
29 Tac. *Agr.* 3; Pliny, *Ep.* 1. 10, 13; 2. 6.
30 Pliny, *Ep.* 1. 12; 2. 11; 3. 5. Such concerns feature throughout the correspondence of Fronto.
31 Veyne 1987, 36; Gleason 1990.
32 *Or.* 14. 1–6; cf. Cicero, *Tusculanae Disputationes* 2. 48.
33 This was generally praised, but could be taken too far, so that generals would lose control over their troops (Tac. *Hist.* 1. 18; Suet. *Galba* 16).
34 Severus recruited his guard from the Danubian legions rather than using the troops who had supported his predecessor. This added to Dio's alienation, but the troops recruited in Italy are not an exception to this discussion.
35 Pliny, *Ep.* 10. 20, 52–3, 100, 103.
36 Hopkins 1983, 1–30; Coleman 1990, 1993.
37 Hopkins 1983, 20–7 and Plass 1995, 72–5 discuss the issue of the anomalous status of gladiators.
38 Bourdieu 1990, 53–74, emphasizes the role of the *habitus* in perpetuating social structures through time, but also allows for the possibility of change in the *habitus* since it exists in part as a generated result of socio-economic factors.

Bibliography

Abu-Lughod, L. (1986), *Veiled Sentiments: Honor and Poetry in a Bedouin Society* (Berkeley etc.).

Adams, W .L., and Borza, E. N. (eds 1982), *Philip II, Alexander the Great and the Macedonian Heritage* (Washington).

Adkins, A. W. H. (1976), '*Polypragmosyne* and Minding One's Own Business', *CP* 71: 301–27.

Ahlberg, G. (1971), *Prothesis and Ekphora in Greek Geometric Art* (Göteborg).

Alessandrì, S. (ed. 1994), *Historie: studi offerti dagli allievi a Giuseppe Nenci in occasione del suo settantesimo compleanno* (Congedo Editore, place of publication not given).

Alexiou, M. (1974), *The Ritual Lament in Greek Tradition* (Cambridge).

Allen, R. E. (1983), *The Attalid Kingdom: A Constitutional History* (Oxford).

Alston, R. (1995), *Soldier and Society in Roman Egypt: A Social History* (London).

Anderson, B. (1991), *Imagined Communities*, 2nd edn (London).

Anderson, G. (1984), *Ancient Fiction: The Novel in the Graeco-Roman World* (London).

—— (1993), *The Second Sophistic: A Cultural Phenomenon in the Roman Empire* (London).

Andersen, O., and Dickie, M. (eds 1995), *Homer's World: Fiction, Tradition, Reality* (Bergen).

Andreski, S. (1968), *Military Organization and Society*, 2nd edn (London).

Andronikos, M. (1968), *Totenkult. Archaeologia Homerica*, vol. W (Göttingen).

Archer, L., Fischler, S., and Wyke, M. (eds 1994), *Women in Ancient Societies. An Illusion of the Night* (London).

Arens, W. (1979), *The Man-Eating Myth: Anthropology and Anthropophagy* (New York).

Arnould, D. (1990), *Le rire et les larmes dans la littérature grecque d'Homère à Platon* (Paris).

Austin, J. (1970), *Philosophical Papers*, 2nd edn (Oxford).

Austin, M. M. (1981), *The Hellenistic World from Alexander to the Roman Conquest* (Cambridge).

—— (1986), 'Hellenistic Kings, War, and the Economy', *CQ* 36: 450–66.

Bagnall, R. S. (1993), *Egypt in Late Antiquity* (Princeton).

—— (1995), *Reading Papyri, Writing Ancient History* (London).

Bagnall, R. S., and Derow, P. (1981), *Greek Historical Documents: The Hellenistic Period* (Society for Biblical Literature: Sources for Biblical Study no. 16: Chico, California).

Bakir, G. (1981), *Sophilos* (Mainz).

Barker, F., Hulme, P., Iversen, M., and Loxley, D. (eds 1985), *Europe and its Others*, 2 vols (Colchester).

Beauvoir, S. de (1949 [1987]), *The Second Sex* (Harmondsworth).

Becher, I. (1966), *Das Bild der Kleopatra in der griechischen und lateinischen Literatur* (Berlin).

Bérard, C. *et al.* (1988), *The City of Images* (Princeton).

Black-Michaud, J. (1975), *Cohesive Force: Feud in the Mediterranean and the Near East* (Oxford).

Bleicken, J. (ed. 1993), *Colloquium aus Anlass des 80. Geburtstages von Alfred Heuss* (Frankfurter Althistorische Studien 13: Kallmünz).

Blier, R. (ed. 1986), *Feminist Approaches to Science* (New York).

Boardman, J. (1955), 'Painted Funerary Plaques and some Remarks on Prothesis', *BSA* 50: 51–66.

—— (1961), *The Cretan Collection at Oxford* (Oxford).

Boatwright, M. T. (1991), 'Plancia Magna of Perge; Women's Roles and Status in Roman Asia Minor', in Pomeroy (ed. 1991), 249–72 .

Boegehold, A .L., and Scafuro, A. C. (eds 1994), *Athenian Identity and Civic Ideology* (Baltimore etc.).

Bookidis, N. (1990), 'Ritual Dining at Corinth', in Murray (ed. 1990a), 86–94.

Bossy, J. (ed. 1983), *Disputes and Settlements: Law and Human Relations in the West* (Cambridge).

Bourdieu, P. (1977), *Outline of a Theory of Practice* (trans. R. Nice) (Cambridge etc.).

—— (1990), *The Logic of Practice* (trans. R. Nice) (Cambridge).

Bourke, J. (1995), *Dismembering the Male. Men's Bodies, Britain and the Great War* (London).

Bourriot, F. (1972), 'La considération accordée aux marins dans l'antiquité grecque – époques archaïque et classique', *Revue d'histoire économique et sociale*, 50: 7–41.

Bowersock, G. W. (1969), *Greek Sophists in the Roman Empire* (Oxford).

Bowie, A. (1993), *Aristophanes: Myth, Ritual and Comedy* (Cambridge).

Bowie, E. L. (1970), 'The Greeks and their Past in the Second Sophistic', *P&P* 46: 3–41.

Bradley, K. (1994), *Slavery and Society at Rome* (Cambridge).

Bradney, A. (1987), 'Transsexuals and the Law', *Family Law* 17: 350–3.

Braund, D. (1994), *Georgia in Antiquity* (Oxford).

Brelich, E. (1969), *Paides e Parthenoi* (Rome).

Bremmer, J. (1980), 'An Enigmatic Indo-European Rite: Pederasty', *Arethusa* 13: 279–98.

—— (1990), 'Adolescents, *Symposion* and Pederasty', in Murray (ed. 1990a), 135–48.

Brijder, H. (ed. 1984), *Ancient Greek and Related Pottery* (Amsterdam).

Bringmann, K. (1993a), 'The King as Benefactor: Some Remarks on Ideal Kingship in the Age of Hellenism', in Bulloch, Gruen, Long and Stewart (eds 1993), 7–24.

—— (1993b), 'Der König als Wohltäter. Beobachtungen und Überlegungen zur hellenistischen Monarchie', in Bleicken (ed. 1993), 83–95.

—— (1995), 'Die Ehre des Königs und der Ruhm der Stadt. Bemerkungen zu königlichen Bau- und Feststiftungen', in Wörrle and Zanker (eds 1995), 93–102.

Brittan, A. (1989), *Masculinity and Power* (Oxford etc.).

Brod, H., and Kaufman, M. (1994), *Theorising Masculinities* (London).

Brodersen, K. (1985), 'Der liebeskranke Königssohn und die seleukidische Herrschaftsauffassung', *Athenaeum* 63: 459–69.

Brown, P. (1988), *The Body and Society: Men, Women and Sexual Renunciation in Early Christianity* (London etc.).

Brownmiller, S. (1975), *Against Our Will: Men, Women and Rape* (Harmondsworth).

Brunt, P. A. (1988), *The Fall of the Roman Republic and Related Essays* (Oxford).

Buckland, W. W. (1966), *A Text-Book of Roman Law* (Cambridge).

Buffière, F. (1980), *Eros Adolescent* (Paris).

Buitron-Oliver, D. (ed. 1991), *New Perspectives in Early Greek Art* (Hanover etc.).

Bulloch, A., Gruen, E. S., Long, A. A., and Stewart, A. (eds 1993), *Images and Ideologies: Self-definition in the Hellenistic World* (Berkeley).

Burkert, W. (1983), *Homo Necans* (Berkeley).

Burstein, S. M. (1982), 'Arsinoe II Philadelphus: a Revisionist View', in Adams and Borza (eds 1982), 197–212.

—— (1985), *The Hellenistic Age from the Battle of Ipsos to the Death of Kleopatra VII* (Cambridge).

Burton, R. (1962), *Pindar's Pythian Odes: Essays in Interpretation* (Oxford).

Butler, J. (1990), *Gender Trouble, Feminism and the Subversion of Identity* (London).

Cairns, D. (1993), *Aidōs. The Psychology and Ethics of Honour and Shame in Ancient Greek Literature* (Oxford).

Calame, C. (1990), 'Narrating the Foundation of a City: The Symbolic Birth of Cyrene', in L. Edmunds (ed. 1990), 277–341.

Caldara, A. (1924), *L'indicazione dei connotati nei documenti papiracei dell'Egitto greco-romano* (Milan).

Cameron, A. (1990), 'Two Mistresses of Ptolemy Philadelphus', *GRBS* 31: 287–311.

Cameron, A., and Kuhrt, A. (eds 1983), *Images of Women in Antiquity* (London).

Campbell, J. B. (1978), 'The Marriage of Roman Soldiers under the Principate', *JRS* 68: 153–67.

—— (1984), *The Emperor and the Roman Army 31 BC–AD 235* (Oxford).

Campbell, J. K. (1964), *Honour, Family and Patronage* (Oxford).

Carey, C. (1981), *A Commentary on Five Odes of Pindar. Pythian 2, Pythian 9, Nemean 7, Isthmian 8* (Salem).

—— (1994), 'Return of the Radish, or Just when you Thought it was Safe to go Back into the Kitchen', *LCM* 18: 53–5.

Carney, E. (1987a), 'The Career of Adea-Eurydike', *Historia*, 36: 496–502.

—— (1987b), 'Olympias', *Ancient Society* 18: 35–62.

—— (1987c), 'The Reappearance of Royal Sibling Marriage in Ptolemaic Egypt', *Parola del Passato* 237: 420–39.

—— (1988a), 'Eponymous Women: Royal Women and City Names', *Ancient History Bulletin* 6: 134–42.

—— (1988b), 'The Sisters of Alexander', *Historia* 37: 385–404.

—— (1991), '"What's in a Name?": the Emergence of a Title for Royal Women in the Hellenistic Period', in Pomeroy (ed. 1991), 154–72.

—— (1992), 'The Politics of Polygamy: Olympias, Alexander, and the Murder of Philip', *Historia* 41: 169–89.

—— (1993a), 'Olympias and the Image of the Virago', *Phoenix* 47: 29–55.

—— (1993b), 'Foreign Influence and the Changing Role of Royal Macedonian Women', *Ancient Macedonia* 5 (Thessalonike) i 313–23.

—— (1994a), 'Olympias, Adea Eurydice, and the End of the Argead Dynasty', in Worthington (ed. 1994b), 357–97.

—— (1994b), 'Arsinoë before she was Philadelphus', *Ancient History Bulletin* 8: 123–31.

—— (1995), 'Women and *Basileia*: Legitimacy and Female Political Action in Macedonia', *CJ* 90: 367–91.

Carson, A. (1990), 'Putting Her in Her Place: Woman, Dirt, and Desire', in Halperin, Winkler, and Zeitlin (eds 1990), 135–70.

Carter, A. (1979), *The Sadeian Woman* (London).

Carter, J. C. (1983), *The Sculpture of the Sanctuary of Athena Polias at Priene* (Reports of the Research Committee of the Society of Antiquaries of London: London).

Carter, L. (1986), *The Quiet Athenian* (Oxford).

Cartledge, P. A. (1985), 'The Greek Religious Festivals', in Easterling and Muir (eds 1985), 98–127.

—— (1987), *Agesilaos and the Crisis of Sparta* (London).

—— (1990), 'Fowl Play: a Curious Lawsuit in Classical Athens (Antiphon xvi, frr. 57–9 Thalheim)', in Cartledge, Millett, and Todd (eds 1990), 41–61.

—— (1993a), ' "Like a worm i' the bud"? A Heterology of Ancient Greek Slavery', *G&R*, 40: 163–80.

—— (1995a), 'The Greeks and Anthropology', *Classics Ireland* 2: 17–28.

—— (1995b), review of Dougherty 1993, *CP*, 90: 74–7.

—— (1996a), review of Loraux 1993, *POLIS* 13, 1–2: 96–103.

—— (1996b), 'Comparatively Equal', in Ober and Hedrick (eds 1996), 175–85.

—— (1997), *The Greeks. A Portrait of Self and Others*, revised edition (Oxford).

Cartledge, P. A., and Harvey, F. D. (1985), *Crux: Essays Presented to G.E.M. de Ste Croix* (Exeter).

Cartledge, P. A., Millett, P., and Todd, S. C. (1990), *Nomos: Essays in Athenian Law, Politics and Society* (Cambridge).

Cartledge, P. A., Millett, P., and von Reden, S. (eds 1998) *KOSMOS* (Cambridge).

Casewitz, M. (1985), *Le vocabulaire de la colonisation en grec ancien* (Paris).

Castriota, D. (1992), *Myth, Ethos, and Actuality: Official Art in Fifth-Century BC Athens* (Wisconsin).

Cavanagh, W., and Mee, C. (1995), 'Mourning Before and After the Dark Age', in Morris (ed. 1995), 45–61.

Chamoux, F. (1953), *Cyrène sous la monarchie des Battiades* (Bibliothèque des Écoles françaises d'Athènes et de Rome 177: Paris).

Chapman, R., and Rutherford, J. (eds 1988), *Male Order: Unwrapping Masculinity* (London).

Charlesworth, J. H. (ed. 1983), *The Old Testament Pseudepigrapha*, i: *Apocalyptic Literature and Testaments* (London).

Chodorow, N. (1978), *The Reproduction of Mothering: Psychoanalysis and the Sociology of Gendering* (Berkeley).

Clark, G. (1993), *Women in Late Antiquity: Pagan and Christian Lifestyles* (Oxford).

Clarke, J. (1991), 'The Decor of the House of Jupiter and Ganymede at Ostia Antica: Private Residence Turned Gay Hotel?', in Gazda (ed. 1991), 90–104.

Clarke, N. (1991), 'Strenuous Idleness: Thomas Carlyle and the Man of Letters as Hero', in Roper and Tosh (eds 1991), 25–43.

Cockburn, J. S. (ed. 1977), *Crime in England, 1550–1800* (London).

—— (1991), 'Patterns of Violence in English Society: Homicide in Kent 1560–1985', *P&P* 108: 206–24.

Cohen, D. (1983), *Theft in Athenian Law* (Munich).

—— (1985), 'A Note on Aristophanes and the Punishment of Adultery in Athenian Law', *ZSS* 102: 385–7.

—— (1989), 'Seclusion, Separation, and the Status of Women in Classical Athens', *G&R* 36: 3–15.

—— (1991), *Law, Sexuality and Society* (Cambridge).

—— (1995), *Law, Violence and Community in Classical Athens* (Cambridge).

Cohen, G. M. (1974), 'The Diadochoi and the New Monarchies', *Athenaeum* 52: 177–9.

Coldstream, J. N. (1968), *Greek Geometric Pottery. A Survey of Ten Local Styles and their Chronology* (London).

Coleman, K. M. (1990), 'Fatal Charades: Roman Executions Staged as Mythological Enactments', *JRS* 80: 44–73.

—— (1993), 'Launching into History: Aquatic Displays in the Early Empire', *JRS* 83: 48–74.

Collins, J. J. (1983), 'Sibylline Oracles', in Charlesworth (ed. 1983), 317–472.

—— (1987), 'The Development of the Sibylline Tradition', in Haase (ed. 1987), 421–59.

Connell, R. W. (1987), *Gender and Power* (Cambridge).

—— (1995), *Masculinities* (Cambridge).

Cook, J. M. (1935), 'Protoattic Pottery', *BSA* 35: 165–219.

Cooke, M., and Woollacott, A. (eds 1993), *Gendering War Talk* (Oxford).

Cooper, K. (1992), 'Insinuations of Womanly Influence; Aspects of the Christianisation of the Roman Aristocracy', *JRS* 82: 151–60.

Corbett, P. E. (1930), *The Roman Law of Marriage* (Oxford).

Cornwall, A., and Lindisfarne, N. (eds 1994), *Dislocating Masculinities: Comparative Ethnographies* (London etc.).

Coulson, W. D. E., Palagia, O., Shear, T. L. Jr., Shapiro, H. A., and Frost, F. J. (eds 1994), *The Archaeology of Athens and Attica under the Democracy* (Athens).

Cretney, S. M. (1984), *Principles of Family Law*, London.

Crielaard, J.-P. (1995), 'Homer, History, and Archaeology. Some Remarks on the Date of the Homeric World', in J.-P. Crielaard (ed.), 201–88.

—— (ed. 1995), *Homeric Questions* (Amsterdam).

Crosby, M. (1937), 'Greek Inscriptions', *Hesperia* 6: 442–68.

Crowther, N. B. (1985), 'Male "Beauty" Contests in Greece: the *Euandria* and *Euexia*', *AC* 54: 285–91.

Csapo, E. (1993), '"Deep Ambivalence": Notes on a Greek Cockfight', *Phoenix* 47: 1–28, 115–24.

Culham, P., and Edmunds, L. (eds 1989), *Classics: A Discipline and Profession in Crisis?* (Lanham).

Dalla, D. (1978), *L'incapacità sessuale in diritto romano* (Milan).

—— (1987), '*Ubi Venus mutatur': omosessualità e diritto nel mondo romano* (Milan).

Damousi, J., and Lake, M. (eds 1995), *Gender and War: Australians at War in the Twentieth Century* (Cambridge).

Dasen, V. (1993), *Dwarfs in Ancient Egypt and Greece* (Oxford).

Davies, J. K. (1967), 'Demosthenes on Liturgies: A Note', *JHS* 87: 33–40.

—— (1971), *Athenian Propertied Families* (Oxford).

—— (1981), *Wealth and the Power of Wealth in Classical Athens* (London etc.).

—— (1984), 'Cultural, Social and Economic Features of the Hellenistic World', in Walbank, Astin, Frederiksen and Ogilvie (eds 1984), 257–320.

—— (1993), *Democracy and Classical Greece*, 2nd edn (Glasgow).

Davies, R. W. (1989), *Service in the Roman Army* (Edinburgh).

Davis, N., and Kraay, C. M. (1973), *The Hellenistic Kingdoms: Portrait Coins and History* (London).

Dawson, G. (1991), 'The Blond Bedouin, Lawrence of Arabia, Imperial Adventure and the Imagining of English-British Masculinity', in Roper and Tosh (eds 1991), 113–44.

Dean-Jones, L. (1994), *Women's Bodies in Classical Greek Science* (Oxford).

Dentzer, J.-M. (1982), *Le motif du banquet couché dans le proche-orient et le monde grec du VIIᵉ au IVᵉ siècle avant J.-C.* (Rome).

Detienne, M. (1977), *The Gardens of Adonis: Spices in Greek Mythology* (Atlantic Highlands).

Dickie, M. (1995), 'The Geography of Homer's World', in Andersen and Dickie (eds 1995), 29–56.

Dihle, A. (1993), 'Response' [to van Straten and Giovannini], in Bulloch, Gruen, Long and Stewart (eds), 287–95.

Dollimore, J. (1991), *Sexual Dissidence: Augustine to Wilde, Freud to Foucault* (Oxford etc.).

Dougherty, C. (1993), *The Poetics of Colonization: From City to Text in Archaic Greece* (Oxford etc.).

—— (1994), 'Archaic Greek Foundation Poetry: Questions of Genre and Occasion', *JHS* 114: 35–46.

Dover, K.J. (1968), *Aristophanes, Clouds* (Oxford).

—— (1972), *Aristophanic Comedy* (London).

—— (1974), *Greek Popular Morality in the time of Plato and Aristotle* (Oxford).

—— (1978), *Greek Homosexuality* (London).

—— (1988), *The Greeks and their Legacy* (Oxford).

duBois, P. (1988), *Sowing the Body: Psychoanalysis and Ancient Representations of Women* (Chicago etc.).

Du Boulay, J. (1974), *Portrait of a Greek Mountain Village* (Oxford).

Dupont, F. (1989), 'The Emperor-God's Other Body', in Feher, Nadaff and Tazi (eds 1989), vol. 3, 396–419.

Durham, E. (1909), *High Albania* (London).

Dyer, R. (1993), *The Matter of Images: Essays on Representation* (London).

Easterling, P. A., and Muir J. V. (eds 1985), *Greek Religion and Society* (Cambridge).

Eck, W. (1984), 'Senatorial Self-Representation: Developments in the Roman Period', in Millar and Segal (eds 1984), 129–67.

Eder, W. (ed. 1995), *Die Athenische Demokratie im 4. Jahrhundert v. Chr.: Vollendung oder Verfall einer Verfassungsform?* (Stuttgart).

Edley, N., and Wetherell, M. S. (1995), *Men in Perspective: Practice, Power and Identity* (Hemel Hempstead).

Edmunds, L. (ed. 1990), *Approaches to Greek Myth* (Baltimore).

Edwards, T. (1994), *Erotics and Politics: Male Sexuality, Masculinity and Feminism* (London).

Ellis, W. M. (1994), *Ptolemy of Egypt* (London).

Ensoli, S. (1990), 'Notizie sulla campagna di scavi del 1987 sulla Terrazza della Myrtusa a Cirene', in *Atti dei convegni Lincei: Giornata Lincea sull' archeologia cirenaica*, Roma 3 Novembre 1987, 157–76.

Erskine, A. (1994), 'The Romans as Common Benefactors', *Historia* 43: 70–87.

Evans, E. (1969), *Physiognomics in the Ancient World* (Philadelphia).

Fantham, E., Foley, H. P., Kampen, N. B., Pomeroy, S. B., and Shapiro, H. A. (eds 1994), *Women in the Classical World: Image and Text* (Oxford).

Farnell, L. (1930), *The Works of Pindar: Translated and with a Literary and Critical Commentary* (London).

Farrell, W. (1994), *The Myth of Male Power. Why Men are the Disposable Sex* (London).

Fee, E. (1986), 'Critiques of Modern Science: the Relationship of Feminism to other Radical Epistemologies', in Blier (ed. 1986), 42–56.

Feher, M., Nadaff, R., and Tazi, N. (eds 1989), *Fragments for a History of the Human Body*, 3 vols (New York).

Fehr, B. (1971), *Orientalische und griechische Gelage* (Bonn).

Fink, R. O. (1971), *Roman Military Records on Papyrus* (Ann Arbor).

Finlay, H. A., and Walters, W. A. W. (1988), *Sex Change: Judicial and Legal Aspects of Sex Reassignment* (Box Hill, Victoria).

Finley, M. I. (1980), *Ancient Slavery and Modern Ideology* (London).

—— (1985a), *The Ancient Economy*, 2nd edn (London).

—— (1985b), *Ancient History. Evidence and models* (London).

—— (1985c), *Democracy Ancient and Modern*, 2nd edn (London).

Fischler, S. S. (1989), *The Public Position of the Women of the Julio-Claudian Household* (D.Phil. dissertation, Oxford).

Fisher, N. R. E. (1990), 'The Law of *Hubris* in Athens', in Cartledge, Millett, and Todd (eds 1990), 123–38.

—— (1992), *Hybris* (Warminster).

—— (1993), *Slavery in Classical Greece* (London).

—— (1998), 'Gymnasia and Social Mobility in Athens', in Cartledge, Millett, and von Reden (eds 1998), 84–104.

—— (1999), 'Symposiasts and other Drinkers in Old Comedy', in Harvey and Wilkins (eds 1999).

Fisher, N. R. E., and Van Wees, H. (eds 1998), *Archaic Greece: New Approaches and New Evidence* (London).

Fleischer, R. (1991), *Studien zur seleukidischen Kunst* i: *Herrscherbildnisse* (Mainz).

Foley, Helene P. (1993) 'The politics of tragic lamentation', in Sommerstein, Halliwell, Henderson, and Zimmermann (eds 1993), 101–43.

Foucault, M. (1978), *The History of Sexuality* i *An Introduction* (trans. R. Hurley) (Harmondsworth).

—— (1984), *Histoire du Sexualité: Le Souci de Soi* (Paris).

—— (1985), *The History of Sexuality* ii *The Use of Pleasure* (trans. R. Hurley) (Harmondsworth).

—— (1986), *The History of Sexuality* iii *The Care of the Self* (trans. R. Hurley) (Harmondsworth).

Fowler, D. P.(1989), 'Taplin on Cocks', *CQ* 39: 257–9.

Foxhall, L. (1989), 'Household, Gender and Property in Classical Athens', *CQ* 39: 22–44.

—— (1992a), 'The Control of the Attic Landscape', in Wells (ed. 1992), 155–60.

—— (1992b), 'Response to Eva Cantarella', in Gagarin (ed. 1992), 297–304.

—— (1995a), 'Women's Ritual and Men's Work in Classical Athens', in Hawley and Levick (eds 1995), 97–110.

—— (1995b), 'Monumental Ambitions: the Significance of Posterity in Ancient Greece', in Spencer (ed. 1995), 132–49.

—— (1996), 'Law and the Lady: Women and Legal Proceedings in Classical Athens', in Foxhall and Lewis (eds 1996), 302–25.

Foxhall, L., and Lewis, A. D. E. (eds 1996), *Greek Law in its Political Setting: Justifications not Justice* (Oxford).

Foxhall, L., and Salmon, J. (eds 1998), *Thinking Men: Masculinity and its Self-Representation in the Classical Tradition* (London etc.).

Foxhall, L., and Stears, K. (1998), 'Redressing the Balance: Dedications of Clothing to Artemis and the Order of Life Stages', in Hurcombe and Donald (eds 1998).

Fraenkel, H. (1950), 'Problems of Text and Interpretation in Apollonius' *Argonautica*', *AJP* 71: 113–33.

Francis, E. D. (1990), *Image and Idea in Fifth-century Greece. Art and Literature after the Persian Wars* (London etc.).

Fraser, P. M. (1972), *Ptolemaic Alexandria*, 3 vols. (Oxford).

French, R. (1994), *Ancient Natural History* (London).

Frühe Zeichner 1500–500 v. Chr. [Catalogue of the H.A. Cahn collection] (Freiburg 1992).

Gabba, E. (ed. 1983), *Tria Corda: Scritti in onore di Arnaldo Momigliano* (Como).

Gabrielsen, V. (1994), *Financing the Athenian Fleet: Public Taxation and Social Relations* (Baltimore etc.).

Gagarin, M. (ed. 1992), *Symposion 1990: Vorträge zur griechischen und hellenistichen Rechtsgeschichte* (Koln).

Gagarin, M., and Woodruff, P. (1995), *Early Greek Political Thought from Homer to the Sophists* (Cambridge).

Gale, M. R. (1997), 'Propertius 2.7: Militia Amoris and the ironies of elegy', *JRS* 87: 77–91.

Gardner, J. F. (1986), *Women in Roman Law and Society* (London).

—— (1993), *Being a Roman Citizen* (London etc.).

—— (1995), 'Gender-Role Assumptions in Roman Law', *Échos du Monde Classique/Classical Views* 39: 377–400.

Garlan, Y. (1988), *Slavery in Ancient Greece* (trans. J. Lloyd) (London).

Garland, R. (1985), *The Greek Way of Death* (London).

—— (1989), 'The Well-ordered Corpse', *BICS* 36: 1–15.

Garnsey, P. (1966), 'The lex Iulia and Appeal under the Empire', *JRS* 56: 167–89.

—— (1970), 'Septimius Severus and the Marriage of Roman Soldiers' *CSCA* 3: 45–73.

Gazda, E. (ed. 1991), *Roman Art in the Private Sphere* (Ann Arbor).

Geagan, D. J. (1979), 'Roman Athens: Some Aspects of Life and Culture I, 86 BC–AD 267', in Temporini (ed. 1979), 371–437.

Geertz, C. (1973), 'Deep Play: Notes on the Balinese Cock-fight', in *The Interpretation of Cultures* (New York), 412–53.

Gehrke, H.-J. (1982), 'Der siegreiche König: Überlegungen zur hellenistischen Monarchie', *AKG* 64: 247–77.

Gellner, E. (1991), 'An Anthropological View of War and Violence', in Hinde (ed. 1991), 62–79.

Georges, P. (1994), *Barbarian Asia and the Greek Experience. From the Archaic Period to the Age of Xenophon* (Baltimore etc.).

Gernet, L. (1981), *The Anthropology of Ancient Greece* (Baltimore).

Giardina, A. (ed. 1993), *The Romans* (Chicago).

Gildersleeve, B. (1885), *Pindar: the Olympian and Pythian Odes* (New York).

Gilmore, D. (1982), 'The Anthropology of the Mediterranean Area', in *Annual Reviews in Anthropology* 11: 175–205.

—— (1987a), *Aggression and Community: Paradoxes of Andalusian Culture* (New Haven etc.).

—— (ed. 1987b), *Honour and Shame and the Unity of the Mediterranean* (Washington).

—— (1990), *Manhood in the Making: Cultural Concepts of Masculinity* (New Haven etc.).

Girard, R. (1977), *Violence and the Sacred* (Baltimore).

Gleason, M. W. (1990), 'The Semiotics of Gender: Physiognomy and Self-Fashioning in the Second Century CE', in Halperin, Winkler, and Zeitlin (eds 1990), 389–415.

Golden, M. (1984), 'Slavery and Homosexuality at Athens', *Phoenix* 38: 308–24.

—— (1990), *Children and Childhood in Classical Athens* (Baltimore etc.).

Goldhill, S. (1986), *Reading Greek Tragedy* (Cambridge).

—— (1990), 'The Great Dionysia and Civic Ideology', in Winkler and Zeitlin (eds 1990), 97–129.

—— (1992), *Aeschylus: The Oresteia* (Oxford).

—— (1995), *Foucault's Virginity: Ancient Erotic Fiction and the History of Sexuality* (Cambridge).

Goldhill, S., and Osborne, R. G. (eds 1994), *Art and Text in Ancient Greek Culture* (Cambridge).

Goodwin, G. (1994), *The Janissaries* (London).

Gordon, R. L. (1979), 'The Real and the Imaginary: Production and Religion in the Graeco–Roman World', *Art History* 2: 5–34.

Gould, J. (1980), 'Law, Custom and Myth: Aspects of the Social Position of Women in Classical Athens', *JHS* 100: 38–59.

Graham, A. J. (1984), 'Religion, Women and Colonization', *Centro ricerche e documentazione sull' antichità classica*, *Atti* 11 (1980–1, published 1984): 294–314.

—— (1992), 'Thucydides 7. 13. 2 and the Crews of Athenian Triremes', *TAPA* 122: 257–70.

Graindor, P. (1927), *Athène sous Auguste* (Cairo).

Granfeld, P., and Jungmann, J. A. (eds 1970), *Kyriakon: Festschrift für Johannes Quasten* (Munster).

Green, J. R. (1995), review of Bulloch, Gruen, Long, and Stewart (eds 1993), *Bryn Mawr Classical Review* 95: 10. 5.

Greenblatt, S. (1991), *Marvelous Possessions: The Wonder of the New World* (New York).

Greenwalt, W. S. (1989), 'Polygamy and Succession in Argead Macedonia', *Arethusa* 22: 19–43.

Gröschel, S.-G. (1989), *Waffenbesitz und Waffeneinsatz bei den Griechen* (Frankfurt am Main).

Gundlach, R., and Weber, H. (eds 1992), *Legitimation und Funktion des Herrschers: vom ägyptischen Pharao zum neuzeitlichen Diktator* (Stuttgart).

Haase, W. (ed. 1987), *Aufstieg und Niedergang der römischen Welt* ii. 20. 1 (Berlin etc.).

Habicht, C. (1995), *Athen. Die Geschichte der Stadt in hellenistischer Zeit* (Munich).

Hänlein-Schäfer, H. (1985), *Veneratio Augusti* (Archaeologia 39: Rome).

Hall, E. (1989), *Inventing the Barbarian. Greek Self-definition through Tragedy* (Oxford).

—— (1993a), 'Asia Unmanned', in Rich and Shipley (eds 1993), 108–33.

—— (1993b), 'Political and Cosmic Turbulence in Euripides' *Orestes*', in Sommerstein, Halliwell, Henderson, and Zimmermann (eds 1993), 263–86.

—— (1996), *Aeschylus. Persians* (Warminster).

Halperin, D. M. (1990), *One Hundred Years of Homosexuality and Other Essays on Greek Love* (London).

Halperin, D. M., Winkler, J. J., and Zeitlin, F. I. (eds 1990), *Before Sexuality: The Construction of the Erotic Experience in the Ancient Greek World* (Princeton).

Handman, M.-E. (1983), *Le Violence et la Ruse: Hommes et femmes dans une village Grec* (Aix-en-Provence).

Hansen, M. H. (1985), *Demography & Democracy* (Copenhagen).

—— (1991), *The Athenian Democracy in the time of Demosthenes* (Oxford).

Hanson, C., and Johnson, F. P. (1946), 'On Certain Portrait Inscriptions', *AJA* 50: 389–400.

Hanson, V. D. (1989), *The Western Way of War* (New York).

—— (1995), *The Other Greeks: The Family Farm and the Agrarian Roots of Western Civilization* (New York).

Haraway, D. (1986), 'Primatology is Politics by Other Means', in Blier (ed. 1986), 77–118.

—— (1989), *Primate Visions: Gender, Race and Nature in the World of Modern Science* (London etc.).

—— (1991), 'Situated Knowledges, the Science Question in Feminism and the Privilege of Partial Perspective', in *Simians, Cyborgs and Women: The Reinvention of Nature* (London), 183–201.

Harris, D. (1996), *Treasures of the Parthenon and Erechtheion* (Oxford).

Harris, E. M. (1989), 'Demosthenes' Speech against Meidias', *HSCP* 92: 117–36.

—— (1992), review of MacDowell 1990, *CP* 87: 71–80.

—— (1995), *Aeschines and Athenian Politics* (Oxford).

Harris, W. V. (1979), *War and Imperialism in Republican Rome, 327–70 BC* (Oxford).

Harrison, A. R. W. (1968), *The Law of Athens* i (Oxford).

Hartog, F. (1980), *Le Miroir d' Hérodote* (Paris).

Harvey, D. (1990), 'The Sykophant and Sykophancy: Vexatious Redefinition?', in Cartledge, Millett, and Todd (eds 1990), 103–22.

Harvey, D., and Wilkins, J. (eds 1999), *Aristophanes and his Rivals* (London).

Hasebroek, J. (1921), *Das Signalement in den Papyrusurkunden* (Schriften Papyrusinstitut Heidelberg 3: Berlin).

Hatzopoulos, M. B. (1996), *Macedonian Institutions under the Kings*, 2 vols. (Meletemata 22: Athens).

Hauben, H. (1983), 'Arsinoé et la politique extérieure de l'Egypte', in van't Dack, van Dessel, and van Gucht (eds 1983), 99–127.

Hawley, R. (1994), 'The Problem of Women Philosophers in Ancient Greece', in Archer, Fischler, and Wyke (eds 1994), 70–87.

Hawley, R., and Levick, B. (eds 1995), *Women in Antiquity: New Assessments* (London).

Hay, D., and Snyder, F. G. (eds 1989), *Policing and Prosecution in Britain, 1750–1850* (Oxford).

Hearn, J. (1987), *The Gender of Oppression: Men, Masculinity and the Critique of Marxism* (Brighton).

—— (1992), *Men in the Public Eye: The Construction and Deconstruction of Public Men and Public Masculinitites* (London).

Hearn, J., and Morgan, D. (eds 1990), *Men: Masculinities and Social Theory* (London).

Heckel, W. (1983/4), 'Kynnane the Illyrian', *Rivista Storica dell'Antichità* 13–14: 193–200.

—— (1989), 'The Granddaughters of Iolaus', *Classicum* 15: 32–9.

Hellström, P., and Alroth, B. (eds 1996), *Religion and Power in the Ancient Greek World* (Uppsala).

Henderson, J. (1991), *The Maculate Muse: Obscene Language in Attic Comedy*, 2nd edn (New York).

Henderson, J. G. W. (1994), '*Timeo Danaos*: Amazons in Early Greek Art and Pottery', in Goldhill and Osborne (eds 1994), 85–137.

Henrichs, A. (1970), 'Pagan Ritual and the Alleged Crimes of the Early Christians', in Granfeld and Jungmann (eds 1970), 18–35.

—— (1972), 'Toward a New Edition of Philodemus' Treatise *On Piety*', *GRBS* 13: 67–98.

Herbert, Y. (1993), 'The Slave', in Giardina (ed. 1993), 138–74.

Herdt, G. (1981), *Guardians of the Flutes: Idioms of Masculinity* (New York).
—— (ed. 1984), *Ritualized Homosexuality in Melanesia* (Berkeley).
—— (1987), *The Sambia : Ritual and Gender in New Guinea* (New York).
—— (1994a), *Guardians of the Flutes* i: *Idioms of Masculinity*, 2nd edn (Chicago).
—— (ed. 1994b), *Third Sex, Third Gender, Beyond Sexual Dimorphism in Culture and History* (New York).
Herman, G. (1993), 'Tribal and Civic Codes of Behaviour in Lysias 1', *CQ* 43: 406–19.
—— (1994): 'How Violent was Athenian Society?', in Osborne and Hornblower (eds 1994), 99–117 .
—— (1995), 'Honour, Revenge and the State in Fourth-century Athens', in Eder (ed. 1995), 43–60.
—— (1996), 'Ancient Athens and the Values of Mediterranean Society', *Mediterranean Historical Review* 11: 5–36.
Herz, P. (1992), 'Die frühen Ptolemaier bis 180 v. Chr.', in Gundlach and Weber (eds 1992), 51–97.
—— (1996), 'Hellenistische Könige. Zwischen griechischen Vorstellungen vom Königtum und Vorstellungen ihrer einheimischen Untertanen', in Small (ed. 1996), 27–40.
Herzfeld, M. (1985), *The Poetics of Manhood: Contest and Identity in a Cretan Mountain Village* (Princeton).
—— (1987), *Anthropology through the Looking-Glass* (Cambridge).
Higgins, R. (1967), *Greek Terracottas* (London).
Hinde, R. A. (ed. 1991), *The Institution of War* (Basingstoke).
Hintzen-Bohlen, B. (1990), 'Die Familiengruppe – ein Mittel zur Selbstdarstellung hellenistischer Herrscher', *JDAI* 105: 129–54.
—— (1992), *Herrscher-repräsentation im Hellenismus* (Cologne etc.).
Hobsbawm, E. J. (1972), *Bandits* (Harmondsworth).
Hoff, M. (1996), 'The Politics and Architecture of the Athenian Imperial Cult', in Small (ed. 1996), 185–200.
Hoffman, H. (1974), 'Hahnenkampf in Athen: Zur Ikonographie einer attischen Bildformel', *RA* 195–220.
Holst-Warhaft, G. (1992), *Dangerous Voices. Women's Laments and Greek Literature* (London).
Honoré, A. M. (1962), *Gaius* (Oxford).
Hopkins, K. (1978), *Conquerors and Slaves* (Cambridge).
—— (1983), *Death and Renewal* (Cambridge).
Hornblower, S., and Greenstock, M. C. (1984), *The Athenian Empire*, 3rd edn (LACTOR 1: London).
Houby-Nielsen, S. (1992), Henrichs' Interaction between Chieftains and Citizens? Seventh-century Burial Customs in Athens', *Acta Hyperborea* 4: 343–74.
Hulme, P. (1985), 'Polytropic Man: Tropes of Sexuality and Mobility in Early Colonial Discourse', in Barker *et al.* (eds 1985), 7–32.
Humphreys, S. C. (1983), 'The Evolution of Legal Process in Ancient Attica', in Gabba (ed. 1983), 229–56.
—— (1985), 'Social Relations on Stage: Witnesses in Classical Athens', *History & Anthropology* 1: 313–69 .

235

—— (1993), *The Family, Women and Death: Comparative Studies*, 2nd edn (Ann Arbor etc.).

Hunt, P. (1998), *Slaves, Warfare, and Ideology in the Greek Historians* (Cambridge).

Hunter, V. J. (1994), *Policing Athens: Social Control in the Attic Lawsuits, 420–320 BC* (Princeton).

Hurcombe, L., and Donald, M. (1998), *Gender and Material Culture* (London etc.).

Hyam, R. (1990), *Empire and Sexuality: the British Experience* (Manchester).

Iakovidis, S. (1966), 'A Mycenaean Mourning Custom', *AJA* 70: 43–50.

Irigaray, L. (1985), *Speculum of the Other Woman* (trans. G. C. Gill) (Ithaca) [originally published in French 1974].

—— (1991), *The Irigaray Reader* (ed. and intro. by M. Whitford) (London etc.).

—— (1993), *je, tu, nous: Toward a Culture of Difference* (trans. A. Martin) (London etc.).

Isaac, B. (1990), *The Limits of Empire: The Roman Army in the East* (Oxford).

Jones, A. H. M. (1957), *Athenian Democracy* (Oxford).

Jones, C. P. (1978), *The Roman World of Dio Chrysostom* (Cambridge, Mass.).

—— (1987), '*Stigma*: Tattooing and Branding in Graeco-Roman Antiquity', *JRS* 77: 139–55.

—— (1993), 'The Decree of Ilion in Honor of a King Antiochus', *GRBS* 34: 73–92.

Jordanova, L. (1980), 'Natural Facts: A Historical Perspective on Science and Sexuality', in MacCormack and Strathern (eds 1980), 42–69.

Just, R. (1989), *Women in Athenian Law and Life* (London).

Kabbani, R. (1986), *Europe's Myths of Orient: Devise and Rule* (Basingstoke).

Kagan, R. L. (1983), 'A Golden Age of Litigation: Castile 1500–1700', in Bossy (ed. 1983), 145–66.

Kampen, N. B. (ed. 1996), *Sexuality in Ancient Art* (Cambridge).

Karaosmanoğlu, Y .K. (1981), *Nur Baba* (Istanbul).

Karydi, E. (1963), 'Schwarzfigurige Lutrophoren im Kerameikos', *AM* 78: 90–103.

Katzoff, R. (ed. 1996), *Classical Studies in Honor of David Sohlberg* (Ramat-Gan).

Keuls, E. (1989), 'Archaeology and the Classics: a Rumination', in Culham and Edmunds (eds 1989), 225–9.

—— (1993), *The Reign of the Phallus. Sexual Politics in Ancient Athens*, 2nd edn (Berkeley).

Kilmer, M. F. (1993), *Greek Erotica* (London).

King, C. (1976), 'More Pots by the *Mesogeia* Painter', *AJA* 80: 79–82.

Kleiner, D. E. E. (1992), 'Politics and Gender in the Pictorial Propaganda of Antony and Octavian', *Echos du Monde Classique* 11: 357–67.

Knight, C. (1991), *Blood Relations* (New Haven).

Knox, B. M. W. (1989), *Essays Ancient & Modern* (Baltimore etc.).

Koenen, L. (1993), 'The Ptolemaic King as a Religious Figure', in Bulloch, Gruen, Long, and Stewart (eds 1993), 25–115.

Kokkinos, N. (1992), *Antonia Augusta: Portrait of a Great Roman Lady* (London).

Kübler, K. (1959), *Kerameikos: Ergebnisse der Ausgrabungen*, vi. 1 *Die Nekropole des späten 8. bis frühen 6. Jahrhunderts: Textband, Erster Zeil* (Berlin).

Kübler, K. (1970), *Kerameikos. Ergebnisse der Ausgrabungen*, vi. 2 *Die Nekropole des späten 8. bis frühen 6. Jahrhunderts: Textband, Zweiter Zeil* (Berlin).

Kurtz, D. (1984), 'Vases for the Dead, an Attic Selection, 750–400 BC', in Brijder (ed. 1984), 314–28.

Kurtz, D., and Boardman, J. (1971), *Greek Burial Customs* (London).

Kyle, D. G. (1992), 'The Panathenaic Games. Sacred and Civic Athletics', in Neils (ed. 1992), 77–101.

Lacan, J. (1977), *Écrits* (London).

Lacey, W. K. (1986), 'Patria Potestas', in Rawson (ed. 1986), 121–44.

Lambert, S. D. (1993), *The Phratries of Attica* (Ann Arbor).

Lane Fox, R. (1994), 'Aeschines and Athenian Politics', in Osborne and Hornblower (eds 1994), 137–55.

Laubscher, H. P. (1991), 'Ptolemäische Reiterbilder', *AM* 106: 223–38.

Laurenzi, L. (1955–6), 'Sculture Inedite del Museo di Coo', *Annuario della Scuola Arch. Ital. di Atene* 33–4: 59–156.

Le Bohec, S. (1991), 'L'idéologie officielle du roi de Macédoine à l'époque hellénistique', in *L'idéologie du pouvoir monarchique dans l'antiquité* (Actes du Colloque de la Société de Professeurs d'Histoire Ancienne de l'Université tenu à Lyon et Vienne les 26–28 juin 1989: Paris), 23–38.

—— (1993), 'Les reines de Macédoine de la mort d'Alexandre à celle de Persée', *Cahiers du Centre Glotz* 4 *Revue d'Histoire Ancienne*, 229–45.

Le Bohec, Y. (1994), *The Imperial Roman Army* (London).

Leigh, M. (1995), 'Wounding and Popular Rhetoric at Rome', *BICS* 40: 195–212.

Lenger, M.-Th. (1980), *Corpus des ordonnances des Ptolémées* (reprint with corrections and additions) (Mémoires de la Classe des Lettres, Académie Royale de Belgique, 2ᵉ Série 64 fasc.2: Brussels).

—— (1990), *Corpus des ordonnances des Ptolémées: bilan des additions et corrections (1964–1988)* (Papyrologica Bruxellensia 24, Documenta et opuscula 11: Brussels).

Lennon, K., and Whitford, M. (eds 1994), *Knowing the Difference: Feminist Perspectives in Epistemology* (London).

Leppin, H. (1992), *Histrionen. Untersuchungen zur sozialen Stellung von Bühnenkünstlern im Westen des Römischen Reiches zur Zeit der Republik und des Principats* (Bonn).

Levensohn, M., and E. (1947), 'Inscriptions on the South Slope of the Acropolis', *Hesperia* 16: 68–9.

Lévêque, P. (1991), 'Monarchie et idéologie: le cas des gréco-bactriens et des gréco-indiens', in *L'idéologie du pouvoir monarchique dans l'antiquité* (Actes du Colloque de la Société de Professeurs d'Histoire Ancienne de l'Université tenu à Lyon et Vienne les 26–28 juin 1989: Paris), 39–50.

Levick, B., and Jameson, S. (1964), 'C. Crepereius Gallus and his gens', *JRS* 54: 98–106.

Lewis, D. M., Boardman, J., Davies, J. K., and Ostwald, M. (eds 1992), *Cambridge Ancient History*, v *The Fifth Century BC*, 2nd edn (Cambridge).

Lintott, A. (1982), *Violence, Civil Strife and Revolution in the Classical City* (London).

—— (1993), *Imperium Romanum: Politics and Administration* (London etc.).

Lissarrague, F. (1988), *L'Autre Guerrier: archers, peltastes et cavaliers dans l'imagerie attique* (Paris etc.).

—— (1989), 'The World of the Warrior', in Bérard *et al.* (eds 1989), 39–51.

—— (1990), *The Aesthetics of the Greek Banquet* (Princeton).

Livrea, E. (1987), 'L'episodio libyco nel quarto libro delle "Argonautiche" di Apollonio Rodio', *Quaderni di Archeologia della Libia* 12: 175–90.

Lloyd A. (ed. 1996), *Battle in Antiquity* (London).

Lloyd, G. (1984), *The Man of Reason: 'Male' and 'Female' in Western Philosophy* (London).

Loizos, P., and Parataxiarchis, E. (eds 1991), *Contested Identities: Gender and Kinship in Modern Greece* (Princeton).

Loraux, N. (1981/1986), *The Invention of Athens: The Funeral Oration in the Classical City* (Cambridge, Mass.)

—— (1984/1993), *The Children of Athena: Athenian Ideas about Citizenship and the Division between the Sexes* (Princeton).

—— (1989/1995), *The Experiences of Teiresias: The Feminine and the Greek Man* (Princeton).

—— (1990), 'Heracles: the Super-Male and the Feminine', in Halperin, Winkler and Zeitlin (eds 1990), 21–52.

Lovibond, S. (1994), 'An Ancient Theory of Gender: Plato and the Pythagorean Table', in Archer, Fischler, and Wyke (eds 1994), 88–101.

Lullies, R. (1946/7), 'Attisch-schwarzfigurige Keramik aus der Kerameikos', *JDAI* 61/2: 55–75.

Lund, H. (1992), *Lysimachus: A Study in Early Hellenistic Kingship* (London).

Lutz, C. E. (1947), 'Musonius Rufus, the Roman Socrates', *YCS* 10: 3–147.

Mac an Ghaill, M. (ed. 1996), *Understanding Masculinities* (Buckingham etc.).

MacCormack, C., and Strathern, M., (eds 1980), *Nature, Culture and Gender* (Cambridge).

McDonnell, M. (1991), 'The Introduction of Athletic Nudity: Thucydides, Plato and the Vases', *JHS* 111: 182–92.

MacDowell, D. M. (1963), *Athenian Homicide Law in the Age of the Orators* (Manchester).

—— (1971), *Aristophanes' Wasps* (Oxford).

—— (1978), *The Law in Classical Athens* (London).

—— (1990), *Demosthenes: Against Meidias* (Oxford).

—— (1995), *Aristophanes and Athens* (Oxford).

Macfarlane, A. (1981), *The Justice and the Mare's Ale: Law and Disorder in Seventeenth-Century England* (Cambridge).

McGregor, M. F. (1987), *The Athenians and their Empire* (Vancouver).

Macurdy, G. (1932), *Hellenistic Queens* (Baltimore).

Magie, D. (1950), *Roman Rule in Asia Minor* (Princeton).

Malkin, I. (1987), *Religion and Colonization in Ancient Greece* (Leiden).

Manfredini, A. D. (1985), '*Qui commutant cum feminis vestem*', *RIDA* 32: 257–71.

Mann, J. C. (1983), *Legionary Recruitment and Veteran Settlement during the Principate* (London).

Marcus, M. (1987a), in Gilmore (ed. 1987), 49–65.

Markle, M. M. (1985), 'Jury Pay and Assembly Pay in Athens', in Cartledge and Harvey (eds 1985), 265–97.

Mason, J. K. (1990), *Medico-Legal Aspects of Parenthood and Marriage* (Dartmouth).

Mattingly, H. B. (1996), *The Athenian Empire Restored* (Ann Arbor).

Meier, C. (1990), *The Greek Discovery of Politics* (Cambridge, Mass.).

Meiggs, R. (1979), *The Athenian Empire* (Oxford).

Meskell, L. (1996), 'The Somatization of Archaeology: institutions, discourses, corporeality', *Norwegian Archaeological Review* 29–1: 1–16.

Meyers, D. W. (1990), *The Human Body and the Law*, 2nd edn (Edinburgh).

Millar, F. G. B. (1981), 'The World of the Golden Ass', *JRS* 71: 63–75.

—— (1984a), 'The Political Character of the Classical Roman Republic, 200–151 BC', *JRS* 74: 1–19.

—— (1984b), 'State and Subject: The Impact of Monarchy', in Millar and Segal (eds 1984), 37–60.

—— (1986), 'Politics, Persuasion and the People before the Social War (150–90 BC)', *JRS* 76: 1–11.

—— (1989), 'Political Power in mid-Republican Rome: Curia or Comitium?', *JRS* 79: 138–56.

Millar, F. G. B., and Segal, E. (eds 1984), *Caesar Augustus: Seven Aspects* (Oxford).

Millett, P. (1989), 'Patronage and its Avoidance in Classical Athens', in Wallace-Hadrill (ed. 1989), 15–47.

—— (1990), 'Sale, Credit and Exchange in Athenian Law and Society', in Cartledge, Millett, and Todd (eds 1990), 167–94.

—— (1991), *Lending and Borrowing in Ancient Athens* (Cambridge).

Momigliano, A. (1975), *Alien Wisdom: The limits of Hellenization* (Cambridge etc.).

Monsacré, H. (1984a), *Les larmes d'Achille. Le héros, la femme et la souffrance dans la poésie d'Homère* (Paris).

—— (1984b), 'Weeping Heroes in the *Iliad*', *History and Anthropology* 1: 57–75.

Montserrat, D. (1996), *Sex and Society in Græco-Roman Egypt* (London).

Morris, C. (ed.1995), *Klados: Essays in honour of J. N. Coldstream* (*BICS* suppl. 63: London).

Morris, I. (ed. 1994), *Classical Greece. Ancient Histories and Modern Archaeologies* (Cambridge).

Morris, I., and Powell B. (eds 1997), *A New Companion to Homer* (New York).

Morris, S. (1984), *The Black and White Style* (New Haven).

Mortensen, K. (1992), 'Eurydice: Demonic or Devoted Mother?', *Ancient History Bulletin* 6: 156–71.

Muccioli, F. (1994), 'Considerazioni generali sull'epiteto Φιλάδελφος nelle dinastie ellenistiche e sulla applicazione nella titolatura degli ultimi Seleucidi', *Historia* 43: 402–22.

Müller, H. (1991), 'Königin Stratonike, Tochter des Königs Ariarathes', *Chiron* 21: 393–424.

Murray, O. (1983), 'The Greek Symposium in History', in Gabba (ed. 1983), 257–72.

—— (ed. 1990a), *Sympotica: A Symposium on the Symposion* (Oxford).

—— (1990b), 'Sympotic History', in Murray (ed. 1990a), 3–13.

—— (1990c), 'The Affair of the Mysteries: Democracy and the Drinking Group', in Murray (ed. 1990a), 149–161.

—— (1994), 'Nestor's Cup and the Origins of the Greek *Symposion*', *Annali di Archeologia e storia antica* (Napoli) 1: 47–54.

Neale, J. E. (1979), *Queen Elizabeth I* (St Albans).

Neils, J. (ed. 1992), *Goddess and Polis. The Panathenaic Festival in Ancient Athens* (Princeton).

—— (1994), 'The Panathenaia and Kleisthenic Ideology', in Coulson *et al.* (eds 1994), 151–60.

Neuberger-Donath, R. (1996), 'Τέρεν δάκρυον: θαλερὸν δάκρυον: Über den Unterschied der Characterisierung von Mann und Frau bei Homer', in Katzoff (ed. 1996), 57–60.

Neumann, G. (1965), *Gesten und Gebärden in der griechischen Kunst* (Berlin).

Nicolet, C. (1980), *The World of the Citizen in Republican Rome* (London).

Nielsen, I. (1994), *Hellenistic Palaces: Tradition and Renewal* (Studies in Hellenistic Civilisation 5: Aarhus).

North, H. (1966), *Sophrosyne: Self-Knowledge and Self-Restraint in Greek Literature* (Ithaca).

Norwood, S. (1945), *Pindar* (California).

Nye, R. A. (1993), *Masculinity and Male Codes of Honor in Modern France* (Oxford).

Oates, J., *et al.* (1992), *A Checklist of Editions of Greek and Latin Papyri, Ostraca and Tablets*, 4th edn (Atlanta).

Ober, J. (1989), *Mass and Elite in Democratic Athens. Rhetoric, Ideology and the Power of the People* (Princeton).

—— (1994), 'Power and Oratory in Democratic Athens: Demosthenes 21 *Against Meidias*', in Worthington (ed. 1994a), 85–108.

Ober, J., and Hedrick, C. W. (eds 1996), *Demokratia: A Conversation on Democracies, Ancient and Modern* (Princeton).

Ogden, D. (1996), 'Homosexuality and Warfare in Ancient Greece', in Lloyd (ed. 1996), 107–68.

Oliver, J. H. (1965), 'Livia as Artemis Boulaia at Athens', *CP* 60: 179.

Osborne, M. J., and Byrne, S. G. (eds 1994), *A Lexicon of Greek Personal Names* ii *Attica* (Oxford).

Osborne, R. (1985), 'Law in Action in Classical Athens', *JHS* 105: 40–58.

—— (1987), 'The Viewing and Obscuring of the Panathenaea Frieze', *JHS* 107: 98–105.

—— (1990), 'Vexatious Litigation in Classical Athens: Sykophancy and the Sykophant', in Cartledge, Millett, and Todd (eds 1990), 83–102.

—— (1992), '" Is it a farm?" The Definition of Agricultural Sites and Settlements in Ancient Greece', in Wells (ed. 1992), 21–8.

—— (1996), *Greece in the Making* (London).

Osborne, R., and Hornblower, S. (eds 1994), *Ritual, Finance, Politics: Athenian Democratic Accounts Presented to David Lewis* (Oxford).

Ostwald, M. (1986), *From Popular Sovereignty to the Sovereignty of Law* (Berkeley etc.).

Parke, H. W. (1988), *Sibyls and Sibylline Prophecy in Classical Antiquity* (London etc.).

Parker, R. (1983), *Miasma: Pollution and Purification in early Greek Religon* (Oxford).

240

Pellizer, E. (1990), 'Outlines of a Morphology of Sympotic Entertainment', in Murray (ed. 1990a), 177–84.

Peremans, W., and van't Dack, E. (1950–1981), *Prosopographia Ptolemaïca*, 9 vols. (Louvain).

Peters, E. L. (1967), 'Some Structural Elements of the Feud among the Camel-herding Bedouin of Cyrenaica', *Africa* 37: 261–82.

Pfeiffer, R. (1968), *History of Classical Scholarship: from the Beginnings to the End of the Hellenistic Age* (Oxford).

Plass, P. (1995), *The Game of Death in Ancient Rome: Arena Sport and Political Suicide* (Wisconsin Studies in Classics: Madison etc.).

Pollitt, J. J. (1986), *Art in the Hellenistic Age* (Cambridge).

Pomeroy, S. B. (1975), *Goddesses, Wives, Whores and Slaves: Women in Classical Antiquity* (New York) [reprinted London, 1994].

—— (1984), *Women in Hellenistic Egypt from Alexander to Cleopatra* (New York).

—— (ed. 1991), *Women's History and Ancient History* (Chapel Hill etc.).

Pope, A. (1715), *The Iliad of Homer, Books I–IX*, in *The Poems of Alexander Pope* vii, (ed. M. Mack) (London 1967).

Powell, A. (ed. 1990), *Euripides, Women and Sexuality* (London).

—— (ed. 1992), *Roman Poetry and Propaganda in the Age of Augustus* (London).

Préaux, C. (1978), *Le monde hellénistique: la Grèce et l'orient (323–146 av. J.-C.)*, 2 vols. (Paris) (3rd edition with additional bibliography 1992).

Price, S. R. F. (1984a), *Rituals and Power: The Roman Imperial Cult in Asia Minor* (Cambridge).

—— (1984b), 'Gods and Emperors: the Greek Language of the Roman Imperial Cult', *JHS* 104: 75–95.

Raaflaub, K. A. (1996), 'Equality and Inequalities in Athenian Democracy', in Ober and Hedrick (eds 1996), 139–74.

Rabinowitz, N., and Richlin, A. (eds 1993), *Feminist Theory and the Classics* (London).

Raubitschek, A. E. (1943), 'Greek Inscriptions', *Hesperia* 12: 12–88.

—— (1946), 'Octavia's Deification at Athens', *TAPA* 77: 146–50.

Rawson, B. (ed. 1986), *The Family in Ancient Rome: New Perspectives* (London etc.).

Rawson, E. (1985), *Intellectual Life in the Late Roman Republic* (London).

Reiner, E. (1938), *Die rituelle Totenklage der Griechen* (Stuttgart etc.).

Reynolds, J. (1982), *Aphrodisias and Rome* (London).

—— (1996), 'Ruler-cult at Aphrodisias in the Late Republic and under the Julio–Claudian Emperors', in Small (ed. 1996), 41–50.

Rhodes, P. J. (1981), *A Commentary on the Aristotelian Athenaion Politeia* (Oxford).

—— (1985), *The Athenian Empire* (*Greece & Rome* New Surveys in the Classics, 17: Oxford).

—— (1992), 'The Delian League to 449 BC', in Lewis, Boardman, Davies, and Ostwald (eds 1992), 34–61, 535–9.

Rice, E. E. (1983), *The Grand Procession of Ptolemy Philadelphus* (Oxford).

—— (1993), 'The Glorious Dead', in Rich and Shipley (eds 1993), 224–57.

Rich, J., and Shipley, D. G. J. (eds 1993), *War and Society in the Greek World* (London etc.).

Richlin, A. (1992), *Pornography and Representation in Greece and Rome* (Oxford).

Ridgway, B. S. (1993), 'Response' [to Smith and Zanker] in Bulloch, Gruen, Long, and Stewart (eds 1993), 231–41.

Ridley, R. T. (1979), 'The Hoplite as Citizen. Athenian Military Institutions in their Social Context', *L'Antiquité Classique* 48: 508–48.

Riedinger, J.-C. (1980), 'Les deux *aidōs* chez Homère', *RPh* 54: 62–79.

Riewald, P. (1912), *De imperatorum romanorum cum certis dis et comparatione et aequatione* (Ph.D. dissertation, Halle).

Ritter, H. W. (1965), *Diadem und Königsherrschaft. Untersuchungen zu Zeremonien und Rechtsgrundlagen des Herrschaftseintritts bei den Persern, bei Alexander dem Grossen, und im Hellenismus* (Vestigia 7: Munich).

Robbins, E. (1978), 'Cyrene and Cheiron: the Myth of Pindar's Ninth Pythian', *Phoenix* 32: 91–104.

Robert, L. (1940), *Les gladiateurs dans l'Orient grec* (Paris).

—— (1960), 'Recherches Épigraphiques', *REA* 62: 276–361.

Roesch, P. (1965), *Thespies et la Confédération Béotienne* (Paris).

Rombos, T. (1988), *The Iconography of Attic Late Geometric II Pottery* (Jonsered).

Romilly, J. de (1995), 'Nature et éducation dans le théâtre d'Euripide' (1986), reprinted in *Tragédie grecque au fil des ans* (Paris), 171–84.

Roper, M., and Tosh, J. (eds 1991), *Manful Assertions: Masculinities in Britain since 1800* (London etc.).

Rose, H. J. (ed. 1924), *The Roman Questions of Plutarch* (Oxford).

Rosivach, V. J. (1994), *The System of Public Sacrifice in Fourth-century Athens* (Atlanta).

Rougé, J. (1970), 'La colonisation grecque et les femmes', *Cahiers d'histoire* 15: 307–17.

Roy, J. (1991), 'Traditional Jokes about the Punishment of Adulterers in Ancient Greek Literature', *LCM* 16: 73–6.

Rubin, N. (1978), 'Narrative Structure in Pindar's Ninth Pythian', *Classical World* 71: 353–67.

Russell, D. A. (1973), *Plutarch* (London).

Said, E. (1978/1995), *Orientalism* (London etc.).

—— (1993), *Culture and Imperialism* (New York).

Sale, W. M. (1994), 'The Government of Troy', *GRBS* 35: 5–102.

Sallares, R. (1990), *The Ecology of the Ancient Greek World* (London).

Saller, R. P. (1994), *Patriarchy, Property and Death in the Roman Family* (Cambridge).

Sanday, P. R. (1986), *Divine Hunger: Cannibalism as a Cultural System* (Cambridge).

Santoro L'Hoir, F. (1992), *The Rhetoric of Gender Terms: 'Man', 'Woman' and the Portrayal of Character in Latin Prose* (Leiden).

Sargent, B. (1984), *L'Homosexualité dans la mythologie grecque* (Paris).

—— (1986), *L'Homosexualité initiatique dans l'Europe ancienne* (Paris).

Šašel Kos, M. (1978), 'A Latin Epitaph of a Roman Legionary from Corinth', *JRS* 68: 22–6.

Saunders, T. J. (1991), *Plato's Penal Code* (Oxford).

Savalli-Lestrade, I. (1994), 'Il ruolo pubblico delle regine ellenistiche', in Alessandrì (ed. 1994), 415–32.

Schauenburg, K. (1975), 'Εὐρυμέδων εἰμι', *AM* 90: 97–121.

Schmidt, H. (1967), 'Frühgriechische Terrakotten aus Kreta', in *Gestalt und Geschichte: Festschrift Karl Schefold* (*AK* Beiheft 4), 168–73.

Schmitt, H. H. (1991), 'Zur Inszenierung des Privatlebens des hellenistischen Herrschers', in Seibert (ed. 1991), 75–86.

Schmitt-Pantel, P. (1992), *La Cité au Banquet* (Paris).

Schofield, M. (1991), *The Stoic Idea of the City* (Cambridge).

Schütrumpf. E. (1995), Discussion, in Eder (ed. 1995), 65–6.

Schulz, F. (1946), *History of Roman Legal Science* (Oxford).

Scott, J. (1986), 'Gender: A Useful Category of Historical Analysis', *American Historical Review* 91: 1053–75 [reprinted in Scott 1988].

—— (1988), *Gender in History* (New York).

Seaford, R. (1990), 'The Structural Problems of Marriage in Euripides', in Powell (ed. 1990), 151–76.

—— (1994), *Reciprocity and Ritual. Homer and Tragedy in the Developing City-State* (Oxford).

Secunda, N. V. (1990), 'IG ii^2 1250: A Decree Concerning the *Lampadephoroi* of the Tribe Aiantis', *ZPE* 83: 149–82.

Segal, C. (1986), *Pindar's Mythmaking: The Fourth Pythian Ode* (Princeton).

Segal, L. (1990), *Slow Motion: Changing Masculinities, Changing Men* (London).

Seibert, J. (1967), *Historische Beiträge zu den dynastischen Verbindungen in Hellenistischer Zeit* (Historia Einzelschriften 10: Stuttgart).

—— (ed. 1991), *Hellenistische Studien: Gedenkschrift für Hermann Bengtson* (Münchener Arbeiten zur Alten Geschichte 5: Munich).

Seidler, V. (1989), *Rediscovering Masculinity: Reason, Language and Sexuality* (London).

Shapiro, H. A. (1986), review of Keuls 1985, *AJA* 90: 361–3.

—— (1991), 'The Iconography of Mourning in Athenian Art', *AJA* 95: 629–56.

Sharpe, J. A. (1984), *Crime in Early Modern England, 1550–1750* (London etc.).

—— (1985), 'The History of Violence in England: Some Observations', *P&P* 108: 206–15.

Shaw, B. D. (1984), 'Bandits in the Roman Empire', *P&P* 105: 3–52.

—— (1987), 'The Family in Late Antiquity: the Experience of Augustine' *P&P* 115: 3–51.

Shaw, M. C. (1983), 'Two Cups with Incised Decoration from Kommos, Crete', *AJA* 87: 443–52.

Shear, T. L. (1981), 'Athens: From City-State to Provincial Town', *Hesperia* 50: 356–77.

Sheedy, K. A. (1992), 'The Late Geometric Hydria and the Advent of the Protoattic Style', *AM* 107: 11–28.

Sherwin-White, S., and Kuhrt, A. (1993), *From Samarkand to Sardis: A New Approach to the Seleucid Empire* (London).

Sinclair, R. K. (1988), *Democracy and Participation in Athens* (Cambridge).

Small, A. (ed. 1996), *Subject and Ruler: the Cult of the Ruling Power in Classical Antiquity* (Journal of Roman Archaeology Supplementary Series 17: Ann Arbor).

Smallwood, E. M. (1967), *Documents Illustrating the Principates of Caius, Claudius and Nero* (Cambridge).

Smith, R. R. R. (1987), 'The Imperial Reliefs from the Sebasteion at Aphrodisias', *JRS* 77: 88–138.

—— (1988), *Hellenistic Royal Portraits* (Oxford).

—— (1993), 'Kings and Philosophers', in Bulloch, Gruen, Long, and Stewart (eds 1993), 202–11.

Sommerstein, A., Halliwell, S., Henderson, J. J., and Zimmermann, B. (eds 1993), *Tragedy, Comedy and the Polis* (Bari).

Spencer, N. (ed. 1995), *Time, Tradition and Society in Greek Archaeology* (London).

Spivey, N. J. (1996), *Understanding Greek Sculpture. Ancient Meanings, Modern Readings* (London etc.).

Stadter, P. (1992), *Plutarch and the Historical Tradition* (London).

Stewart, F. H. (1994), *Honor* (Chicago).

Stone, L. (1985), 'A Rejoinder' *P&P* 108: 216–24.

—— (1987), 'Homicide and Violence', in *The Past and the Present Revisited*, 2nd edn (London), 295–310.

Strauss, B. S. (1996), 'The Athenian Trireme, Cradle of Liberty', in Ober and Hedrick (eds 1996), 313–26.

Stucchi, S. (1975), *Architettura Cirenaica* (Rome).

Svenbro, J. (1988/1993), *Phrasikleia. An Anthropology of Reading in Ancient Greece* (Ithaca).

Swain, S. (1996), *Hellenism and Empire* (Oxford).

Syme, R. (1979), 'Some Imperial Salutations', *Phoenix* 33: 308–29.

Szegedy-Maszak, A. (1978), 'Legends of the Greek Lawgivers', *GRBS* 19: 199–210.

Taaffe, L. K. (1993), *Aristophanes and Women* (London).

Taplin O. (1987), 'Phallology, *Phlyakes*, Iconography and Aristophanes', *PCPS* 30: 92–104.

—— (1993), *Comic Angels and other Approaches to Greek Drama through Vase-Painting* (Oxford).

Tazelaar, C. M. (1967), 'Παῖδες καὶ Ἐφήβοι: Some Notes on Spartan Stages of Youth', *Mnemosyne*, 4th Series, 20: 127–53.

Temporini, H. (ed.1979), *Aufstieg und Niedergang der römischen Welt* ii. 7. 1 (Berlin).

Thomas, R. F. (1982), *Lands and Peoples in Roman Poetry: The Ethnographical Tradition* (Cambridge).

Thompson, D. B. (1973), *Ptolemaic Oinochoai and Portraits in Faïence: Aspects of the Ruler Cult* (Oxford).

—— (1980), 'More Ptolemaic Queens', *Antike Kunst* Beiheft 12: *Eikones* (Festschrift H. Jucker), 181–4.

Thompson, H. A. (1966), 'The Annex to the Stoa of Zeus in the Athenian Agora', *Hesperia* 35: 171–87.

Tod, M. (1951), 'An Ephebic Inscription from Memphis', *Journal of Egyptian Archaeology* 37: 86–102.

Todd, S. (1990a), '*Lady Chatterley's Lover* and the Attic Orators', *JHS* 110: 146–73.

—— (1990b), 'The Purpose of Evidence in Athenian Courts', in Cartledge, Millett, and Todd (eds 1990), 19–39.

—— (1993), *The Shape of Athenian Law* (Oxford).

Toner, J. P. (1995), *Leisure and Ancient Rome* (London).

Tosh, J. (1991), 'Domesticity and Manliness in the Victorian Middle Class: The Family of Edward White Benson', in Roper and Tosh (eds 1991), 44–73.

Tomaselli, S., and Porter, R. (eds 1986), *Rape* (Oxford).

Trexler, R. C. (1995), *Sex and Conquest: Gendered Violence, Political Order and the European Conquest of the Americas* (Oxford).

Turner, B. S. (1984), *The Body and Society* (Oxford).

Van Bremen, R. (1983), 'Women and Wealth', in Cameron and Kuhrt (eds 1983), 223–42.

—— (1996), *The Limits of Participation: Women in Civic Life in the Greek East in the Hellenistic and Roman Periods* (Dutch Monographs on Ancient History and Archaeology: Amsterdam).

Van Compernolle, R. (1983), 'Femmes indigènes et colonisateurs', in *Modes de contact et processus de transformation dans les sociétés antiques: Actes du colloque de Cortone (24–30 mai 1981)* (Collection de l'École française de Rome 67: Rome), 1033–49.

Van't Dack, E., van Dessel, P., and van Gucht, W. (eds 1983), *Egypt and the Hellenistic World* (Studia Hellenistica 27: Louvain).

Van Wees, H. (1994), 'The Homeric Way of War: The *Iliad* and the Hoplite Phalanx (I) and (II)', *G&R* 41: 1–18, 131–55.

—— (1995), 'Princes at Dinner. Social Event and Social Structure in Homer', in Crielaard (ed. 1995), 147–82.

—— (1996), 'Heroes, Knights, and Nutters. Warrior Mentality in Homer', in Lloyd (ed. 1996), 1–86.

—— (1997), 'Homeric Warfare', in Morris and Powell (eds 1997), 668–93.

—— (1998), 'Greeks Bearing Arms. The State, the Leisure Class, and the Display of Weapons in Archaic Greece', in Fisher and van Wees (eds 1998), 333–78.

Vermeule, C. C. (1968), *Roman Imperial Art in Greece and Asia Minor* (Cambridge, Mass.).

Vermeule, E. (1991), 'Myth and Tradition from Mycenae to Homer', in Buitron-Oliver (ed. 1991), 98–121.

Vernant, J. P. (1977), 'Introduction', in Detienne 1977, i–xxxv.

Veyne, P. (1978), 'La famille et l'amour sous le Haut-Empire romain', *Annales (ESC)* 33: 35–63.

—— (1987), 'The Roman Empire', in Veyne (ed. 1987), 1–233.

—— (ed. 1987), *A History of Private Life: From Pagan Rome to Byzantium* (Cambridge, Mass. etc.).

Vickers, M. (1990), 'Attic *Symposia* after the Persian Wars', in Murray (ed. 1990a), 105–21.

—— (nd), *Greek Symposia* (London).

Vidal-Naquet, P. (1981/1986), *The Black Hunter: Forms of Thought and Forms of Society in Ancient Greece* (Baltimore etc.).

—— (1986), 'The Black Hunter revisited', *PCPS* 32: 126–44.

von Hesberg, H. (1989), 'Temporäre Bilder oder die Grenzen der Kunst: Zur Legitimation frühhellenistischer Königsherrschaft im Fest', *JDAI* 104: 61–82.

Waern, I. (1985), 'Der weinende Held', *Eranos* 83: 223–9.

Walbank, F. W. (1957–1979), *A Historical Commentary on Polybius*, 3 vols. (Oxford).

—— (1967), *Philip V of Macedon* (reprinted with new foreword) (place of publication not given).

—— (1984), 'Monarchies and Monarchic Ideas', and 'Macedonia and Greece', in Walbank, Astin, Frederiksen, and Ogilvie (eds 1984), 62–100, 221–56.

—— (1992), *The Hellenistic World* (3rd impression with amendments) (London).

—— (1993), 'Response' [to Bringmann and Koenen], in Bulloch, Gruen, Long and Stewart (eds 1993), 116–24.

Walbank, F. W., Astin, A. E., Frederiksen, M. W., and Ogilvie, R. M. (eds 1984), *Cambridge Ancient History*, vii. 1 *The Hellenistic world*, 2nd edn (Cambridge).

Wallace-Hadrill, A. (ed. 1989), *Patronage in Ancient Society* (London).

Weber, G. (1993), *Dichtung und höfische Gesellschaft: die Rezeption von Zeitgeschichte am Hof der ersten drei Ptolemäer* (Hermes Einzelschriften 62: Stuttgart).

—— (1995), 'Herrscher, Hof, und Dichter: Aspekte der Legitimierung und Repräsentation hellenistischer Könige am Beispiel der ersten drei Antigoniden', *Historia* 44: 283–316.

Webster, G. (1980), *The Roman Invasion of Britain* (London).

Weeks, J. (1989), *Sexuality and its Discontents: Meanings, Myths and Modern Sexualities* (London).

Wehrli, C. (1964), 'Phila, fille d'Antipater et épouse de Démétrius, roi des Macédoniens', *Historia* 13: 140–6.

Weinstock, S. (1971), *Divus Iulius* (Oxford).

Wells, B. (ed. 1992), *Agriculture in Ancient Greece: Proceedings of the Seventh International Symposium at the Swedish Institute at Athens* (Stockholm).

West, M. (1995), 'The Date of the *Iliad*', *MusHelv* 52: 203–19.

Whitehead, D. (1983), 'Competitive Outlay and Community Profit: *Philotimia* in Democratic Athens', *C&M* 34: 55–74.

—— (1986), *The Demes of Attica* (Princeton).

—— (1993), 'Cardinal Virtues: The Language of Public Approbation in Democratic Athens', *C&M* 44: 37–75.

Whitehorne, J. (1994), *Cleopatras* (London).

Whitley, J. (1991), *Style and Society in Dark Age Greece: The Changing Face of a Pre-Literate Society 1100–700 BC* (Cambridge).

—— (1994), 'Protoattic Pottery: a Contextual Approach', in Morris (ed. 1994), 51–70.

Wickersham, J. (1994), *Hegemony and Greek Historians* (Lanham).

Wiedemann, T .E. J. (1981), *Greek and Roman Slavery* (London).

—— (1987), *Slavery* (*Greece and Rome* New Surveys in the Classics, 19: Oxford).

Wikander, C. (1986), 'Religion, Political Power and Gender – the Building of a Cult-Image', in Hellström and Alroth (eds 1996), 183–8.

Wilkins, J., and Hill, S. (1994), *Archestratus: Life of Luxury* (Newton Abbot).

Will, E. (1979, 1982), *Histoire politique du monde hellénistique*, 2 vols., 2nd edn (Nancy).

—— (1984), 'The Fountain of the Hellenistic Kingdoms', in Walbank, Astin, Frederikson, and Ogilvie (eds 1984), 101–17.

Willcock, M. M. (1986), Review of Monsacré 1984a, *JHS* 106: 203.

Williams, C. (1993), *Pope, Homer and Manliness: Some Aspects of 18th Century Classical Learning* (London).

Williams, W. (1990), *Pliny: Correspondence with Trajan from Bithynia (Epistles x)* (Warminster).

Wilson, P. J. (1991), 'Demosthenes 21 *against Meidias*: Democratic Abuse', *PCPS* 37: 164–95.

Wilson, S., (1988), *Feuding, Conflict and Banditry in Nineteenth-century Corsica* (Cambridge).

Winkler, J. J. (1980), 'Lollianos and the Desperadoes', *JHS* 100: 155–81.

—— (1990a), *The Constraints of Desire: the Anthropology of Sex and Gender in Ancient Greece* (London etc.).

—— (1990b), 'The Ephebes' song: *Tragoidia* and *Polis*', in Winkler and Zeitlin (eds 1990) 20–62

Winkler, J. J., and Zeitlin, F. I. (eds 1990), *Nothing to do with Dionysos? Athenian Drama in its Social Context* (Princeton).

Wirszubski, C. (1950), *Libertas as a Political Idea at Rome during the Late Republic and Early Principate* (Cambridge).

Wiseman, T. P. (1979), *Clio's Cosmetics: Three Studies in Greco-Roman Literature* (Leicester).

Woodbury, L. (1982), 'Cyrene and the *Teleuta* of Marriage in Pindar's Ninth Pythian Ode' *TAPA*, 112: 245–58.

Woodman, A. J. (1988), *Rhetoric in Classical Historiography* (Beckenham).

Wörrle, M. (1978), 'Epigraphische Forschungen zur Geschichte Lykiens II', *Chiron* 8: 201–46.

Wörrle, M., and Zanker, P. (eds 1995), *Stadtbild und Bürgerbild im Hellenismus* (Kolloquium, München, 24. bis 26. Juni 1993: Munich).

Worthington, I. (ed. 1994a), *Greek Rhetoric in Action* (London).

—— (ed. 1994b), *Ventures into Greek History* (Oxford).

Wyke, M. (1987), 'Propertius' *Scripta Puella*', *JRS* 77: 47–61.

—— (1989), 'In Pursuit of Love: the Poetic Self and a Process of Reading Augustan Elegy in the 1980s', *JRS* 79: 165–73.

—— (1992), 'Augustan Cleopatras: Female Power and Poetic Authority', in Powell (ed. 1992), 98–140.

Zanker, P. (1983), *Provinzielle Kaiserporträts zur Rezeption der Selbstdarstellung des Princeps* (Munich).

—— (1995), *The Mask of Socrates. The Image of the Intellectual in Antiquity* (Sather Classical Lectures 59: Berkeley etc.).

Zeitlin, F. I. (1986), 'Configurations of Rape in Greek Myth', in Tomaselli and Porter (eds 1986), 122–51.

Zschietzschmann, W. (1928), 'Die Darstellungen der Prothesis in der griechischen Kunst', *AM* 53, 17–47.

Zweig, B. (1993), 'The Primal Mind: Using Native American Models for the study of Women in Ancient Greece', in Rabinowitz and Richlin (eds 1993), 145–79.

Index of ancient authors

References to ancient works are in parentheses; page numbers of this volume are outside parentheses. Abbreviations are as used in the *Oxford Classical Dictionary*, 3rd edn.

Achilles Tatius, *Leukippe and Kleitophon* (3.15), 200; (6.21), 198; (6.22), 198
Aesch. *Cho.* (24–5), 48 n25; (423–4), 53 n73; (24–5), 17–18; *Pers.* (302–432), 67 n37
Aeschin. (1.60–1), 94 n29; (1.61), 94 n23; (1.62), 95 n37; (1.107), 96 n61; (1.135–6), 75; (2.150–1), 67 n26; (2.156), 47 n21; (2.181), 96 n66; (3.51–3), 85, 95 n47; (3.52), 94 n36
[Andoc.] (4.20–1), 94 n22
Anth. Pal. (5.202),132 n65, 132 n74; (5.210), 132 n74; (12.155, 210), 164 n6
Ap.Rhod. (2.502–5), 108 n16; (2.505), 107 n4; (2.505–6), 102, 108 n21; (4.1551–63;1731–64), 109 n23, n28; (4.1731–45), 108 n14; (4.1731–64,1733–7), 109 n24; (4.1733–7), 102; (4.1755–8), 102
Apollod. (3.14.3–4), 52 n66
Apul. *Met.* (4.21), 202; (7.13), 197; (9.39–42), 217
Ar. *Lys.* (510–21), 94 n32; (556–64), 95 n69; *Nub.* (206–9), 6 n81; (1083–5), 95 n38; *Plut.* (168), 95 n38; *Vesp.* (605–9), 94 n32; (1060–3), 62; (1076–6), 62; (1295–8), 77; (1299–325), 94 n22; (1299–363), 77
Archestratos (Fr.4), 108 n13
Archil. (Fr.13 West), 18
Arist. *Eth.Nic.* (4.1125a5–9), 83; (4.1126a2–8), 83; (4.1126a20–8), 95 n44; (5.1132b32-a2), 83; *Gen.an.*

(1.716a4–8, 730a25–30), 106; (1.716a20–4, 730a15), 106; (1.729b9–19), 106; (1.729b17–19;2.730b12–21), 106; (1.730a14–16), 106; (4.777b28–30), 110 n40; *Pol.* (1.1252a35-b9), 53 n71; (1268b33–69a3), 87; (2.1268b40), 86; (2.1269b12), 169; (4.1289b36–9,4.1297b12–28,6.1321a5 –25), 66 n21; (4.1291b4,5,1304a22), 55; *Rh.* (1.1368b24), 95 n44; (2.1382b1–2), 83
[Arist.] *Ath.Pol.* (2.5–6), 109 n36; (7.4), 67 n23; (9.1), 88; (25.4), 93 n19; (52), 89; (53), 96 n79; (56.2), 96 n84
Arr. *Anab.* (7.11.5), xii; (7.14.3), xii
Ath. (36b=101 K-A), 76; (36b-c=93 K-A,) 94 n25; (36d-e=46 K-A), 76; (3.111e), 108 n13; (5.201d-e), 129 n38; (259e), 52 n65; (443c-d), 76; (12.517–18), 194 n3; (555a), 94 n24; (13.576e-577a, 577f-578b, 589f-590a, 593d-e, 596e), 132 n71; (13.576e-f), 132 n73; (13.577f-578a), 132 n71; (13.603d-e), 132 n70
Augstus *Res Gestae* (1), 203 n5, 222 n7; (34), 213
August. *Conf.* (9.9.19), 94 n32; *De Civ.D.* (4.4), 204 n31

Callim. *Hymn 1* (1.78–89), 129 n39; *Hymn 2* (55–7), 110 n41; (63–8) 103; (63–8), 108 n8; (90–2), 99, 106, 107

248

BIBLE

General Index

Achilles 11, 13, 14, 15, 46
Acropolis, Athenian 57, 66 n14, 172, 173
Adonis 42, 43, 44
adoption 139, 144
adultery 79, 82, 84
adulthood 141–3, 209
Aegisilaos 16
Agamemnon 11, 17, 18
agora 172
Agrippina (Elder and Younger) 166, 167, 168, 175, 176–8
Alexander the Great xii, 5, 6, 111, 117, 192
Amazons 57, 107
anal sex 155
andron 43
Antiochos III 112, 118, 120
Aphrodisias 176–8
Aphrodite 99, 197
Apollo 61, 98–103, 172
arbitration 89–92
Arcesilas IV of Cyrene 104
archegetes 104, 105, 106
Archilochos 18
Ares 172, 199, 200
Argeads 117
Argonauts 102, 191
Aristaios 102
aristocracy 91, 214–15
Artemis 173
Athena 61, 83
Athenian empire 54–67 *passim*
Athens 45, 54–97 *passim*; Roman 171–4
athletics 104
atimia 71, 84
Attalos II 113

Augustus 166, 167, 169, 172, 173, 178, 206, 212–14, 216, 217

Baal 45
banditry 195–204 *passim*
barbarian 42, 44, 45, 46, 57, 62, 217, 218, 219
battle 62
Battos 98, 100, 103–6
beard 153, 158–9, 162
beasts 202
benefaction 114, 121, 122, 131 n61, 169–70
body, the 5–6, 137, 138, 140, 147–8, 153–64 *passim*
Boiotia 184–94 *passim*
Bourdieu, Pierre 220

cannibalism 200–1
castration 137, 139, 141, 144–6, 147
Chaironea 184, 192
chaos 195–7
chariot procession 21, 33, 35, 36
childbirth 62, 187
children 69, 77, 137, 139, 140, 143, 153, 159
Cicero 142, 207, 211
citizen, citizenship 55, 75, 79–80, 83, 90, 146, 153, 169, 170, 192, 193–4, 201, 207–8, 209, 211
city 114, 118, 170, 172, 178, 192–4
Claudius 166, 172, 174, 175, 176
Cleopatra *see* Kleopatras
clothing 43, 136, 146–7, 178
cockfighting 68–9, 75, 77
colonialism 54–5, 56, 60
colonisation 54–5, 98–110 *passim*

254

Lightning Source UK Ltd.
Milton Keynes UK
UKOW032205240912

199565UK00003B/84/P